STUDIES IN ANTIQUITY AND CHRISTIANITY

The Roots of Egyptian Christianity
Birger A. Pearson and James E. Goehring, editors

The Formation of Q: Trajectories in Ancient Wisdom Collections
John S. Kloppenborg

Saint Peter of Alexandria: Bishop and Martyr
Tim Vivian

STUDIES IN ANTIQUITY AND CHRISTIANITY

The Institute for Antiquity and Christianity
Claremont Graduate School
Claremont, California

STUDIES IN ANTIQUITY & CHRISTIANITY

ST. PETER OF ALEXANDRIA
BISHOP AND MARTYR

Tim Vivian

FORTRESS PRESS   PHILADELPHIA

Library of Congress Cataloging-in-Publication Data

Vivian, Tim.
  Saint Peter of Alexandria.

  (Studies in antiquity and Christianity)
  Revision of the author's thesis (Ph. D.—University of California)
  Bibliography: p.
  Includes index.
  1. Peter, of Alexandria, Saint, d. 311.
2. Christian saints—Egypt—Biography. I. Title.
II. Series.
BR1720.P427V58   1988   270.1'092'4   86-46425
ISBN 0-8006-3102-1

2534H87   Printed in the United States of America   1-3102

To

APOSTOLOS N. ATHANASSAKIS

H. A. DRAKE

BIRGER A. PEARSON

JEFFREY B. RUSSELL

of

the University of California at Santa Barbara

Professors, Colleagues, Friends

Contents

Foreword

As director of the Roots of Egyptian Christianity research project of the Institute for Antiquity and Christianity, I take great pleasure in the publication of this book, the second volume to be published as part of the Roots of Egyptian Christianity project of The Institute for Antiquity and Christianity. My special pleasure in this book has another basis, too. I served as Tim Vivian's dissertation advisor at the University of California, Santa Barbara, when the first version of this book was accepted as a Ph.D. dissertation and given the grade "passed with distinction." The volume here published is a revised version of that excellent dissertation, made all the better for the revisions since undertaken. I do not doubt that it will be widely acknowledged as the definitive work on Saint Peter of Alexandria.

The Roots of Egyptian Christianity project has, as its long- term goal, the publication of a comprehensive history of Christian Egypt, from the beginnings of Christianity in Egypt until the Arab Conquest in the seventh century. As part of the unfolding work of the project we have envisioned the publication of spin-off volumes, apart from the comprehensive history itself. This study fits into that category, and we expect others to follow. The high standard of scholarship exhibited in this book by Dr. Vivian augurs well for the future of the Roots of Egyptian Christianity project and the Studies in Antiquity and Christianity series.

BIRGER A. PEARSON, *Project Director*
Institute for Antiquity and Christianity, Claremont
Professor of Religious Studies
University of California, Santa Barbara

Acknowledgments

This book, now considerably revised, began as the dissertation for an interdisciplinary Ph.D. at the University of California, Santa Barbara. In the dedication I have tried to express my deep thanks to the members of my committee, who generously read each chapter, sometimes several times; their criticism and advice helped me to make considerable improvements.

I especially wish to thank Professors Apostolos Athanassakis and Birger Pearson. Professor Athanassakis directed the dissertation in its early stages and was of invaluable assistance with the translations from the Greek. Professor Pearson directed the final stages of the dissertation. I profited greatly from his vast knowledge of the Alexandrian church and, as the project grew in size, it was he who most encouraged me to follow the study to its conclusion. He has been unfailingly generous, both with regard to this work and in our joint effort on the Coptic homilies attributed to St. Peter.

I wish to thank Professor Pearson and the editorial board of the Roots of Egyptian Christianity project at the Institute for Antiquity and Christianity at Claremont College, Claremont, California, for their decision to publish the work as part of their series on Egyptian Christianity. I would also like to thank John A. Hollar of Fortress Press for his guidance and assistance. The editors of Fortress Press through their painstaking help in the editing of this work have saved me from many errors of omission and commission. I wish especially to thank Stephanie Egnotovich.

I am grateful to the Committee on Research at the University of California, Santa Barbara, for a grant which allowed Professor Pearson and me to study the manuscripts of the Coptic homilies at the Morgan Library in New York. I am grateful also to the Church Divinity School of the Pacific in Berkeley, California, for scholarships which allowed me time amid my seminary studies to continue the research for this book.

Professor Rebecca Lyman of the Church Divinity School of the Pacific read the completed dissertation before I began to revise it for this book. Her careful comments and suggestions have saved me from mistakes and helped me nuance a number of judgments.

I wish to thank the libraries at the University of California, Santa Barbara, and at the Graduate Theological Union in Berkeley for their help. At the latter, Paul Clay was unfailingly helpful during a hectic summer.

I wish also to thank Bill Countryman, Sally Hall, Claudia Schmidt, Marcia Thompson, Miriam Raub Vivian, and Naomi Yavneh for their assistance.

I am grateful to Rick Kennedy and Bill Donahue for their assistance in reading two sets of proofs, and to Gwen Vergeer for her help with the index.

Finally, some personal notes. The late Right Reverend Robert C. Rusack, Episcopal bishop of Los Angeles, died as this book was going to press. Bishop Rusack's support, both financial and pastoral, was of great importance to me, and it is my hope that this book on one of his episcopal predecessors will in a small way do honor to his memory.

Because of the generosity of Anne and Apostolos Athanassakis, I was able to stay at Santa Barbara and finish my studies. I wish to thank both the Reverend Gary Commins, vicar at Saint Michael's Episcopal Church in Isla Vista, California, who freed me from parochial duties that I might concentrate on my research, and Rick Kennedy, friend and fellow historian, to whom I am indebted in numerous intangible ways.

Last, I wish to thank Miriam Raub Vivian, herself a historian, who listened to my talk about Saint Peter more than even the most ardent historian should have to. Even though writing her own dissertation, she has been unfailingly patient in her attention to my work.

Tim Vivian

Berkeley
August 1986

Abbreviations

ACO	*Acta Conciliorum Oecumenicorum*, ed. E. Schwartz (Strassbourg 1914–).
AnBol	*Analecta Bollandiana.*
ANF	Ante-Nicene Fathers.
ANRW	*Aufstieg und Niedergang der römischen Welt*, ed. H. Temporini and W. Haase (Berlin).
AS	*Analecta Sacra*, ed. J. B. Pitra (repr. Paris [1883] 1966).
BHG	*Bibliotheca Hagiographica Graeca.*
BHL	*Bibliotheca Hagiographica Latina Antiquae et Mediae Aetatatis.*
BHO	*Bibliotheca Hagiographica Orientalis.*
DCB	*Dictionary of Christian Biography*, ed. W. Smith and H. Wace (London 1877).
DSp	*Dictionnaire de spiritualité, ascetique et mystique, doctrine et históire*, ed. M. Viller et al. (Paris 1934–).
GCS	*Die griechischen christlichen Schriftsteller der ersten drei Jahrhunderte* (Leipzig and Berlin 1897–).
HE	Eusebius, *Ecclesiastical History.*
HTR	*Harvard Theological Review.*
JAC	*Jahrbuch für Antike und Christentum.*
JEA	*Journal of Egyptian Archaeology.*
JEH	*Journal of Ecclesiastical History.*
JTS	*Journal of Theological Studies.*
Lampe	*A Patristic Greek Lexicon*, ed. G. W. H. Lampe (Oxford 1961, 1978).
LCL	Loeb Classical Library.
LSJ	*A Greek-English Lexicon*, ed. H. G. Liddell and Robert Scott, rev. by H. S. Jones (Oxford 1968).
LXX	*Septuaginta*, ed. Alfred Rahlfs (Württemberg 1935).

Mu	*Le Muséon.*
NCE	*New Catholic Encyclopedia.*
NHLE	*The Nag Hammadi Library in English,* ed. J. M. Robinson (New York 1977).
NGG	*Nachrichten von der Gesellschaft der Wissenschaften zu Göttingen, phil-hist-Klasse.*
NPNF	Nicene and Post-Nicene Fathers.
NTApo	*New Testament Apocrypha,* ed. Edgar Hennecke and Wilhelm Schneemelcher (Philadelphia 1965).
OrChr	*Oriens Christianus.*
ODCC	*Oxford Dictionary of the Christian Church* (2d ed.; Oxford 1974, 1983).
PG	*Patrologia Graeca,* ed. J. P. Migne (Paris 1857–66).
RS	*Reliquiae Sacrae,* ed. M. J. Routh (2d ed.; Oxford 1846).
TDNT	*Theological Dictionary of the New Testament,* ed. G. Kittel and G. Friedrich (Grand Rapids, Mich. 1964–76).
TU	Texte und Untersuchungen.
ZNW	*Zeitschrift für die neutestamentliche Wissenschaft und die Kunde des Urchristentums.*

The Martyrdom of Saint Peter of Alexandria, miniature in the eleventh century Menologian of Basil II (Vat. Gr. 1613). From the Vatican library.

Introduction

Peter of Alexandria was seventeenth[1] bishop of the great Egyptian city and Christian see that produced Clement, Origen, Dionysius, Athanasius, Cyril, and a number of lesser luminaries. Although Peter was bishop from 300 to 311 and was later held in great esteem in the East because of his martyrdom, he has remained an obscure figure. Eusebius of Caesarea praised him for his glorious death, but said very little else about him. This near silence by one who was in a good position to chronicle the saint's life certainly helped doom him to obscurity; and Socrates and Sozomen, in their *Ecclesiastical Histories*, and Jerome, in his *De viris illustribus*, say little or nothing about him.

---

1. This is the traditional reckoning. See J.-M. Sauget, "Pietro I," *Bibliotheca Sanctorum* 10:762, for a discussion of Peter's place as sixteenth or seventeenth bishop of Alexandria. The list of Alexandrian bishops going back to Saint Mark is based upon legend. See E. R. Hardy, *Christian Egypt: Church and People* (New York 1952) 3–41, for a brief discussion of the Alexandrian church before Peter's time. The list of Alexandrian bishops may be found in Eusebius's *Ecclesiastical History*; for the passages, see A. von Harnack, *Geschichte der altchristlichen Literatur* (1893; repr. Leipzig 1958) 2/1:205ff. See also Walter Bauer's famous discussion in chap. 2 of *Orthodoxy and Heresy in Earliest Christianity* (Philadelphia 1971), esp. 45 n. 2, for the passages in Eusebius.

The first designation of Peter as "*arch*bishop" was apparently that of Epiphanius (315–403) in *Adversus haereses (Panarion)* 68.1 (*PG* 42:185A; see also *Adv. haer.* 69.1), but since he refers also to Melitius as "archbishop" (69.3; *PG* 42:208A), it is not exactly clear what he means by the term. The earliest use of the term "archbishop" is apparently found in a list of Melitian bishops presented to Alexander of Alexandria and reported by Athanasius in his second *Apology, Contra Arianos* 71 (*PG* 25:377A). The archbishop there is also Melitius, and once again it is not clear precisely what the term designates. It is ironic that the first attested uses of "archbishop" should designate Melitius—the foe of Peter who at Alexandria was the chief (*arch-*) bishop of Egypt. Since the term is first employed in Melitian documents (Epiphanius relies on Melitian sources; see chap. 1, "The Beginning of the Melitian Schism," 20–36), is it possible that "archbishop" is a Melitian, or at least an upper Egyptian, coinage? By the time of the Council of Ephesus in 431 the title was being applied to Cyril of Alexandria. See Lampe, 237B. Despite Epiphanius, the term "archbishop" should not be anachronistically used for Peter.

This virtual silence is unfortunate, because Peter's life, much like those of Dionysius and of Athanasius, although on a significantly smaller scale, makes an interesting—and sometimes exciting—story. He was bishop when the decrees of the Great Persecution in effect shut down the church in large areas of the East. He went into exile, probably twice, and from there managed his see and had to face one of the most crucial problems in the fourth-century church, that of the confessors who were challenging church order by their forgiveness of those who lapsed during persecution. Upon his return to Alexandria when the Great Persecution was over, he was arrested and beheaded, becoming the "seal of the martyrs" in Egyptian church tradition.

Scholars of church history have for the most part been content with this meager outline. However, church tradition, especially that of the Coptic church, has had much more to say about Peter than the "authorized" version handed down by Eusebius. A great number of *Martyrdoms* and *Lives* attest to the popularity of Peter's story in the centuries after his death. Severus's *History of the Patriarchs* and an *Encomium* on Peter falsely attributed to Alexander of Alexandria also show an interest—albeit largely hagiographical—in Peter of Alexandria that one would never guess existed if we had only the accounts of Eusebius.

Unfortunately most church historians have ignored what these sources may have to offer. In this work I have attempted to reclaim Peter both from the hagiographical tradition and from the silence of scholarship. My purpose has been first to reconstruct what we may reasonably know about the life of Saint Peter and then to discuss the writings that have been attributed to the bishop of Alexandria.

L. B. Radford, with his *Three Teachers of Alexandria* (1908), was the first scholar in this century to offer a major treatment of Saint Peter, but his interests were primarily theological. In the mid 1930s F. H. Kettler in Germany wrote his inaugural dissertation on the Melitian schism, and much of that work focused on Peter; during the same period he contributed a long encyclopedia article on the bishop of Alexandria. About ten years earlier H. I. Bell and W. E. Crum, in *Jews and Christians in Egypt,* had published a number of fragments on the Melitian schism with a brief discussion of Peter's role in the controversy.

Crum really began, at the turn of the century, the scholarly exploration of the fragmentary writings attributed to Peter. Many of the scholars who have written on this bishop have been concerned with the publication and discussion of the extant writings; Tito Orlandi, Marcel

Richard, and Henry Chadwick (with J. Barns) have been foremost among them. William Telfer offered the first systematic appraisal of the *Martyrdom of St. Peter*; he has been followed in this area most conspicuously by Orlandi.

As bishop during the Great Persecution, not to mention during the lifetimes of Melitius and Arius, Peter has had a secure—albeit small— niche in the many volumes of early church history, both those which focus on Alexandria and Egypt, and those concerned with the early church as a whole.[2] W. H. C. Frend, in particular, has discussed Peter's place within the many themes of early church history.

Despite all these scholarly endeavors there has not been, up to now, a comprehensive collection of Peter's writings and a thoroughgoing study of this Alexandrian bishop. Scholarship has generally limited itself to a discussion of Peter vis-à-vis some other topic, for example, Arius, the Melitians, martyrdom, or apostasy and penance. Scholarship has not yet successfully placed Peter within church history: it has generally ignored the biographical; it has not located the bishop's penitential canons, known as the *Canonical Letter*, within the context of a developing penitential discipline in the church; it has, for the most part, erroneously seen Peter's theology as anti-Origenist.

I have attempted here to gather together all but obviously spurious works attributed to Peter, and have offered new or first translations of them. In the process, I also offer a new appraisal of Peter's theological writings (chap. 2) and the *Canonical Letter* (chap. 3). Through a study of the penitential writings of Cyprian and Dionysius, I have attempted to place the *Canonical Letter* more firmly within the history of the fourth-century church and the development of a penitential system for apostates. With regard to the theological fragments, I have followed their history through the fifth and sixth centuries, especially as they were used against Origen. It is hoped, then, that this work will give the fullest account yet of Peter's life and death, that it will help in the reevaluation of long-held positions about his theology, and that it will give us a better understanding of the *Canonical Letter*.

It could be said of Saint Peter—not unfairly—that "Nothing in his life/Became him like the leaving it."[3] We know very little that is trustworthy about his life and even less about the effect of his *Canonical*

---

2. The most reliable history of the Christian church in Egypt remains that of E. R. Hardy. O. Meinardus is often good but sometimes less reliable; the *History* of C. A. Papadopoulos is not trustworthy.

3. Shakespeare *Macbeth* 1. 4. 7–8.

Letter with regard to the Melitian schism. There is no need to deny that Peter's fame is almost entirely posthumous: after his martyrdom he seems to have been immediately venerated, and it also seems that it was precisely because of that veneration (and *only* because of it?) that Peter's theological writings were handed down—in tatters to be sure—from the fourth to the sixth centuries, and into the ninth-century collection of Photius.

Peter, then, becomes important in tradition, in the church's retrospective self-understanding as it underwent immense changes during the time of Constantine and Chalcedon, and afterward. Saint Peter becomes important for one or two very specific reasons. In Egypt, Athanasius was fusing together two traditions, Coptic and Greek, and it is during this time that Peter's place of eminence in the church became secure.

As far as we can tell, however, Peter's "canonization" does not seem to have followed any plan. Athanasius mentions Peter relatively rarely, and when Socrates and Theodoret report on the later compromise between the orthodox and the Melitians they make no mention of Bishop Peter.[4] Peter did live on in two traditions: first, as a martyr, and second, as a great warrior (and implicitly, theologian) against Origen and Origenism. These two traditions later merged, but the evidence indicates that in the fourth century they were still separate.

The later *Lives* and *Martyrdoms* of Peter attest to the importance of this saint in the Egyptian church. This importance needs to be precisely defined. In the Greek tradition, it is the *Canonical Letter* and theological fragments that are most important, along with the *Life* of Peter, but only one fragment of a homily exists. By contrast, no theological writings by Peter survive in Coptic, only homilies and letters attributed to the bishop—and, once again, the accounts of his life. Athanasius in his *Life of Antony* probably intuited the Coptic interest in Peter and extoled him as a "martyr of blessed memory" (*Life* 47). This definition of Peter as martyr, not theologian, is the one that came down in the Coptic church: Peter was remembered primarily as a pious and humble pastor, one who gave up his life for his flock.

Pachomius, like Antony, was probably not interested "in the niceties of orthodox doctrine as a theological system."[5] One story in the *Life of Pachomius* illustrates wonderfully both the difference in Coptic and

4. Socrates *HE* 1.9.1–14; and Theodoret *HE* 1.9.2–13.
5. Henry Chadwick, "Pachomius and the Idea of Sanctity," *History and Thought of the Early Church* (London 1982) 14:18.

Greek interests and the apparent later fusion of those interests—in this case around the figures of Athanasius and Peter. It also serves as a perfect example of what happened in later church tradition to the figure of Peter the martyr.

Peter is primarily remembered in the Greek tradition as an anti-Origenist, and in this guise he makes an appearance in the *Life of Pachomius*. The famous anti-Origenist passage in the first Greek *Life* (*Vita Prima*: G¹) occurs in par. 31. Pachomius, according to this account, hated Origen as a blasphemer and a corrupter both of scripture and the ignorant: "Therefore the great Pachomius emphatically ordered the brothers not only not to dare to read that man's writings but not even to listen to his sayings. One day, having found a book of Origen, he threw it into the water and destroyed it."[6]

This passage is suspect for a number of reasons. First the transition from par. 30 is not a smooth one: the subject of that paragraph is the attempt by Athanasius to ordain Pachomius and the latter's humble refusal. If one compares the Greek version with the Bohairic (par. 28), it becomes clear that the Coptic emphasizes the refusal of Pachomius and the speech of Athanasius accepting this modest decision of the monk.

Paragraph 30 of the *Vita Prima* cuts out much of this and instead ends the paragraph by placing the emphasis on Athanasius:

> But [Pachomius] gazed at [Athanasius] on the boat, and recognized him as a holy servant of God, all the more as he had heard of the trials which Athanasius had endured for the sake of the Gospel and of his right faith for the sake of which he was also going to suffer later on.[7]

This emphasis on Athanasius the heretic fighter leads naturally into an attack on Origen who, along with Melitius and Arius, is made part of the great trinity of evil. The Bohairic version has none of this.

In the *Vita Prima* par. 31, after Pachomius speaks of burning heretical books, the narrative continues: "The holy man gave to the orthodox bishops and successors of the apostles and of Christ himself the heed of one who sees the Lord ever presiding upon the episcopal throne in the church and teaching through it."[8] Thus, Pachomius—as well as the monks and the Coptic communities—shows obeisance to the (Greek) hierarchy in Alexandria.

A later editor was still not satisfied with this. The editor of G³ expands

6. A. Veilleux, ed., *Pachomian Koinonia* (Kalamazoo, Mich. 1980) 1:317–18.
7. Ibid., 317.
8. Ibid., 318.

the above passage with even more pro-Athanasian material: "The holy Athanasius used to see the Savior in his church upon the throne, as also did the holy Peter, the bishop and martyr of the same Church, as we have learned from the orthodox bishops his successors."[9] The editor of G³, not content with the vagueness of "orthodox bishops and successors of the apostles" in the *Vita Prima*, has identified Athanasius as the chief of these successors. To praise Athanasius's sanctity and to ensure both his orthodoxy and the authority of the episcopacy (of Alexandria), the editor has borrowed a scene from the *Life* of Peter and attributed it to Athanasius, the successor of Peter. Thus Peter's own sanctity, strengthened by martyrdom (as Athanasius also suffers "martyrdom" for the truth in par. 30), is called upon in support of the current struggles against heretics, particularly Origen.

I have given this story in detail because, aside from its intrinsic interest to the historian, it exemplifies fully what was to happen in the later church tradition, specifically in the tradition surrounding Peter. As I shall show in chapter 2, Peter's authentic writings have nothing of anti-Origenism in them; later interpolations and accretions *seem* to make him an anti-Origenist. The same thing appears to have happened in the accounts of Peter's life (see chap. 1). In the story recounted above from the *Life of Pachomius*, we can see this process being acted out before our eyes.[10]

In this way, Peter the martyr becomes Peter the opponent of heretics, and this is the way later tradition has remembered him up to our day. The Greek tradition preserved a few fragments of Peter's writings that opposed some of Origen's teachings and were read as opposing Origenism in general. The Coptic tradition at first seemed content with the name of the blessed martyr and some of his marvellous deeds; later, as a soldier of Christ, Peter naturally enlisted in the ongoing wars—past, present, and future—against heretics, especially Origen. These two traditions, martyr and anti-Origenist, eventually came together: as we

---

9. Ibid., 411; G¹ par. 31 n. 3.
10. For a discussion of the various recensions of the *Life of Pachomius*, see ibid. 1–21 and notes, which refer to the Coptic, Greek, and Arabic critical editions. See also P. Rousseau, *Pachomius* (Berkeley 1985) 44, who concludes that we should be "distinctly nervous" about an incident that occurs only in the *Vita Prima*. On Origen, see ibid. 81 n. 21: "but there is little early evidence for later preoccupations, for example, with the works of Origen. . . ." For another "Pachomian" anti-Origenistic piece, see *Paralipomena*, chap. 4 (par. 7), in Veilleux 2:28–29, where a great stench comes from some anchorites who read Origen. A similar story occurs in G²; see F. Halkin, *Sancti Pachomii Vitae Graecae* (Brussels 1932) 241.

have seen in the later recensions of the *Life of Pachomius*, as well as in the later versions of the *Life of Peter*.

Saint Peter is important both for who he was and what he became. In this study I attempt to discuss both of these figures and try to separate them where they have become too closely joined. Finally, in each chapter I discuss this bishop of Alexandria within the broader context of church history. This study takes us from the third century, the time of Cyprian, Origen, and Dionysius, up through the time of Justinian in the sixth; geographically it ranges from Carthage in the West to Cappadocia in the East.

It would have been desirable to present a discussion of Peter the bishop and his role in ancient society along the lines set by Henry Chadwick and Peter Brown, but so little information survives about Peter as a civic and ecclesiastical administrator that this is not possible.[11] Nevertheless, it has been my intention to broaden the scope of this inquiry, that in focusing on early fourth-century Alexandria we might also range over a wider area. Thus I hope this study will be of interest not only to the historian of the Alexandrian church but also to all who are interested in the early church, both for its own story and for what it has to say about our own.

11. See H. Chadwick, "The Role of the Christian Bishop in Ancient Society," *Protocol of the Colloquy of the Center for Hermeneutical Studies* (Berkeley 1979), and Peter Brown's response.

1

Life and Works of Saint Peter

Peter I, bishop and martyr, occupied the see of Alexandria from 300 to 311. According to Eusebius (*HE* 9.7.2), Peter "presided with the greatest distinction" and was "a truly divine example of a bishop on account of his virtuous life and his earnest study of the holy scriptures. . . ."[1] Eusebius, however, mentions no details of the bishop's life.[2]

Eusebius's account symbolizes all too well the problem for the historian who wishes to investigate the life, writings, and times of Bishop Peter, the "seal of the martyrs": unlike Dionysius and Athanasius, the former a predecessor and the latter a successor in the Alexandrian see, Peter has left almost no biographical details. He became bishop in 300, wrote the *Canonical Letter* in 306 and another letter in 309, and was martyred in 311. Little more than this can be established for certain.

Yet the period of Peter's episcopacy was marked by a number of significant happenings—the persecution first under Diocletian and, later, under Maximin Daia, Peter's flight from Alexandria, the beginning of the Melitian schism, and Peter's return, arrest, and execution. In addition to these events, we should like to know about the church of Alexandria in Peter's day, its theology and ecclesiology, as expressed by its bishop and those to whom he addressed himself. Fortunately, many materials for this task have come to light in this century, and a large volume of scholarship has helped bring those materials to greater clarity.

Here I wish to build on this work and give as full a discussion as

1. All citations from Eusebius's *Ecclesiastical History* are from vol. 1 trans. Kirsopp Lake, vol. 2 trans. J. E. L. Oulton (LCL; Cambridge, Mass. 1926).
2. It is possible that Eusebius had no first-hand information on Peter; however, his reports on the martyrs and their persecutors are often stereotyped—the good are very good, and the bad very bad. Moreover, in a list of martyrs he may not have been interested in supplying details of the martyrs' lives.

possible of the life and writings of Peter of Alexandria. In the first part of the chapter I shall treat Peter's early life, the episcopacy, the beginning of the Melitian schism, and Peter's martyrdom. In the second part I shall discuss the works by and about Saint Peter: letters, theological and homiletical writings, and the *Martyrdom of Saint Peter*.

THE LIFE OF SAINT PETER[3]

Early Life

Nothing certain is known about Peter before he became bishop of Alexandria in 300. Since Eusebius says nothing about Peter's early life, we must rely on the tenth-century Arabic *History of the Patriarchs* by Severus (Ibn el Moqaffa), bishop of El Eschmounein, and on the seventh-century (?) Coptic *Encomium* on Saint Peter attributed to Alexander of Alexandria (see appendix 4, 78–84).[4] Although both of these works are highly hagiographical, it may still be possible to gather from them a few facts about the early life of the saint.

Both works frame the begetting and birth of Saint Peter with the stories of John the Baptist and the prophet Samuel. Peter's mother Sophia is a devout but barren wife, like Elizabeth, the mother of John, and Hannah, the mother of Samuel; however, through prayer and entreaty, she is blessed with a child whom, like the great prophets of old, she dedicates to God. In these works, almost nothing occurs in Peter's life that does not have scriptural parallel or warrant. It is just possible

3. For late illustrations of Saint Peter, see J.-M. Sauget, "Pietro I.," *Bibliotheca Sanctorum* 10:763, 766, 769–70; and H. Musurillo, "Peter of Alexandria, St.," *NCE* 11, 209. Professor H. A. Drake informs me that there is also an early fifteenth-century fresco, apparently fragmentary, entitled *The Vision of Saint Peter of Alexandria* in the Kanellopoulos Museum in Athens.

4. Severus, *History of the Patriarchs of the Coptic Church of Alexandria*, trans. B. Evetts, *Patrologia Orientalis* 1:103–211, 383–518. The history of Peter occupies pages 383–401. On Severus, see W. Telfer, "Episcopal Succession in Egypt," *JEH* 3 (1952) 6–7. Tito Orlandi, "La versione copta (Saidica) dell' 'Encomio di Pietro Alesandrino,'" *Rivista degli studi orientali*, 45 (1970) 151, says that Severus's *History* is partly realistic and partly legendary. The Bohairic encomium may be found in Henri Hyvernat, *Les actes des martyrs de l'Égypte* (Hildesheim and New York 1977) 247–62. I translate this in appendix 4, 78–84. Further references will be to the translation. See Orlandi, "La versione," for the Sahidic version of the encomium. Orlandi shows (151) that the Sahidic and Bohairic versions are essentially the same. He gives a summary of the contents (152), a discussion of the differences (152–53), the Coptic text (157–70), and a Latin translation (170–75). He states (154) that the attribution to Alexander is "certainly false."

The word "martyrology" ($\mu\alpha\rho\tau\upsilon\rho\text{o}\lambda\text{o}\gamma\iota\text{o}\nu$), 261 of Hyvernat's text, might give some indication of a date. Lampe (830b) cites for this word only the Trullan Synod (692), Canon 63—coincidentally the synod that accepted Peter's canons as canonical.

that Peter's mother did bear him late in life, and thus she was seen to be like Elizabeth and Hannah. We should be careful not to dismiss the reasonable possibility that early Christians understood their own lives in terms of the biblical saints and expressed themselves accordingly. Nevertheless, from a historian's viewpoint the hagiographical nature of the details given above makes them stereotypical and, therefore, suspect.

However, the *History* and *Encomium* share some common traditions that may have historical reminiscences behind them. Both "histories" agree that Peter was from an Alexandrian family. In the *Encomium* Peter's father is Theodosios, a (or the) senior presbyter (*protopresbyteros*) of Alexandria.[5] Socrates testifies (*HE* 6.9.3) that there was such an ecclesiastical position in Alexandria a hundred years after Peter's death, and it seems reasonable that it existed at the time of his birth.[6] Peter's mother Sophia is "of those who are honored"; this description may suggest that she came from Alexandrian nobility.[7]

In Severus's *History* Peter's parents are unnamed, although there too his father is "archpriest." The history of the episcopacy of Theonas, Peter's successor and "father," gives prominent position to the story of Peter's birth, and Peter's life as a whole, a story remarkably similar to the one given by the author of the *Encomium*.[8] The *History* also gives us a date for Peter's birth: the fifth of Abib (12 July, according to the Gregorian calendar).

Both the *History* and the *Encomium* reliably place Peter's birth in Alexandria. It also seems possible that local tradition may have preserved the names of his parents and of their station.[9] If this tradition is accurate, Peter was, like Athanasius, "presented" as a child, and, like Dionysius, well-born.[10] He may also have come from the highest ecclesiastical circles in Alexandria.[11]

According to the *Encomium* Peter was presented as a "gift" to the

---

5. *Encomium*, 79.

6. On *protopresbyteros* see Lampe, 1201a. A. C. Zenos, in NPNF 2:144 n. 2, cites Bingham's *Antiquities of the Christian Church* 2.19.18 for a discussion of the functions of this office.

7. *Encomium*, 79.

8. Severus, 206–11. See also pp. 81–82 and n. 170 below.

9. The Ethiopic Synaxery preserves their names. See E. A. Wallis Budge, *The Book of the Saints of the Ethiopian Church* (Hildesheim and New York 1976) 300.

10. J. Quasten, *Patrology* (Westminster, Md. 1984) 2:101; C. L. Feltoe, *DIONYSIOU LEIPSANA: The Letters and Other Remains of Dionysius of Alexandria* (Cambridge 1904), xii–xiii (hereafter, *Dionysius: Letters*).

11. It is odd, however, that when Sophia goes to see Archbishop Theonas he does not know her. See *Encomium*, 80.

church when he was seven years old; he was trained in both secular wisdom and in scripture, and by the age of thirteen was a lector and "knew how to recite in such a way that everyone came early to church because of the sweetness with which he read the lessons."[12] In Severus's *History* the child is even more precocious: at five he is given instruction, at seven he is made a reader, at twelve a deacon, and at sixteen a priest.[13] His learning is matched only by his ability to work wonders and silence heretics, notably Sabellius. When one reads these accounts, one is constantly reminded of the canonical and apocryphal acts of the boy Jesus and of the apostles and evangelists, upon which the acts of young Peter are certainly based, whether in conscious imitation or from popular piety and storytelling.

Nevertheless one must be careful not to dismiss these accounts too quickly. Tradition often connected Peter with Sabellius, but this is so implausible that one quickly dismisses it: the *Encomium* has Peter defeat Sabellius during the episcopacy of Theonas (282–300), which gives an impossibly late date for Sabellius. However, some later Greek writers, notably Basil and Timothy of Constantinople, place Sabellius in Libya or the Pentapolis, and Sabellian Christology persisted in Egypt into the fifth century.[14] Therefore, this account, although certainly wrong in having saint and heretic meet, may reflect a historical reminiscence of the bishop's confrontations with Sabellians.[15]

Only one other thing may be said about Peter before his accession to the see of Alexandria in 300. It is possible that at the end of the third century he was head of the catechetical school at Alexandria, the same school which Clement and Origen had directed. Harnack reports that according to Philip Sidetes Peter was director of the school, but says that it is impossible to give a chronology and does not commit himself on the truthfulness of Philip's report.[16]

---

12. *Encomium*, 80.

13. Severus, 208–9. John Mason Neale, *A History of the Holy Eastern Church*, vol. 1, *The Patriarchate of Alexandria* (London 1847) 90, remarks, "The infancy of Peter is, by the oriental writers, ornamented with many fables."

14. See the *ODCC*, 1218a, and W. H. C. Frend, *The Rise of Christianity* (Philadelphia and London 1984) 495. According to Eusebius (*HE* 7.6) Dionysius had confronted Sabellians. One might also note that Arius called Alexander a Sabellian.

15. Severus, 394, is more accurate. There Peter speaks of Sabellius as being alive during the time of Dionysius. Note that Sabellius is seen as having been active in Egypt.

16. Adolf von Harnack, *Geschichte der altchristlichen Literatur* (2d ed.;/Leipzig [1894] 1958) 2/2: 71–72. There is a problem with Philip's list. Harnack says that Peter was head of the school after Pierius, Theognostus, and (the unknown) Serapion. He sees Serapion as the one mentioned by Epiphanius, *Adv. haer.* 69.2 (*PG* 42:205A): "The church of Dionysius, and that of Theonas, and that of Pierius, and that of Serapion

Otto Bardenhewer, however, believes that Peter was at the catechetical school at the same time as Pierius and Achillas.[17] There is little to
choose between these views. Neither Severus's *History* nor the *Encomium* makes any mention of Peter and the school, but their silence does
not exclude the possibility. It is likely that Peter was in some way
associated with the famous Christian academy, and it is certainly possible that he, like Dionysius, was elected bishop while directing its
affairs.

Bishop of Alexandria

Both the *Encomium* of Alexander and the *History* of Severus report
that Peter was a presbyter or priest at the time of Archbishop Theonas's
death, but they give no clear indication how long he had been one or
how old he was at that time.[18] Eusebius puts matters very succinctly (*HE*
7.32.30): "After Theonas had given his utmost service for nineteen years,
Peter succeeded to the episcopate of the Alexandrians, and he too was
especially prominent for twelve entire years."

It is likely that Eusebius had nothing more than chronological information. That Peter and Theonas were "especially prominent" is a nice bit
of eulogizing, but almost nothing is known about Theonas. Even the
portion of Severus's *History* given to him is almost entirely dedicated to
Peter. A tradition, however, exists throughout the ancient literature on
Peter that Theonas was a "father" to him and "raised him," and that
Peter was particularly devoted to the memory of the old bishop.[19]

Eusebius's report (*HE* 7.32.30) that Peter "ruled" the church for less
than three entire years before the persecution" allows his accession to be
dated to 300, a date with which both the *Encomium* and the *History*
agree:

[Σεραπίωνος], etc." Such a church is not known, but there was at least one, and
probably two churches, built in the Serapeum after its destruction. Serapion may be a
misreading of Serapeion. See note 17. My thanks to Professor Birger Pearson for this
suggestion.

17. Otto Bardenhewer, *Geschichte der altchristlichen Literatur* (2d ed.; Freiburg 1914)
2:239. Bardenhewer agrees that Serapion is not to be identified and adds that Philip
Sidetes "arouses mistrust." Sauget (764) also doubts Philip's report. The relevant passage
of Philip, as quoted by Bardenhewer, reads: "after this one [Pierius], Serapion; after this
one, Peter the great bishop who was a martyr." The passage may be found in *PG* 39:229.

18. *Encomium*, 82; Severus, 383.

19. See par. 12 of P. Devos, "Une passion grecque inédite de S. Pierre d'Alexandrie et
sa traduction par Anastase le Bibliothécaire," *AnBol* 83 (1965). For my translation, see
appendix 3, 70–78, and 73 for Theonas. Further references will refer to this translation.
On Theonas, see Walter Ewing Crum, "Texts Attributed to Peter of Alexandria," *JTS* 4
(1902–03) 392–93. In a fragment of a letter (frag. A₈) attributed to Peter, Theonas is "he
that nourished me." See also 56–57 below.

When Abba Theonas, the patriarch, went to his rest, the clergy of Alexandria assembled with the people and laid their hands upon Peter the priest, his son and disciple, and seated him upon the episcopal throne of Alexandria, as Theonas, the holy father [had] bade them; and that was in the sixteenth year of Diocletian the prince.[20]

Both the *History* and the *Encomium* state that Theonas died on the second of Tobi (10 January, Gregorian). If this is accurate, and there seems to be no reason to doubt it, Peter was probably consecrated shortly thereafter.[21]

According to these two accounts, Theonas himself appointed Peter as his successor. The author of the *Encomium* reports that Theonas was instructed to do so by the Lord: "'You who water well the spiritual garden, give the garden to Peter the presbyter so he can water it, and come and rest with your fathers.'"[22] It is a nice image. Whoever wrote it had the sensibility of a poet along with the thinking of a churchman: the Lord's command clearly represents an attempt to lend authority to the see of Alexandria and its bishops. It is not so clear, however, whether it is a justification, or even an accurate description, of the process by which new bishops succeeded to their post.[23]

According to Severus, Theonas had come to the episcopal throne in a much less visionary way: "after the people had assembled, and had come to an agreement upon his fitness for the office."[24] Although this description is a little vague, the mention of "the people" is similar to the description given above of "the clergy and the people." This phrasing suggests that Peter was elected and then consecrated by presbyteral rather than episcopal laying-on of hands.

Jerome, in a famous passage, notes the unusual procedure at Alexandria: "For at Alexandria, from Mark the Evangelist up to the bishops Heraclas and Dionysius, the presbyters always nominated one chosen

20. *HE* 7.32.30; Severus, 207 and 383. See also Harnack, *Geschichte* 2/2:71; and Bardenhewer 2:239.

21. Severus, 207. *Encomium* 82. Epiphanius's statement, *Adv. haer.* 69.11 (*PG* 42:220B) is relevant: "It is the custom in Alexandria that when a bishop dies, there is no delay in appointing his successor, but it takes place at once, for the sake of peace in the church, and so that disturbances may not arise among the people, some wanting this man for bishop, and some that." Quoted by Telfer, "Episcopal Succession," 5. But see Eric Waldram Kemp, "Bishops and Presbyters at Alexandria," *JEH* 6 (1955) 132–33, for a moderating of Telfer's position. See 14–15 below.

22. *Encomium*, 82.

23. See the *Encomium*, 84, and also par. 6 of the *Passio* (ed. Devos); appendix 3, 72, for the visions of Peter, in which he is told to appoint Achillas and Alexander as his successors. See also n. 168 below.

24. Severus, 206.

from among themselves to be placed in the highest position."[25] Eutychius, a tenth-century Melchite patriarch of Alexandria, gives a history of the "presbyteral college" and traces its origin to Mark the evangelist, the patron saint of the Egyptian church, adding that this custom continued until the time of Alexander.

> S. Mark along with Anianas, ordained twelve presbyters, to remain with the patriarch, so that when the chair should become vacant, they might elect one out of the twelve on whose head the other eleven should lay their hands, give him benediction, and constitute him patriarch. . . . This custom continued at Alexandria till the time of the Patriarch Alexander . . . who forbade the presbyters in future to ordain their patriarch, but decreed that on a vacancy of the see the neighboring bishops should convene for the purpose of filling it with a proper patriarch, whether elected from those twelve presbyters, or from any others.[26]

Eutychius's report, however, is highly legendary, and untrustworthy.[27] Nevertheless, Eutychius does preserve a tradition of which he does not approve (before Alexander, he implies, the patriarchs were not "properly" elected). His statement also receives support from Severus's description of the consecration of Peter.[28] William Telfer concludes that "there is no longer room for doubt that early popes of Alexandria took office without intervention of other sees."[29]

If this is so, then did the presbyters also perform the laying-on of hands, as Severus says, in order to consecrate the new bishop? Telfer suggests that Severus's words "laid their hands on," "may simply render ἐχειροτόνησεν, and mean nothing different from Jerome's nominabant ['nominated'; see above, 13]."[30] Telfer conjectures that the city's presbyters elected the new bishop, but that the new bishop, through a prescribed ritual, took the authority of his office directly from the old bishop (see below, 47–49):

---

25. Jerome, Ep. 146, ad Evagrium (PL 22:1194A). For fuller discussions, see Telfer, "Episcopal Succession"; and also his "Meletius of Lycopolis and Episcopal Succession in Egypt," HTR 48 (1955) 227–37.

26. Neale, 9, modernized slightly. See Neale's discussion on 9–12 for an interesting insight into Anglican-Presbyterian disputes in the nineteenth century: "The above-quoted passage from Eutychius was first published by the learned Selden, with a very prolix commentary, as a prop to the falling cause of Presbyterianism" (10).

27. See ibid., 10–12; and esp. Telfer, "Episcopal Succession," 6–7. Kemp, 138, says, "Gore rightly objects, however, that Eutychius is so reckless and ignorant a writer that nothing can be taken for history because Eutychius says it."

28. Telfer, "Episcopal Succession," 7.

29. Ibid.

30. Ibid., 10. Kemp, 138, says that the term is ambiguous and may mean either "appoint" or "consecrate." See Lampe, 1522–23.

The probability is that th[is] old custom was undisturbed until Nicea [whose fourth Canon would render it obsolete], that Alexander was the last Alexandrine pope to take office without the imposition of living episcopal hands, and that a new order came in with Athanasius.[31]

E. W. Kemp, however, has shown that Severus's testimony is more ambiguous than Telfer seems willing to allow. He quotes eight separate passages on the consecration of bishops from the *History* which have, variously, the people (or laity), the laity and presbyters, and the presbyters alone, enthrone the new pope.[32] The examples Kemp cites also do not make clear who does the laying-on of hands.[33]

Although Kemp does not have much confidence in the ritual Telfer describes (which is discussed below, 47–49), he nevertheless agrees that the evidence shows "the survival at Alexandria to a later date than elsewhere of a presbyteral college with episcopal powers, such as some have suggested was usual in the great sees of Christendom in the earliest period."[34] Therefore, it would seem that Severus's description of Peter's consecration may be reasonably accurate. Eutychius, although guilty of pious flights of fancy when he envisions the twelve "tribes" (i.e., presbyters) of Alexandria established by Saint Mark, nevertheless seems to be accurate when he speaks of the presbyteral election of bishops at Alexandria. This appears to have been the custom which lasted until the lifetime of Bishop Alexander—who was probably himself a witness to Peter's election and consecration.

The Beginning of the Melitian Schism: 304–6[35]

Nothing is known of Peter or his episcopacy from 300 until the outbreak of persecution in 303. The bishop's flight sometime after that

31. Telfer, "Episcopal Succession," 10–11.
32. Kemp, 133–34.
33. Ibid., 134.
34. Ibid., 140; see also 142. Although Kemp offers a searching critique of both Telfer's methodology and intentions, he nevertheless does not refute Telfer's main points. The dispute to which their articles testify grew out of ecumenical studies in England in the mid-fifties, and centered on the definition and validity of the episcopacy and apostolic succession. See ibid., 140–42.
35. The Melitian schism is a complex subject, and the literature large. Here I deal with Melitius only as he comes into contact with Peter. I do not treat the question of Melitius's immunity from arrest, his alleged lapse, his being sentenced to the mines, or the subsequent fate of his party. This section will cover only the years 304–6, the years within which the schism occurred. Three important early essays on the Melitian schism are Edouard Schwartz, "Zur Geschichte des Athanasius," *NGG* (1905) 164–87; H. I. Bell, "The Melitian Schism," in *Jews and Christians in Egypt* (London 1924) 38–99; F. H. Kettler, "Der melitanische Streit in Ägypten," *ZNW* 35 (1936) 155–93. More recently, L. W. Barnard, William Telfer, Tito Orlandi, S. L. Greenslade, W. H. C. Frend, Henry

date, however, led to the schism caused by one of his bishops, Melitius of Lycopolis.[36] Before one studies the nature of this schism, however, it is necessary first to look briefly at the beginning of the Great Persecution and what its effect may have been upon Alexandria.[37]

Eusebius gives the following account of the beginning of the persecution under Diocletian:

> It was the nineteenth year of the reign of Diocletian [303], and the month Dystrus, or March, as the Romans would call it, in which, as the festival of the Savior's Passion was coming on, an imperial letter was everywhere promulgated, ordering the razing of the churches to the ground and the destruction by fire of the Scriptures, and proclaiming that those who held high positions would lose all their civil rights, while those in households, if they persisted in their profession of Christianity, would be deprived of their liberty. Such was the first document against us.[38]

The "first document" Eusebius speaks of is the first edict of Diocletian, promulgated 23 February 303, in the imperial city of Nicomedia.[39] Given the lack of contemporary witnesses to the effect of this law on the Alexandrian church, it is difficult to reconstruct what individual Christians there must have felt. The effect, however, must have been immediate: some, perhaps many, stayed away from church; others continued to worship, but in secrecy and fearful of detection; scriptures were hidden.

It is possible that the first edict was not enforced or was not effective, for those in power decided it was necessary to pass a second edict

---

Chadwick, and, most recently, Rowan Williams have made important contributions. Consult the bibliography for these authors' works. For brief narratives and chronological summaries independent of, but largely in agreement with, the present study, see L. W. Barnard, "Athanasius and the Meletian Schism in Egypt," *JEA* 59 (1973) 181–89; S. L. Greenslade, *Schism in the Early Church* (London 1953) 51–54; and R. Williams, "Arius and the Melitian Schism," *JTS*, n.s., 37.1 (1986) 35–52. Barnard's other article on this subject, "Some Notes on the Meletian Schism," *Studia Patristica* 12 (1971) 399–405, does not propose to discuss the origins of the schism.

36. Most recent scholars affirm that "Melitius," rather than "Meletius" is the correct spelling. See Bell, 39 n. 1; and Schwartz, 164. For the sake of consistency, I use "Melitius" throughout this work, and, wherever necessary, silently change the spelling in quotations, although not in titles of works.

37. This outline of the Great Persecution is largely drawn from N. H. Baynes, "The Great Persecution," chap. 19 in *Cambridge Ancient History* (Cambridge 1971), esp. 12:665ff.; for bibliographical information, see 789–93, esp. 789–90 for the Melitian schism. See also Geoffrey de Ste. Croix, "Why Were the Early Christians Persecuted?" *Past and Present* 26 (1963) 6–38; W. H. C. Frend, *Martyrdom and Persecution in the Early Church* (1965, 1981) esp. 491ff.

38. Eusebius *HE* 8.2.4. See also Eusebius *Martyrs of Palestine* (shorter recension) Praefatio; citations from this work are from *The Ecclesiastical History and the Martyrs of Palestine*, ed. H. J. Lawlor and J. E. L. Oulton (London 1928, 1954).

39. Baynes, 665, gives the provisions of the first edict.

directed specifically against church leaders. Whatever its motivations, the government published the second edict in the spring or early summer of 303. Eusebius reports: "But not long afterwards we were further visited with other letters, and in them the order was given that the presidents of the churches should all, in every place, be first committed to prison, and then afterwards compelled by every kind of device to sacrifice."[40]

Anyone who reads through Eusebius's *Ecclesiastical History* or *Martyrs of Palestine* will quickly learn what "every kind of device" meant in the Roman world: "On others, the noses, ears, and hands were mutilated, and the remaining limbs and parts of the body cut up, as was done at Alexandria."[41] Again, it is unclear what the exact events were in Alexandria at this time; it is not known how strictly the law was enforced nor how many suffered. But in September or November 303, the third edict was published, offering amnesty to those who sacrificed to the gods. Some must have done so and apostatized; some must have refused and died.

> Such was the course of action in the first year, when the presidents of the Church were alone menaced by the persecution. But when the second year came around and, further, the war against us increased in intensity (Urban being at that time governor of the province), imperial edicts then visited us for the first time in which by a general ordinance the command was given that in the several cities all the people in a body should sacrifice and offer libations to the idols.[42]

Eusebius, curiously, does not mention the most important feature of this "general ordinance" of January or February 304. This edict, the fourth and most terrible, dictated that all inhabitants were to sacrifice to the gods on pain of death. All Christians were now liable to prosecution if they did not sacrifice. Particular days were probably appointed for provinces or towns or parts of cities in which all the inhabitants were required to show their allegiance to the state by worshiping publicly the state gods. After these appointed days, those who had not sacrificed were immediately subject to arrest, imprisonment, torture, and death.[43]

Christians were now enemies of the state. Many were jailed—including at Alexandria the bishops Hesychius, Pachomius, Theodorus, and

---

40. Eusebius *HE* 8.2.4. See also *Martyrs* Praefatio and 1.1
41. Eusebius *HE* 8.12.1.
42. Eusebius *Martyrs* 3.1.
43. Geoffrey de Ste. Croix, "Aspects of the 'Great' Persecution," *HTR* 47 (1954) 80 and 96.

Phileas, all of whom were later martyred.[44] Mass apostasies undoubtedly took place. Many fled. One of these was Bishop Peter, Bishop of Alexandria, who went into exile probably at the beginning of 304.[45]

Why did Peter flee? And where did he go? Harnack is close to the truth when he says that at the beginning of the Melitian schism "everything is in an impenetrable fog."[46] Nevertheless, there are some clues as to where Peter went and what he did while he was there. The *Martyrdom of Saint Peter* gives the following account:

> Peter, avoiding the madness of the persecutors, went as a fugitive from place to place. Hiding himself, he passed most of the time in Mesopotamia, and in like manner concealed himself in Syria of Phoenicia. He continued his wandering for a longer time in Palestine, and then stayed for some time in the islands. In all these places he did not cease from writing by night or day, strengthening not only the clergy but also the laity in the unity of Christ.[47]

The *Encomium* of Alexander testifies also to the tradition that Peter fled to Mesopotamia because of the persecution of Diocletian.[48]

There is nothing in this account that is inherently improbable. Dionysius, some forty years earlier, "was able in his banishment to hold services and even make converts, and carried on the affairs of the Church by letter . . . until he could return to Alexandria."[49] In Ep. 20.2, Cyprian tells of having sent thirteen letters while in flight: "In them neither advice was wanting to the clergy, nor exhortation to the confessors."[50]

The "Veronese fragments," two letters and a short narrative piece, are the most important contemporary witness to events in Alexandria at this

44. See the "Letter of Phileas" in James Stevenson, *A New Eusebius* (London 1963) 290–92; and M. J. Routh, *RS* 4:91. See also Peter's *Canonical Letter* (chap. 3 below) and Cyprian *De Lapsis* 7 and 8. See also the "Acts of Phileas," in Herbert Musurillo, *The Acts of the Christian Martyrs* (Oxford 1972) 328–53.

45. Harnack, *Geschichte* 2/2:72; and Frend, *Martyrdom*, 498, agree that Peter fled after the fourth edict, at the beginning of 304. Bardenhewer prefers to place his flight in 303 after the second edict. Either date could be correct, although I prefer the former.

46. Harnack, *Geschichte* 2/2:72: "Alles [ist] in einem undurchdringlichen Nebel."

47. William Telfer, "St. Peter of Alexandria and Arius," *AnBol* 67 (1949) 126.

48. *Encomium*, 83. Interestingly, the details of Peter's flight are given in the first person plural—analogous to the "we" passage of Acts—and the narrator is Alexander who, along with Achillas his "father," is with Peter in his wanderings. Frend, *Rise of Christianity*, 447 and 458, says that Peter fled in 303 for Oxyrhyncus, and cites Schmidt, TU 6–7. This text published by Schmidt has serious difficulties, and one can not rely on it. See 57 below, and the notes ad loc. Most of the evidence points to a journey by Peter in Mesopotamia.

49. E. R. Hardy, *Christian Egypt* (New York 1952) 28.

50. *Letters of St. Cyprian*, trans. Sister Rose Bernard Donna, C.S.J. (Washington, D.C. 1965) 54.

time.[51] One of these, the "Letter of Phileas," actually a letter written from prison by the bishops Hesychius, Pachomius, Theodorus, and Phileas to Melitius, strongly suggests that Peter was in control of ecclesiastical matters at Alexandria—even if from a distance.[52] Temporary replacements had been appointed for the jailed bishops, while the latter advised Melitius to wait "for the judgment of the superior father [Peter]." The tone of this letter, the continued obedience of the bishops to their bishop, and their firm belief that church order was being maintained (under Peter's supervision *in absentia*) does not suggest that Peter left in haste or that he had lost control of the situation.[53]

Peter's exact motives for flight are unknown, but to suggest that he may have thought discretion the better part of valor does not make him a Falstaff.[54] He probably left seeking personal safety and a secure place from which he could continue to administer his church, or, like Cyprian, Peter fled to avoid provoking further actions by the authorities against the church (see below, 157–59). The bishop did indeed have precedent for his actions. Although Origen early in life may have sought out martyrdom, he later said that "Jesus taught his disciples not to be rash,

51. Kettler, "Streit," 159–63, gives the Latin texts of the Veronese fragments, with a critical apparatus. An English translation may be found in Stevenson, 290–93, who has improved on the one in the ANF. See William Telfer, "The Codex Verona LX (58)," *HTR* 36 (1943) 169–246; he says that the author is Athanasian. See Williams, 38ff., for a discussion and modification of Telfer's work. Williams concludes (38) that the Veronese fragments give us "the clearest picture available" on the origins of the Melitian schism. On the Veronese fragments, see also Tito Orlandi, "Ricerche su una storia ecclesiastica alesandrina del IV sec.," *Vetera christianorum* 11 (1974) 287–96. See also n. 193 below.

52. Stevenson, 290. Severus preserves a tradition that these bishops were in contact with Peter. In the *History*, 392ff., he has Peter say: "And my heart was greatly grieved; but in spite of all this I did not neglect the care of Phileas and Hesychius and Pachomius and Theodorus, who were imprisoned for the faith in the Lord Jesus Christ, and merited grace from God; for I used to write to them, and to speak of them in my epistles from Mesopotamia. And I suffered great troubles and torment for their sakes, lest anything should happen to them together with the priests who were in prison; for more than six hundred and sixty souls became martyrs." Telfer omits this passage from his Urtext, but whoever put these words in Peter's mouth had access to written or oral records of events during the persecution.

53. Stevenson, 291; *RS* 4:91. The bishops refer to Peter as "our great bishop and father Peter, on whom we all depend in the hope which we have in the Lord Jesus Christ." This reverence from men who probably knew they were going to die does not suggest the "chicken-heartedness" imputed to Peter by Frend, *Martyrdom*, 498.

54. Telfer, "St. Peter and Arius," 125, concludes: "The first impact of persecution in Egypt was very severe. Notwithstanding that Egyptian Christians scattered far and wide, many were caught and martyred abroad. The price on Peter's head is sure to have been heavy. If, at the outset, he fled till he crossed the imperial frontiers, there was time enough in three years for his cautious return through Syria and Palestine to a secret hiding place in Egypt. Melitius, as a trusted suffragan of Peter, would know where to find him. And that is what the confessors imply. There seems, therefore, no ground for stigmatizing the list of Peter's hiding places as 'legend.'. . ."

saying to them, 'If they persecute you in this city flee to another; and if they persecute you in that, flee again to yet another.' And he gave them an example of his teaching by his tranquil life; he was careful not to meet dangers unnecessarily or at the wrong time for no good reason."[55]

Such a text was probably taken much to heart during the persecution. Peter himself uses it in Canon 9 of the *Canonical Letter*, where he indirectly justifies his own flight:

> He also wishes us to move about from place to place when we are being persecuted for his name, as we again hear him saying: 'And when they persecute you from this town, flee to the next.' For he does not wish us of our own accord to go over to the supporters and accomplices of the Devil, for if we did so we would become the cause of many deaths and would be forcing them to become harsher and to carry out their works of death.[56]

The four bishops in the "Letter of Phileas" say nothing about Peter's flight; all we know from them is that Melitius had performed illegal ordinations during the absence of the bishop.

The chronology for this time is as obscure as Peter's precise motives for leaving Alexandria. We know that he left the city and that he returned, but it is impossible to be exact as to the sequence of events for the years 304–06. I suggest the following chronology:

304	Peter flees.
304–5	Melitius comes to Alexandria.[57]
305–6	Peter returns; he writes the *Canonical Letter*.
306(?)	Peter flees again.

Melitius, bishop of Lycopolis (Asiout) in the Thebaid, has never had a good press from church historians.[58] Athanasius says that he "was convicted of many crimes and among the rest of offering sacrifice to idols," although this is unlikely.[59] Epiphanius, on the other hand, influ-

---

55. Origen, *Contra Celsum*, trans. Henry Chadwick (Cambridge 1980) 1.65. The scripture he refers to is Matt. 10:23.

56. See chap. 3, 157–59 and 200–202 below for a detailed discussion.

57. B. J. Kidd, *A History of the Church* (Oxford 1922) 1:531, suggests that the schism took place in 306; Harnack, *Geschichte* 2/2:72, prefers 306; F.-J. Foakes-Jackson, "Meletianism," *Encyclopaedia of Religion and Ethics* (London 1915) 8:538, places the schism in 305 or 306; Bell, 38, prefers 305; Hans Lietzmann, *A History of the Early Church*, vols. 2–3, *The Founding of the Church Universal* (Cleveland, Ohio 1961) 3:104, dates it to the end of 305; Telfer, "Meletius," 227, argues for 306, and cites Lawlor and Oulton, *Eusebius* 2:267.

58. See, e.g., Bardenhewer 2:240, who says that he was a "man of doubtful character."

59. Athanasius *Apologia contra Arianos* 11, in *PG* 25:256ff., and trans. in Stevenson, 379–81. Bell, 38, rightly points out that it is very improbable that Melitius apostatized: "The accusation [that one sacrificed] was one that came readily to controversialists on

enced by Melitian sources, goes out of his way to emphasize that
Melitius was not a heretic, and, in fact, says that he "was thought to be
first among [the bishops] throughout Egypt and was second only to
Peter in the archbishopric [of Egypt]."[60]

Epiphanius's statement certainly seems like Melitian propaganda; he
has, however, had his supporters among church historians. J. M. Neale is
willing to accept Epiphanius's report, and concludes that Lycopolis
"appears to have possessed some honorary pre-eminence," while F. H.
Kettler sees Melitius as an agent or representative of the Alexandrian
bishop for all of Egypt.[61] Neither of these suppositions, however, can be
proved.

If Melitius had been of such high position, it might help to explain his
audacity at usurping the power of his bishop. Neale was willing to
accept some sort of preeminence for Melitius because he thought it
helped to explain the rapid spread of the schism.[62] Although this
explanation does not seem likely, one can sympathize with Neale,
because establishing a motive for Melitius has been a vexing problem
(see below). Whatever his character and motivation, it is clear that
Melitius, sometime in 304-6, left Lycopolis and was ordaining presbyters
in other dioceses; finally, he came to Alexandria and assumed some of
the powers of the absent bishop.

Is it possible that the imprisoned bishops wrote their letter at Peter's
behest? There is no direct evidence for this in the letter itself, but it is

---

the morrow of a great persecution." Such an accusation by Athanasius is reminiscent of
the charges of communist sympathies tossed about in the 1950s. For a detailed
comment, see C. J. Hefele, *History of the Ecclesiastical Councils* (repr., New York [1894]
1972) 1:346ff. See also Williams, 37.

60. Epiphanius *Adv. haer.* (*Panarion*) 68 (*PG* 42:184B–189B). See appendix 5, 84–86 for
a translation. Telfer, "St. Peter and Arius," 125ff., believes that Epiphanius's sources are
Melitian, as do Kidd 1:531; and Williams, 36. Neale, 91 n. 1, says that Epiphanius is
"unconsciously using Melitian documents"; as does W. Bright, "Petrus I., St.," *DCB* 4:332.
Hefele 1.350, says that Epiphanius was influenced by Melitians in his home town of
Eleutheropolis. Foakes-Jackson, 538, sees this as "special knowledge." On Epiphanius
and Eleutheropolis, see Telfer, "Meletius," 229.

Athanasius also suggests indirectly that Melitius was not a heretic. He has Antony
call the Melitians "schismatics" rather than "heretics" like the Arians. See the *Life of
Antony,* pars. 68 and 89; and Kettler, "Streit," 156–57. For a general discussion of schism,
see Greenslade, esp. 15–29 for a definition of schism.

61. Neale, 90–91; Kettler, "Streit," 166. But Kettler, with K. Müller, and against E.
Schwartz, insists that Melitius was not archbishop or metropolitan of the Thebaid.
Greenslade, 53, concurs, and emphasizes that the imprisoned bishops make no mention
of any special authority for Melitius. He sees the importance given Melitius in the
Epiphanian documents as an "attempt to justify Melitius."

62. Neale, 91 n. 1: "it affords some grounds for the rapid spread of the schism, if we
allow the superior dignity of the first mover."

clear that they are speaking as bishops who owe their allegiance to the
bishop of Alexandria:

> But you [they say to Melitius], neither taking any account of these things,
> and with no regard for the future, and the law throughout of our blessed
> fathers and those who have been taken to Christ in succession, nor the
> honor of our great bishop and father Peter, on whom we all depend in the
> hope which we have in the Lord Jesus Christ . . . have ventured on
> subverting all things at once.[63]

In addition to charging Melitius with disrespect of authority, they
accuse him of ordaining priests "in parishes other than his own,"
because he has given "such strenuous attentions to the deceits of certain
parties and their vain words."[64] C. J. Hefele made the perceptive judgment that Melitius was probably ordaining in the dioceses of the bishops
who wrote the letter.[65] That Melitius was ordaining illegally is corrob-
orated by a later synodical letter of the Egyptian bishops which orders
that those so ordained must be properly reconsecrated.[66]

What were Melitius's motives in this illegal act? The salutation of the
bishops' letter, unless excessively politic or polite, shows that Melitius
was, at the time of the letter, in good standing within the Christian
community.[67] The bishops do not say how long Melitius has been about
his illicit business; they do, however, provide a motive when they
rhetorically suggest (they do not mean it) that he might excuse himself
by saying that the flocks, because of the persecution, were without their
pastors. In agreement with the excuse offered by the bishops, W. Telfer
suggests that after the clergy of lower Egypt had "gone underground"
because of the persecution and Christian liturgy had ceased, Melitius
"set out to secure its revival. Where he found men willing to defy
imperial orders by restoring the liturgical gatherings, he ordained them
presbyters."[68]

---

63. Stevenson, 290–91.
64. Ibid., 291.
65. Hefele 1:343.
66. See Socrates *HE* 1.9; and Theodoret *HE* 1.9. Hefele 1:352 gives the text: "and as
for the clergy ordained by him, it is necessary to lay hands upon them again, that they
may afterwards be admitted to communion with the Church, to give them their work,
and to restore to them the honors which are their due; but in all dioceses where these
clergy are located, they should always come after the clergy ordained by Alexander. . . ." Hefele also suggests that the many offenses Athanasius speaks of represent
"an allusion to these ordinations, and consequently it would be untrue to say that
Athanasius and the original documents are at variance" (1:347).
67. They address Melitius as "Melitio dilecto et comministro in Domino." *RS* 4:91;
Kettler, "Streit," 159.
68. Telfer, "Meletius," 227–28; see also Williams, 37.

The bishops, however, say that the flocks have not been left destitute, "because there are many going about (to) them . . . in a position to act as visitors."[69] According to Kettler, the term for "visitors," *circumeuntes*, denotes not the later office of "chorepiscopus," but a layperson commissioned to visit the parishes because of extraordinary conditions.[70] If these visitors had no sacramental authority, then conditions in the churches were probably as Telfer suggests.

It is important to note that the bishops say nothing about any kind of disagreement between Peter and Melitius concerning those who had fallen (the *lapsi*) during the persecution; it is this disagreement which Epiphanius was to see as the main reason for the schism. At this point, the bishops see only one offense by Melitius: he is ordaining outside of his diocese. According to the second, anonymous Veronese fragment, Melitius had not yet set foot in Alexandria; it states that he did so only after the deaths of the bishops.[71]

After their deaths, Melitius came to Alexandria and enlisted the aid of Isidore and Arius.[72] The account in the second Veronese fragment does not say whether Isidore and Arius were clergy or laypersons.[73] According to Epiphanius *Adv. haer.* 69.1–2 Arius was presbyter in the church of Saint Mark (the Baucalis church), while Sozomen *HE* 1.15 says only that it was a church in Alexandria.

Is the Arius mentioned here the famous heretic and foe of Athanasius?[74] An extensive tradition has Peter involved with the heretic Arius, and the *Passio S. Petri*, edited by Telfer, certainly links the two.[75] The Greek *Martyrdom* edited by Devos is even more explicit: Arius had been excommunicated by Peter, and when he heard that Peter had been jailed, Arius sent others to intercede for him. After hearing their intercessions, Peter denounces Arius and later has a vision about him.[76]

69. We should probably understand that the bishops are saying, quite reasonably, "in *our* dioceses."

70. Kettler, "Streit," 160, under 1.14 in the *apparatus criticus*. The second Veronese fragment, however, speaks of them as presbyters. See ibid., 162.

71. Stevenson, 292–93; Routh, *RS* 4:94; Kettler, "Streit," 161–62. Eusebius *HE* 8.10 testifies to the martyrdom of these bishops.

72. See Stevenson, 292.

73. On divining their possible motives in the ambiguous phrasing of the Veronese fragment—*doctoris habens desiderium*—see Williams, 35 and n. 4 ad loc.

74. Greenslade, 52 n. 44, says that it is probable, but not certain.

75. See par. 3, Telfer, "St. Peter and Arius," 128–30, and appendix 2, 69–70 below.

76. See 70–78 below for a translation. The images for the story of Peter's vision of a child with his seamless robe torn asunder by Arius may go back to a letter of Alexander. See Williams, 44 and n. 42 ad loc. This entire section of the *Martyrdom* is extremely untrustworthy.

However, T. Orlandi views the antiheretical portions of the *Passio* as later additions.[77] The *Passio*, he says, was written in two different periods: one not long after Peter's death, the other, legendary, about a century later.[78] Neither the Bohairic *Encomium* nor the Greek *Martyrdom* edited by Devos connects Arius with Melitius.[79] The *Encomium* says nothing more than that Melitius and Arius were contemporaries. This is significant, because if the writer had known of a tradition linking the two, he certainly would have used it.

Athanasius, in *Apologia contra Arianos* 6, says that Alexander excommunicated Arius. In 11 the Melitians and Peter are mentioned, but no mention is made of Melitius *and* Arius. In 59 Athanasius says that Melitius was deposed by Peter and that the "Arian heresy began" during Melitius's lifetime.[80] Whether this was during Peter's episcopacy remains doubtful. Athanasius also says that Melitius caused trouble for Achillas and Alexander, Peter's immediate successors, and the context suggests that Arianism arose after Peter's lifetime. In *Epistula ad episcopos Aegypti* 22 (NPNF 4.234–35), Athanasius states that the Melitians and Arians have joined forces, but he does not say they were related in Peter's day. These texts from Athanasius must be regarded as serious evidence against a connection between Melitius and Arius, and Arius—at least the heretical Arius—and Peter.

The accounts of Socrates and Sozomen on this issue are difficult to reconcile. According to Socrates *HE* 1.6, Alexander says that the problems with Arian troublemakers have "recently" arisen. Alexander does not number Melitius in his list of Arian apostates, and Socrates says that Melitius and Arius came together only during the time of Alexander. Sozomen's account differs. Contrary to the Veronese fragment, he says in *HE* 1.15 that Arius followed Melitius *before* he was a deacon, and that after abandoning his Melitian opinions he was ordained deacon by Peter.[81] Peter later cast out Arius because Arius sided with the Melitians when the archbishop anathematized them and invalidated their baptism. Sozomen concludes that after Peter's death Arius was restored by Achillas to deacon and later presbyter.

77. Orlandi, "Ricerche," 299–304.

78. Orlandi, *Omelie copte*, 27.

79. See Devos, par. 8; appendix 3, 73–74 below.

80. Translated in Stevenson, 379. On Athanasius and his treatment of Melitius, Arius, and Peter, see T. Orlandi, "Sull' Apologia secunda (contra Arianos) di Atanasio di Alessandrina," *Augustinianum* 15 (1975) 49–79.

81. For Sozomen's possible source, see appendix 2, 69–70, below; and see Williams's detailed discussion, 39–45.

Rowan Williams, however, after a careful study has concluded that Sozomen's account also has difficulties—the gravest of which was first recognized by Valesius, the seventeenth-century editor of Sozomen and Socrates: No fourth-century writer refers to Arius's alleged excommunication by Peter. And, as Williams points out, "several 'cues' occur for the mention of such a subject in the polemics of the period: not once is it even hinted at."[82]

Later polemic, it seems, joined together the two "traitors," Arius and Melitius, and would have been glad to see the Arius of the Veronese fragment as the archheretic. However, the fact that the various *Martyrdoms* of Peter vary suggests that at least in some circles little or nothing was known of a connection between the later heretic Arius and Melitius during Peter's lifetime. If one combines this with the silence of Alexander, Athanasius, and Epiphanius, the early evidence is overwhelming against a "Melitian Arius."[83]

Williams, in fact, concludes that the stories of two persons named Arius have been conflated: the heretic Arius had been ordained deacon by Peter; the Melitian Arius was a layperson who was later excommunicated by Peter.[84] At the very least, from Williams's study and the present one, it must be concluded that there is very little solid evidence to show a Melitius-Arius connection. More important, since none of the earliest sources locates Arianism during Peter's episcopacy, it seems clear that the heresy postdates the bishop's death.[85]

82. Williams, 45.
83. Williams's term. I find now that he has independently reached the same conclusions as I, though by a slightly different path. See ibid., 46–47.
84. Williams, 49–50; he points out that the name "Arius" was common. Williams's reasons are complicated, and one, the issue of Peter's invalidation of Melitian baptism (only Sozomen mentions this), is very speculative. Nevertheless, Williams has done a valuable service in showing the many difficulties and great complexity of this subject.
85. L. W. Barnard, "The Antecedents of Arius," *Vigiliae Christianae* 24 (1970) 184, suggests that Peter could have influenced Arius because of their common literalist biblicism which was opposed to the allegorism of Origen and his followers. Based on Peter's extant writings, such a speculative suggestion is not warranted. It is not certain that Peter was either a literalist or against allegory. See the discussion of this in the section on anti-Origenism, 110–26 below.

One final—again, contradictory—note is of interest. Socrates relates that after Peter's death Arius returned to the church. If he had been at odds with Peter, what might have caused his change of heart? It is possible that he was a witness to the events surrounding Peter's martyrdom. As noted above, Epiphanius places Arius in the Baucalis church in Alexandria. According to one tradition concerning Peter's martyrdom, his last hours were spent at the tomb of Saint Mark in Baucalis, and it is just possible that Peter was in fact buried there (see 45–46 and notes ad loc.). As Frend has suggested (see 38 below), Peter's death may have brought many Melitians back to the orthodox fold. If one accepts the "one Arius hypothesis," it is just possible that one of these Melitians was Arius.

According to the second Veronese fragment, Isidore and Arius led Melitius to two "presbyters, then in hiding, to whom the blessed Peter had given powers to act as parish-visitors." Melitius wins them to his side and then ordains two others, one in prison and one in the mines.[86] Peter's response to this is worth quoting in full:

> Peter, to the brethren who are loved and established in the faith of God, greetings in the Lord.
>
> I have learned that Melitius does nothing for our good. He is not satisfied with the letter of the most blessed bishops and martyrs, and moreover has invaded my parish and has arrogated so much to himself that he even attempts to separate from my authority the presbyters and those whom I have appointed to visit the needy. He has also given proof that he desires to be preeminent since he has ordained to himself certain ones of those in jail.
>
> Now, be on your guard, and do not associate with [or: be in communion with] [ne ei communicetis] him until, with our wise men in attendance, I can meet with him and see what he is planning. Farewell.[87]

Peter here attacks Melitius for the same reasons the bishops did: Melitius has usurped the bishop of Alexandria's authority and has performed illegal ordinations, "invading" the bishop's parish. Peter imputes no motives to Melitius; more important, he says nothing about a disagreement between them with regard to the lapsed. It is possible that the bishop is being cautious or that he honestly does not know what Melitius's designs are. Peter clearly has, or knows of, Phileas's letter, and therefore would know of the motives that letter suggests—but the bishops' suggestions there may be rhetorical and based on guesswork. Unfortunately, the documents examined so far do not supply the cause for the origins of the Melitian schism.

Is Peter's letter a letter of excommunication? Probably, but in precisely what sense is uncertain. "Ne ei communicetis" must be a translation of (ἵνα) $\mu\grave{\eta}$ $\alpha\mathring{\upsilon}\tau\tilde{\wp}$ $\kappa o\iota\nu\omega\nu\tilde{\eta}\tau\epsilon$, which does not necessarily mean "excommunicate." Its primary meaning in this context would be "associate, have fellowship with." More specifically, it could mean "associate in Christian fellowship with, hold communion with," and one could translate the sentence under discussion with "Do not be in communion with him."[88]

But does this mean that Melitius is excommunicate? It is clear that, de

---

86. Stevenson, 292.

87. *PG* 18:509; my translation. Kettler, "Streit," 175, accepts Peter's letter and says that unfortunately the conclusion does not say whether he would come to Alexandria or to Melitius to conduct an inquiry. See Cyprian Ep. 15.1 for a statement similar to the one Peter makes. For a striking parallel to Peter's letter, see Dionysius's lament over a certain Germanus, in Eusebius *HE* 7.11.18–19.

88. See Lampe, 762.

facto, he is now separated by the bishop from the orthodox, but has he been excommunicated de jure? Epiphanius, interestingly, employs the closest parallel to the phrase used here; in *Panarion* 68.3 he discusses the separation between the Melitians and the orthodox (see 84–86 below): "And the two opposing sides were not in communion [ἀλλήλοις ἐκοι-νώνουν] with each other." The use of κοινωνοῦν by Epiphanius here does not automatically mean "excommunication" in the formal sense, although there was certainly no communion—in every sense of the word —between the two parties. Moreover it seems likely that by the time to which Epiphanius is referring both sides had "excommunicated" each other. By contrast, the context of Peter's letter suggests that he has not yet officially cast out Melitius: the bishop explicitly states that he hopes to meet with the usurper, and such a statement does not seem likely if Melitius were already outside the orthodox fold. It seems best to regard this letter as a provisional excommunication: the recipients are to have nothing to do with Melitius—including liturgically and sacramentally— until Peter can come to judge matters.[89]

Until very recently Epiphanius was the only source able to offer a motive for Melitius's actions and, since his information is based on Melitian sources and is otherwise full of inaccuracies, his testimony has largely been dismissed. For example, he places Peter and Melitius in prison together; this makes for good drama, but is historically extremely unlikely.[90] B. J. Kidd neatly summarizes both Epiphanius's report and

89. See Williams, 36, who has reached the same conclusion.
90. A surprising number of scholars are willing to accept Epiphanius's account: W. H. C. Frend, *The Donatist Church: A Movement of Protest in North Africa* (Oxford 1952) 22 (following Lietzmann); *Martyrdom*, 539; and "The Failure of the Persecutions in the Roman Empire," in *Town and Country in the Early Centuries* (repr., London 1980) x, p. 280. Ramsey MacMullen, *Christianizing the Roman Empire (AD 100–400)* (New Haven 1984) 92 n. 17, 160; C. A. Papadopoulos, *Historia tēs Ekklēsias Alexandrias* (Alexandria 1935) 154; Bell, 39; J. Lebreton, in J. Lebreton and J. Zeiler, *The History of the Primitive Church* (New York 1949) 1048–49. Lebreton as well as Frend also accept the story that Peter put up his cloak to separate himself from Melitius. Most recently, Robin Lane Fox, *Pagans and Christians* (New York 1987), 609–10, gives credence to the tale, as does Peter Brown in his review of Fox's book, "Brave Old World," *New York Review of Books*, 12 March 1987, 25. While this story is extremely doubtful, it vividly symbolizes the schism. Whoever created it had a fine sense for poetic, if not historical, truth. T. D. Barnes, *Constantine and Eusebius* (Cambridge 1981) 184, correctly says that Epiphanius "was deceived by a story that he [Peter] had been cast into prison with the schismatic Melitius." That the prison story comes initially from Melitian sources is patent. The Veronese fragments say nothing about a meeting between Peter and Melitius, nor does either the Coptic *Encomium* or the Greek *Martyrdom*—and such a scene would fit gloriously in those accounts. None of these sources even knows of an imprisonment of Peter other than the one immediately prior to his death. Greenslade, 53–54; and Williams, 36 (citing Hefele), do not accept the prison story. Williams, 36, says "there is no reason to think that Melitius was in captivity at all before 311." See 32 and n. 105

the scholarly consensus on it. According to Epiphanius's account, Kidd writes,

> The origin of the schism was a difference in regard to the treatment of the lapsed, between Peter inclined to laxity and Melitius to stricter measures. But the Epiphanian documents are Melitian, and their account is inconsistent with well-ascertained facts. Thus, according to Epiphanius, Melitius and Peter were in prison together; whereas, according to the Verona fragments neither was in prison at all. Again, according to Epiphanius, Peter was too 'considerate'; but his own penitential canons show that he knew how to apportion the penance to the sin.[91]

Epiphanius, despite his flaws, has long had one thing in his favor: he offers a plausible explanation for the Melitian schism. Does it matter if it is from the Melitians' point of view? If they, following Melitius, were the ones to go into schism, their simple statement that there were differences between themselves and Peter regarding apostasy and penance would be of great value—and this, when the excesses of sectarianism are stripped away, is precisely what they do say.

Presumably, Epiphanius's sources were written after Peter's initial conflict with Melitius and show a certain amount of reflection upon the subject. They have, therefore, broadened the disagreement between the two bishops to include a dispute over how to deal with the lapsed. As was shown above, this does not seem to have been at issue initially. But it seems likely that it was already an issue with Melitius when he set out to correct matters in lower Egypt: things were generally in a bad way, he thought, and it was up to him to change them.

All this may plausibly lie behind Epiphanius's Melitian sources. F. J. Foakes-Jackson concludes that Epiphanius "is full of inaccuracies, and contradicts the earliest evidence. . . . But he may have been correct as to the underlying cause of the schism, Melitius being, like Novatian at Rome and the Donatists in Africa, the representative of the severe disciplinarians."[92]

Until recently such a conclusion was the best available. However, two remarkable Coptic fragments have since come to light which may be very important to the understanding of the Melitian schism. In 1973

---

below. A. Martin, "Athanase et les Mélitiens (325–335)," in *Politique et theologie chez Athanase d'Alexandrie*, ed. C. Kannengiesser (Paris 1974) 40 n. 24, has observed that Epiphanius omits Achillas as bishop between Peter and Alexander and perhaps confuses this Achillas with a later one, or places him at a later time.

91. Kidd, 1:531–32. See Epiphanius *Adv. haer.* 68, for very similar language to Peter's on lapsed clergy.

92. Foakes-Jackson, 538; Lebreton, 1047, concurs.

John Barns and Henry Chadwick published a report of a trial and a letter which "has authentic elements or is even (which is possible) an authentic document from Peter's pen."[93]

In this letter Peter, angry and feeling betrayed, attacks a certain Apollonius, bishop of Asiout (Lycopolis):

> As for you, poor wretch . . . I am at a loss about you, where your wits have gone, that you have not had the wit to exercise yourself and escape by means of [others] who have their wits about them, before you were ruined. . . . I wonder at you, that you should join in debate [συνζητεῖν] with the enemies of Him in whose holy Name you were baptized. Who has put this beast's heart in you? . . .What has happened to you? Tell me! . . .It is truly a shame, the denial [ἄρνησις] which has caught you in a trap, and something from which there is no escape. Who suggested to you treason [παράδοσις] like this?[94]

There can be no doubt that the bishop of Lycopolis has done something dreadful. Although absolute certainly is impossible, his crime seems to have been apostasy. Early in the letter Peter speaks of "the idolatry of [those whom] I consider to fall away through a fateful misstep [?] and to have betrayed their own selves."[95] Such words as "idolatry" (-ειδωλον), "betray" (παραδιδόναι), and "denial" and "treason" in the excerpt above, strongly suggest that Apollonius has apostatized. "Join in debate" (συνζητεῖν) might also suggest that the bishop has acted as a zealot, forced the issue with the authorities, and then fallen. Peter strongly condemns such actions in Canon 9 of the *Canonical Letter*, and his attitude here about "treason," though expressed far more strongly, is consistent with his order in the *Canonical Letter* that apostate clergy are not to retain or regain their office.[96]

This much in itself would be far from conclusive evidence, especially given the condition of the manuscript. But Chadwick makes a very important connection: he suggests that this Apollonius is the same man as the bishop named in another fragment of independent tradition.[97] In

---

93. J. Barns and Henry Chadwick, "A Letter Ascribed to Peter of Alexandria," *JTS* 24 (1973) 443–55. The quotation is from 449. Kettler, "Petros 1.," in *Realencyklopedie der klassischen Altertumswissenschaft* (1938) 19/2:1288, says the letter is not authentic, but does not discuss it. Tito Orlandi, "La raccolta copta delle lettere attribuite a Pietro Alesandrino," *AnBol* 93 (1975) 131–32, discusses the letter but does not commit himself.

94. Barns and Chadwick, 454. See 450 for the beginning of the text; the word "Peter" is preserved, but unfortunately "archbishop" has to be largely restored (but seems certain), and "Rakote," i.e., "Alexandria," completely restored. "Apollonius" too has to be partially restored, but the reading of "bishop" after his name is certain.

95. Ibid., 450–55.

96. See Canon 10 of the *Canonical Letter*, chap. 3., 189–90.

97. Pierpont Morgan Coptic Codex XXVIII. See Barns and Chadwick, 448. See also

this second fragment, a Roman persecutor tries to persuade a Christian, Coluthus by name, to sacrifice. He explains that two bishops have already done so and that one, Plutarch of Sbeht (Apollinopolis Minor), "remained in full possession of his episcopal office without having lost face at all."[98]

The other bishop is named as Apollonius, bishop of Lycopolis! Is this the same man as the bishop in the letter attributed to Peter? The chances are good that it is. If the trial of Coluthus took place in 305, that would suggest that Apollonius's apostasy occurred in 304–5, and Chadwick suggests that Melitius may have succeeded Apollonius at Lycopolis.[99] It is even possible that Peter himself consecrated Melitius. Given the fact that Melitius was bishop of Lycopolis when he interfered in Alexandria, probably in 304–5, this would suggest a date for Peter's letter at a time before Melitius was bishop and before Peter fled: c. 305.

Chadwick further suggests that if Melitius did succeed an apostate at Lycopolis, it "would go far to explain the impassioned puritan zeal of his schismatic actions."[100] Chadwick goes on to say that this letter attributed to Peter,

> with its indictment of the bishop of Lycopolis, provides *an otherwise lacking motive* [emphasis added] for the origination of the schism led by Melitius of Lycopolis. Melitius went into schism because he thought, no doubt with reason, that too many Egyptian churches were taking compromise with the authorities lightly—bishops (like Peter of Alexandria) were abandoning their flocks and lying low or even leaving the country altogether until the persecution abated; or (like Plutarch of Apollinopolis Minor) were being left in undisputed possession of their sees even after they had offered sacrifice.[101]

Given the evidence Chadwick and Barns present, this hypothesis is very plausible. It becomes even more so when one realizes that the motive is

E. A. E. Reymond and J. W. B. Barns, *Four Martyrdoms from the Pierpont Morgan Coptic Codices* (Oxford 1973) 8–18, 25–29.

98. Barns and Chadwick, 448. For the text, see "[The Martyrdom of] S. Coluthus," in Reymond and Barns, 27–28 (Coptic), 147 (English). The governor says to Coluthus that Apollonius "is not at all ashamed, and every one honors him. . . ."

99. Barns and Chadwick, 449–50. Neale, 91, says that Melitius's immediate predecessor was Alexander, "who during the time of Theonas had filled that see, had distinguished himself by a work against the Manicheans, which work still exists." However, Alexander of Lycopolis was neither a Christian nor a bishop, but was a Platonist philosopher. See now A. Villey, *Alexandre de Lycopolis: Contre la doctrine de Mani* (Paris 1985), esp. 16–19, 341–42.

100. Barns and Chadwick, 449.

101. Ibid. If one allows Chadwick's hypothesis about events at Lycopolis, one must still question whether Melitius would have immediately been an opponent of Peter who, after all, had deposed Apollonius.

not "otherwise lacking," but has been given by Epiphanius in *Adv. haer.* 68. As has been discussed, Epiphanius's testimony is generally dismissed as untrustworthy, full of inaccuracies, and based on Melitian information. There is no doubt that the last two charges are true. But Walter Crum has made a suggestion with regard to the Coptic Petrine material that may also be of great value here: he suggests that a historical substratum probably lies under later hagiographical and erroneous accretions.[102] Chadwick, in his discussion of the Petrine fragments, concurs with this sentiment: "We cannot exclude the possibility that some authentic stuff may have served as a substratum."[103]

I would suggest that we apply this principle to Epiphanius's report. If we strip away the unconscious Melitian viewpoint and the parts based on hearsay and rumor, we are left with an account that confirms Chadwick's suggestion and gives further support to the authenticity of the letter from Peter to Apollonius. Reduced to its essentials, Epiphanius's report testifies to a difference (or differences) between Peter and Melitius. This far Epiphanius can be trusted; however, we must examine closely the exact reasons given by Epiphanius for the schism.

Epiphanius says that each side, the orthodox and the Melitians, presented their arguments concerning apostates. The former, led by Peter, argued for strict mercy and readmission of the fallen to the church after suitable penance; the latter argued that the fallen "no longer had the courage to be athletes in the struggle" and were unworthy of repentance. Epiphanius concludes:

> Therefore, because of the reasons presented and thought godly by both men, the schism occurred, some saying this and some saying that. For when Archbishop Peter saw that the Melitians opposed his counsel of brotherly love, and bore an excessive godly zeal, he himself, by spreading out his himation (that is, his cloak or pallium), set up a curtain dividing their prison and proclaimed through his deacon, 'Let those who are of my opinion come forward to me and let those who hold the view of Melitius go to him.' The majority of the bishops and monks and elders and those of other orders sided with Melitius. Only a few altogether went with Archbishop Peter, a few bishops and some others. These prayed by themselves, and the others [the Melitians] by themselves. Likewise, as concerning the other holy offices, each side completed them by themselves.[104]

---

102. Crum, "Texts," 387.
103. Barns and Chadwick, 445. William Telfer works with the same principle in his reconstruction of the Urtext of the *Passio S. Petri*. See his "St. Peter and Arius," 118.
104. See appendix 5, 84–86.

In this account, based on Melitian documents, Epiphanius is undoubtedly wrong when he places Melitius and Peter in prison at the same
time; his tale of Peter using his cloak to divide the two factions shows
the later embroidery which commonly changed the simple fabric of
saints' lives into fabulous tapestries.[105] (That Epiphanius's account is a
fabrication does not discount the symbolic value of the story, see 27
above.)

Epiphanius's report that Peter and Melitius divided over the question
of penance—mercy vs. rigorism—must be considered carefully. As
Foakes-Jackson suggested (above, 28), the dispute between the Donatists and Cyprian in North Africa offers a very close parallel to the
situation in Alexandria. In the East, Athanasius spent much of his life
fighting schismatic groups that grew out of this dispute in Alexandria in
305. It is probably not an exaggeration to say that the conflict over
penance dramatized by Epiphanius was the single most pressing and
divisive ecclesiastical issue (if we regard the christological controversies
as theological) in the early church. Therefore, that such a division should
split the church in Alexandria and throughout Egypt should come as no
surprise.

It is precisely because of these reasons that Epiphanius's report is not
to be trusted. He is reading back into the early days of the schism (more
accurately, before there probably was a full "schism") divisions articu-
lated later.[106] In fact, the end of the passage quoted above has the
Melitians and orthodox already fully divided and not in communion
with each other; this situation is the same as Epiphanius's *concluding*
description about the separation of the two parties, and almost certainly
reflects later conditions. The differences Epiphanius describes may have
been latent earlier, but our best evidence does not indicate that they
were decisive in the beginning.

To summarize, Telfer is probably correct in saying that Melitius
moved out of his see to restore liturgical services and sacramental

105. Reymond and Barns's comment about the martyrdom literature is appropriate
here also: "Considered as literature, some at least of the Egyptian martyr acts seem
hardly as contemptible as the outraged sensibilities of the historian would make them;
there are moments . . . which achieve something like poetic imagination" (1). See also n.
60 above. Perhaps the most tell-tale sign that the source for the prison scene is Melitian
is that most of those in jail sided with Melitius—although this is not impossible. Those
in jail facing death might indeed be inclined to rigorism. We know from Athanasius
that the schism was later widespread.

106. Bell, 38: "The situation described by Epiphanius is entirely different from that
presupposed by the [Veronese] documents . . . but it is easy to reconcile them if we
suppose them to present different stages in the growth of the schism." Williams, 38,
states that the division over the lapsed was not the origin of the schism.

practices in lower Egypt. That this betokens dissatisfaction with the state of affairs seems clear. As Chadwick suggests, Melitius undoubtedly would have been unhappy with clergy who had "deserted" their flocks, and it is reasonable to conclude that this unhappiness would extend especially to the bishop of Alexandria. But as the Veronese fragments testify, Melitius first worked in the provinces, and only later came to Alexandria and acted against Peter. Nevertheless, such actions would have been an affront to the chief bishop of the Egyptian church.

Melitius, like Tertullian, may have scorned flight, and despised those who, like Peter, took Matt. 10:23 to heart. If this was so, nor would he have looked with favor upon those who lapsed. Undoubtedly, it was the last difference that led to formal schism (and was remembered), but that schism cannot be dated to the first contact between Peter and Melitius. I suggest this as the most reasonable way to reconcile the conflicting evidence and present the beginnings of the schism. This summary does not depend on the authenticity of the letter to Apollonius of Lycopolis. That it is authentic seems to be at least possible, if not probable. Melitius's actions, however, can be explained without it.[107]

The events of Peter's life during 305–6—indeed until his death in 311—are very obscure and can for the most part only be guessed at or sketchily outlined. Nothing is known about his return to Alexandria or any later confrontations with the Melitians. Even the fact the he returned at all is not certain, but is probable. Most scholars connect the publication of the *Canonical Letter* to a return in 306. As Telfer concludes: "The fact that Peter's *Canonical Epistle* was issued after the persecution had been raging for more than three years fits the supposition that in 306 A.D. he was again in Egypt after a long absence."[108]

It is also possible that the persecution was not enforced in any systematic way, thus allowing Peter to return to the episcopal city.[109] As the opening of the *Canonical Letter* shows, persecution was still going on, but the tone of the canons is not one of impending destruction.[110] The canons were probably written during a lull, when Peter was in the process of gathering his flock together, ministering to their needs, and administering the necessary regulations to govern a church torn by the question of apostasy and penance.[111]

107. Williams, 38, is willing to accept the possibility that Apollonius preceded Melitius, but regards the matter as too speculative.

108. Telfer, "St. Peter and Arius," 125.

109. Hardy, 44; Ste. Croix, "Aspects," 99.

110. See Canon 1 of the *Canonical Letter*, 185.

111. Hardy, 45, says that these canons lend "some support to the report that the

A vexing question arises concerning the penitential canons of Peter. Were they directed *at* Melitius? And if so, was Melitius punished by the Alexandrian church for not adhering to them? It is very difficult to answer this question, partly because the chronology of the years 305–6 is so uncertain, and partly because the canons themselves do not say.

Epiphanius, *Panarion* 68.3 (see 84–86 for a translation), says that Melitius was "banished and exiled" to the mines, but he places this after Peter's death (in 311). Athanasius declares in his *Apologia contra Arianos* 59 that Peter excommunicated Melitius and repudiated Melitian baptism, but he does not say why this took place or when. If Melitius was deposed by Peter—and it is by no means certain—then it took place after the deaths of the four imprisoned bishops.[112] In his letter to them Peter says that he will meet with Melitius.[113]

Once again, we are thrown back upon Epiphanius, and this, as we have seen, creates numerous difficulties. Barnard and Bell, following Schwartz, have concluded that neither the Melitians nor the orthodox led by Peter proposed that the lapsed be permanently excluded, and that this is made certain by the canons of Peter.[114]

It is true that Peter allows for no permanent exclusion. However, it is important to note that his canons do not say what the Melitian position is; they oppose confessor forgiveness, and this *may* be directed at the Melitians. Schwartz based his conclusions on Epiphanius *Panarion* 68.2–3. However, the Epiphanian report is contradictory: he has the Melitians first allowing no possibility of repentance for those who lapsed, and then during a time of peace allowing communion after appropriate penance.[115] (It is possible that Epiphanius is preserving a reminiscence that there were factions among the confessors.)

I have argued above that this report by Epiphanius represents a secondary stage in the origins of the Melitian schism. The first stage would have been 303–5, when Melitius was ordaining outside of Alex-

---

schism launched by Peter's impulsive suffragan, Melitius of Lycopolis, took as one of its grounds the need for a stricter discipline in the treatment of the lapsed.' This would suggest that by 305–6, a year or two after Melitius's initial actions, his disagreements had broadened.

112. Athanasius is the only early source to mention Melitius's excommunication by Peter. Socrates *HE* 1.6 vaguely says that Melitius "was deposed," and adds the Athanasian charge that he had sacrificed. Epiphanius says nothing, which is not surprising if he is using Melitian documents.

113. Stevenson, 293.

114. Barnard, "Athanasius and the Meletian Schism," 181; Bell, 39; Schwartz, 172–73.

115. Interestingly, "waiting for peace" is also one of Cyprian's requirements. See 149 below.

andria and Peter was in exile; the second would date to 305–6, when Melitius and Peter were both in Alexandria. During the first stage the question was one of Melitius's illegal ordinations, not apostasy and penance.[116] What was at issue in the second stage?

If we follow Epiphanius, then neither Melitius nor Peter opposed eventual readmission for repentant apostates. What, then, were their differences? It had to have been the immediacy with which penance was to begin and the mildness of the penance assigned.[117] As I shall discuss in chapter 3, the two main characteristics of the mildness of Peter's canons are that the penalties imposed are relatively light and that, as opposed to the Melitians who wished to wait for a time of peace, the time of penance was to begin immediately.

It is reasonable to suggest, then, that the two parties might have split over this issue. Perhaps Peter saw the lull in the persecution in 306 as a "time of peace," while the Melitians did not. Frend has suggested that up to 306 the persecution in Egypt had not been severe and that Peter's canons in their mildness "fitted the situation." However, Canon 1 (see 185) acknowledges that the lapsed were not at first received back into communion, and this seems to define the position of the Alexandrian church, and not just part of the Melitians (perhaps the church in Peter's absence?). Since Dionysius had not taken such a position (see 163–73 below), perhaps this "rigorism" was a temporary measure following the outbreak of persecution and that Peter—to the disgust of the Melitians —was not changing this position. The "increasing horrors" of 306–11 and Peter's renewed absence probably helped the Melitian cause to gather support.[118] During such extreme times, moderation such as Peter's was probably not welcome.

We are still left with the question of Melitius's "excommunication." Was he removed from the church because of his opposition to Peter's canons, therefore *after* the promulgation of the canons?[119] Or was he ousted *before* Easter 306 because of his illegal ordinations? Because of the uncertainty in the second Veronese letter by Peter (see 21–22 above) it is impossible to be certain. Given the fact that the question of the lapsed was remembered as the crucial difference between the orthodox and the Melitians, the first hypothesis seems more certain.[120]

116. Greenslade, 54, 117, concurs.
117. Greenslade, 117; Barnard, 181.
118. Frend, *Rise of Christianity*, 493. See Greenslade, 54.
119. Bell, 39; Greenslade, 54.
120. Telfer, "Melitius," 230 and n. 18, 19, believes that Melitius was condemned *in absentia*, and appeals to Athanasius *Apol. contra Arianos* 59, but the evidence for this

Given the discussion above, I suggest the following chronology:

I. 303   The beginning of systematic persecution.
    303–4   Apollonius of Lycopolis apostatizes.[121]
    303–4   Peter writes to Apollonius.
                 Melitius succeeds Apollonius as bishop of Lycopolis (conse-
                 crated by Peter?).
    304   Peter flees Alexandria.
                 Melitius illegally ordains priests in the countryside.
    304   The "Letter of Phileas."
    304–5   Phileas and the other imprisoned bishops are martyred.
II. 305   Melitius comes to Alexandria.
    305–6   Peter returns to Alexandria.
                 Peter issues the *Canonical Letter*.
                 Peter excommunicates Melitius (?).
    306   Peter flees again.

To this point we have examined the narrower context of the origins of
the Melitian schism: the surviving documents and the establishment of a
chronology. But what was the broader context of the schism, that is, its
setting in Egypt, and what might a discussion of this context add to an
understanding of the Melitian schism? From the above discussion, it
seems clear that the origins of the Melitian schism are not to be sought
either in doctrinal disputes or in a difference over policy with regard to
the lapsed.[122] Melitius was, at least initially, unhappy with the state of
the church during the Great Persecution and left his diocese, as he
thought, to restore order.

Behind such a precipitous move may have lain years—and even
centuries—of dissatisfaction on the part of upper Egyptians with the
way things were done in the north. Recent scholarship has emphasized
the difference between upper and lower Egypt, and such discussion has
brought a good deal of light to an area where detail, such as those
supplied by Epiphanius, have often been lost in shadow.

It has been emphasized recently that the Melitian schism was con-

---

view appears to be very uncertain.
    121. Reymond and Barns, 145 n. 3, also date the trial of Coluthus (according to his
Martyrdom), at which Apollonius's apostasy is mentioned, to 304, which supports my
suggestion of 303–4 for Apollonius's "fall."
    122. Kidd 1:532; and Bell, 38, say that the schism was not over doctrinal matters. See
Epiphanius *Panarion* 68.1, 3 (84–86 below), who emphasizes that the differences were
not doctrinal. However, one should remember that this may be special pleading in the
Melitian sources to protect Melitius from the taint of Arianism.

fined to Egypt and the Thebaid.[123] In 327, the year before Athanasius's election, one out of six episcopacies in the Delta was Melitian, while one out of every two or three in the Coptic-speaking Thebaid was; Athanasius, within eight months of his consecration, went to the Thebaid to win the respect of Pachomius.[124] Frend has seen much of Athanasius's genius in that he created an "unbreakable alliance" between the Coptic and Alexandrian Christians, and "transformed the none too popular hegemony of the Church of Alexandria over the rest of Egypt."[125]

The division that Frend sees certainly existed a generation earlier during Peter's time: a division between "town and country" (Frend), Hellenized and Egyptian, Greek-speaking and Coptic-speaking, order and prophecy. This division extended, quite naturally, to matters of faith: "Just as Alexandria and the remainder of Egypt represented different, indeed contrasting cultures, so the Christianity that developed in these two areas was also radically different."[126] A language boundary could become a theological boundary.[127] This boundary could then be symbolically represented in a story: Saint Peter, while in prison, places his cloak between himself and the Melitians, "the one representing Alexandrian orthodoxy, the other, the emergent Coptic Church."[128]

When one thinks of the Coptic-speaking Egyptian church one thinks of Antony and Pachomius, while Clement and Origen often symbolize the Greek-speaking Alexandrian church. And Athanasius was the chief architect of the bridge between the two churches. At the turn of the fourth century, a generation before Athanasius, the hierarchy at Alexandria, both in church and state, would have been made up of Greeks or Hellenized Romans or Egyptians; as such, they would have favorably looked upon Greco-Roman institutions. Such was not the case in the countryside.[129] When persecution came, the hierarchy at Alexandria, as Dionysius and Peter show, did not offer open resistance. The attitude of native Egyptians was quite different. Although Peter's canons show that there was opposition to the persecution at Alexandria, most resistance

123. See, e.g., H. Chadwick, "The Council of Nicea," in *History and Thought of the Early Church* (London 1982) 12:189–90; and the works of W. H. C. Frend cited immediately below.
124. Frend, *Rise of Christianity*, 525. See Athanasius *Apol. contra Arianos* 71, for the list of Melitian clergy given to Alexander.
125. W. H. C. Frend, "Religion Popular and Unpopular," in *Religion Popular and Unpopular in the Early Christian Centuries* (repr., London 1976), 16:22.
126. Ibid., 25.
127. Frend, "The Winning of the Countryside," in *Town and Country* 2:9.
128. Frend, "Religion," 28.
129. See Frend, "Countryside," 9–10.

came from the countryside.[130] In Judaism (witness the Maccabees) and in primitive Christianity (as the Book of Revelation testifies) persecution often aroused intense eschatological expectations. Such fervor seems to have been the case with the Egyptian provincials, but appears to have been lacking among the Alexandrian hierarchy.[131] Peter's *Canonical Letter*, written in the midst of persecution, shows no sign of eschatological fervor.

As a bishop from the Coptic-speaking countryside, a region antagonistic toward both Rome and Alexandria, Melitius had "relatives" in the Maccabees in Palestine and the Donatists in North Africa. It is possible that his opposition, at least initially, was to the world rulers and not with the Alexandrian bishop or hierarchy. However, when his actions met with their disapproval, he was prepared to number them among his enemies.[132]

This period in church history of persecution from without and conflict from within, the "Era of the Martyrs," was when the Coptic church was born.[133] Peter was twice in exile, and Melitius was arrested, sent to the mines, and thus became a "confessor." Had things continued this way, the "Church of the Martyrs," as the Melitians called themselves, might have triumphed; had Melitius been martyred before his conflict with Peter and his associations with Arius, he might today be a saint in the Coptic church.

But the persecution ended early in 312, and Peter died a martyr's death late in 311. Did Peter's death effectively "check" Melitius's progress, as Frend and Telfer suggest?[134] Given the fact that the Melitians plagued both Alexander and Athanasius, fifty years after Peter's death, their statement seems overdrawn. However, Frend is correct when he says that Peter's death "set the seal of divine approval on his policies."[135] The martyrdom of Peter gave the Alexandrian church its own hero,

130. See W. Telfer, "Melitius," 227; and Frend, "Failure," 280: "That there were really numerous Egyptian (i.e. southern) confessors is shown by the fact that in 308 parties of more than 100 each were being sent up north to work in the mines of Palestine and Cilicia. . . ."
131. See Frend, *Town and Country* 8:59.
132. See Telfer, "Melitius," 229.
133. Frend, "Religion," 29.
134. Telfer, "Melitius," 231; Frend, "Religion," 29. Telfer writes: "Peter could have done nothing so effective for his cause, against that of Melitius, as in dying under the executioner's sword" (231).
135. Frend, "Religion," 29. Orlandi, "Sull' Apologia secunda," 58–59, argues that Athanasius in the *Second Apology* passed over the conflict that Peter's canons caused, and instead emphasized the bishop's martyrdom, which helped justify the polemics of his supporters.

"bishop *and* martyr," who would soon enter (via the monasteries?) the ranks of the Coptic saints.

What can we conclude about Melitius? S. L. Greenslade has made the suggestion that the origins of the Melitian schism are to be found in large part in the personal ambitions of the bishop of Lycopolis.[136] This is an interesting suggestion, but impossible to prove. Greenslade bases his thesis on the extreme presumptuousness of Melitius's actions: leaving his see and invading the see of the primate of all of Egypt. He is certainly right to point to Melitius's extraordinary action and to suggest a motive that would have led him to such a point, but I think we need to look for more certain motives.

The terms "puritan" and "indigenous" are often applied to the Melitians and to their founder.[137] It is reasonable to suggest that Melitius, like Novatian and Hippolytus in Rome and Tertullian in North Africa, opposed what he considered to be the lax policy of the church hierarchy. If with the term "indigenous" we follow Frend's suggestion that Melitius, as an upper Egyptian, was reacting against both Roman persecution and the perceived pusillanimity of the Alexandrian hierarchy, then we are on sure grounds.[138]

Melitius deserves more respect than he has received. He lived in awful times, and his actions and motives apparently were justifiable to large numbers of his fellow Christians. The later Athanasian unification of Egypt had as one of its results the "canonization" of Peter in the Greek and Coptic churches and the concomitant vilification of Melitius (who was to be joined with Arius and Origen in an evil trinity). But as Epiphanius clearly shows, Melitius was long venerated in many of the churches and monasteries of upper Egypt.

If there was a lull in 306, the storm broke with renewed intensity sometime in that year—and it was to last until 312:

> For indeed a second attack was directed against us by Maximin in the third year [306] of the persecution of our day, and a rescript from the tyrant then for the first time was published abroad, to the intent that the magistrates of every city should make it their earnest endeavor that all the people in a

---

136. Greenslade, 48, 52; Barnard, "Athanasius and the Melitian Schism," 182, says that this thesis has "some probability," but he adds as an important factor the conflict between upper and lower Egypt.

137. E.g., Barnard, "Athanasius and the Meletian Schism," 188; and Greenslade, 108.

138. See also Barnard, "Athanasius and the Meletian Schism," 188, but his other conclusions that Melitius was "anti-Alexandrian, anti-imperial," need to be made clearer. Are these to be taken together, and if so, how is "anti-imperial" to be understood in 306 as opposed to 313 and after?

body at absolutely one time should sacrifice. Throughout the whole city of Caesarea by the order of the governor heralds were calling up men, and women and children too, to the temples of the idols; and, in addition, the military tribunes were summoning every individual by name from the census list.[139]

Undoubtedly the situation was the same in Alexandria as in Caesarea and, as Eusebius says, there too "no small confusion hung over all; men were dispersed, one this way, one that, seeking earnestly to escape the danger; and dire commotion universally prevailed."[140]

The blow to Christianity was intended to be a mortal one. Many must have died in Alexandria, and the church must indeed have been confused, with a schism dividing the faithful, many bishops and clergy dead, and the bishop of Alexandria, long in exile, once again lost to flight. Except for an Easter letter written in 309, Peter too is lost amid this confusion.[141] Peter disappeared in 306, and almost nothing is known of him until he returned to Alexandria, probably in 311, and there was martyred for his faith.

The Martyrdom of Saint Peter

Diocletian abdicated in 305 and Galerius became Augustus in the East with Maximin Daia as his Caesar. Throughout the uneasy history of Roman-Christian relations, the prosecution of anti-Christian edicts always depended on local authorities. In the West at this time, Constantius did little to disturb the church; in the East, however, Maximin Daia was a relentless persecutor of Christianity. Eusebius, understandably, saw in him an implacable enemy: "Maximin Caesar, the moment he came to the principate, displayed to all the tokens, as it were, of his innate enmity with God and his impiety by setting to work with greater vigor than his predecessors on the persecution against us."[142]

There can be little doubt that Peter was forced to remain in exile during the years 306–11. In 309 the persecution worsened, either be-

---

139. Eusebius *Martyrs of Palestine* 4.8 (shorter recension). See also Ste. Croix, "Aspects," 97. He continues: "There can be little doubt that the edict of 306 was the first of its kind during the whole persecution, and not merely during Maximin's reign. Eusebius has already said that Maximin set to work on the persecution with greater vigor than his predecessors. When recording E[dict] 4, he does not mention any instructions such as he quotes Maximin as giving in 306 and 309, and the steps taken in 306 to prepare registers would not have been necessary had they been taken a year or two previously. Eusebius also speaks of the roll-calls as if they were unprecedented" (98).

140. Eusebius *Martyrs of Palestine* 3.4.

141. See chap. 2, 101–2.

142. Eusebius *Martyrs of Palestine* 3.4.

cause of new orders or because existing statutes were now being enforced. Eusebius reports that the new "edict of Maximin" dictated

> that those idol temples which had fallen should be rebuilt with all speed; that care should be taken that all the people in a mass, men with their wives and households, even babes at the breast, should offer sacrifice and libations and taste with scrupulous care the accursed sacrifices themselves.[143]

Once again, it is very difficult to determine what took place in Alexandria at this time, but it is probably safe to say that Eusebius's description accurately represents events in that city, at least for sporadic periods during the persecution. The church in the East lay under this state of siege until sometime in 310 when "a seventh year of the conflict against us was nearing its end, and our affairs having taken a quieter and more peaceful turn—a state of things which continued until the eighth year [311]."[144]

Eusebius is describing here what for many Christians must have been the calm before the final calm—for on 30 April 311, in the edict commonly called the "Palinode of Galerius," peace came at last to the church.[145] This edict essentially gave the Christians legal recognition, or was, as N. H. Baynes has put it, an "amnesty"—an amnesty that Maximin reluctantly, and briefly, accepted.[146]

> In the Eastern provinces Maximin had unwillingly accepted the Edict issued just before his death by Galerius. The text of the Edict was not published by him, but he gave verbal instructions to his Praetorian Prefect, Sabinus, to write to the provincial governors: of that letter we possess a Greek translation: the authorities are directed that if any Christian be found following the religion of his nation he should be set free from molestation and from danger and should henceforth not be deemed punishable on this charge. The administration welcomed the permission to stay the persecution: the Christian prisoners were released: those relegated to the mines returned with joy, and the pagans themselves shared in the general rejoicing.[147]

In Eusebius's words, the Christians "went through every city, full of unspeakable mirth and a boldness that cannot be expressed in words."[148]

---

143. Ibid. 9.2.
144. Ibid. 13.1.
145. Harnack, *Geschichte* 2/2:71 dates it to April–May 311. See Bright, 333; Baynes, 671 (text on 672); Frend, *Martyrdom*, 510–11; Eusebius *HE* 8.17.2, 9.1.10.
146. Baynes, 671; Frend, *Martyrdom*, 510–11.
147. Baynes, 686–87.
148. Eusebius *HE* 8.17.2. Baynes comments: "Eusebius realized that it was a historic moment: with the text of the palinode issued by the author of the persecution he closed the first half of his history" (673).

The mirth and rejoicing lasted scarcely six months, for by October or November 311, the persecution had begun anew.[149] Why it began again is beyond the scope of this discussion.[150] It is important, however, to conclude that with the calm of April 311 Peter, bishop of Alexandria, returned to his episcopal see and city. He died in the fierce storm of persecution that was to follow a few months later.

Exactly why Peter was arrested is unknown; the early sources offer a number of suggestions. Eusebius says that the bishop "was seized for no reason at all and quite unexpectedly; and then immediately and unaccountably beheaded, as if by the command of Maximin. And with him many others of the Egyptian bishops endured the same penalty."[151]

Other early historians of the church are silent on this question, but the chroniclers of the saint's life do offer reasons:

> After his return, the blessed Peter, through his teaching, separated many from the worship of idols and united them to the Church of Christ. Hearing of this, Maximin immediately ordered a tribune to the city of Alexandria. He found the blessed Peter, who was celebrating the commemoration of the holy martyrs with a great multitude of Christians. [The tribune] immediately seized him.[152]

Another *Martyrdom* offers this reason for the arrest:

> This man, because of his blameless way of life—both in his excellent spiritual discipline and in his continency—had been considered worthy to hold the throne of the high priesthood of Mark the most holy apostle and evangelist who had spread the Good News and taught the Gospel there, shepherding the people of the Lord. Since, then, this man was conspicuous and famous for his great and most noble way of life and teaching, the fame of his virtue reached the Emperor Diocletian.[153]

The details of this last account are vague enough and pious enough—and wrong on at least one account—that the writer probably had no first hand knowledge or report of the arrest; what he has given us is pious guesswork. It is important to note, however, that none of the three accounts above mentions a failure on Peter's part to sacrifice to the

---

149. Harnack, *Geschichte* 2/2:71 says that "alone in Maximin Daia's territory the peace lasted only six months." See Frend, *Martyrdom*, 514; and Eusebius *HE* 9.1.2.

150. See Eusebius *HE* 9.6; and Baynes, 686–87.

151. Eusebius *HE* 9.6.2. Frend, *Martyrdom*, 515, accepts Eusebius's statement. See also Harnack, *Geschichte* 2/2:71.

152. Telfer, "St. Peter and Arius," 127. See appendix 2, 68. For a parallel to the account of the tribune, see Eusebius *HE* 6.40.2, where a *frumentarius*, a centurion acting as an agent, is sent out to arrest Dionysius.

153. Devos, par. 1; see appendix 3, 70–71.

Roman gods.[154] If that had been the reason for Peter's arrest, it would surely have been remembered. This suggests two things: that Peter returned to Alexandria—and was taken captive—after the Edict of Galerius and that the arrest may well have been arbitrary.

Some scholars have suggested that the arrest grew out of disputes between the Catholic church and the Church of the Martyrs, that is, the Melitians: "celebrating the commemoration of the holy martyrs," if the list of martyrs conspicuously omitted Melitians, could have led to riots between the two churches which the civil authorities would have suppressed with force.[155] As we know from Augustine's accounts of pitched battles between the Catholics and Donatists in North Africa, such conflict was certainly possible. However, it seems that if this had been the reason for Peter's arrest and execution, it would have been remembered by the orthodox.

Severus offers the only specific reason for Peter's arrest, a complicated tale of storm and miracles, where Peter is arrested for baptizing the children of a woman whose husband is a nonbeliever.[156] This account is so legendary and hagiographical that it is impossible to recover any

154. Ste. Croix, "Aspects," 80–81, comments: "The hagiography of the fourth and subsequent centuries came to be written with diminishing restraint and increasing contempt for historicity; and the stories of the martyrs of the Great Persecution were, as we should say, 'written up' according to a pattern which became ever more standardized. Refusal to comply with a demand to sacrifice, with or without a reference to an imperial decree to that effect, became a stock feature and was included in virtually all *Passions*, even of martyrs who suffered under emperors other than Decius or the tetrarchs." The *Martyrdoms* of Peter, however, have an unusual feature: they give very little or no attention to the arrest and trial of Peter. See, e.g., appendix 3, 70–78. It would seem likely, then, that Peter was not arrested for refusing to sacrifice. Ste. Croix's comments about the increasingly stereotyped nature of the *Martyrdoms* should alert us to the unique details in the accounts of Peter.

155. Telfer, "Meletius," 231; and "St. Peter and Arius," 124.

156. Severus, 384–85, offers this account: "Now the reason for the prince's [Diocletian's—wrongly] command to seek and put to death this father and patriarch was as follows . . ."; he then tells the story of Irene and her sons, a tale as marvellous as anything in Gregory of Tours: Irene, a Christian, is married to a certain Socrates of Antioch who has renounced the faith. When he refuses to allow her to have their children baptized, she makes for Alexandria by boat. While at sea, a storm arises. She prays to God, cuts herself on the breast, and with three drops of blood baptizes her children. The storm stops, and three days later they arrive safely in Alexandria. By chance, it is the time of the baptizing of infants. She takes her children to the cathedral, where Peter tries three times unsuccessfully to baptize them. Each time the water congeals like stone because, he discovers, the children have already been baptized. Finally, he hears the story from Irene, and blesses her. She returns to Antioch, is betrayed by her husband, and is burned alive—with her children. Peter is accused as the perpetrator of these baptisms, and Diocletian orders his death. Reymond and Barns observe: "One of the permanent features of the Egyptian mind was its taste and talent for romantic story-telling" (1). The Ethiopic Synaxarium also preserves the story; see Budge, 300–303.

historical substratum. The translation of the *Martyrdom of Saint Peter* attributed to Anastasius Bibliothecarius, although a later one, offers a simple reason: Peter "was a leader and holding chief place among the Christians; and he [Diocletian—wrongly], inflamed with his accustomed iniquity, on the instant ordered Peter to be apprehended and cast into prison."[157]

What happened to Peter between the time of his arrest and imprisonment and his death (and even after his death; see below) is very uncertain. The various *Martyrdoms* offer a wealth of detail: plans, plots, nocturnal rendezvous, the appearance of a boy-Christ, soliloquies that anathematize heretics (including, prominently, Origen), and near riots. Most of this, however fascinating it may be to the student of the early church, is more the stuff of a Gothic romance than the history of a man's life and death. Yet these histories of the saint's life are not wholly hagiographical—a bedrock of first hand information may underlie the pious and fantastic. The narrative that follows will give only the few aspects of Peter's last days that seem at least plausible.[158]

All of the *Martyrdoms* agree that Peter, once condemned to death, voluntarily gave himself up to the soldiers rather than bring risk to his flock:

> He did not hold his life to be of more worth [than the lives of his flock], but called one of his attendants and sent him to the tribune saying, 'Come secretly to the back of this jailhouse at night a make a small entrance in the wall, big enough for one person. There you will hear a signal from inside, at which sign your executioner will cut off my head with his sword. You will take it to your ruler.' Eagerly heeding this advice, the tribune cut off his head with a sword.[159]

That Peter sacrificed himself for his flock is not unlikely: that he did so in the manner described above is more problematic, given the legendary aspects of the story. However, Tito Orlandi believes that the earliest part

157. ANF 6:262; PG 18:451–66. The Greek *Martyrdom* edited by Devos has much the same theme. There Peter is "adorned with all piety and resplendent with all virtue," and is "blameless." See appendix 3, 70.

158. See appendices 2 and 3 for the texts of these *Martyrdoms*, from which details are drawn. Scholars, too skeptically in my opinion, have generally rejected out of hand any evidence the *Martyrdoms* offer. T. D. Barnes, *Tertullian: A Historical and Literary Study* (Oxford 1971) 184, for example, says they offer "bogus detail." Frend's conclusion, *Martyrdom*, xi–xii, is more nuanced: "Even more difficult, however, has been a rational assessment of the *Acta Martyrum* . . . and the historian's task is to decide whether any kernel of truth underlies these stereotyped and florid discourses. . . . Despite the work, however, of H. Delehaye and the Bollandists in attempting to apply rules for assessment and categories of verisimilitude to each *Acta Martyrum*, the historian has still to decide each case for himself."

159. Telfer, "St. Peter and Arius," 127–28. See appendix 2, 69.

of the *Passio Sancti Petri* is a narrative that emphasizes the secrecy surrounding Peter's death and the voluntary nature of his sacrifice. These two themes seem to be based on historical fact.[160]

Another difficulty is that the stories vary. However, they play variations on the same theme, and a historical element may lie behind the stories. The key, perhaps, to understanding the different recensions of the *Passio S. Petri* lies in one feature of the tradition: the hole in the wall of the prison.[161] The shortest versions, like the one quoted immediately above, have the hole made in the wall so the soldiers could get *in*; in the longer version, the hole was made so Peter could get *out*—not in order to escape, but to go with the soldiers away from the people:

> The blessed one knew that they stood there waiting; he entered unafraid into the inner part of the prison where he thought he would go undisturbed and so that those in prison would not know what was happening. He knocked on the wall from the inside and those outside recognized the blessed one's signal. Immediately they dug where he was knocking and made an entrance. The holy one crossed himself, went out to them and said that it was better for him to hand himself over than have the people perish by the sword.[162]

In this version, instead of murdering Peter in prison, the soldiers take him to Boucalia where lay the tomb of Saint Mark, the traditional founder of Alexandrian Christianity.[163] Many of the events that transpire there, according to this *Martyrdom*, are clearly legendary—thereby causing scholars to dismiss the whole episode as pious fiction.[164] It is improbable indeed that Peter's captors would have allowed him to be taken to the most sacred shrine of the Alexandrian church. But it is not improbable that Peter's body was taken there *after* his murder. Otto Meinardus has noted that according to "Coptic tradition, the body of the

160. See Orlandi, "Ricerche," 301. See 66 below.
161. J. B. Pitra, *Analecta Sacra* (Paris 1883) 4:429, preserves a Syriac manuscript which has an interesting title. He comments: "In B this fragment is given under the title 'Of Peter, bishop of Alexandria and martyr, of him who pierced through the wall. . .'" (429 n. 5). Whoever copied this manuscript or translated it into Syriac knew of the tradition relating to Peter and the prison wall.
162. Devos, par. 10; appendix 3, 74. See also Severus, 397.
163. Neale, 7, is willing to accept the legend about Saint Mark and says that "it was, apparently in 49, that S. Mark returned to Egypt; and there, till the time of his decease, the first church in Alexandria is said to have been built, at a place called Boucalia, near to the sea shore, and thence called Boucalis, or Baucalis. The name Boucalis arose, if we may believe Strabo, from the fact that, in former times the spot had been appropriated for the pasturage of cattle." The earliest witness to Mark's evangelization of Alexandria is Clement, in the fragment preserved as the "Secret Gospel of Mark." See Morton Smith, *Clement of Alexandria and a Secret Gospel of Mark* (Cambridge, Mass. 1973).
164. See Devos, pars. 11–18, "Une passion grecque," 19–28. See also Hardy, 11.

Evangelist [Saint Mark] still reposed in the Church of St. Mark at Baucalis in 311 at the time of the martyrdom of St. Peter."[165]

The longest recensions of the *Martyrdom of St. Peter* give varying legendary accounts of what happens to Peter after he is taken to the tomb: the scene includes either a long monologue by Peter addressed to the spirit of the evangelist Mark or a voice calling out from heaven. After his prayer, Peter gives himself up and is killed. When his body is found there is a great tumult:

> The people were milling about in great confusion: some from Dromos wanted to take him to where Theonas had been buried; others from other parts wanted to take him to where Saint Mark had been perfected. There was a great uproar, and the people were about to fight. Some from Dromos saw the uproar among the people and were afraid that there was going to be a great battle. They ran and found a ship and got it ready very near the place—for it was near the sea—and after a great deal of time and arguing among the people, quickly seized the martyr and ran and placed him in the ship. They put off from shore and sailed away."[166]

This account does not appear to be hagiographical, especially if one compares it to the story of Peter at the tomb of Saint Mark, which is pious myth making. If one follows the suggestion that the *Martyrdoms* may preserve some historical knowledge of what happened to Peter after he was killed, then the events reported above could have taken place. Here is a realistic and detailed account (by someone from Dromos?) which would more likely be cut from, rather than added to, the life of a saint.

The story certainly does no honor to the Alexandrians—but it does reflect an accurate knowledge of them. The Alexandrian mob was famous for its disorder.[167] Because of this "excitability and readiness to riot," Epiphanius reports, "it is the custom in Alexandria that when a bishop dies, there is no delay in appointing his successor, but it takes place at once, for the sake of peace in the church, and so that disturbances may not arise among the people, some wanting this man for bishop, and some that."[168]

---

165. Otto Meinardus, *Christian Egypt Ancient and Modern* (Cairo 1977), 32. There is a possibility that the relics of Saint Mark are really those of Saint Peter. For the history of Saint Mark and Saint Peter, see ibid. 25–55.

166. See Devos, pars. 15–18; appendix 3, 76–78, and Anastasius Bibliothecarius's translation in ANF 6:261–68.

167. Hardy, 10: "The people of Alexandria had throughout the ancient history of the city a reputation for excitability and readiness to riot for any cause or almost for none." Kidd, 1:381, comments: "No fact is better established than the turbulence of the mob of Alexandria."

168. Epiphanius *Adv. haer.* 69.11 (PG 42:220B), cited in Telfer, "Episcopal Succession,"

The *Martyrdom* clearly shows that Bishop Peter was buried quickly—largely because of the mob—and his successor quickly appointed.[169] The description follows the story of Peter being taken away by sea; according to this account, he was buried in the "cemetery which he had established in the western part of the city in the suburbs." It seems reasonable, then, to suggest that Peter was taken to Boucalia after his death rather than before; after some disturbance among the people whether to bury him at the tomb of Saint Theonas or Saint Mark, he was taken to a cemetery to the west where Theonas lay.[170]

But before Peter's burial, the *Martyrdom* reports, the people placed their martyred bishop upon his episcopal throne. Only after they had done this would they proceed with the consecration of the new bishop and finally the burial of his predecessor (possibly seated on his *kathedra*):

> The ministers of the Levitical priesthood with haste entered the sanctuary and, putting on the emblems of their office, took the holy martyr; with the crowd gathered around the bishops and elders of the city, they set him on the throne.[171]

One wonders whether this description could come from the imagination of a hagiographer. Nor does it appear to be a *topos* in any other saint's life. Could it have possibly occurred? The *Martyrdom* explains that this was done because Peter had refused to sit on his throne during his life but out of humility sat instead on the footstool.[172] This detail too is also unique among *Martyrdoms*, and may well be true.

---

5. Henry Chadwick, "The Role of the Christian Bishop in Ancient Society," *Protocol of the Colloquy of the Center for Hermeneutical Studies* (Berkeley 1979) 8, has observed that "it is hardly surprising that episcopal elections were normally a source of unrest and disorder. . . . It was common for bishops nearing their end to try to avert a riot by nominating their successor, as Augustine himself tried (unsuccessfully) to do." Severus's report (392), then, that Peter hand picked Achillas and Alexander as his successors, may be historical. See further Orlandi, "Ricerche," 303.

169. Devos, par. 18; appendix 3, 78.

170. The Church of Saint Theonas was in the western part of Alexandria, that of Saint Mark in the eastern. A transport by boat to the Church of Saint Theonas is plausible. My thanks to Professor Birger Pearson for this observation. It seems reasonable to suggest that Peter would have established a cemetery at the Church of Saint Theonas in order to honor his "father," and that the people would have wanted to bury him there.

171. Devos, par. 18; appendix 3, 78. See also Budge, 303: the Ethiopic Synaxerium preserves a garbled account of the enthroned burial. Telfer, "Episcopal Succession," 12, says that a study of enthroned burial "awaits an adequate monograph." See 12–13 for a brief note on the practice.

172. See Devos, par. 17; appendix 3, 77–78. Peter says: "For, beloved, whenever I ascend the episcopal chair and come near to the throne while standing in prayer—as you see—and I look on the throne and see what radiant and inexpressible power resides there, fear mixed with joy comes over me. . . ." The theme occurs in the "Epiphany Homily" attributed to Peter, par. 29; see 62–64 below. This tradition is

More important, after Peter's "enthronement," and before his burial, the *Martyrdom* describes the ritual of passing the episcopacy on to Peter's successor:

> Then all the bishops took the holy Achillas and stood him near the throne where they had also seated the martyr. And they took the pallium of the most holy and famous Bishop Peter and placed it upon him.[173]

This description is straightforward and has nothing legendary about it, as does the story of Peter's enthronement. W. Telfer is willing to accept it and suggests, "conjecturally," the following ceremony at Alexandria in Peter's time:

> the dead pope's body is washed, vested, and carried into church to be seated in the chair of St. Mark; the city presbyters elect his successor and bring him to the throne where he kneels and lifts the dead man's right hand to lay it on his head (thus taking the authority of his office directly from his predecessor); the presbyters now transfer the omophorion to the new pope's shoulders and take their seats on the bench; the living pope, standing beside the dead, now presides over the liturgy and finally completes the obsequies.[174]

The Greek *Martyrdom* supports much of Telfer's conjecture,[175] as does the *History* of Severus; while Severus's account narrates the transfer of the omophorion or pallium, it conspicuously lacks the details of "posthumous consecration" by the dead bishop.

E. W. Kemp has criticized Telfer for equating "the principle of apostolic succession with the idea of consecration by a series of monarchical bishops"; he does not believe that the actual imposition of the dead bishop's hand was necessary. Although he disagrees with Telfer as to the *method* of succession, he too suggests that the fact that "the mode of appointment of the early bishops of Alexandria was unusual is also evidence that there was a carefully regulated succession, albeit a succession through a presbyteral college."[176] Given the evidence, one must

---

remembered also in the *Vita Pachomii; The Life of Pachomius*, trans. Apostolos N. Athanassakis (Missoula, Mont. 1975) 42 (par. 57): "Saint Athanasius used to see in his church the Savior seated upon the throne, as did Saint Peter, the bishop and martyr of the same church. . . ."

173. Devos, par. 18; appendix 3, 78. The use of "bishop" in this paragraph, especially, "bishops . . . of the city," reflects later terminology used by someone who did not understand presbyteral succession at Alexandria.

174. Telfer, "Episcopal Succession," 10. Kemp, 142, says that the rite suggested by Telfer is "macabre."

175. See Severus, 400.

176. Kemp, 141–42. Eutychius (tenth c.) reports that up to the time of Alexander the bishop of Alexandria was ordained by the presbyters; see *PG* 111:982. See E. W. Brooks,

agree with Kemp. That there was a tradition at Alexandria of presbyteral consecration which included the transfer of the omophorion, the symbol of episcopal office, seems likely. When the practice ended, the reason for its existence became lost, and later writers had difficulty explaining it. Its very unusualness suggests that it took place.

Whatever one may think about the details from the *Martyrdom* concerning Peter's burial and the consecration of his successor, one thing remains clear: the tradition surrounding Peter holds him to have been a man of great piety and humility. Peter became known as "the last of the martyrs" or "the seal of the martyrs," and his name, naturally enough, became closely associated with Saint Peter the disciple. The *Martyrdom* preserves the tradition that "Peter [was] the first of the apostles, Peter [shall be] the last of the martyrs."[177]

Unfortunately, this was not to be so. As W. H. C. Frend says, Peter was just one victim at the bitter end of the persecution against the church:

> Silvanus of Emesa was thrown to the beasts in the late autumn, Peter of Alexandria executed on 25 November 311 and 'many other Egyptian bishops with him' [says Eusebius], also the bishop and author Methodius of Olympus in Lycia, and the theologian, Lucian, presbyter of Antioch at Nicomedia on 7 January 312. The final savage outburst lasting from November 311 to January 312 deprived the Christians of some of their ablest leaders who had hitherto escaped molestation.[178]

A year and a half after Peter's death, the church and the Roman Empire officially made peace, although the war had ended sometime earlier. On 13 June 313, Constantine's Edict of Toleration was published at Nicomedia, the city where the earlier edicts had been promulgated, and the city from which Maximin probably had issued orders for Peter's death.[179]

It is unfortunate that so few records of Saint Peter's life have survived; we are deprived not only of the details of an interesting life, but also of better insight into an important period of church history. Almost all of

---

"The Ordination of the Early Bishops of Alexandria," *JTS* 2 (1901) 612–13. Brooks cites Severus of Antioch (c. 465–538), who had studied at Alexandria and was exiled there after 518. In a letter written from Egypt, Severus confirms that "the bishop also of the city renowned for its orthodox faith, the city of the Alexandrines, used in former days to be appointed by presbyters. . . ."

177. Devos, par. 15; appendix 3, 76–77. Anastasius Bibliothecarius makes a pedestrian correction: "Peter was the first of the apostles, Peter is the last of the martyred bishops of Alexandria." See ANF 6:266.

178. Frend, *The Rise of Christianity*, 515.

179. See ibid., 518.

Peter's episcopacy took place during the last persecution of Christianity, and the meager evidence shows that he must have spent much of his time encouraging his flock during such terrible times; his *Canonical Letter* shows great pastoral care and admirable moderation. Peter lived in the last years before the "peace of the church," and he died at the end of a long, bitter war waged by the Roman state against the church. He lived in a time of transition: the councils would soon follow his death, and the Catholic church, soon to become a close relative to the Roman state, would change greatly in the next few years.

Saint Peter escaped the wars of neither church nor state. Many of the major problems of the church existed at Alexandria during Peter's episcopacy: it was divided both ecclesiastically and theologically over how it saw itself. The Melitian schism began during Peter's lifetime, and the Arian heresy would begin shortly after. Peter, however, has come down in history as one of those who embodies the strengths of the church: toughness tempered with compassion, perseverance, and personal piety. In this saint perhaps one can see those traits which have helped the church survive wars and persecutions—internal as well as external—for two thousand years.

Peter seems to have been immediately venerated as the last of the martyred bishops (see Athanasius *Life of Antony* 47), and it is reasonable to suggest that he came to symbolize, both to Greek and Copt, the end of the terrible years of persecution and the beginning of the "Great Peace."

Sozomen records that "it was the custom of the Alexandrians to celebrate with great pomp an annual festival in honor of one of their bishops named Peter, who had suffered martyrdom. Alexander, who then conducted the Church, engaged in the celebration of this festival."[180] The Coptic and Ethiopic churches venerate Peter as "the preacher of the Faith, the counterpart of Paul."[181] His feast day in the Greek Orthodox church is 25 November, in the Roman Catholic church 26 November, in the Coptic church 29 Athor (25 November, Julian; 8 December, Gregorian), and in the Ethiopic church 29 Khedar (5 December).[182]

---

180. Sozomen *HE* 2.17.

181. Budge, 303.

182. For the various dates on which Peter is commemorated, see Sauget, 768. The Greek *Martyrdom of Saint Peter* says that Peter died on the twenty-ninth of Athyr (Athor) which "according to the Romans is November 25th." See Viteau, 81; and 76 below (Devos, par. 14). The Coptic *Encomium* attributed to Alexander also has the twenty-ninth of Athyr; see 79 below. M. Chaîne, *La chronologie des temps Chrétiens de l'Égypte et de l'Éthiope* (Paris 1925) 251, lists Peter's day of death as 25 November, but

THE WORKS OF SAINT PETER

Writings attributed to Peter of Alexandria are extant in Greek, Latin, Syriac, Coptic, and Armenian. Writings about Peter, that is, the *Martyrdom of Saint Peter* (also called the *Passio Sancti Petri*), the *Encomium* about Peter attributed to Alexander of Alexandria, and the portions of the *History of the Patriarchs* given to Peter, exist in Greek, Latin, Coptic (Sahidic and Bohairic), Arabic, Armenian, and Syriac. W. E. Crum and Tito Orlandi have shown that collections of works by and about Peter exist in Coptic, and if the "Veronese fragments" in Latin and the Syriac collection edited by J. B. Pitra are added to these, one must certainly agree with D. B. Spanel's observation that Peter's life, work, and martyrology "enjoyed considerable popularity."[183]

Although Peter's *Canonical Letter* (see chap. 3) and various fragments had long been known, it was Crum, at the beginning of this century, who began the systematic listing and publication of works attributed to the bishop of Alexandria.[184] Crum identified two Coptic codices from the White Monastery, which he designated "A" and "B," folios of which are located in Paris, London, and Rome. "A" contains eight pieces ("A_α" to "A_η"), of which Crum edited four, while "B" has two pieces ("B_α" and "B_β"), the first of which he edited and the second for which he gave an abstract. These ten fragments are a miscellaneous lot: five letters, three homiletical fragments, and two biographical pieces.

In 1973 J. W. B. Barns and Henry Chadwick summarized Crum's work and edited one fragment, a letter by Peter to Bishop Apollonius of Lycopolis.[185] D. B. Spanel has recently edited the two remaining pieces, a fragment of a letter and a biographical fragment.[186] In the meantime, Tito Orlandi identified six codices from the White Monastery which contain two homilies by Peter, the *Encomium* on Peter attributed to

---

he also has the year as 310.

Sauget, 767, accepts 25 Nov. as the date of Peter's martyrdom, as do most scholars. Recently, T. D. Barnes, *Constantine and Eusebius* (Cambridge, Mass. 1981), 159 n. 79, following F. H. Kettler, proposes 26 Nov. as the true date. Kettler, "Petros 1," 1283, says that in 311 the twenty-ninth of Athyr fell on 26 Nov., not the twenty-fourth or twenty-fifth; however, he does not explain how he knows this.

183. D. B. Spanel, "Two Fragmentary Sa'idic Coptic Texts Pertaining to Peter I, Patriarch of Alexandria," *Bulletin de la Société d'Archéologie Copte* 24 (1979–82) 91.

184. Walter Ewing Crum, "Texts Attributed to Peter of Alexandria," *JTS* 4 (1902–3) 387–97.

185. Barns and Chadwick, 443–55.

186. Spanel, 85–102.

Alexander, the *Martyrdom* of Peter, and a collection of letters.[187] Thanks also to Orlandi's painstaking work, which has followed the initial research of W. Telfer, we now have a clearer picture of the almost bewildering number of recensions of the *Martyrdom* of Peter.[188]

The first question confronting the scholar who deals with these writings is, of course, their authenticity. Crum was aware of the difficulty in ascertaining the genuineness of the fragments he published, but felt that they should not be dismissed out of hand.[189] Harnack believed that the authenticity of all the pieces printed by Crum was "prejudiced" by the spuriousness of one from the same collection printed earlier by C. Schmidt; however, Harnack was willing to concede that Crum was right when he said that an authentic base might underlie them.[190]

The difficulties that Crum and Harnack recognized concerning the Coptic fragments apply to virtually all of the writings attributed to, or about, Peter. They are beset with many problems: redactional elements, polemical interpolations, and hagiographical accretions. Nevertheless, following Telfer and Chadwick I believe that there is much that can be gained by following Crum's suggestion: we should look for what might be authentic and historical underneath the polemical, pious, or fantastic.[191]

In the discussion that follows, writings by and about Peter are grouped thus:

1. Letters
2. Theological works
3. Homiletical works
4. The *Martyrdom of Saint Peter*

Within each group, I shall discuss the authenticity, contents, and significance of the writings. Some of these, such as the *Canonical Letter* and the theological fragments, are dealt with in detail later in this work; for

187. Tito Orlandi, "La raccolta copta delle lettere attribuite a Pietro Alesandrino," *AnBol* 93 (1975) 127–32. On 129 Orlandi terms Crum's codex "A" as "U," and Crum's "B" as "BI."

188. Orlandi, "La versione," 151–75. Telfer, "St. Peter and Arius," 117–30.

189. Crum, "Texts," 387 n. 1: "It would be difficult to maintain the genuineness of these texts after Delehaye's criticisms ([Untitled Review], *AnBol* 20 (1901) 101), though certain of the passages which I here publish may indicate interpolated, rather than wholly apocryphal compositions."

190. Harnack, *Geschichte* 2/2:75. Bardenhewer 2:244 was not optimistic that they would prove authentic.

191. Telfer, "St. Peter and Arius," 117–30; Barns and Chadwick, 448.

these, therefore, only brief summaries will be given in this chapter. The discussion of other works, such as the homilies, will be fuller. The purpose of this section is to bring together for the first time, in an annotated list, all of the writings related to Peter of Alexandria.[192]

Letters

The *Canonical Letter*.

Written in 306 and edited after Peter's death, this "letter" is a collection of fourteen canons in which the bishop of Alexandria determined the appropriate penance for those who lapsed during persecution. The work may have been an Easter letter, but was more likely an encyclical written after Easter. It is also possible that it was not a true letter but was instead a treatise *De paenitentia*, but since it has long been referred to as the *Canonical Letter* (or *Epistle*), it seems best to place it among his letters. It is unanimously agreed that the *Letter* is authentic. A full discussion of this work, the most important of Peter's writings, and of its significance to the history of the Church's teaching on apostasy and penance appears in chapter 3.

A Letter from Peter concerning Melitius.

This letter, extant only in Latin, is one of the "Veronese fragments" and is of considerable importance with regard to the Melitian schism. In the letter Peter attacks Melitius for invading his diocese and performing illegal ordinations. It can be dated to c. 304–5 and is widely regarded as authentic.[193] See above 15–40 for a discussion of the Melitian schism and 26 for a translation of the letter.

---

192. Obviously spurious works, such as the "Mystagogia," are omitted. See Harnack, *Geschichte* 2/2:71–75; and Kettler, "Petros 1.," 1281–88, for earlier surveys.

193. See Harnack, *Geschichte* 2/2:72–73; Hefele 1:341; Quasten 2:116; Orlandi, "Ricerche," 287–96; Bell, 38 n. 3. In 1963 M. Richard published two fragments from Codex Ochrid, Musée National 86, attributed to Saint Peter ("Quelques nouveaux fragments des pères antenicéens et nicéens"); see *Opera Minora* (Turnhout Brepolis 1976) 1:76–83 [#5]. Concerning the second fragment (#5) Richard later corrected himself and said that "without a doubt" it belonged to Peter II and not Peter I. See "Le Florilège Eucharistique du codex Ochrid, Musée National 86," *Opera Minora* 1:47 n. 1 (#6); and see *Opera Minora* 1:80–81 [appendix 5, s.v. 5 (72)]. The first fragment (#4) concerns Melitius and has the title "From the letter of Peter, Bishop of Alexandria and martyr, to his own clergy": "You know how much evil Melitius of Lycopolis has shown me, cutting in two the Church of God which the Word of God obtained through his own blood and on whose behalf he gave his own life." This fragment, in fact, is from the *Martyrdom* and is not from a letter; see Devos, 167 (par. 6); 73 below; and Viteau, 73.

A Letter concerning Persecution and the Celebration of the Eucharist.

This Coptic fragment from an "Epistle or Homily" was published by Crum as fragment A$_a$ and is addressed to the church community as a whole, possibly during a pause in the persecution.[194] Orlandi identifies it as the first in a collection of six letters.[195] Barns and Chadwick give the following opinion of it:

> The text cannot possibly belong to the beginning of the fourth century. But the exhortation to the community to be unprovocative under the persecution could be based on some authentic fragment of Peter. It fits exactly with what is known of his policy. There is therefore a possibility that the text is not a free invention but is based on some genuine information which has been richly embroidered.[196]

The part of this fragment which deals with the persecution certainly seems to be authentic or to be based on a genuine historical reminiscence. We know from Canons 12 and 13 of the *Canonical Letter* that Peter advised prudent actions during persecution and did not encourage zealotry. Such is what this letter encourages:

> Beloved sons, be not severe with these godless ones, lest . . . we be delivered into their hands. . . . Be not reckless; because if we appear in the streets of the cities, our enemies will talk against us, saying: 'Whence [sic] are they thus so proud and come not to worship the king's gods?' And thus a great disorder and disturbance shall befall the faithful.[197]

The second part of the letter directs that "the eucharist is not to be celebrated twice on the same altar on the same day" and relates a miraculous vision to explain why this should be so.[198] There is a clear seam in the text between the earlier exhortation about what to do during persecution and this story. While the latter is clearly an interpolation, there seems to be no reason to regard the first part of the letter as inauthentic.

A Letter Written during Persecution.

This Sahidic Coptic fragment, the second in Orlandi's collection, announces the beginning of the persecution.[199] It was transcribed and printed by Carl Wessely and is translated here for the first time:

194. Crum, "Texts," 388.
195. Orlandi, "La raccolta," 130–31.
196. Barns and Chadwick, 443.
197. Crum, "Texts," 390.
198. Barns and Chadwick, 443.
199. So believes Orlandi, "La raccolta," 130.

[. . .] and when the holy Archbishop Abba Peter received [the letter], he wept, saying this: "There is woe on account of these persecutions which have arisen against the children of peace. Our fathers in their time lived together (in peace) with the emperors, but now, on the other hand, behold, the emperors have broken the law! I write to them (the Christians) to console (them) while they are in grief, knowing that it is an important thing that is happening in the city as a result of it (the persecution).

Almighty Lord, do not humiliate us again beneath the bloodshedders, for they have exalted themselves over us and have brought in upon us (the) worship (of) idol(s), that which casts us aside from (the) worship (of) God alone (and) which is appropriate (only) to the evil demons [. . . .]"[200]

If this letter is authentic it must be dated to sometime after Diocletian's third edict (September or November 303) which called for Christians to sacrifice to the gods. By his use of "again," Peter seems to be referring to the persecutions by Decius and Valerian, c. 250 and 260; the fifty intervening years was the time of peace for "our fathers."

The beginning of the fragment seems to show that this letter formed part of a narrative, possibly about Peter. The letter that Peter is said to have received must have reported to him troubles in Alexandria and not, it seems, the beginning of persecution, since Peter already is aware of troubles. The letter also assumes, interestingly, that Peter is not in Alexandria. If authentic, it would belong then to the time of his exile, sometime after 305.

A Letter from Peter to Diocletian.

This Sahidic Coptic fragment, the third in Orlandi's collection, is purportedly part of a letter from Peter to Diocletian. It was published by Wessely with the preceding fragment and is first translated here.[201]

The third letter which Saint Peter, archbishop of Alexandria, wrote to Diocletian until he (Diocletian) (became) angry, sent (for him), and beheaded him. It is written in this way. In the peace of God. Amen.

I expect, O King, that you are a lover of the wise God in everything that is good. I have inquired, and I understand that you have given yourself over to the demons. Glorify God Almighty, this one who (holds) your lifebreath in his holy hands! Keep yourself from this evil lawlessness. Do not make these children of God worthless. Do not obey your thoughts, and do not scatter the sheep of Emmanuel [. . .] himself.

Yet now you have put enmity between yourself and the God who made you. O force, O violence! They are doing us evil, trampling divinity and

200. Carl Wessely, *Studien zur Palaeographie und Papyruskunde* (repr., Amsterdam [1914] 1967) 15:143 (K9429, No. 245a).
201. Wessely, 144 (K9429, No. 245b).

worshiping things which are only lifeless beings, having done evil to the nature of true worship. Know the murderers of the prophets and the patriarchs, O King. Know the ones who kill the holy Gospels which honor the noble estate of Christianity, not with sinful anger but with an open spirit. Did not Christ pity (and) bear with us, and did he not mediate for us with his father? If we follow his words, O King of this world (according to your mind), it is not because you are not a lord [. . . .]

The colophon to this letter indicates that there was a collection of letters purportedly from Peter to Diocletian, and there might be a hint in the Sahidic version of the *Encomium* attributed to Alexander of such correspondence. In the *Encomium* Diocletian's name appears, but the text there is badly preserved.[202]

This letter does not seem to be authentic. It is difficult to imagine a bishop telling the emperor that he had given himself over to demons, and one wonders what Diocletian would have made of "prophets and patriarchs." It seems more likely that such chastisement as we have here directed toward the emperor would have been written after the empire was "Christian" and Diocletian was remembered by the church with opprobrium. The letter would be welcome in a community which was also reading Lactantius's *De mortibus persecutorum*.

A Letter from Peter to Bishop Apollonius of Lycopolis.

This Coptic fragment was listed as frag. A$_\beta$ by Crum and was first published by Barns and Chadwick; it is the fourth letter in Orlandi's collection.[203] The letter purports to be one from Peter in which he severely rebukes Apollonius, possibly for apostasy, and, if authentic, is of considerable importance with regard to the Melitian schism. See pp. 28–30 above for a full discussion.

A Letter during Persecution concerning Heretics.

This Coptic fragment was published as frag. A$_\delta$ by Crum and is the fifth letter in Orlandi's collection.[204] It is addressed to the orthodox community during a persecution and exhorts them to avoid heretics. The fragment speaks of a heretical church (Melitians?) and then relates a story about Theonas, Peter's "father," and his encounter with heretics:

202. Orlandi, "La raccolta," 130. For the *Encomium*, see Orlandi, "La versione," 164 (Coptic), 174 (Latin).
203. Crum, "Texts," 387; Barns and Chadwick, 445–55; Orlandi, "La raccolta," 130.
204. Crum, "Texts," 391; Orlandi, "La raccolta," 130–31.

Theonas, apparently, did not wash after becoming a bishop, "since he was spotless," but when the shadow of a heretic touched him, he washed three times.

The story about Theonas is clearly legendary, and one cannot place much confidence in the fragment's authenticity. The reference to persecution might give the fragment some historical basis.

A Letter about a Visit to Oxyrhynchus.

In 1901 Carl Schmidt first published as authentic two fragments from this letter (sixth in Orlandi's collection), but H. Delehaye showed conclusively that they are not genuine.[205] Crum felt that after Delehaye's criticism they could not be counted as authentic, and Chadwick and Barns summarize the evidence against them: the work "twice borrows phrases from the *Acta* of Peter's martyrdom, speaks of Diocletian as still persecuting at a date years after his abdication, and presupposes an attitude to Sunday observance characteristic of the period after c. 450 rather than of 311. It cannot possibly be a genuine piece of Peter of Alexandria."[206]

Theological Works

It is interesting to note that except for the *Canonical Letter*, none of the works just discussed has survived in Greek; the one "Veronese fragment" is in Latin, and the remainder survive only in Coptic translations. Exactly the opposite is true with those writings attributed to Peter that deal with theological subjects: they survive in Greek, Syriac, and Latin; none has come down in Coptic. One cannot escape the conclusion that with regard to Peter, and to Coptic literature in general, those writings which are of a more "popular" nature—homilies, letters, and biographies —were more important to Coptic-speaking Christians and therefore were translated and handed down. Theological works, so it seems, were not.[207]

Be that as it may, a number of fragments from theological writings attributed to Peter have survived in Greek, and in Syriac and Latin translations. It is clear, however, that these fragments come from early

205. Carl Schmidt, "Fragmente einer Schrift des Martyrerbischof Petrus von Alexandrien," TU n.f., 5/4 (1901) 1–50; Delehaye, 101–3; Orlandi, "La raccolta," 131.

206. Crum, "Texts," 387 n. 1; Barns and Chadwick, 444. Orlandi, "La raccolta," 131 n. 1, says Barns and Chadwick incorrectly call it a homily.

207. This is a major point in T. Orlandi's discussion of Coptic literature, "The Future of Studies in Coptic Biblical and Ecclesiastical Literature," in *The Future of Coptic Studies*, ed. R. McL. Wilson (Leiden 1978) 143–63.

epitomes—the major one perhaps being made at the Council of Ephesus in 431—and that no theological work by Peter survived extant into the 6th century.

Of the surviving fragments, the Latin and Syriac are demonstrably later or interpolated, or both; therefore, only the Greek have primary value in determining the nature of Peter's theology. As best as can be determined, the fragments come from four theological works:

1. *On the Deity and Humanity* [*of Christ*]
2. *On the Soul*
3. *On the Resurrection* (*Paschal Letter*)
4. *On Easter* (A Paschal homily ?)

The fragments from *On the Deity* and *On the Soul* survived because they were quoted in the christological battles of the fifth and sixth centuries, and they were often quoted against Origen. For a full discussion of the theological fragments and the question of Peter's alleged "anti-Origenism," see chapter 2.

Homiletical Works

Three homiletical works have come down to us. One, in Greek, is merely a short fragment, while two in Coptic are substantially complete. None of them can be securely claimed as belonging to Peter of Alexandria, although the evidence suggests that two of them may be by the bishop. Attribution is a very difficult problem with regard to patristic literature in Coptic, and one must be very careful in assigning authorship.[208]

"The Teaching of Our Father Peter Archbishop of Alexandria, Who Is among the Saints."

In 1902 J. M. Heer published a Greek fragment of a "*didaskalia* in homiletical form."[209] Because of its opening sentence, an address in the second person plural, Heer suggested that it might be a fragment of a homily.[210] Its authenticity is not certain. The external evidence is not conclusive; the internal evidence neither proves nor disproves its genuineness. If it is authentic, it would be important as the only surviving

---

208. On the problem of attribution, see ibid., 152–53. "Some homilies attributed to Peter of Alexandria [in the Morgan collection] . . . may be authentic only in part" (ibid., 153 n. 46).

209. J. M. Heer, "Ein neues Fragment der Didaskalie des Martyrerbischofs Petros von Alexandrien," *OrChr* 2 (1902) 344–51.

210. Ibid., 346.

example in Greek of homiletical material by Peter. I offer the following translation:

Carefully pay heed to the discourse, and incline your ears to the utterances of my mouth, all you who are clothed in and wear the baptism through the explication of the word, and understand what is spoken to you, and preserve it so that you may be saved. For (I am not speaking) about anything difficult. It is not burdensome for me to speak concerning the kingdom of heaven and judgment and retribution on the day of Christ our God, but (it is difficult) for you to receive the secure oil and unguent of immortality. The Lord cried out, 'Why do you call me "Lord, Lord," and do not do what I say?' [cf. Matt. 7:21] This is to say, 'Will to learn my will.'

He who wishes to be saved will do these things: love one another and forgive each other's sins [cf. Matt. 6:14]. Do not let the sun go down upon your anger [Eph. 4:26]. Love your brother [cf. Matt. 6:15]. But if you hate your brother, I hate you also. Why, man, do you call me, saying, 'Father, forgive us our debts as we also forgive our debtors?' [cf. Matt. 6:8 and 12]. Why do you lie? Do you not know that I am a knower of hearts? And how have you dared to lie about this matter? Have I not said to you through my prophet that I will send into flaming fire all those who speak lies? [Ps. 5:7]. Why do you pray by yourself? May you [not?] cast yourself into eternal fire and destruction! O wretched, empty, and corrupt man! You have forgiven no one, and how you entreat me and dare to open your mouth and speak, asking (me) to forgive your sins, your voluntary and involuntary errors done knowingly and in ignorance, done in word and deed, by night and by day, by the hour and by the minute![211]

A Homily on Riches.

This Coptic homily, also less correctly referred to as a homily or encomium on Saint Michael, was discovered in 1910 at the ancient monastery of Saint Michael at Hamouli in the Fayyum, and is now at the Morgan Library in New York.[212] Fragments of the Sahidic version from the White Monastery exist in Paris, Vienna, and Naples, and another small fragment is in the Amherst collection of papyri in the Morgan Library.[213] The Morgan manuscript is missing a quire of eight leaves

---

211. Text in ibid., 350–51.

212. M. 602. See H. Hyvernat, *A Checklist of Coptic Manuscripts in the Pierpont Morgan Library* (New York 1919); idem, "The J. P. Morgan Collection of Coptic Manuscripts," *JBL* 31 (1912) 54–57; idem, *Bibliothecae Pierpont Morgan Codices coptici photographice expressi. . .* (Roma 1922), esp. vol. 25, which has M. 602.

213. Crum, "Texts," 395–97, published two fragments from an unknown homily (frags. A$_\eta$ and B$_a$ [A = Orlandi U; B = BI]) which we now know belong to the "Homily on Riches." Crum published the papyrus fragment, but erroneously associated it with four other frags. from an unidentified sermon. See his *Theological Texts from Coptic Papyri* (Oxford 1913) 56ff. (no. 10, fol. 5). For the codices from the White Monastery, see Orlandi, "La raccolta," 129; and "La versione," 155–56.

(sixteen pages of text), but fortunately a complete Bohairic version (unedited) resides in the Vatican library.[214] Fragments of the Bohairic version are in Leipzig and Leningrad.[215] Birger A. Pearson and I have edited and translated this homily.[216]

The homily, as it now stands, was intended to be read on one of the festival days of Saint Michael, specifically 12 Athor (22 November). Although the material on Michael is a later interpolation, the homily is frequently referred to as an "Encomium on Saint Michael." The attribution of the Michael material to Saint Peter may be due to the proximity of the feast days of Michael and Peter, the latter's being 25 November, (but celebrated as early as 23 November); however that may be, the survival of the main part of the homily is probably due to its being joined with the Michael material.[217]

The homily may be outlined as follows (the numbers refer to paragraph divisions made by the editors):

1. Proemium	1–13	
2. Address to the Rich	14–54 [44–49: interpolation of "bestiary" material]	
3. Address to the Poor	55–69 [60–61: interpolation of "bestiary" material]	
4. Special Application to Church Leaders	70–74 [interpolation?]	
5. On Judgment and Resurrection	75–81; 118–19	
6. Encomium on the Archangel Michael	82–117	
7. Peroration	120	
8. Doxology	121	

The basic themes of the homily are the proper use of wealth and the attitudes which should be adopted by the wealthy and the poor. The

214. Vat. 61, 3.
215. For a complete list of mss., see A. Hebbelynck and A. van Lantschoot, *Codices Coptici Vaticani Barberiniani Borgiani Rossiani* (Vatican City 1937) 1:420–21.
216. As well as an Epiphany homily attributed to Peter (see below, 62–64). The publication of a Coptic transcription and English translation of the "Homily on Riches" and of a translation only for the "Epiphany Homily" (see n. 222 below) will take place in the series Corpus dei manoscritti copti letterari, edited by Tito Orlandi in Rome. Most of the discussion of the two homilies is taken from Birger A. Pearson, "Two Homilies Attributed to St. Peter of Alexandria," forthcoming in the *Proceedings* of the Third International Congress of Coptic Studies, Warsaw, August 1984, to be published by the Polish Academy of Sciences. I am indebted to Professor Pearson for the use of this paper.
217. On the feast days for Saint Peter, see Sauget, 769–70.

author says that it is God who has created both the rich and the poor, and that it is God who will regard the righteous, rich and poor alike, and punish the wicked, whether rich or poor.

In reading the text, one can readily see that it has been subject to considerable editorial expansion. Possible expansions are: (1) the special admonitions to fellow clergy found in the unusually lengthy proemium which focused originally on Solomon; (2) the special applications to church leaders, pars. 70–74, where the subject of riches is not once mentioned. Certain interpolations include: (1) the material on Michael, pars. 82–117; (2) references to the "Alloe," a mythical creature, and to the dung-beetle, pars. 44–49 and 60–61. This "bestiary" material may have been taken from an Egyptian recension of the *Physiologos*.

After the removal of the suspicious interpolations and expansions, what remains is a well-constructed discourse in diatribe style, such as a fourth-century Alexandrian church leader could easily have written. The homily continues some themes already set forth by Clement of Alexandria in the *Quis dives salvetur?* In par. 14 of the homily, the speaker addresses the rich man:

> You will say to [me], "God is the one who gave me this wealth." Yes, I [say] to you, [God] is the one who gives [wealth] and poverty. But [he did not give you wealth in order for] you [to speak it wickedly (κακῶς)] but (rather) benevolently (καλῶς).

Clement has:

> (Riches) have been prepared by God for the welfare of men. . . . You can use (wealth) rightly (καλῶς); it ministers to righteousness. But if one uses it wrongly (κακῶς), it is found to be a minister of wrong.[218]

In addition to the rhetorical skills of the diatribe, the author of the homily possesses a vivid imagination and a skill in using examples. The story of Lazarus and Nineve (i.e., Dives), pars. 20–29, includes an artfully imagined recreation of the conversation between Abraham and the rich man who is now in hell:

> Lying down in Amente, it says, he raised his eyes; he saw Abraham, (and) Lazarus reclining on [his] bosom. He spoke, begging, "[My] father Abraham, [have mercy upon me]. Send [Lazarus] to me that he might only [dip]

---

218. *Quis dives salvetur* (= *Q.d.s.*) 14 (ed. Loeb, trans. Butterworth). Other parallels: Par. 51 // *Q.d.s.* 21–22; Par. 52 // *Q.d.s.* 31; Par. 74 // *Q.d.s.* 36; Par. 80 // *Q.d.s.* 3. Other similarities consist mainly in the use of the same scriptural passages to make similar points: Matt. 19:29; 10:42; 5:13; 1 Cor. 15:52. These references are from Pearson's Warsaw Paper.

the [end] of his [finger in water and put it] upon my tongue, [for I am burning] in [these flames." That wretch] was panting greatly from thirst on account of the fire, his lips burning from the fire, his heart pounding, his eyes looking this way and that in the hope that he would find a single drop of water. And he did not find it. He was crying out, "My father Abraham, have mercy on me."

And this man did not obtain it, but rather other reproaches which he heard from Abraham who said, "Remember that you have already received your good things in your lifetime and remember that you wore linen and purple on earth while this man, on the other hand, wore ragged clothes. But now, fire is what will be a garment for you instead of the fine clothing which you wore upon the earth (pars. 26–27).

The rhetorical skills evident in the homily are certainly worthy of an Alexandrian bishop, and it lacks the blatantly hagiographical or fantastic elements so prominent in Coptic literature attributed to the saints. Is it—or at least the part on riches—by Peter? In the proemium (par. 9), the speaker states in the first person that he is in hiding from the persecution. The passage could be part of an editorial expansion intended to make more explicit a traditional attribution of the homily "On Riches" to Peter of Alexandria. On the other hand, since it is virtually certain that Peter spent much of his episcopacy in hiding, it cannot be ruled out that the statement goes back to Peter himself.

At the least we should say that the core material of the homily, pars. 1–44, 50–59, 62–69, 75–81, 118–21, probably goes back to the fourth-century Alexandrian church. It seems reasonable to accept Peter as the author.[219]

An Epiphany Homily.

The superscription to this Coptic work, ms. 611, 1 in the Morgan Coptic Manuscript Collection, says that it is "a homily delivered by the holy Abba Peter, archbishop of Alexandria and martyr, concerning the day on which our Savior received baptism in the Jordan River by John the Baptist, which is the eleventh of Tobi" (trans. Pearson and Vivian).

Like the "Homily on Riches," the "Epiphany Homily" is from the monastery of Saint Michael; other copies of the same homily are attested in Coptic fragments from the White Monastery now kept in Paris.[220]

219. Kettler, "Petros 1," 1288, says the homily is not authentic, but does not discuss it. See Harnack, *Geschichte* 2/2:75.
220. For the codices of the White Monastery, see Orlandi, "La raccolta," 129. On the fragments, see Enzo Lucchesi, *Répertoire des manuscrits coptes (Sahidiques) publiés de la Bibliothèque Nationale de Paris* (Geneva 1981). For ms. 611, 1 see Hyvernat, *Bibliothecae* 31. Lucchesi plans to publish an edition of this homily soon.

Paragraph 40 of the parenesis was later separated from the homily and used, also with an attribution to Peter of Alexandria, as a catechesis for the morning office of the fourth day of Holy Week. As such, it is attested in a number of Bohairic manuscripts.[221]

The homily may be outlined as follows (the numbers refer to paragraph divisions made by the editors):

1.	Proemium	1–3
2.	Exposition (centered upon Matt. 3:13–17)	4–20
2a.	Encomiastic Apostrophe of John the Baptist	4–8
2b.	Marvels at the Jordan	9–17
2c.	Purpose of Christ's Coming and Redemption	18–20
3.	Parenesis	21–40
4.	Peroration	41–43
5.	Doxology	44

The provenience of the homily is certainly Egypt and may be Alexandrian. A clue to the homily's origins may lie in the opening of the account of the marvels at the Jordan: "Do you wish to know about the marvels which happened by the Jordan? Listen, I will teach you. Only, listen to me not with the exterior ears only but with ears of the heart and soul" (par. 9). The turning back of the river Jordan is then described.

This motif, interestingly, is found earlier in the *Testimony of Truth*, an Alexandrian gnostic text addressed "to those who know to hear not with the ears of the body but with the ears of the mind."[222] The motif of "spiritual hearing" doubtless had a long history in Alexandria, originating in Alexandrian Judaism, of which Philo was representative.[223]

There is evidence again in the parenetical section (pars. 21–40) of traditional exegesis rooted in Alexandrian Judaism:

> Therefore, then, let us not offer sacrifice to God with animals that are crippled or blind or maimed or (with) the tongue cut or with any blemish on it. For God does not accept their sacrifice, nor does he pay heed to them.

The reference is to moral defilement and impurity, as symbolized by the

---

221. See O. H. E. Burmester, "The Homilies or Exhortations of the Holy Week Lectionary," *Mu* 45 (1932) 21–70, esp. 50ff. (Bohairic) and 68ff. (English).
222. *Testimony of Truth*, NHL, 407.
223. See Philo *Decal.* 35; and Pearson's discussion in "Two Homilies."

maimed sacrificial animals referred to in Lev. 22:22. The same kind of exegesis of Lev. 22:22 may be found in Philo of Alexandria.[224]

Although it seems reasonably certain that the homily originally came from Alexandria, it is not possible to determine whether it is by Peter of Alexandria. In addition to the superscription, there is one other piece of evidence which links the work with Peter: in par. 29 Peter refers to his custom of not sitting in his episcopal chair. This is a recurrent motif in hagiographical works on the bishop (see 47 above); even though the tradition may be based on a historical reminiscence, its inclusion here is probably hagiographical.

In terms of content the homily clearly reflects an Alexandrian provenience, and could possibly go back to the late fourth century in its original Greek form. Even if Peter was not the author, the homily would be of considerable interest since it would be a very early example of an Epiphany homily—perhaps the first, if those attributed to Hippolytus and Gregory Thaumaturgus are spurious—although it is impossible to be certain about both its date and author.

The Martyrdom of Saint Peter

As early as Tillemont (eighteenth c.), scholarly opinion has been nearly unanimous about the Martyrdom of Saint Peter, also called the Passio Sancti Petri and the Acta Sancti Petri—and it has been almost entirely negative.[225] Bardenhewer, Hardy, Harnack, Altaner and Stuiber, Quasten, and Musurillo have all dismissed it as spurious, late, legendary, and worthless.[226] The language used by some of these scholars in their dismissals, however, suggests that they may have accepted a time-honored opinion without researching the matter anew.[227] Although Herbert Musurillo includes Theonas's letter and Acta in his edition of the Acts of the Christian Martyrs, as well as material after Peter's time, he does not include the Martyrdom of Saint Peter.[228] This omission symbolizes the general scholarly opinion towards the Martyrdom of Peter.

W. Telfer, however, has argued that the Martyrdom, although largely legendary and interpolated, rests upon a historical bedrock. By comparing Greek, Latin, and Arabic versions, he arrives at a short recension

---

224. Philo Spec. leg. 1.166–67; and Pearson's discussion.
225. See Severus, 384 n. 1. On Tillemont, see Williams, 39; and Sauget, 766. See also Telfer, "St. Peter and Arius," 117–30, for a detailed discussion. For lists, see BHL 2:973 (6692–98); BHG 2:197–98 (1502–03).
226. See Bardenhewer 2:240; Hardy, 218; Harnack, Geschichte 2/2:73; Altaner and Stuiber, 213; Quasten, 117.
227. See, e.g., Quasten, Bardenhewer, and Altaner and Stuiber, loc. cit.
228. Herbert Musurillo, The Acts of the Christian Martyrs (Oxford 1972).

which he believes preserves the earliest—and historical—material on Saint Peter.[229] He concludes that this material goes back to a "Jubilee Book," dated to 368, that was gathered together as part of the celebration of the forty-year jubilee of Athanasius as bishop of Alexandria. Cyril of Alexandria, in 419, sent a copy of this book to Carthage, perhaps acting upon a request to supply that church with the history of the Alexandrian see. Telfer suggests that this book was perhaps the best, or the only, history that Cyril had: "If Cyril could find nothing better than this Jubilee Book to serve his purpose in 419, it argues an acute dearth of Christian local records at Alexandria in the early fourth century."[230]

Given that the persecution in Alexandria up to 312 called for the destruction of Christian churches and writings and that ecclesiastical disorder followed the Peace of Constantine (schism and heresy were to plague the entire episcopacies of Alexander and Athanasius), this hypothesis is very possible. Telfer concludes: "Now, part of the hagiography concerning Peter of Alexandria, 'the seal of the martyrs,' seems to draw upon a historical source. There is little reason for thinking that anything existed capable of serving such a purpose apart from the Jubilee Book."[231] Acting on this hypothesis, Telfer has compared the various versions of the *Martyrdom* and has boiled them down to a Latin Ur-text which he believes is based on the original Greek of the Jubilee Book.[232] I give a translation of this text in appendix 2, 68–70.

In his study, Telfer begins with the version of the *Martyrdom* preserved by Severus, the tenth-century bishop of El Eschmounein, and rightly concludes that the bishop had two recensions at hand.[233] The shorter (S) recension ends with the beheading of Peter in prison while "the people . . . sitting by the door of the prison . . . knew not what had happened to him."[234] Severus remarks that "in another copy, however, it is said that he came out through the hole in the wall, and the soldiers took him away to a place called Boucalia."[235] This longer recension (L) has Peter being taken out of prison to Boucalia and the tomb of Saint Mark. Telfer regards this longer version as inauthentic and does not include it in his reconstructed text.

P. Devos, writing after Telfer, published a Greek version of the

---

229. Telfer, "St. Peter and Arius," 117–30. Crum, "Texts," 387–97; and Barns and Chadwick, 443–55, have views toward the material that are similar to Telfer's.
230. Telfer, "St. Peter and Arius," 117–18.
231. Ibid., 118.
232. Ibid., 117.
233. Ibid., 118. See Severus, 383–401.
234. Severus, 397.
235. Ibid., 397.

Martyrdom which he says is "pre-Metaphrastic" (i.e., before 960).[236] This text is longer than that preserved by Severus, yet shorter than the Latin translation attributed to Anastasius Bibliothecarius.[237] Devos divides the text into eighteen paragraphs. Paragraphs 1–10 coincide with Severus's short (S) version, 11–14 with Severus's long (L) version, while 15–18 add new material: the enthronement of the martyred bishop in his episcopal chair, his burial, and Achillas's succession. I have called this version the longest (LL) recension.

More recently, T. Orlandi has emphasized the importance of Telfer's hypothesis, but differs with him on several points.[238] Orlandi disagrees with Telfer's theory that the Latin and Arabic short versions derive from the Greek short version. He believes instead that the Arabic and Latin short versions are interpolations into the long versions, which also exist in Greek. He concludes that thus it is possible that a given long version is earlier than a given short version.[239]

Orlandi goes on to distinguish three parts to the *Martyrdom*: "A" is the "true" story of the martyrdom, as opposed to the parts that attack heretics and schismatics. He labels anti-Arian additions as "B" and anti-Melitian additions as "C."[240] He also suggests that the two versions of the *Martyrdom* have different authors with different purposes.[241]

Orlandi suggests that the original author of the *Passio* relied on a narrative on the death of Peter, the purpose of which was to underline the secrecy of Peter's death, the fact that he was not martyred publicly, and the voluntary nature of his death which gave his martyrdom special merit.[242] He suggests further that perhaps the *Passio* comes from that part of the "Alexandrian History" which narrates the imprisonment and death of Peter.[243] This tradition, Orlandi believes, may be rooted in a historical context, partly local (Alexandrian) and partly "popular."[244]

---

236. Devos, 159. See also the version published by J. Viteau in *Passions des Saints Ecaterine et Pierre d'Alexandrie* (Paris 1897). The *Martyrdom* of Peter occupies 70–81.

237. For "Anastasius's" version, see *PG* 18:451–66 (Latin) and ANF 6:261–68 (English). P. Devos has argued that this translation in fact belongs to Guarimpotus (ninth c.). See Williams, 40; and Sauget, 765.

238. Orlandi, "Ricerche," 296 ff.

239. Ibid., 297–98.

240. Ibid., 299–304. Compare this with Telfer's version, appendix 2, 69–70, which includes antiheretical material.

241. Orlandi, "Ricerche," 304.

242. Ibid., 301.

243. Ibid., 311.

244. Ibid., 296. Three Coptic fragments listed by Crum, "Texts," 394 (A_γ, A_F, and A_ζ), belong to the *Martyrdom*. Spanel published the first two of these. See Spanel, 92–93 (Coptic) and 93 (English). A_ζ is the same as pars. 7–8 of the Greek *Martyrdom*, ed.

Appendix 1 gives a list of the major versions of the *Martyrdom of Saint Peter*.[245]

In this chapter I have attempted to provide a setting for Peter's life and writings by examining the biographical details of his life; such an overview—made necessarily brief by the paucity of reliable information—helps to place the bishop more firmly within the history of the fourth-century church. This has been followed by a brief survey of works attributed to Peter. In the chapters that follow, I discuss more fully many of these writings and hope to show their importance for the history of the church. In chapter 2, I discuss Peter's surviving theological works and the question of Origenism and anti-Origenism at Alexandria. In chapter 3, I discuss the *Canonical Letter* and its importance in the development of a penitential system in the church.

Appendix 1
LIST OF THE MAJOR VERSIONS OF
THE MARTYRDOM OF SAINT PETER

S: Short version. Ends with Peter's death in jail.
L: Longer version. Has Peter taken to Boucalia and the tomb of Saint Mark, where he dies.
LL: Longest version. Has Peter's enthronement and burial.

1. W. Telfer, "St. Peter of Alexandria and Arius," *AnBol* 67 (1949) 117–30 (S: Latin. Reconstructed "Ur-text.").
2. Severus, from the *History of the Patriarchs of the Coptic Church*, in *Patrologia Orientalis* 1/4:383–400 (S and L: Arabic).
3. Surius, *De probatis sanctorum historiis*, BHL 6696, under 25 November (S: Latin).
4. P. Bedjan, *Acta Martyrum et Sanctorum* (Paris 1895) 5:543–61 (L: Syriac).
5. R. Basset, "Synaxaire Arabe Jacobite," *Patrologia Orientalis* 3 (1909) 353–59 (L: Arabic).
6. Anastasius Bibliothecarius (or Guarimpotus), *PG* 18:451–66; ANF 6:261–68 (LL: Latin).

Devos. See appendix 3, 73. See Orlandi, "La raccolta," 131. Fragment A_f, according to Crum, "Texts," 394, a "biographical fragment," narrates a legendary confrontation of Peter with a certain Diogenes, a philosopher. See Spanel, 86–88 (Coptic) and 88–90 (English). One can compare this story with ones similar to it in Severus's *History*, the *Encomium*, and the *Martyrdoms*. See the synoptic table given by Orlandi, "La versione," 156; apparently he sees the stories of Sabellius and Diogenes as related.
245. See Spanel, 97–98, for a list of *Martyrdoms*.

7. J. Viteau, *Passions des Saints Ecaterine et Pierre d'Alexandrie.* . . (Paris 1897) (LL: Greek).

8. P. Devos, "Une passion grecque inédite de S. Pierre d'Alexandrie et sa traduction par Anastase le Bibliothécaire," *AnBol* 83 (1965) 157–87 (LL: Greek).

9. E. A. W. Budge, *The Book of the Saints of the Ethiopian Church* (Hildesheim and New York 1976) I/II:300–303 (LL: Ethiopic).

Appendix 2
THE RECONSTRUCTED UR-TEXT OF
THE MARTYRDOM OF SAINT PETER

Translated from the Latin of W. Telfer, "St. Peter of Alexandria and Arius," *AnBol* 67 (1949) 117–30. [Numbers in brackets indicate pagination in Telfer.]

Peter under Persecution [126]

Peter, avoiding the madness of the persecutors, went as a fugitive from place to place. Hiding himself, he passed most of the time in Mesopotamia, and in like manner concealed himself in Syria of Phoenicia. He continued his wandering for a longer time in Palestine, and then stayed for some time in the islands. In all these places he did not cease from writing by night or day, strengthening not only the clergy but also the laity in the unity of Christ. Indeed, because of (his concern for) the blessed bishops, great tribulation shook him lest their defection scandalize many into denying the faith. More than 660 of the clergy and laity denounced the pagan ritual, were thrown into jail, and, enduring many kinds of punishment, earned the crown of martyrdom. But the good-for-nothing Melitius split apart the church of God. He did not cease to torment and afflict even the holy bishops Phileas and Hesychius, Pachomius and Theodore, who were being held as prisoners in jail and who soon after were martyred and entered heaven.

Peter's Martyrdom [127–28]

After his return, the blessed Peter, through his teaching, separated many from the worship of idols and united them to the church of Christ. Hearing of this, Maximin immediately ordered a tribune to the city of Alexandria. He found the blessed Peter, who was celebrating the commemoration of the holy martyrs with a great multitude of Christians. (The tribune) immediately seized him, bound him with chains, ordered him put in jail under guard, and condemned him to the deadly ruin (?) of leg irons. When the Christians saw this they remained along with their shepherd under guard in jail, for they would not allow the teacher of salvation to suffer any evil.

When Maximin was apprised of this he sent a letter to his tribune to take Peter's life quickly. When the tribune read this he went with a band of soldiers to the guard of the jail. When the people saw that he wished to take Peter from jail by force and kill him, they said, "You know that we are not in any way going to allow our teacher and the physician of our souls to suffer anything." When the tribune heard these words, he had the blessed Peter taken outside with great restraint and without any bloodshed. (There) he struck him just as the sentence from Maximin had dictated. The blessed Peter knew that the tribune had received his death sentence by letter. He did not hold his life to be of more worth (than the lives of his flock), but called one of his attendants and sent him to the tribune saying, "Come secretly to the back of this jail house at night and make a small entrance in the wall, big enough for one person. There you will hear a signal from inside, at which sign your executioner will cut off my head with his sword. You will take it to your ruler." Eagerly heeding this advice, the tribune cut off his head with a sword.

Peter, Melitius, and Arius [128–30]

Peter lived almost his whole life during persecution. During that time he ordained fifty-five bishops. Then Melitius, black in mind and name, was made bishop in the city of Lycopolis. He split the Catholic church, not only throughout the cities of Egypt, but also throughout the villages, ordaining his followers as bishops. He had no concern at all for Peter, nor indeed for Christ who was in Peter. Arius, when as a layperson was not yet distinguished by the clerical tonsure, had been loyal; he was to him quite the dearest person of his household [perhaps: bishopric]. However, when (Peter) learned (of Melitius's actions), the man of God, consumed with sorrow, affirmed that this persecution was worse than (the one) before. Although he was concealing himself in various hiding places he sent exhortatory letters while there on behalf of many, preaching the unity of the church of God and urging them on against the ignorance and wicked recklessness of Melitius. Therefore it happened that not a few were roused to action by his saving admonitions and removed themselves from the Melitian ungodliness. At about this time Arius, as if he were deserting the Melitians, fled to Peter who, when asked by the bishops, raised him to the rank of deacon. To be sure, he was ignorant of the extent of Arius's hypocrisy.

Meanwhile, the detestable abomination of the Melitians grew beyond bounds. The blessed Peter, afraid that the heretical plague would invade the entire flock entrusted to him, by letter excommunicated the Melitians from the church. Immediately Arius, because he saw that his supporters had been separated from the dignity of the church, groaned and gave himself up to sorrow—which he scarcely concealed from the most holy man. Immediately Peter expelled Arius from the body of the church and ordered that he be banished from communion with the faithful. When these things were done, the gusts of persecution had blown away, and peace—although a short one—shone forth. Then the bishop shone upon the people more clearly and the faithful began to turn in masses to the commemoration of the martyrs.

Suddenly a storm of paganism thundered against them and buffeted the serenity of the church with the force of a winter storm. After the death of Diocletian, certain persons reported to Maximin concerning the above-mentioned archbishop that he was the leader and standard-bearer of Christianity. At that very moment he ordered that Peter be seized and cast into jail. When it was discovered that so great a man had been shut up in a prisonlike workhouse, the multitude ran in disbelief and haste and stood watch so that none of the pagans would have the opportunity of entering. But the man of God was confined for several days in that prison while the tribune asked for instructions from the emperor concerning him. He ordered that he be punished for a capital crime.

Arius [130]

Therefore, after Peter had entered the heavenly kingdom through the triumph of martyrdom, Achillas received the reins of the bishopric. Then Arius, whose wish had been fulfilled, began to exclaim repentance with a sorrowful voice. At length Achillas, his soul overcome by compassion, received him. After not more than five months had passed in the administration of his episcopate, he died, and Alexander was ordained bishop. Alexander promoted Arius to the dignity of the priesthood. This latter began, under the pretense of scriptural authority, to expound doctrine to the people, having the congregation come to church on Wednesday and Friday so as to hear the Word of God.

He gradually vomited forth the poison from his breast covered with the honey of deception for the ears of his listeners. His unapostolic teachings continually grew, so much so that not only did he persist in church, but in foreign meetings and councils also he impudently preached the devices of his wickedness. Alexander excommunicated Arius, who was once again cut off from the body of the church. But this raging madman began to give birth to the strife of schismatic persecution and, joining with those who agreed with him, did not cease from calling opposing councils hither and yon in his war against the church.

Appendix 3
THE LIFE AND MARTYRDOM OF THE HOLY
AND GLORIOUS "HOLY MARTYR" OF CHRIST,
PETER ARCHBISHOP OF ALEXANDRIA

Translated from the Greek text of P. Devos, "Une passion grecque inédite de S. Pierre d'Alexandrie et sa traduction par Anastase le Bibliothécaire," *AnBol* 83 (1965) 157–87.

1. There was great trouble, like a winter storm, throughout the entire world while the ungodly lawbreaker Diocletian was ruling in the famous and brilliant city of the Nicomedians. For there was confusion and grief, not only in this city where the enemy of godliness ruled, but also in the other cities—wherever, in fact, his bloodstained and ungodly edict was promulgated. Things were no better than being caught in a great storm.

There was at that time in the city of the Alexandrians a man by the name of Peter who was adorned with all piety and resplendent with all virtue. This man, because of his blameless way of life—both in his excellent spiritual discipline and in his continency—had been considered worthy to hold the throne of the high priesthood of Mark the most holy apostle and evangelist who had spread the good news and taught the gospel there, shepherding the people of the Lord.

Since, then, this man was conspicuous and famous for his great and most noble way of life and teaching, the fame of his virtue reached the emperor Diocletian. The emperor summoned five men from among those who are called tribunes and sent them with many soldiers to put the most holy archbishop Peter in chains and send him to the city of the Nicomedians.

2. When the above-mentioned tribunes came to the great city of the Alexandrians and entered the holy church, they found the most holy bishop Peter while he was celebrating the service, standing before the holy altar, teaching the people and enlightening them with his holy words. After the dismissal and perfection of the faithful, as he was leaving the church, the tribunes came up to him and seized him, saying, "Diocletian, the ruler of the world, has need of you." The most holy archbishop Peter said to them, "Let us go, my children, wherever you wish. Let us go. Only, may the will of the Lord be done."

As the holy one was about to go with them, suddenly all of Alexandria was stirred up against them; some were throwing rocks at them, while others were crying out, saying, "Why are you taking away from us our chief priest and good shepherd?" Therefore, because all of the people of the city stirred up no small riot, the tribunes ordered him to be guarded in the jail near the most holy church until they could tell the emperor everything that had happened concerning him. While they turned back and went off to the emperor, the whole city stood outside the gates of the prison in nightly vigil, performing services and glorifying God on his behalf.

3. When the emperor heard from the tribunes about the riot and disturbance caused by all the people concerning the holy man, he became very angry and sent them a second time, commanding them with the words, "Go immediately and cut off with the sword the bishop's head! And if any of the Christians oppose you or speak a single word concerning him, severely strike them down right there so that they, because of their attempt, learn not to oppose the laws of the emperor!" The tribunes received the emperor's order and hastened to execute it.

They came to Alexandria and were going to take [Peter] from prison in order to fulfill their orders when all the people who were sitting near the prison cried out in one voice, saying to them, "First murder us his children, then you can take our father!" The tribunes were in great doubt as to how they were going to get him out of prison without causing any harm to the people. When they saw them persisting in their riot and shouting in disorder—for the whole city was there, the old with the young, women and children with those women who were living in lifelong chastity, and the monks, all were weeping and wailing—they planned how they could go in, take him, and murder any of the people who opposed them.

4. When Arius, who was one of the elders, came to know and pondered this— Arius who was the enemy of the true and blameless *homoousios* Trinity—he was afraid that Archbishop Peter would be perfected in martyrdom and that he himself would remain excommunicate. For not long before this time he had been banished and driven out of the most holy church because he would not hold correct opinions concerning the Holy Trinity. He ran and gathered the elders and deacons and other honored clergy and, exhorting them, persuaded them to

enter the prison and fall before the bishop so that he might have pity on him and free him from his excommunication.

The most pious clergy, thinking this plan to be pious, entered the prison and entreated Archbishop Peter on Arius's behalf. While they were meeting with the most holy father and clasping his hand, they fell at his feet; after his blessing they cried out and said, "Have mercy on us, we beg you; intercede on behalf of our request." Commanding them to rise, he enquired from them the reason they had done this. They said to him, "We entreat your holiness, father, since our common lord Christ has called you to the honor and glory of confessing him and becoming a partner in his sufferings, unto death fighting for the truth. For you, our holy father, also are worthy of the crown of martyrdom. It happens that you, by the will of God, are quickly going to martyrdom. We bring to you this prayer: that you release Arius from his excommunication from the church."

5. When the archbishop heard these things from them, he gave a loud cry and said to them, "You entreat me concerning Arius?" And immediately he stretched forth his hands and said, "Both in this present age and in the time to come Arius will be excommunicate from the glory of Jesus Christ the Son of God." After the most blessed Archbishop Peter said this, a great fear seized all of them and no one dared to answer him anything. They were afraid, for they knew that he had replied this way because of some sure knowledge.

When the blessed one saw that they were completely stunned and had become silent, he entered into the midst of the clergy and chose two of the elders, old men, Achillas and Alexander by name. The blessed Peter took them aside to another part of the prison and announced to them, speaking in this way, "It is necessary for me—as God has given me the power—to be perfected in this martyrdom. This I know. But you, elder Achillas, after me will be my successor to the priesthood and to the throne. And after you, the throne will pass in succession to brother Alexander. Thus it was made clear to me by the Lord. And do not think that I am without sympathy and pity. I myself am a sinful man—I have kept secret the deceit of Arius. I have not anathematized him thus through my (power but through God's)."

6. "For this night when I had finished the service according to my usual practice, I was standing and praying when it happened that I saw a child come through the door of this cell. He was about twelve years old, and his face was shining like light, as if he were lighting up the entire building. He was wearing a short-sleeved linen garment, split in two from his neck and breast in front on down to his feet; with his two hands on his breast, the two parts of the garment drew together and covered his nakedness. When I saw him thus, I was taken aback suddenly. I opened my mouth and cried out in a loud voice, saying, 'Lord, why have you torn your tunic in two?' He answered and said to me, 'Arius has torn me in two. But see to it that you do not accept him into fellowship. They are going to entreat you on his behalf, but see that you are not persuaded by them. Appoint the presbyters Achillas and Alexander to succeed you in shepherding my church on behalf of which I became like a child and died, although I live always. Make it their duty that they in no way accept him into communion. For yours is the lot of martyrdom.' At this point the vision ended. I have indeed informed you and announced to you the orders (I have received)."

7. "But you, my brothers, know that I have lived with you all the years of my life, with trials and tears because of the misfortunes that have befallen me due to the plots of these crazy idolaters. I have gone about from place to place in Mesopotamian Syria, in Phoenicia and Palestine, and I have been on various islands. And I never stopped writing secretly and strengthening my people with the power of Christ. Concern for the flock which has been entrusted to me has never left me, day or night—rather, my heart would have worn away except that I have entrusted everything to him. And I have not even for a moment ceased from caring, especially for the blessed bishops Phileas, Hesychius, Pachomius, and Theodorus who were imprisoned on behalf of our common faith in Christ. They also have been worthily called by the grace of God. I was not slow in writing them many letters from Mesopotamia. For a great burden and struggle was placed upon me concerning them lest it turn out otherwise, because they were the heads, and there were snares (coming) from the multitudes of laity and clergy inside the prisons. For more than 660 have borne witness, as you know, before these very days.

"With this thought in mind, I could not bear to stand idle. When I heard of the perfection of these people through martyrdom, I rose and worshipped Christ who gives power to them, who perfects them and numbers them among the ranks of the holy martyrs. But you know how much evil Melitius has shown me; he who is from Lycopolis in the Thebaid has split asunder the church of God which the Logos of God had obtained by his very blood. He laid down his life on behalf of the church in order to ransom her from the treachery and deceit of the devil. Melitius has divided this church, and has not ceased from distressing and oppressing and waging war against all the holy confessors and bishops who are in chains. See that you keep yourselves away from him.

8. "For, as you see, I go bound by the love of God; I leave myself to his will. They are already chattering—so I've heard—about my murder, and these tribunes think that I am afraid since a writ has been dispatched which threatens me with death. These things are no concern of mine and I do not consider my life to be an honorable one if I do not complete in joy the course my ruler has decreed for me and the ministry which I have received from my Lord and God Jesus Christ. And now I know that henceforward you will no longer see me in the flesh here. Therefore, I confess to you today that my conscience is clear in all things. For I have not shrunk from telling you what was told to me, and whatever was good for your souls. For the rest, look to yourselves and to the entire flock which the Holy Spirit has given to you as bishops, that you might shepherd the Church of Christ which he obtained through his own blood.

"I know that after my death some of the clergy will rise up and speak perverse things; they will once again divide the Lord's church, just as Melitius has done, in order to drag away the people behind them. Therefore I entreat you: be watchful, stand firm in the faith, be brave, because you are going to enter once again into times of trouble. You know how many dangers Theonas endured at the hands of those who are mad for idols—he who raised me, my father and bishop, from whom I received my throne, whose way of life I hope for. So, too, the great Dionysius suffered, hiding from place to place on account of these crazy idolaters; and, in addition to this, Sabellius caused him grief. And what shall I say about Heracleon and Demetrius, those blessed bishops, who bore so many trials under that madman Origen who caused schisms in the church which to this day have raised up confusion and disorder? And not only these, but also how many temptations and trials the fathers before them endured in their care and attention for the church. But his grace, which guided those men and watched over them, will also guide and watch over you through the wings of his care. And now, my brothers and priests, I give you to God and to the Word of his grace. He is able to build up both you and his flock."

9. After he said these things, he knelt with them and prayed. After the prayers Achillas and Alexander kissed him and then in like manner kissed his hands and wept because he was telling them that they would no longer see him in the flesh. The blessed one went to where the remaining clergy and those of the laity were sitting; speaking comforting words to them and praying, he dismissed them in peace.

Achillas and Alexander departed and secretly reported to the legitimate clergy the things said to them by the blessed Peter their archbishop. And all were astonished when they heard these things. But almost all knew that it was not without a message from God that he had excommunicated Arius. Arius, that wicked and terrible person, knew this; he dissembled by concealing his deceit, and placed his hopes in Achillas and Alexander.

10. The blessed Peter knew the tribunes' scheme and plot and, fearful of the danger to the people, thought it better to hand himself over, thereby keeping the people unharmed. He sent to the tribunes a trusted old man, one of those faithful to him, who said, "Come tonight to the south side of the prison, under the guards' wall. When I knock from inside, dig through from outside and meet me and you will fulfill the orders of him who sent me to you." When these men heard this from the old man who had been sent, they seized on what had been ordered.

The five tribunes went alone, without an escort of soldiers and without a crowd; they took only stonecutters to cut through the wall, and that night met at the place. The blessed one knew that they stood there waiting; he entered unafraid into the inner part of the prison where he thought he would be undisturbed and so that those in the prison would not know what was happening. He knocked on the wall from the inside and those outside recognized the blessed one's signal. Immediately they dug where he was knocking and made an entrance. The holy one crossed himself, went out to them and said that it was better for him to hand himself over than have the people perish by the sword.

It was a strange and wonderful thing which happened that night! For a great wind suddenly rose up—it being winter—and no one was able to hear throughout that hour either the sound of the wall being cut or the sound of metal. In this way the blessed and holy Peter handed himself over to death, and fulfilled the Gospel saying which says, "It is better for one to die rather than have the people destroyed." He imitated his Lord who had said that the good shepherd gives his life for his flock.

11. While the people were sitting by the doors of the prison, the bishop was being held and was hastening quickly to fulfill for them what had been com-

manded. He did this so none of the people would find out and cause a disturbance or riot. The tribunes took him and went away to the place called Boukolos where the holy and blessed evangelist Mark attained perfection through martyrdom. Fear and trembling seized the men when they saw the courage of the blessed and famous Peter in the face of death and the firmness of his holiness. The blessed bishop asked them, saying, "If it is agreeable to you and your hearts are not hardened, I would like to go down to the tomb and bid farewell to Mark the holy apostle and evangelist of Christ." They answered, bowing their faces to the earth, ashamed before the sight of the blessed one, "As you command. Only, do it quickly."

12. The archbishop went down and opened the tomb of the blessed apostle Mark and—in very truth—while he was sitting there and speaking, he saw the evangelist of Christ before him. Weeping, he cried out, saying, "Honored father and evangelist of the only-begotten Son of God, and witness of the sufferings of Christ the redeemer of us all who chose you as the foundation and first bishop of this see. You taught the proclamation of faith throughout all of Egypt and round about the environs of this city. You fulfilled the ministry entrusted to you, and as reward for this, you were crowned with the crown of martyrdom, worthy to be an evangelist and archbishop and martyr of the great God and our Savior Jesus Christ. Then the blessed Anianas was chosen to be proclaimed your successor. He was indeed worthy. Melius followed, and the rest in succession. Then Demetrius and Heraclas, and after these Dionysius and Maximus and the blessed Theonas who raised me.

"The succession after my father Theonas then came to wretched me although I was a sinner and unworthy of this burden. In addition to the many mercies he wrought in me, our common Lord allowed me to be a true witness of his cross and resurrection, placing in me the sweet smell of his passion and resurrection so that I too might be made worthy to become the sweet fragrance of sacrifice, pouring out my own blood for him.

"Therefore, holy and revered father, the time urges me forward to advance to this. Pray for me, I beg you, so that with the power he gives me, I might enter this arena rejoicing with unwavering heart. I commend to your care the flock entrusted to me by (apostolic) succession; you commended them to those who went before me, and our God and Savior placed them in your hands. For you are indeed the teacher and instructor for me and for all those after me, since you, as the successor of the Lord himself, our Savior Jesus Christ, possess also the prerogatives of the (apostolic) see."

13. Rising from the tomb of the blessed and holy evangelist Mark, [Peter] stretched forth his hands to heaven and said, "Son and Logos of God, Jesus Christ, hear me your suppliant. Silence the storm that rises against your church, make as a seal of the persecution of your flock the pouring out of my blood who am your servant."

Then was fulfilled the vision of the virgin. For in that very hour a certain most holy virgin who had a monastery in a private suburban house near the resting place of the holy Mark was finishing her evening service; while praying she heard a voice from heaven come and say, "Peter (was) the first of the apostles, Peter (shall be) the last of the martyrs."

And after the most holy archbishop Peter completed his prayer, he kissed the tomb of the holy evangelist Mark and of the holy bishops resting there who had come before him. He went up to the tribunes, and they saw his face as if it were truly the face of an angel. Filled with fear, they hesitated to speak with him.

It is true in every way that the Lord does not forsake those who have faith in him. For by chance there were two coming from the countryside, one an elderly man and one an elderly virgin. The two entered the city, the old man to sell a hide covering and to go away again, the old woman to sell a pair of winding sheets. They came to the attention of Peter, the martyr of God; he who had been sealed (in the Lord) knew that this was the plan of God. He called to them, saying, "Are you Christians?" They said, "Yes, by the will of God." The holy martyr said to them, "And where are you going?" They answered, saying, "To the city to sell our goods." The holy one said to them, "Faithful children, God has sent you." Immediately they knew that he was the archbishop Peter. It was early in the morning. The archbishop said to them, "Stay with me here a while." They said, "As you have ordered."

14. Then the most holy archbishop said to the tribunes, "Come here, my children, since it is still early, that you might fulfill what has been arranged by our King." Taking him from the south side of the commemorative chapel of the holy evangelist Mark, they stood him in a deep valley where there were tombs. The blessed one said to the old man as they stood there, "Stretch out the hide you have on the earth, and likewise the two winding sheets." When he had willingly done this, Peter went above them and stood looking to the east; kneeling three times to the earth, and stretching his hands to heaven, he gave thanks to God and made the sign of the cross over his entire body. He said "Amen," and loosening his pallium and baring his honored throat, he inclined his neck for Christ. He stretched forth his head and said to them, "Do quickly, my children, what has been commanded you."

But they were afraid of the courage of the holy one, and turned to one another, each urging on the other. But no one dared to touch him and none dared to go forward to murder him with his own hands. They made this resolve, as trembling seized them and they became very afraid: "Let each of us put up five gold aurei, and the one who strikes him takes them all." One of them who had a fair amount of money in gold placed before his companions the twenty-five pieces of gold. One of them, chosen by lot to play the part of Judas, undertook the task and, coming up beside the holy head of Archbishop Peter, beheaded him on 25 November. And taking the blood money, they ran away in flight. They feared the greater numbers of the people, for they were alone.

The body of the holy martyr Peter—as the fathers have said who saw these things—remained standing there after they had beheaded him. It was there until the daylight hours, until what had been done was made known to the people at the prison.

15. For all the people were gathered there watching the outer doors of the prison. When they heard about and saw the tunnel (that had been dug through) the wall of the enclosure, they ran to the place and found the old man and the woman vowed to virginity who was the abbess of virgins sitting there and keeping watch over the body of the blessed martyr Peter. Those of the people

who got there first found the body of the holy one standing upright. They laid the martyr Peter upon the winding sheets as upon a bed. Wrapping the body in the sheets and sponging off the blood, they prepared it as they wept. The entire city was running together to view the martyr for Christ; as they met one another they cried out and mourned for what they had suffered. All the people were one in their tears and cries of mourning.

Those from the city who had gotten there first in haste wrapped the body in the hide which was lying beneath him. They bound fast the body because the people were tearing away pieces from his clothing. For his sacred figure had always worn white clothing: a shirt, short-sleeved tunic, and pallium. The people were trying to tear these and would have finally stripped the body if those who had hastened there had not with difficulty taken charge. These latter parted the crowd, moved the greater part away, and kept watch over the body.

16. The people were milling about in great confusion: some from Dromos wanted to take him to where Theonas had been buried; others from other parts wanted to take him to where Saint Mark had been perfected. There was a great uproar, and the people were about to fight. Some from Dromos saw the uproar among the people and were afraid that there was going to be a great battle. They ran and found a ship and got it ready very near the place—for it was near the sea—and after a great deal of time and arguing among the people, quickly seized the martyr and ran and placed him in the ship. They put off from shore and sailed away.

And once hidden from sight and beyond Pharos, they sailed through the place called Leukas and went to the cemetery which [Peter] had established in the western part of the city in the suburbs. While a large crowd of people mourned greatly and sought their shepherd, they occupied the cemetery. However, once all the people were gathered there, (those who had taken Peter) did not allow the martyr to be buried until they had brought him into the holy sanctuary and had enthroned him, seating him on his own throne. And the people saw and rejoiced when they viewed the dead man seated on the throne as if he were living. The reason for the enthroning was as follows.

17. For some time the blessed one did not sit on the throne of the churches, but mounting the raised step of the throne, he made his prayer for the people, and in this way would sit on the footstool of the throne. Because of this the people would oftentimes grumble and complain. One day, at the end of a great feast, he mounted the raised seat of the bishop and again was going to sit on the footstool when the people became angry and cried out, saying, "Bishop, sit on your throne. Where you were ordained, there you should also sit."

While they were crying out, the blessed one stood silent, bowing his head. The clergy were calling on him along with the people. He nodded to the clergy to keep silent, calmed down the people with soothing words, crossed himself, and once again sat on the footstool of the throne. Then finally all the people grew quiet; no longer did they try to force him to do this, but allowed him to act contrary to their wishes.

After he dismissed the congregation, he went into the council chamber and ordered that no one should come in except the bishops and elders and deacons. When this was done as he wished, he rebuked them, saying, "Why did you distress me along with all the people? Do you not know the fear and trembling my heart feels, and how much that oppresses me? For, beloved, whenever I ascend the episcopal chair and come near to the throne while standing in prayer—as you see—and I look on the throne and see what radiant and inexpressible power resides there, fear mixed with joy comes over me and mightily crushes my bones, and I am unable to do anything. And besides, on account of the people, lest they be led into sin, I sit on the footstool—as often you have seen and witnessed. And, as I have said before, it is with daring that I do this, suppressing my conscience for the edification of the people. When the time is opportune, I sit there according to custom. I have given assurance to your love, revealing what was hidden in my heart. For the rest, when the people try to force me to sit on the throne, you will silence them with consoling words since you know the intent of my conscience."

18. Here, then, is the end of the account which explains why the people, by enthroning the archbishop and martyr Peter after his death, fulfilled what they had asked for. The ministers of the Levitical priesthood with haste entered the sanctuary and, putting on the emblems of their office, took the holy martyr; with the crowd gathered around the bishops and elders of the city, they set him on the throne. And all the church rejoiced, saying, "Even if while living, thrice-blessed and holy father, you refused to sit on your throne, now you have been perfected with Christ and have not refused, but have been seated. Therefore pray also on our behalf, father, holy one of God."

Then all the bishops took the holy Achillas and stood him near the throne where they had also seated the martyr. And they took the pallium of the most holy and famous bishop Peter and placed it upon him. And saying to the people, "Peace be with you," and after praising for many hours the pious and most excellent Peter, the holy martyr of God, he [or: they] hastened to place him in the tomb.

The people had brought many special winding sheets and linen graveclothes, along with silk clothing and an abundance of aromatic herbs. All of them honorably attended to the holy martyr Peter and buried him in the cemetery which he had established and where many miracles had also occurred, and by the grace of Christ are still fulfilled even to the present day. For if the blessed one cared so much for the people before his perfection, he certainly did do much more after he was crowned in martyrdom and attained a great measure of freedom to appear with the ruler and king of all.

Appendix 4
AN ENCOMIUM PROCLAIMED BY
ABBA ALEXANDER ON SAINT PETER

Translated from the Coptic text edited by Henri Hyvernat, *Les actes des martyrs de l'Égypte* (Hildesheim and New York, 1977), 247–62. [Numbers in brackets indicate pagination in Hyvernat.]

An encomium proclaimed by Abba Alexander, archbishop of Alexandria, on Saint Peter, virgin and archbishop of this same city who was martyred for the name of our Lord Jesus Christ. He proclaimed it in the chapel to the west of the city when the day of his glorious commemoration was being celebrated, which is the twenty-ninth of Athor. In the peace of God. Amen.

While your glorious commemoration begins for us today, O my holy father, virgin and archbishop and martyr of Christ, holy Abba Peter, its dazzling rays have illumined my heart, encouraging me to speak your praises. And knowing the poverty of my thought and the weakness of my tongue, I am afraid to proceed toward the boundless ocean of your honors, on the ground that I will not be able to recount them as I should.

But I also know, O our all-holy one, that you will receive what we will say according to our ability by seeing our whole intention in the little which we will say according to the abundance of our poverty, (since) you are like our Lord Jesus Christ who received the poor widow's two pennies—for that was all her wealth. I will not delay any further saying that which we will be able to attain— or, rather, that which your grace will grant to us.

O glorious, excellent one, you who were born as a consequence of a vow as was John the Baptist! O, you who were given as a gift from God like the prophet Samuel, being worthy like that one of the gift of prophecy and wondrous revelations from the time of your childhood! O you who were called to the high priesthood like the priest Aaron—or rather (you who) have been exalted above Aaron, for he was (a priest) figuratively, while you are one in truth.

O you were worthy of the gift of healings, like Peter, head of the apostles, your namesake, from whom you have inherited the power which he was given of binding and loosing in heaven! O you who, like Paul, have preached, strengthening also the hearts of your flock by your catholic letters! O you who, like John the theologian, have closed the mouths of heretics! O you who, like James the holy apostle, were killed by the sword for Christ, you are likened to him when he willingly went before the Jewish officials, saying to them, "I am the one whom you seek," giving his life for his sheep. You have taken the likeness of this one in everything, laying down your life for your flock by robbing it from them [249] and entrusting it to the sword for them. Come now, let us provide the conclusion, O my faithful children, just as we have heard and seen.

The saint whom we are celebrating today, Abba Peter, was begotten, as I have said, in the same way as John the Baptist, from a holy father whose name was Theodosios, who was senior presbyter [πρωτοπρεσβύτερος] of the clergy of this city. And his blessed wife was of those who are honored (and her) name was Sophia. The two of them were righteous and walked in all the commandments and righteousness of the Lord, being blameless. And they had no children, for indeed the woman was barren and both were of advanced age. And, if it is appropriate to say, they were like Zachariah and Elizabeth, faithful servants of God.

Now, it happened one day that they were taking part in the Holy Eucharist in the place of the holy apostles Peter and Paul on the day of their commemoration which is the fifth of Epep. This blessed woman stood before the sanctuary and prayed in this way, saying, "Almighty God, (you) who do all things in abundance, more than the things we ask, who heard his servant Anne. And you favored her with Samuel the prophet whom she in return gave to your holy temple. Listen to me also, [250] give me offspring, and I believe that he will be for you a servant always." When she had said these things, she went forward and took part in the holy mysteries in the fear of God.

The following night she had a dream (which) she told to her husband. "I saw," she said, "two men standing before me in resplendent dress in the likeness of our father the patriarch, and when I saw them I was very afraid. They said to me, 'Do not be afraid. We are the ones in whose sanctuary you prayed to God yesterday, Peter and Paul. We took (your) prayer up to his presence; he heard it and had pity on you, O faithful woman! Tomorrow morning, therefore, go to the archbishop and he will pray on your behalf, and what you ask will quickly be fulfilled.' Behold, this is what I saw (and) said to your holiness. If, therefore, it pleases you, I will go to the archbishop, and I believe that if he prays for me, God will hear me." The holy presbyter said to her, "God be with you."

She rose, then, first thing in the morning and went to the patriarchate's door. She sent a subdeacon, saying, "Tell my father the archbishop, 'I wish to kiss your holy feet.'" When (the subdeacon) informed (the archbishop), he commanded that she come in. She worshiped his holy feet. The archbishop said to her, "What is it, [251] my daughter? Where are you from?" She said, "I am the wife of your servant Theodosios the presbyter, of whom I am not worthy. Because of my sins, God has deprived me of the fruit of my womb. Therefore, I beseech your holiness to pray for your servant and I believe that God will grant me an offspring (who will) be pleasing to him with his goodness." Then the patriarch replied and said to her, "May it be (done) just as you have believed. May the Lord Jesus Christ fulfill your request just as (he did) Anne's, the mother of the prophet Samuel." And in this way he blessed her and she went away from him in peace.

Before long, she conceived and bore a son. It was reported to the archbishop. He said, "Call him by the name of the chief of the apostles, Peter, for I believe that this one will be a solid foundation of the orthodox faith, and a leader for all Christians."

When he was seven years old, his father and mother took him and gave him as a gift to the church like the prophet Samuel whose parents took him up to the temple of God (and presented him) before Eli the priest. And they said to the archbishop, "Here is the child of your prayers; may he always be a servant of God!" The archbishop said, "May the Lord Jesus Christ bless you and exalt the horn of your offspring like Peter the apostle."

[252] And in this way (the archbishop) kept him near him like a beloved son. He sent him to school and in a short time he was well-instructed in secular wisdom. Then he made him (a) lector and kept him near him, in a tranquil place, so he could learn by heart the old and new scripture, and, by the grace of God, he learned in six years. The Holy Spirit of God filled the child and he knew how to recite in such a way that everyone came early to church because of the sweetness with which he read the lessons.

Now, it happened one day that a woman with an unclean spirit came to the church. (The spirit) cried out in her, "Unless Peter the lector comes and prays, I will not leave." The archbishop called him and said to him, "Peter, go and heal this woman." But he wept, saying, "Forgive me, my holy father, I have not yet attained that degree (of perfection); this demon is mocking me."

The archbishop said to him, "Listen to me, my son, and do not disobey (me)." Then Saint Peter, in humility of heart, and as one completing an act of obedience, took water, had the archbishop bless it with the sign of the holy cross, went out, and threw it on the woman, saying, "In the name of our Lord Jesus Christ, Son of the Living God, who was crucified [253] to save the whole world, and by the prayers of my holy father, come out of her and never be able to come back to her!" And immediately the demon, like a flaming fire, left her, while everyone watched him, and those who were watching glorified God, saying, "Truly, the hand of the Lord is with this child!"

Now, in those days there arose an apostate named Sabellius who had raised up a godless heresy which limited the Godhead to a single substance and a single person. He spoke with a mouth that deserved to be shut, (saying,) "The Father himself is the Son and the Holy Spirit, a single substance." Therefore he commanded in his godlessness not to say "And in the Holy Trinity," but rather to say, "The Father and the Son and the Holy Spirit," as if there were but a single person.

Now, his error disturbed many in the city. These (i.e., his followers) came with great arrogance to the door of the church, wishing to dispute, and the archbishop sent Peter out to them to make a defense against them. When he came out, the godless ones mocked him, saying, "See how this one (i.e., the archbishop) acts toward us? For not only does he not come out to speak with us, but he also sends out the youngest and (most) despised of them (i.e., the clergy)."

Saint Peter replied [254] in a prophetic voice. He said, "If you have anything to say, say it; if not, be quiet and do not blaspheme." Immediately, as if struck by lightning, all (their) tongues were silent, their faces twisted into a curse (and) they became frightful to everyone who saw them. And the crowd of faithful who saw what had happened threw them out of the city, saying, "Throw these impious ones from our midst, frighten these wolves away from us."

Then the archbishop sent a decree throughout all Egypt: "May he who says that the Holy Trinity—Father, Son, Holy Spirit—is a single person be anathema! As for us, we say: 'The Father and the Son and the Holy Spirit are three substances, indeed persons, but (they are) a single divinity, one essence, one Lordship, a trinity in unity.'"

Because the grace of God resided in this holy Peter, he was called to the (various ecclesiastical) ranks, even to the presbyterate, by the succeeding archbishops through Saint Theonas whom he succeeded in the archbishopric. O how many were the gifts of healing which God granted to him because of the purity of his body and his soul and his spirit, so that many times he was worthy to see the Son of the living God upon [255] the holy altar, giving (the eucharistic elements) by the hand of the archbishop to those who were worthy.

Now, it happened one day that a man came to receive the holy mysteries of our Lord Jesus Christ, and when the archbishop stretched forth his hand to give (them to) him, immediately he saw the hand of the Son of God which held back his hand from giving (them) to him, (the Son of God) saying to him, "Archbishop, do not give to him, for he is not worthy to partake of my holy body."

Then the archbishop said to the man, "My son, you cannot receive these fearful mysteries if you have not first been purified from such and such sin. As often, therefore, as the good God, out of his love for men, grants you (pl.) repentance, purify yourselves first before you approach this place, lest you receive great punishment instead of pardon." No one saw this wonder revealed except the archbishop and Saint Peter, the two (of them).

But after these things, Archbishop Theonas became ill. When he was about to die—as all men—the clergy gathered to him with practically the entire city, weeping and saying, "Where are you going, our father, abandoning us in this time of trouble? To whom will you give us?"

He said to them, [256] "Be comforted, my children, for God has already chosen someone who will govern you well. What I am about to tell you (may seem) foolish; nevertheless, I cannot hide it. It happened to me that in this night I was awake because of (my) illness and was reciting some psalms. When I had finished the short office according to my strength, I lay down to sleep on the bed, praying to the Lord on behalf of his flock that he might help them. Immediately the King, the Lord of Glory, appeared to me and said, 'You who water well the spiritual garden, give the garden to Peter the presbyter so he can water it, and come and rest with your fathers.'

"And forgive me, O my beloved children, because I was foolish, but I cannot conceal the righteousness of God in my heart for his great congregation which is you. Behold, therefore, I did not hinder my lips; I have proclaimed to you the righteousness of the Lord." And all of them cried out together, saying, "Worthy, worthy, worthy, for he is truly worthy of the rank of the patriarchate." Then the archbishop said to Peter, "Have courage, my son, and be strong, and work well the garden of your Lord."

But he prostrated himself, weeping and saying, "I am not worthy, nor will I be able to do this [257] great thing." The archbishop said, "It is Christ who commands you. Let no one oppose the one who has chosen you. It is he who will give you strength." And when he had said these things, Abba Theonas said, "May peace be with all of you," and he looked upwards to heaven and spoke thus: "Behold, the King of Glory and his holy angels." And thus he went to him whom he loved, our Lord Jesus Christ, on the second day of Tobi, in the peace of God. Amen.

After these things, Saint Peter was seated on the throne of the high priesthood by the decree of God Almighty. He possessed the rudders of the spiritual ship (and) he made the passengers seated in it equal in the riches of the good God by having them sail into good harbors—I mean the holy Gospels—and he made them do business by its holy commandments. He made the poor equal to the rich through their (i.e., the rich) charity, and the rich differed not at all from the poor in all the good things which pleased the Lord, according to what is written.

Come, therefore, let us tell you about this other wonder which was brought about through him for the glory of God. There was a man in the [258] city whose hands were twisted so that he could not straighten them at all. And (when) there was a service, he went to the church and he desired to receive the holy mysteries from the hands of the archbishop, and because his hands were crippled he opened his mouth to receive (them). The archbishop said to him, "My son, stretch forth your hands and take for yourself." Immediately his hands became straight and he stretched them forth and received the holy mysteries, and glorified God.

Now, they were still at peace and the Christians spoke somewhat openly. The devil could not bear it (and) he raised up a terrible persecution against us through the ungodly emperor Diocletian. He (caused) a great deal of blood to flow on account of the name of Christ, in Africa and Mauritania and Egypt and in the East. Because of this persecution, therefore, Saint Peter fled to Mesopotamia with me and my father, Achillas.

Now, when he had come into a city in order to rest there, the ruler found out (about it) and he sent for us. He asked the archbishop, "What is your profession? Why have you come here?" [259] Saint Peter said to him, "I am a general going from place to place, arming soldiers for Christ, my king." The ruler said to him, "Where are the provisions which you give to them, and the arms of your army? (Where is) your king?" The blessed archbishop said to him, "The arms of our army are the holy seal and the baptism of 'rebirth,' and the provisions that he gives to them now are the manifestation of the Holy Spirit according to what is profitable for men: to one, a word of wisdom; to another, a word of knowledge; to yet another, gifts of healing. When they have finished their struggle, then he gives them the good things of heaven, for he himself, my king, is in heaven."

The ruler of all (the people of) that city said, "Since you have said that your king gives the gift of healing, behold, we will bring to you a blind man. If you open his eyes, we will believe in Christ—all of us." And they brought the blind man. Then Saint Peter touched his eyes, saying, "In the name of my Lord Jesus Christ, the Son of the Living God, see!" His eyes were opened. Oh, how great was the shouting there! Everyone cried out, "One is Christ, the god of the Christians is the only (god)! Give us the seal of Christ! Arm us (as) soldiers for him, the true king, Jesus [260] Christ our Lord!" And he spent the rest of that day instructing all of them in the name of the Father and the Son and the Holy Spirit. They numbered 10,000 souls.

While we were still in that place, Satan raised up yet a little trouble against the church, for there was a certain Melitius, a bishop of Lycopolis—he wished to seize the archbishopric. Now, he saw an opportunity while Abba Peter was in flight, (and) went to Alexandria and sat on the (episcopal) chair. He had the audacity to do this lawless act shamelessly. But God said to him, "There is no place for you (here), nor anything to be gained by this act." And again (God said), "I will put a bridle on you; I will put a ring in your nose and I will turn you away from the path which you desired. Moreover, this little bit which you have, I will take away from you." And this happened, for when there was a little peace, Saint Peter returned to Alexandria and threw Melitius out. Now, that miserable fellow fled and did things contrary to the canon(s), but soon he was punished for his lawlessness—as you know.

Now, again, there was another, a certain Arius, a priest among the clergy of this city—this detestable man who afflicts us now. You know how he openly worked against God, going astray in the error of Origen, saying with his mouth—which he should have kept shut—that the Son of God is a "creature."

Although I could not fail to say it, your (pl.) greatness [the text of the preceding phrase is uncertain] knows how Father Peter excommunicated him. Moreover, the Son of the Living God appeared to him and said to him, "Command your sons who follow after you"—that is, Achillas and me, though I am unworthy—said the Lord Jesus Christ, "that they are not to accept him, for he is a stranger to me in this age and (the age) to come."

Our most holy father spoke these things while he lay in prison (awaiting) holy martyrdom. For he finished his course and saved the orthodox faith. Thereafter, the good God wished to add a third crown to that of his angelic way of life and high priesthood, that is, that of martyrdom. And this he was worthy of—as you know. Now, concerning the cause of his martyrdom and the manner in which he commanded us concerning that madman Arius, and the way in which Saint Peter gave himself to death in his own love for Christ—you know all these things; they are written in his martyrology.

We, according to the measure of our weakness, have set before you these few things, putting aside many details so that the discourse might not be prolonged. Some of (these things) were heard from those who went before us; and yet others we saw with our eyes. [262] Thus we have not sought to add to the glory of that holy one, but rather to procure benefit for us, for those who speak and those who listen. For that one has already obtained ineffable honors in heaven.

May it happen for all of us that through his holy intercession, by completing our lives in sinlessness, we may be worthy of these things. To the glory of the Father and the Son and the Holy Spirit who gives life, now and always, forever and ever. Amen.

Lord, be merciful to your servant, the deacon Gabriel Kosmet. Amen.

Appendix 5
EPIPHANIUS, "THE SCHISM OF
MELITIUS IN EGYPT"

Translated from *Adversus Haereses* (*Panarion*) 68 (*PG* 42:184B–189B).

1. There is a certain community of Melitians in the land of the Egyptians in the Thebaid which arose from one Melitius, of the Catholic church and true faith—for his faith did not change at any time from that of the Catholic church. This Melitius was a contemporary of and flourished at the same time as the above-mentioned Hierakas whom he succeeded and who was also a contemporary of Saint Peter, bishop of Alexandria. All of these men lived at the time of the persecution of Diocletian and Maximian. The subject of Melitius can be treated in this way.

He caused a schism—but indeed he did not become one who changed his faith. Melitius was seized at the time of the persecution together with Peter the holy bishop and martyr along with other martyrs. He was seized by those whom the emperor had appointed as rulers of Egypt and Alexandria at this time. Culejanus was procurator of the Thebaid, Hieroklas of Alexandria. Melitius himself had been confined in prison together with the above-mentioned martyrs and the above-mentioned Peter, archbishop of Alexandria. Melitius was also thought to be preeminent throughout Egypt and was second only to Peter in the archbishopric (of Egypt).

He was his helper although, being under him, he referred ecclesiastical matters to him. For it is the custom that the archbishop in Alexandria have ecclesiastical control of all Egypt and the Thebaid, Mareotis and Libya, Ammoniaka, Mariotis and Pentapolis. Therefore, once these were seized they remained in prison in order to bear witness for Christ, and their imprisonment lasted a long time. Others before them had been handed over and bore witness (or: were martyred); they received the rewards of perfection and fell asleep. These were revered thereafter as emminent and great persons.

2. And while some have borne witness (or: been martyred), others have lapsed from witnessing. They have under compulsion offered sacrifice and have committed the sinful act of worshiping idols. Therefore, they fell and sacrificed. Having transgressed, they went to those who had confessed and borne witness [martyrs] in order to obtain mercy through repentance. Some were from the rank and file of the church, while others were from various orders of the clergy— some elders, some deacons, and others.

Now, there was an extraordinary commotion among those who were ready to bear witness for Christ. Some were saying that those who fell once and denied Christ and because of their lack of bravery did not put up a struggle should not be considered worthy of repentance. (They said this) so that those who still remained steadfast would not swerve from the path and join the God-denying and impious idolaters, paying little heed to penance and seeing how swiftly forgiveness could be obtained.

And what was said by those who had confessed was reasonable. For they were saying this—Melitius and Peleus and many of the witnesses [martyrs] and confessors with them. It was obvious, then, that those who were saying these things had demonstrated their zeal for God and had suffered. They said that during a time of peace, after the persecution was over, and after a sufficient period of time, repentance should be allowed to those mentioned above, if they truly repented and showed the fruit of their repentance—not, to be sure, so that each might be received back into his own clerical order, but rather that after an interval of time they might be gathered together in the church and in fellowship [communion], in the church body but not in the clergy. This (decision) was full of truth and of the zeal for God.

3. The most holy Peter, since he was merciful and was the father of all, pleaded and entreated (in their behalf), saying, "Let us receive them as repentants and set penance for them, so they might remain in communion with the church. And, since the Word has come to us and embraces us, let us not turn them away, not even the clergy, for fear that those who through cowardice and weakness were at one time set upon and shaken loose (from the faith) by the devil be irrevocably turned away and never healed. As it is written, 'Do not turn away the lame, but rather heal them.'" Peter's words were words of mercy and love for his fellow man; Melitius's and those with him were words of truth and zeal.

Therefore, because of the reasons presented and thought godly by both men, the schism occurred, some saying this and some saying that. For when Archbishop Peter saw that the Melitians opposed his counsel of brotherly love and bore an excessive godly zeal, he himself, by spreading out his himation, that is, his cloak or pallium, set up a curtain dividing their prison and proclaimed through his deacon, "Let those who are of my opinion come forward to me and let those who hold the view of Melitius go to him." The majority of the bishops and monks and elders and those of other orders sided with Melitius. Only a few altogether went with Archbishop Peter, a few bishops and some others. These prayed by themselves, and the others (i.e., the Melitians) did likewise. In like manner, with regard to the other holy offices, each side completed them by themselves.

It happened that Peter was martyred, the blessed one was perfected, and Alexander succeeded him in Alexandria. For this man succeeded to the see after the above-mentioned Peter. Melitius and many others were banished and exiled to the mines of Phainos. After this time Melitius himself, with all those who professed his cause and had been swept away with him, founded their own churches. Whether they were in jail or on the road, going through every land and every place they established clergy—bishops, elders, and deacons. And the two opposing sides were not in communion with each other.

Each side gave a name to its own church. Those who succeeded Peter, in possession of what was ancient in the church, (called theirs) the Catholic Church; the Melitians (called theirs) the Church of Martyrs [or: Witnesses]. Therefore, Melitius himself, as he traveled, ordained many men in Eleutheropolis and in Gaza and in Aelia [Jerusalem]. It happened that he spent time in the above-mentioned mines. But afterwards the confessors were freed from the mines, those of Peter's party—for there were still many—and those of Melitius's. They did not have fellowship with each other in the mines, nor did they pray together. It happened that Melitius lived on for quite some time; therefore he flourished at the same time as Alexander, the successor of Peter, and was his friend. He cared for the affairs of the church and faith, for he said many times that he held nothing at variance (with church doctrine).

2

The Theological Fragments and Peter's Alleged Anti-Origenism

None of the theological works attributed in antiquity to Saint Peter survives intact. Even the *Canonical Letter*, Peter's longest extant work, exists only as an epitome (see 139–40 below). Of the theological writings, fragments survive in Greek, Latin, Syriac, and Armenian. The titles given to these pieces vary, but these predominate: *On the Deity* (Περὶ θεότητος), *On the Soul* (Περὶ ψυχῆς), and *On the Resurrection* (Syriac), the last of which is also the subject of Greek fragments from a paschal letter. The fragments of all these works are scattered throughout many volumes and are gathered together here for the first time (see the tables below, 90 and 91).

Since all the literature on Peter employs the traditional titles given above, I have retained these headings. The discussion of the fragments, then, is divided into the following headings:

I. *On the Deity and Humanity [of Christ]*
II. *On the Soul*
III. *On the Resurrection* (Paschal Letter)
IV. *On the Resurrection* (Syriac)
V. *On Easter*
VI. Miscellaneous Fragments

The fragments are grouped under the works to which they belong. This was by no means easy to decide in some cases: some fragments are very brief, and little can be concluded from them. In making this division for the sake of clarity, I have had to wrench some pieces, misplaced or mistitled, from their published order and regroup them. Also, in some of the collections, especially the Syriac collection of Pitra, but also in the *PG*, several fragments have been placed under one heading or number. These have had to be renumbered.

The numeration in this chapter follows the model of I.1a:

I. Section heading, here, *On the Deity and Humanity [of Christ]*.

1 A fragment within that heading.

a A version of the fragment.[1]

In treating Peter's theological works I examine, under each heading, the provenance, authenticity, and texts of the fragments, and then discuss their theology. Also, a note at the beginning of each heading directs the reader to a brief overview of patristic works that have similar titles or that deal with subject matter similar to those of Peter.[2] Because so much of the discussion of Peter's fragmentary writings—indeed, even the preservation of the fragments themselves—involves "anti-Origenism," this chapter will conclude with a study of Peter's theological works and anti-Origenism. An appendix at the end of the chapter gives a new translation of all the fragments under discussion.

Table 1 (p. 90) gives the numbering system used in this chapter, the source of each fragment, and, wherever necessary, the numeration employed by other editors. A second table follows which gives a synoptic view of the fragments in groups I and II (p. 91).

THE THEOLOGICAL FRAGMENTS

I. On the Deity and Humanity [of Christ][3]

The full Greek title (Πέτρου τοῦ ἁγιωτάτου ἐπισκόπου ᾽Αλεξανδρείας καὶ μάρτυρος. ᾽Εκ τοῦ περὶ θεότητος βιβλίου) of a work *On the Deity*

---

1. Such a system may seem cumbersome, but I felt that it was better to follow as closely as possible the groupings that have been used in the scholarship on the saint's writings, while at the same time renumbering the fragments based on new research and study. My numbering allows one to distinguish smaller fragments within larger collections, which has not always been done before, and thus allows one to see more clearly later variants, translations, and interpolations. Many of the fragments are duplicates, and therefore the actual number of fragments preserved is smaller than past collections would seem to indicate.

2. Because of the extremely fragmentary nature of the writings attributed to Saint Peter, they can not be compared at length to other works of the same title. Therefore, only an overview will be attempted here in the notes.

3. *On the Deity and Humanity [of Christ]* as a christological work has precursors as early as Justin (*1 Apol.* 22). Novatian, in the mid-third century, wrote a work *On the Trinity*. According to J. Quasten, *Patrology* (Westminster, Md. 1984) 2:218, "the second part, comprising chapters 9–28, is a defense of the two natures and their union in Christ, the Son of God and the Son of Man." At Alexandria Origen discussed the nature of Christ in book 1 of the *De principiis*. Theognostus, the head of the catechetical school shortly before Peter, wrote a wide-ranging work, the *Hypotyposeis*, the fifth and sixth books of which dealt with the incarnation of the Savior. Apparently these two books

attributed to Peter is clearly secondary;[4] furthermore, the designation *On the Deity* is so general that it may not be the title of a work, but rather indicates the contents of a work by Peter whose title is unknown. Of the six groups of fragments that clearly belong to *On the Deity* (I.1–5), only three (I.1, the Syriac frags. of Pitra, and I.4–5) preserve a title referring to deity, while the others bear such titles as *From a Sermon of Theology* (I.2a) or *On the Resurrection* (I.2b), or are untitled (I.A1–5). Because Syriac fragments I.1a, 2c, and 3a are a translation of I.1–3 (see below), the title under which they were collected is a borrowed one. Therefore, only frag. I.1 offers evidence of a work by Peter entitled *On the Deity*, while I.4–5 suggest *Concerning Deity and Humanity*.[5] The other fragments (I.6, I.6a, and I.6b) considered here have no designated relationship with *On the Deity*, but by virtue of their subject matter might belong to that work.

Given such scanty evidence, is it possible to establish the title of this theological work attributed to Peter? Although the title of frag. I.1, which calls Peter "most blessed bishop of Alexandria and martyr," is hagiographical, its report that Peter's work was called *On the Deity* may be accurate.

If this were the only evidence, it would not be possible to reach a firm conclusion, but two other fragments offer more evidence. Fragments I.4–5, from Vatican codex Vatopédi 236, a florilegium on the corruptible and incorruptible, preserve one piece, I.4, which is a series of scripture citations from a work by Peter entitled "Concerning Deity and Humanity" (Περὶ θεότητος καὶ ἀνθρωπότητος). In the codex this fragment follows two pieces from a paschal letter by Peter (frag. III.1– 2). Since it was not lumped in with the paschal address, one might conclude that the ancient editor knew it was from another source, namely *Concerning*

---

set out to prove the possibility of the incarnation and may have been a "philosophical proof." Harnack sees in this work an "anticipation" of the conflict between Christianity and Neoplatonism. See L. B. Radford, *Three Teachers of Alexandria: Theognostus, Pierius and Peter. A Study in the Early History of Origenism and Anti-Origenism* (Cambridge 1908) 28–29. Pierius, in his work on the *theotokos*, perhaps wrote a "treatise on the fact of the Incarnation and in particular on its method, the Virgin Birth" (Radford 56). After Peter, Athanasius, who was undoubtedly a more systematic theologian than Peter, wrote *On the Incarnation* as part of his *Adversum gentes duo libri*. It is much more ambitious than previous works on the incarnation and resurrection in that its subject is a broad defense of the Christian faith and its theology of redemption (Quasten 3:24). The Arian controversy, with its rancorous debates over the nature of Christ, saw a proliferation of christological treatises. For an overview of the theology of the Alexandrians and of the contending parties in the Arian struggles, see G. W. H. Lampe, "Christian Theology in the Patristic Period," chaps. 5–7 in *A History of Christian Doctrine*, ed. Hubert Cunliffe-Jones (Philadelphia 1980).

4. PG 18:509A; RS 4:46.

5. Quasten 2:114, along with many others, takes the title to be *On the Deity*.

TABLE 1

Abbreviations: *A* =Armenian
G = Greek
S = Syriac
Exp = Expansion
T = Testimonium

I.   *On the Deity and Humanity* [*of Christ*]
I.1–3   On the Deity (*PG* 18:509–512A).
I.2a   Ex Sermone de Theologia (*PG* 18:521D–522D).
I.2b   On the Resurrection (Pitra IIA: *AS* 4:189).
I.1a
I.2c   } From the Book "On the Deity" (Pitra IA–D: *AS* 4:187– 88).
I.3a
I.3 (*S* Exp)
I.A1–5   Five Armenian Fragments (Pitra I–V: *AS* 4:194– 95).
I.4–5   Concerning Deity and Humanity (Richard 15: *Le Muséon* 86 (1973) 268–69).
I.6   On the Advent of Our Savior (*RS* 4:48).
I.6a   On the Advent of Christ (*PG* 18.511A–512A).
I.6b   On Matthew (*PG* 18:521C).
I.T   On the Union of Two Natures (*RS* 4:50).

II.   *On the Soul*
II.1   That the Soul Did Not Preexist the Body (*PG* 18:520C– 521A; *RS* 4:48–50).
II.1a   From the First Sermon Concerning the Soul (that it did not preexist) (*ACO* 3:197; *PG* 86^1:961B).
II.1b   Concerning the Soul: that it did not preexist or sin before (*Kleronomia* 5 (1973) 311–12).
II.2   That the Soul Did Not Preexist (Pitra III: *AS* 4:193– 94).
II.T   From the First Sermon on the Soul (*RS* 4:50).

III.   *On the Resurrection* (*Paschal Letter*)
III.1–2   From the Paschal Letter of Saint Peter of Alexandria (*Le Muséon* 86 (1973) 267–69).

IV.   *On the Resurrection* (Syriac)
IV.1–7   On the Resurrection (Pitra IIB–H: *AS* 4:189–93).

V.   *On Easter*
V.1–5   That the Jews Correctly Fixed the Date of Easter (*PG* 18:512B–520B).

VI.   Miscellaneous Fragments
VI.1   From the Teaching of Peter of Alexandria (*PG* 18:521B).
VI.2   Untitled Fragment (*AS* 4:194).

TABLE 2

Synoptic Table

I.	*On the Deity and Humanity [of Christ]*
I.1	I.1a
I.2	I.2a; I.2b; I.2c
I.3	I.3a
I.2a	see I.2
I.2b	see I.2
I.1a	see I.1
I.2c	see I.2
I.3a	see I.3
I.3 (*S* Exp)	Spurious
I.*A*1	see I.2c
I.*A*2	see I.2c
I.*A*3–5	Spurious
I.4–5	
I.6	I.6a; I.6b
I.6a	see I.6
I.6b	see I.6
I.T	Testimonium
II.	*On the Soul*
II.1	II.1a; II.1b
II.1a	see II.1
II.1a (*G* Exp 1–2)	Spurious
II.1b	see II.1
II.1b (*G* Exp 1–2)	Spurious
II.2	Spurious (?)
II.T	Testimonium

Deity and Humanity. The material under this title exists in Greek independently of the other fragments of *On the Deity*. By their subject matter, these fragments (I.4–5) belong with those of *On the Deity* and suggest that the full title of a christological work by Peter was *On the Deity and Humanity [of Christ]*.

Fragment II.1, from a work entitled *On the Soul*, also offers an important clue to the title. It begins with what looks like a transition sentence: "We have explained earlier (or: previously) (ἐν πρώτοις) the things *concerning the divinity and humanity* (περὶ τῆς θεότητος καὶ ἀνθρωπότητος) of the Second Man [i.e., Jesus Christ], according to the blessed Apostle. It is necessary also to relate and set down the things concerning the First Earthly Man [i.e., Adam]." Ἐν πρώτοις can mean "in the first part," which would suggest that Peter wrote a two-part work. The first part of this work could be on the nature of Christ, and the second part on the nature of Adam, that is, mankind.[6] Ἐν πρώτοις can also mean "earlier," "previously," therefore, "in the first or earlier work." Since the manuscript tradition has preserved separate titles for the fragments of group I and group II, it seems best to understand ἐν πρώτοις as referring to a separate, earlier work. Thus, Peter probably wrote a christological work, *On the Deity and Humanity [of Christ]*, and a work *On the Soul*.[7]

The only fragment(s) preserved in Greek, I.1–3, where three small pieces are collected under one title, come from the Council of Ephesus in 431.[8] Fragment I.2a, preserved only in Latin, is a quotation from frag. I.2 by the Emperor Justinian in his *Contra Monophysitas*.[9] The Latin text cannot repeat the play on words found in the Greek ("the Lord came [γενόμενον] into the womb and thus became [γενόμενον] flesh"), but otherwise closely follows the Greek, quotes from John 1:14, Luke 1:28, 35, and also preserves the chief theological point of the passage: God the

6. The designation of *On the Soul* as the "first sermon" (λόγου) (see frag. II.1a) might come from a misreading of ἐν πρώτοις: the sentence which designates the second part of the work was misconstrued to mean the first. Since the subject of the piece seemed to be "On the Soul," the fragment was called the first sermon (λόγος) on the soul. This conclusion is, however, highly speculative and not likely. Theognostus's *Hypotyposeis*, in seven books, offers a possible parallel to a two-part work by Peter. See Radford, 4ff.; and Otto Bardenhewer, *Geschichte des altkirchlichen Literatur* (2d ed.; Freiburg 1914) 2:246.

7. It is not clear precisely what ἐν πρώτοις means. See LSJ, 1535A s.v. πρότερος, B.II.2, "first part, beginning." In the passages cited there, ἐν πρώτοις, with the article, means the earlier part of a work; see, e.g., Plato *Rep.* 392e2. In others places, it clearly refers to the beginning of the *same* dialogue, e.g., Plato *Gorg.* 460e2 (with λόγος), and *Sym.* 221d7. Professor Robert Renehan of the University of California at Santa Barbara suggested in conversation that ἐν πρώτοις would need to be in the singular, i.e., ἐν τῷ πρώτῳ (sc. λόγῳ) in order to signify an earlier work (cf. Acts 1:1). Thus, it would seem that in frag. II.1 ἐν πρώτοις shows that Peter is referring not to an earlier work, but to an earlier part of the same work (so Bardenhewer 2:246). In literature more contemporary with Peter, however, the evidence is not so clear. While Origen, in the *Contra Celsum*, seems regularly to use the singular to refer to an earlier book of the *Contra Celsum*, and not to a *separate* work (see 3.1 and 2.1 in the latter of which τῷ πρώτῳ τόμῳ = "in the first book"), I could not find an example of ἐν πρώτοις in the *Contra Celsum*, but ἐν τοῖς πρὸ τούτων [8.2 and 8.6.2] does mean "earlier," that is, in the same work; see also 2.25 and 2.29). In Eusebius HE 6.24.1, πρότερα refers to individual works within a larger work, but the phrase τὰ πρότερα πέντε is not parallel with the one under discussion. In HE 7.24.3, πρότερα essentially means "former," while in 6.25.3 ἐν δὲ τῷ πρώτῳ refers to an independent work as part of a series: ἐν δὲ τῷ πρώτῳ εἰς τὸ κατὰ Ματθαῖον. . . . Given the evidence just presented, it is just possible that ἐν πρώτοις refers to an earlier part of one work, but in the absence of an exact parallel where the phrase means this, it seems better to stay with the traditional divisions (see, e.g., Quasten 2:114–15; and Adolf von Harnack, *Geschichte der altchristlichen Literatur* [2d ed.; Leipzig (1893) 1958] 1/1:445–46) and see in this passage a reference to an earlier, separate work.

8. *PG* 18:509A; *AS* 4:425 n. 2.

9. *PG* 18:521C.

Word (ὁ θεὸς λόγος, Deus verbum) is with you, which identifies the human Jesus with the Logos. It is likely that Justinian did not have an independent work of Peter before him, but quoted one of the three fragments preserved at Ephesus.

A Syriac fragment (I.2b), preserved under the title *De resurrectione*, is actually a translation from *On the Deity*, as Pitra observed.[10] Since the Syriac fragment (Pitra IIA) preserves the name of the angel Gabriel (cf. I.2), which the Latin (I.2a) does not, it is probably translated from the Greek frag. I.2. Nevertheless, once again it is likely that the author worked from an epitome of Peter's work (most likely the Ephesian one) rather than from a complete text by the bishop of Alexandria.

Fragments I.1a, I.2c, I.3a, and I.3 (S Exp) form a collection of four Syriac fragments (Pitra IA–D) from a book *On the Deity*.[11] Pitra noted that one of the manuscripts states that these fragments, "testimonia from the synod of Ephesus," are the work of "Saint Peter, bishop and martyr."[12] This confirms that, once again, what we have does not come directly from a work by Peter, but from an epitome of his work made by a council—which is also true for the *Canonical Letter*.

Of the four Syriac pieces, I.1a is the same as frag. I.1. Fragment I.2 is omitted, except for part of the last sentence, a quotation from Luke 1:35. Syriac frag. I.2c begins with this quotation, then goes on to add material not found in frags. I.1–3. Pitra suggested that frag. I.2c (IB by his designation) might give a Syriac translation of material immediately following frag. I.2.[13] This is possible, but frag. I.2c reads like a creedal confession and is probably an interpolation. This last conclusion is made more likely by the fact that frag. I.3a (Pitra IC) is clearly a translation of frag. I.3 which begins immediately after the passage from Luke 1:35. It must be concluded that these Syriac pieces are translations of the Greek text preserved in I.1–3, and that the Syriac translator did not have a work of Peter before him, but only the three small pieces preserved at Ephesus. Fragment 3 (S Exp) (Pitra ID), preserved in the same Syriac collection, does not exist among the pieces of frags. I.1–3 and must be a Syriac addition: it is a natural theological expansion of frag. I.3 glorifying the Virgin. Consequently the term "Mother of God" given to Mary can not, on the strength of this fragment, be attributed to Peter.[14]

10. See *AS* 4:426 n. 4, 189ff. for a detailed discussion. The text is in *AS* 4:189ff. (Syriac); 426 (Latin).
11. *AS* 4:187–88 (Syriac); 425–26 (Latin).
12. *AS* 4:425 n. 2.
13. *AS* 4:426 n. 1.
14. Daniélou, *The Theology of Jewish Christianity* (Chicago 1964) 31, points out "that

Only the first two pieces of frags. I.*A*1–5, preserved in Armenian, are possibly authentic; the last three pieces are clearly monophysitic.[15] Fragments I.*A*1–2, however, do not go back to the Greek fragments preserved at the Council of Ephesus, but come, rather, from one of the Syriac fragments (I.2c). The two pieces insist on the reality of Jesus' nature, and frag. I.*A*1 expands the text with an antidocetic statement, "and truly he suffered torments for us." The Armenian text is an expansion of a Syriac text which is an expansion of the Greek text. It is clearly secondary (or tertiary).

Of the fragments of a work by Peter on the deity discussed above, only three, frags. I.1–3, are of primary importance. The Syriac, Latin, and Armenian translations add nothing authentic to the pieces preserved in Greek. The *terminus post quem* for these fragments is 431, the date of the Council of Ephesus. Did the church fathers at that council have before them a work by Peter, from which they quoted three small pieces, or did they, even at that date, have only these three pieces? It is impossible to be sure, but given the poor state of preservation of Peter's writings, I believe that the bishop's work had already been epitomized. Whatever the case, it was the fate of that work to survive only in small quotations.

One other group remains to be considered. The fragments edited together as I.4–5 and bearing the title *Concerning Deity and Humanity* preserve independently two pieces from Peter's work. The first (I.4) is a catena showing that Jesus was truly human; the second is only one line— "By the will of God the Word—and it was given life by the Spirit"—and appears to be an editorial summary. The theology of both pieces is compatible with frags. I.1–3.

The fragments from *On the Deity* were quoted in later times against both the Nestorians and the Monophysites, which would indicate that those quoting them believed them to hold a middle, orthodox position. The fragments, in fact, are so orthodox that they at first seem to be only a catena of biblical quotations—there are nine quotations from scriptures in a very short space. Peter asserts, quoting John 1:14 and Phil. 2:7, that although "'the Word became flesh,' 'being found in human form,' it was not deprived of its deity" (I.1). This is a statement of two natures in one person; although it must be emphasized that Peter does not use the technical post-Chalcedonian vocabulary.

---

an emphasis on the divine motherhood of Mary was a characteristic of Syrian thought," going back to the *Ascension of Isaiah* and the *Odes of Solomon*.

15. For text, see *AS* 4:194–5 (Armenian), 430 (Latin). See *AS* 4:430 n. 1. Bardenhewer rejects these fragments out of hand, declaring that they have no attestation. Indeed, they do not even possess a title.

Peter, following Origen and Alexandrian theology, identifies the Logos with the Son:

> the angel greeted the Virgin, saying, "Hail, O favored one, the Lord is with you." Now when Gabriel said, "The Lord is with you," he meant "God the Word [ὁ θεὸς λόγος] is with you." He means that the Lord came [γενόμενον] into the womb and thus became [γενόμενον] flesh. (frag. I.2)

Peter emphasizes (referring to 2 Cor. 8:9) that the Son, the Logos, loses nothing by the incarnation; he becomes incarnate in order to redeem humanity: "Although he was rich, he became poor, not in order to be separated completely from his power or glory, but in order to take death upon himself on behalf of us sinners" (frag. I.1). In fragments I.1 and I.2 he emphasizes that this act of atonement was by grace, "without need of man's help, and (without his) presence."

One cannot, unfortunately, draw many conclusions about Peter's theology from these fragments from *On the Deity and the Humanity [of Christ]*. Although the fragments were preserved for polemical reasons, nothing here seems especially pointed, as if aimed at Gnostics or Origenists. What survives is strongly incarnational, with an emphasis on the Logos.

Three other fragments (I.6, I.6a, and I.6b)—which actually are only one—remain to be discussed. The Greek title, given by Leontius of Byzantium (c. 500–543) in his *Contra Nestorianos et Eutychianos*, is Ἐκ τοῦ περὶ τῆς Σωτῆρος ἡμῶν ἐπιδημίας (frag. I.6);[16] the piece is a brief comment on Luke 22:48. The title is also given in a Latin fragment (I.6a) of the *Contra Monophysitas* of Leontius of Jerusalem (sixth c.).[17] Justinian, in his *Contra Monophysitas*, preserves the fragment under the title "On Matthew" (I.6b. See Mt. 26:47; it's possible that Justinian's text of Matthew borrowed Jesus' reply from Luke).[18] Photius, in the *Bibliotheca*, quotes Ephrem of Antioch's (bishop 527–45) comment that Peter affirms the "union of two natures"; this is also the subject of the fragments preserved by the Leontii and Justinian.[19] M. Richard has pointed out the close connection between Ephrem's anthologies and those of Leontius of Byzantium, Leontius of Jerusalem, and Justinian. These latter three all quote one passage from Peter, "without doubt the one quoted by Ephrem."[20]

16. *RS* 4:48.
17. *PG* 18:511A–512A.
18. *PG* 18:521C.
19. *RS* 4:50.
20. M. Richard, "Pierre Ier d'Alexandrie et l'unique hypostase du Christ," *Mélanges de science religieuse* 2 (1946) 358.

All of these citations come from the sixth century except Photius's, and he is quoting a sixth-century father. The passage by Peter affirms that Jesus Christ was both God and human by nature. Photius (ninth c.) speaks of "nature," "hypostasis," and "person" (frag. I.10). Ephrem could have used this terminology, but did Peter? M. Bardy believes so: "As to Peter the Martyr, one cannot say anything else on the subject except the evidence of Ephrem of Antioch reported by Photius: his doctrine proved that the belief in the union in Christ, of the two natures in one person (μίαν ὑπόστασιν καὶ πρόσωπον ἕν) was orthodox and apostolic."[21]

M. Richard, however, argues that Peter did not recognize one *hypostasis* and one *prosopon*.[22] Richard shows that Photius gives his resume of Ephrem's statement in a section demonstrating ὅτι δὲ δύο φυσέων ἕνωσιν καὶ μίαν ὑπόστασιν καὶ πρόσωπον ἐν ὁμολογεῖν τοῦ ὀρθοῦ φρονήματος ἔστι καὶ τῶν πατέρων κήρυγμα, and that Peter is cited in support of this theology—and listed between Ambrose and Basil![23] Richard points out that of the five patristic quotations preserved by Photius, "only one contains the word ὑπόστασις," and he goes on to say that "as in all the similar anthologies, certain texts insist first of all on the unity of the person of Christ, others on the duality of his nature, and not necessarily in technical terms."[24]

Since no technical theological vocabulary exists in the sixth-century citations of Peter, one must agree with Richard and conclude that "it is a question neither of person nor of hypostasis."[25] It must be added that it is not even a question of union. All that can be concluded from this one fragment is that Peter affirmed that Christ had two natures. Peter, it seems, saw in the "signs and miracles," and probably in Jesus' foreknowledge of Judas's actions, the divine nature of Christ, and in the kiss

21. M. Bardy, *Didyme l'Aveugle* (Paris 1910). Quoted by Richard, "Pierre Ier," 357. For R. MacMullen's criticism of M. Bardy's "generalizing," see his *Christianizing the Roman Empire* (New Haven/London 1984) 7–8, and 8 n. 20.

22. Richard, "Pierre Ier," 357. Πρόσωπον = *persona* probably came into Eastern usage under the influence of Latin theology (Tertullian, Leo, etc.). It became standard at Chalcedon. See Lampe, 1188A. It is possible that Valentinus, the second-century Gnostic, was the first to use *hypostasis* in its technical sense. The attribution, however, is suspect. Fragment 9, from Anthimus' *De sancta ecclesia*, states "and they teach three hypostases, just as Valentinus the heresiarch himself first conceived in that book of his which bears the title 'On the three natures.' For he was the first to conceive of three hypostases and three persons, the Father, the Son, and the Holy Spirit" (Werner Foerster, *Gnosis: A Selection of Gnostic Texts* [Oxford 1972] 1:243). The Greek text may be found in Giovanni Mercati, "Note di letteratura biblica e cristiana antica," *Studi e Testi* 5 (1901) 96.

23. Richard, "Pierre Ier," 358.

24. Ibid., 358.

25. Ibid., 358.

(that is, in Jesus' betrayal and death) the human. No more than this can be said. From fragments I.6, I.6a–b, and I.T, it can not be concluded that Peter used the technical theological vocabulary of Nicea and Chalcedon. It is possible that frags. I.6 and I.6a–b come from a work *On the Deity and Humanity [of Christ]*, but it is not demonstrable.

II. On the Soul[26]

Four groups of fragments, in Greek and Syriac, have come down with titles that indicate that Peter wrote a work *On the So⌐   ⌐l*. Of the four, the three in Greek (II.1, II.1a–b) are concerned with the question of the soul's preexistence, while the fourth, in Syriac, is concerned with the resurrection body. The Greek fragments are preserved by Leontius of Byzantium (frag. II.1), the emperor Justinian, (frag. II.1a), and, in a twelfth-century codex, an anti-Origenistic florilegium on the "Corruptible and the Incorruptible" (frag. II.1b).[27]

All of the titles appear to be tendentious. The shortest, preserved by Leontius (II.1), is "From the (Work) 'The Soul Did Not Preexist the Body'." Both the florilegium (II.1b) and the Syriac (II.2) expand the title with the statement that the soul did not sin before. Interestingly, Justinian (frag. II.1a), while reporting the longest title (adding that the soul was not, on account of its sins, cast into the body), adds that the work is

26. In Greek thought, speculation on the soul is as old as the pre-Socratics and Plato (e.g., *The Timaeus*). Justin had to deal with such Greek thought, and Eusebius reports (*HE* 4.18.5) that he did so in a work "in which he propounds various questions concerning the problems under discussion and adduces the opinions of the Greek philosophers; these he promises to refute and to give his own opinion in another work." Tertullian's work *On the Soul* is apparently indebted to the *On the Soul* of Soranus of Ephesus, a non-Christian who lived in Rome at the beginning of the second century (Quasten 2:289). In the *De anima* Tertullian speaks of a *De censu animae* in which he spoke of the divine origin of the soul (Quasten 2:287). The second part of the *De anima* (23–37.4) investigates the origin of the soul. Before Peter's time there were apparently no works written in Alexandria specifically titled *On the Soul*. Immediately after Peter, there is a sermon *On the Body and Soul* attributed to Alexander (Quasten 3:17) and to Athanasius; see E. A. Wallis Budge, *Coptic Homilies in the Dialect of Upper Egypt* (London 1910), 115ff. (258–74 for Eng. trans.). Quasten (3:17) believes that the sermon is influenced by Melito's *Homily*; Eusebius *HE* 4.26.2 does credit Melito with a work entitled *On the Soul and Body*. T. Orlandi, in a paper delivered in Claremont, California, attributes the work to Melito: "The homily was divided into two parts: the fi[r]st one, found only in Coptic and Syriac, contains a remarkable piece of theology on the problem of the relation of Soul and Body, which is very far from the theology which would have been acceptable for a follower of the Alexandrian school." See Orlandi, "Coptic Literature," in *The Roots of Egyptian Christianity*, ed. Birger A. Pearson and James E. Goehring (Philadelphia 1986) 58–59.

27. For Leontius, see the *New Catholic Encyclopedia* 8:660–61; for the origin of frag. II.3, see W. Bienert, "Neue Fragmente des Dionysius und des Petrus von Alexandrien aus Cod. Vatop. 236," *Kleronomia* 5 (1973) 308–9.

from the first sermon or treatise (λόγου) on the soul by Saint Peter. This information corresponds, at least in part, to what is probably the oldest mention of the title, that by Procopius of Gaza (c. 475–528). In his *Commentary on Genesis* Procopius speaks of "the bishop and martyr Peter" and the First Sermon (*sermo*) on the Soul." Since Procopius says nothing about preexistence, sinning, or falling, and since the title of the work tends to expand from Leontius to Justinian, one must conclude that the shortest appellation is closest to the original.

Which of the texts appears to be the most original? Fragment II.1 has the shortest text and is the one that preserves a transition sentence (see below 130). In all important respects it is the same as the text preserved by Justinian (frag. II.1a)— except at the beginning and end.

The beginning of frag. II.1a is clearly secondary: gone is the transition sentence of II.1, and in its place is "we note (ἡγούμεθα) that the things concerning the First Earthly Man . . . are provided." The ending of each fragment offers an instructive difference:

II.1

For if the earth, at (God's) command, brought forth the other living animals, much greater was the dust, raised by God from the earth, which received life according to the will and working of God.

II.1a

For if there had been a union, why was it also written, "it was made"?

Given only these two fragments, it is difficult to judge which of these endings is authentic. The ending preserved by Justinian (II.1a) makes sense; in fact, it is clearer than the one in frag. II.1. The sense of frag. 2.1a seems to be that the earth, through God's agency (a reference to Gen. 1:26), is capable of producing man; therefore, there is no need for a preexistent being. Fragment II.1a may be, therefore, an attempt by Justinian to simplify Peter's thought, since it seems to refer to God's acts of making and creating (ποιεῖν) in Genesis.

In addition, while frag. II.1 ends with the passage quoted above, frag. II.1a goes on to add two more pieces. The first of these is a polemical piece which goes beyond the denial of preexistence and denies also the possibility of precorporeal sin:

So that it is not possible for souls to sin in heaven before they assume corporeal form, nor for that matter is hypostasis (ὑπόστασις)[28] possible

---

28. See Lampe, 1467, s.v. ὑφίστημι, B2. The word is in use before Peter's time.

before corporeal existence. This teaching is a precept of Greek philosophy which is foreign and alien to those who desire to live piously in Christ.

Justinian finishes his citations of Peter with a legendary, anti-Origenistic speech by Peter from the *Vita Sancti Petri* that can not possibly go back to the archbishop.[29] It seems reasonable then to suggest that these last two additions came from the same source. At any rate, neither can be by Peter. Since it is clear that Justinian changed the beginning of his text, it seems reasonable to assume that he changed the end also.

Finally, corroboration for the text of frag. II.1 comes from a fragment preserved in the *Sacra parallela* (ἱερά) of John of Damascus (eighth c.). This text carries the same title and preserves the exact text of frag. II.1.[30] This in itself does not, of course, prove that the fragment preserved by Leontius is earlier than that preserved by Justinian, but it does show that in the eighth century a text existed that was independent of Justinian's.

Fragment II.1b comes from an anti-Origenestic florilegium containing three pieces. It begins with the quotation from Gen. 1:26 which both frags. II.1 and II.1a contain. It also, like them, follows with an attack on preexistence. This attack, it is important to note, is identical in wording to the fragment preserved by Justinian (II.1a). Instead of $\tau\iota\nu\grave{o}s$ $\dot{\epsilon}\tau\acute{\epsilon}\rho o\upsilon$ $\tau\acute{o}\pi o\upsilon$ as in frag. II.1, it has $\tau\iota\nu\grave{o}s$ $\dot{\epsilon}\tau\acute{\epsilon}\rho o\upsilon$ $\kappa\alpha\grave{\iota}$ $\dot{\alpha}\phi'$ $\dot{\epsilon}\tau\acute{\epsilon}\rho o\upsilon$ $\tau\acute{o}\pi o\upsilon$ as in Justinian's text, thereby showing that the florilegium preserves the later, and not the earlier, text. Also in the florilegium, a new fragment intrudes between the two given by Justinian. This piece is clearly polemical and is probably directed against Origenists (or, possibly, Gnostics).[31] The third fragment begins in the same way as Justinian's second piece, but then goes on to expand it with material extant in neither frag. II.1 nor II.1a.

Clearly, then, both the florilegium and Justinian represent an expanding text, while the fragment preserved in the *Sacra parallela* of John of Damascus does not. It is not possible to accept as authentic the additional material not preserved by Leontius of Byzantium. One could argue that Leontius, an Origenist, deleted material unfavorable to

29. Justinian terms this speech a "mystagogia." See PG 86/1:961C. See also 130–31 below; and J. Viteau, *Passions des Saints Ecaterine et Pierre d'Alexandrine* (Paris 1897) 75. Aimé Solignac, "Pierre I d'Alexandrie," *Dictionnaire de spiritualité*, fasc. 80–82 (Paris 1985) 1499, has made the same observation.

30. K. Holl, "Fragments Vornicänisher Kirchenvater aus den Sacra Parallela," TU 5.2 (1899) 210 (frag. 460).

31. K. Papadopoulos, "Eis Petron Alexandreias," *Kleronomia* 6 (1974) 235–36, acknowledges (235) that the second fragment printed by Bienert, "Neue Fragmente," 308–14, is defective, and proposes a number of emendations. In reply, "Zu den neuen Petrusfragmenten aus Cod. Vatop. 236," *Kleronomia* 6 (1974) 237, Bienert rejects all but one of the suggested emendations. See ibid., 241 for Bienert's revised text. The discussion here is moot: the fragment in question is a later interpolation.

Origen. This is possible, but his text does preserve a clear denial of one of Origen's chief tenets: the preexistence of the soul. The material preserved by the later anti-Origenists is clearly tendentious and polemical. It is very unlikely that it goes back to Peter.

If fragment II.1 is authentic, and there seems to be no good reason to doubt it (since it was quoted by both Origenists and anti-Origenists), Peter's view here is clearly opposed to the preexistence of the soul: God created both body and soul at one time and in one place, that is, from the earth, when he said "Let us make man in our image." Procopius of Gaza (c. 475–c. 528) provides further evidence that Peter held this view. In his commentary on Genesis, Procopius says that Peter, in a work called "The First Sermon on the Soul," speaks against the allegorical interpretation of the leather tunics (see Gen. 3:21).[32] Without the existence of frag. II.1, it would be difficult to accept Procopius's statement. But when it is taken with Peter's denial of preexistence, one can reasonably conclude that Peter denied the allegorical interpretation of Gen. 3:21 because that interpretation presupposes a preexistent celestial being. This Peter rejects while affirming the traditional teaching on Genesis that humanity was created by God from the earth.

III–IV. On the Resurrection[33] (Paschal Letter[34] and Syriac Fragments)

A very close connection exists in the manuscript tradition between works attributed to Peter entitled *On the Deity, On the Soul,* and *On the*

---

32. *RS* 4:50.

33. The oldest known patristic work on the resurrection is attributed to Justin in the *Sacra parallela* of John of Damascus. Three small fragments, whose authenticity is doubtful, are preserved there (see Quasten 1:205). See Justin *1 Apol.* 19. Athenagoras (second c.) is credited with *On the Resurrection of the Dead,* a philosophical appeal from reason to a Greek audience, which has few citations from scripture (only one from 1 Cor. 15, the usual Christian text on the resurrection). See William R. Schoedel, *Athenagoras: Legatio and De Resurrectione* (Oxford 1972) xxv–xxxii (especially xxvi–xxvii), and 97 n. 3, 4, for the arguments for a much later dating of the work. According to Jerome *De viris illustribus* 61, Hippolytus wrote a work *On the Resurrection* (or *On God and the Resurrection of the Flesh*). See Quasten 2:196–97. Tertullian wrote two closely related works on the resurrection, *De carne Christi* and *De resurrectione carnis,* in which he argues for the resurrection of the body and against docetism. *De carne Christi* is concerned per force with the nature of Christ and his body, while *De resurrectione carnis* discusses the bodily resurrection of all humans. "Thus the real topic of the treatise is: The resurrection of the body according to the Old and the New Testament (chs. 18–55)" (Quasten 2:283–84). Eusebius reports (*HE* 6.24.2–3) that Origen wrote two volumes or books (τόμοι) of a work on the resurrection. For the fragments, see *PG* 11:91–100. Methodius's *On the Resurrection,* although fragmentary, is the longest surviving pre-Nicene work on the resurrection; it is cast in the form of a dialogue. For texts, see *PG* 18:265–329; and G. N. Bonwetsch, *GCS* 27 (1917) 217–424.

34. "Up to the ninth century it was a custom among the bishops of Alexandria to

Resurrection. J. B. Pitra collected eight Syriac fragments from a work attributed to Peter called *On the Resurrection*.[35] Of these the first fragment (I.2b of this work) is the same as frag. I.2, a Greek fragment entitled *On the Deity*. The other Syriac fragments on the resurrection body fit their title (IV.1–7). Another Syriac fragment (frag. II.2) published by Pitra with the title "That the Soul Did Not Preexist (the Body), Nor Did It Sin (Before)" seems not to be related to the Greek fragments of *On the Soul*, but is rather a fragment on the resurrection.[36] Thus, a fragment from *On the Deity* is subsumed under fragments from *On the Resurrection*, while a fragment that is actually concerned with the resurrection is mistitled *On the Soul*. From this one can conclude that all three titles were known to the Syriac tradition, although there was confusion as to what pieces came from what works.

The Greek manuscript tradition does not preserve a title *On the Resurrection*. Nevertheless, it does hand down, from a florilegium on the perishable and imperishable, a work on the resurrection entitled "From the Paschal Letter of Peter, Archbishop of Alexandria and Martyr" (frags. III.1–2).[37] It is preserved in the same collection, Vatican codex Vatopédi 236, as the one that preserves frags. II.1b, *On the Soul*, and clearly shows the same secondary characteristics of expansion and tendentiousness.

Although this is so, the codex nevertheless offers some valuable information about Peter's writing. The title states that it is from the *Paschal Letter* (ἐξ ἑοραστικῆς ἐπιστολῆς) of Saint Peter, and the second

---

send every year to all the Churches of Egypt an announcement of the date of Easter and the beginning of the preceding fast. This took the form of a pastoral epistle exhorting the congregation to observe the Lenten and the Easter season carefully. Dionysius of Alexandria is the first bishop known to have sent such a letter" (Quasten 2:108). Eusebius (*HE* 7.20.1) reports that Dionysius "composed at that time also the festal letters (ἑοραστικάς) which are still extant, in which he gives utterance to words specially suited to a solemn occasion with reference to the festival of the Pascha." Dionysius shows that "it is not proper to celebrate the festival of the Pascha at any other time than after the vernal equinox." Dionysius's Easter letters are given by Charles Lett Feltoe, *DIONYSIOU LEIPSANA: The Letters and Other Remains of Dionysius of Alexandria* (hereafter: *Dionysius: Letters*) (London/New York 1918) 64–91; and the Eng. trans. in idem, *St. Dionysius of Alexandria: Letters and Treatises* (Cambridge 1904) 63–76. The subjects of the letters are wide-ranging. Apparently none of Alexander's letters survives (Quasten 3:14–16). Only fragments remain in Greek of Athanasius's letters, but thirteen are preserved in Syriac and seventeen in Coptic (see Quasten 3:52–53).

35. *AS* 4:426–29 (IIA–H).

36. *AS* 4:193–94.

37. M. Richard, "Le Florilège Du Cod. Vatopédi 236 Sur Le Corruptible et L'incorruptible," *Mu* 86 (1973) 267–69.

piece (frag. III.2) states that as part of the paschal observance, "We will cease (our) fasts in the evening on Saturday when holy Sunday begins to dawn four days before the Ides of April, which is the fifteenth of Pharmouth."[38] This date is reckoned by M. Richard to be 10 April 309, and fits with the known chronology of Peter's life.[39]

The inclusion of a sentence setting the date of Easter follows the form of the Easter letters sent out by Alexandrian bishops. In his "Festal Letter" of 332 Athanasius declares:

> The beginning of the fast of forty days is on the fifth day of Phamenoth [1 March]; and when, as I have said, we have first been purified and prepared by those days, we begin the holy week of the great Easter on the tenth of Pharmuthi [1 April].[40]

The two pieces preserved of Peter's *Paschal Letter* have the rhetorical elements of an address. Immediately preceding the passage setting the date for Easter, the speaker exhorts his flock and himself: "Let us lift up 'holy hands without anger and arguments,' being hopeful that we are being brought to life on every side even while we are alive, and will live again."[41] If these homiletical fragments are authentic—and they certainly seem to be—they provide evidence that Peter did write a work on the resurrection, although it may not have borne that title. Therefore the Greek manuscript tradition supports the Syriac tradition.

Fragments III.1–2 discuss the resurrection body. In the first piece, Peter affirms that "all the dead will rise, changing the(ir) form and being conformed ($\mu\epsilon\tau\alpha\sigma\chi\eta\mu\alpha\tau\iota\zeta\acute{o}\mu\epsilon\nu\omicron\iota$ $\kappa\alpha\grave{\iota}$ $\sigma\upsilon\mu\mu\omicron\rho\phi\omicron\acute{\upsilon}\mu\epsilon\nu\omicron\iota$) 'to his body of glory'" (Phil. 3:21), and then quotes 1 Cor. 15:53: "For it is necessary that this perishable (nature) be clothed with immortality." Peter quotes Paul (including Hebrews and Colossians) six times in a very brief passage—

38. For $\dot{\epsilon}\omicron\rho\alpha\sigma\tau\iota\kappa\acute{o}s$, see Lampe, 504B: "pertaining to a festival, hence paschal; of letters of bishops of Alexandria announcing date of Easter." See Eusebius *HE* 7.20.1 and 7.22.11; and n. 34 above.

39. Richard, "Le Florilège," 267. See also idem, "Le comput pascal par octaétéris," *Opera Minora* 1:307 (#21). He says that this date "is, in effect, the most ancient paschal date directly attested for Alexandria."

40. Quoted in Quasten 3:53. For Athanasius, see Quasten 3:52–55. For an edition of the Coptic texts see L.-Th. Lefort, *S. Athanase: Lettres festales et pastorales en Copte* (2 vols.; Louvain 1955). For the Syriac, *The Festal Letters of Athanasius*, ed. William Cureton (London 1848); and the English trans., *The Festal Epistles of S. Athanasius, Bishop of Alexandria* (London 1854); and NPNF, 2d ser., 4:506–53.

41. Again, a comparison with the festal letters of Athanasius quoted earlier is instructive. During Holy Week Athanasius exhorts his audience, "my beloved brethren, we should use more prolonged prayers and fastings, and watchings, that we may be enabled to anoint our lintels with precious blood, and to escape the destroyer" (Quasten 3:53).

this seems typical of Peter's authentic writings—and does not go beyond Paul's statements on the nature of the resurrection body.

In frag. III.2 Peter again quotes 1 Cor. 15:53 to emphasize the point that there will be a change at the resurrection. Peter asserts that "when we arise from the dead we receive a different body (τὸ σῶμα ἀλλοῖον), not according to substance (οὐσίαν), but according to the quality (ποιό-τητα) made manifest" in Jesus. A little later he reemphasizes this point: Paul "does not teach" that Jesus "changed the substance of (his) body (οὐ γὰρ τὴν οὐσίαν τοῦ σώματος μεταβεβλῆσθαι)."

From these statements it might seem that Peter is arguing for a materialistic understanding of the resurrection body, especially when he says that "the Lord gave life (ζωοποίησας) to his own body (τὸ ἴδιον σῶμα)." However, he defines this life-giving process not as revivifica-tion, but as a change of quality: "he made (it) imperishable (ἄφθαρτον ἐποίησε), that is, impassible and eternal (ἀπαθὲς καὶ ἀθάνατον)." Peter calls this the "change" (ἀλλαγήν) to which the Lord submitted. In the hortatory part of the fragment, Peter tells his audience that Jesus' change and resurrection serve as symbol and reality in their own lives: "we are being brought to life (ζωοποιούμεθα) on every side even while we are alive, and will live again (ζησόμενοι)." Peter says nothing here about resurrection bodies, but instead sees the resurrection as "realized."

In the final part of frag. III.2 Peter talks about the resurrection appear-ances of the risen Jesus (cf. Luke 24:39–41) and emphasizes again that because of this change the disciples did not recognize him. It seems that Peter understood the resurrection body of Jesus to be different enough that he was not recognized: he was now "clothed with imperishability." Nowhere in these two pieces does Peter argue for the absolute identity of the resurrection body with the earthly body.

The Syriac fragments attributed to Peter on the resurrection (IV.1–7) show quite a different understanding of the resurrection body. Fragment II.1 (which is entitled *On the Soul* and has no Greek counterpart), although not attributed to a work on the resurrection, asserts that the body "also arises united again with the soul in order that both might receive retribution in judgment for those things which they did in this life."[42] Fragment IV.1 echoes this understanding and alludes to 1 Cor.

---

42. Pitra, *AS* 4:429 n. 5, notes that "this fragment is given under the title 'Of Peter, Bishop of Alexandria and martyr, of him who pierced through the wall. . . .'" This refers to Peter's imprisonment as recorded in the *Acta Sancti Petri* (see 44–45 above). Whoever wrote the title to the Syriac fragment had access to the *Acta* or had heard this story from it. Perhaps the fragment came into the hands of the Syriac redactor together with the *Acta*, or a portion of it.

15:53 to support it: "We are able to return from the dead since it is known that at the resurrection our mortal bodies put on immortality in order that the body united with the soul might receive the reward which it deserves." This cannot be a translation—unless it has been drastically altered—of the Greek fragments on the resurrection.

Syriac fragment IV.2 has many similarities to the two fragments from the *Paschal Letter* (frags. III.1–2): both quote or refer to 1 Cor. 15:20, Luke 24:39, and John 20:27. Christ is the first fruits of the dead, makes a resurrection appearance, and convinces Thomas. Fragment IV.2 could be a translation of frags. III.1–2 but if it is, it too is much altered: gone are quotations from Colossians and Hebrews and added are quotations from John 3:2 and Gen. 1:26. It is possible that the Syriac is a loose translation and thorough rewriting of the Greek text. Major additions, however, have been made:

III.1

"The first fruit of those who sleep" [1 Cor. 15:20] has become *"also the first-born of the dead"* [Col. 1:18] in order that he might cause us to rise together with him, and (that) he might sit *"at the right hand of greatness among the most high"* [Heb. 1.3] [italics added].

IV.2

In the likeness of *"the first fruits of those who have fallen asleep"* [1 Cor. 15:20]. For we know that Christ is our *first fruits*, therefore the first fruits which (we will have) afterward are Christ's through his advent. When the dead arise in his likeness . . . it is clear that this body also, which was in the grave, will be resurrected, made perfect in its members [italics added].

The emphasis in the Syriac fragment is on the resurrection of the body from the grave, whereas Peter makes no mention of this in the extant Greek fragments. None of the remaining Syriac fragments (frags. IV.3–7) can be shown to be related to the *Paschal Letter*. They go on at length, with many references to 1 Cor. 15:42ff., to argue the identity of the resurrection body with the mortal body.

Given the fragmentary evidence, it is impossible to conclude whether the Greek and Syriac works on the resurrection are related. Since the Greek tradition (frags. III.1–2) shows that Peter wrote on the resurrection, it is possible that the Syriac presents material which is no longer extant in Greek. In all likelihood the Syriac fragments go back to a work by Peter on the resurrection, but are heavily interpolated and expanded. If so, one must conclude either that the *Paschal Letter* is far in the background or that the Syriac represents a separate work by Peter on the resurrection. Of course, it is also possible that the Syriac is falsely attributed to Peter. Given these difficulties, the Syriac fragments should not be used in determining Peter's thought on the resurrection.

V.1–5 On Easter (Περὶ τοῦ πάσχα)[43]

Two sources offer evidence that Peter wrote a piece entitled *On Easter* against a certain Tricentius: the Alexandrian *Paschal Chronicle* and the manuscripts of the *Canonical Letter*.[44] The *Paschal Chronicle* preserves frags. V.1–4 and a piece not by Peter while some manuscripts of the *Canonical Letter* append a fifteenth canon and say it is from περὶ τοῦ πάσχα.[45]

Modern critical scholarship is unanimous that the work is authentic.[46]

---

43. The most famous patristic work on Easter is the *Paschal Homily* of Melito of Sardis, which gives in beautiful Greek the typology of the Passover and the Passion. Eusebius *HE* 6.22.1 records that Hippolytus wrote a treatise (σύγγραμμα) Περὶ τοῦ πάσχα, "in which he sets forth a register of the times and puts forward a certain canon (κανόνα) of a sixteen-year cycle for the Pascha." Eusebius also reports here that Hippolytus wrote another work on Easter. According to Quasten (2:178–79), one of these is a homily (although not termed that by Eusebius) which, though greatly expanded after Hippolytus's time, has its "prototype" in the third century. If Quasten is correct, we have a work at Rome very similar to the paschal addresses given at Alexandria. In the treatise attributed to Hippolytus, the author gives the date of Easter and uses the occasion, as in Peter's letter on the resurrection (frags. III.1–2), to deliver a sermon. For the text and a full discussion of a paschal homily attributed to Hippolytus, see Pierre Nautin, *Homélies Pascales*, vol. 1, *Une homélie inspirée du traité Sur la Pâque d'Hippolyte* (Paris 1950). In *HE* 6.13.9 Eusebius also states that Clement of Alexandria wrote a work on Easter: "And in his book *On the Pascha* he professes that he was compelled by his companions to commit to writing traditions that he had heard from the elders of olden time, for the benefit of those that should come after; and he mentions in it Melito and Irenaeus and some others, whose accounts also of the matter he has set down." For the fragments, see O. Stählin, *Clemens Alexandrinus*, vol. 3 [*Stromata* 7–8] (Leipzig 1909), 216–18. A papyrus found at Toura, Egypt, in 1941 preserves a work or works with the title Περὶ πάσχα, attributed to Origen. See O. Guérard, "Note préliminaire sur les papyrus d'Origène découverts à Toura," *Revue de l'histoire des religions* 131 (1946) 85–108, on the discovery of the papyrus. The work is exhaustively treated in O. Guerard and P. Nautin (eds.), *Origène: Sur la Pâque* (Paris 1979). The editors (108–9) date the work to c. 245. They give an overview of early Christian works on Easter on 96–100. Origen states (245) that "most—and perhaps even all—of the brethren" understand that the Pascha (πάσχα) is called that because of the suffering (πάθος) of Christ, a belief found already in Melito's *Pachal Homily* (par. 46). For three "Origenist" paschal homilies, see Nautin, *Homélies Pascales*, vol. 2, *Trois homélies dans la tradition d'Origène* (Paris 1953).

44. F. H. Kettler, "Petros 1," *Realencyklopaedie der klassischen Altertumwissenschaft* 19.2 (1938) 1285. Quasten 2:116 mistakenly says it was "dedicated to a certain Tricenius [sic]." The letter is clearly addressed *against* someone (see frag. V.2, 136).

45. O. Bardenhewer 2:243; Kettler, "Petros 1," 1285. The earliest collection of the canons, that by Photius (ninth c.), has only fourteen canons, lacking the fifteenth canon wrongly included in the PG. See Mai, *Specilegium Romanum*, v. 7, pp. 444–55.

46. Bardenhewer 2:243; Kettler, "Petros 1," 1285; Harnack, *Geschichte* 1/1:445; Quasten 2:116.

F. H. Kettler says that the *Chronicon* preserves four pieces (frags. V.1–4 of this work) which *PG* prints as I–VI (18:512B–517A); he adds the misplaced Canon 15 from the *Canonical Letter* as the fifth piece (frag. V.5 here).[47] Kettler further states that *PG* frag. VII (following frag. V.4 in this work) is by Athanasius and that *PG* in printing it with the fragments by Peter has erred in following Gallandius.[48] This fragment does contain a creedal statement with technical vocabulary such as "homoousios" (ὁμοούσιος), "Mother of God" (θεοτόκου), and "ever-virgin" (ἀειπαρθένου) not found elsewhere in Peter's writings and belonging more likely to the time of Athanasius.[49]

In *On Easter* Peter is apparently arguing for Anatolius's dating of Easter.[50] Anatolius (d. c. 282), bishop of Laodicea, was, according to Eusebius (*HE* 7.32.6), "by race an Alexandrian" and wrote a treatise on the dating of Easter.[51] Peter follows Alexandrian custom, which always celebrated Easter after the vernal equinox:[52]

> Therefore it has been rightfully established by law that after the most proper and suitable songs of praise have been given, from the time of the vernal equinox the Passover is to be celebrated in whatever week the fourteenth day of the first month falls. (frag. V.1)

Fragment V.5 is often printed as Canon 15 of the *Canonical Letter*. Following a tradition as old as the early second century, it affirms that fasting is to be done on Wednesday and Friday. *Didache* 8.1 enjoins: "Do not let your fasts be with the hypocrites [i.e., the Jews], for they fast on

---

47. Kettler, "Petros 1," 1285.

48. Ibid. See also M. Richard, "Le fragment XXII d'Amphiloque d'Iconium," *Opera Minora* 2:204–5 (#36). Richard concurs that the first four fragments (I–VI in *PG*) should not be joined with the last, which "is in effect the work of a chronologist." Richard concludes that there is "no reason" to suspect the authenticity of the other fragments.

49. On "Theotokos" see W. J. Burghardt, "Mary in Eastern Patristic Thought," in *Mariology*, ed. J. B. Carol (Milwaukee, Wisc. 1957) 2:117ff.

50. Kettler, "Petros 1," 1285. On the subject of Anatolius and the dating of Easter at Alexandria, see M. Richard, "Le comput pascal par octaétéris," *Opera Minora* 1:307–39 (#21); and M. Chaîne, *La chronologie des temps Chrétiens de l'Égypte et de l'Éthiope* (Paris 1925). Chaîne, 28, says that "according to the testimony of St. Peter the martyr . . . in hearing him speak of the Jewish computation [of Passover], that the latter used the cycle of 19 years. The Patriarch of Alexandria does not indeed criticize the Jewish computation except for its erroneous date of the equinox; only this point seems to distinguish it from the computations which he himself then follows and which was that of Anatolius." With regard to Peter, see also Chaîne, 38 n. 1 and 40. According to Chaîne, 52, the Alexandrian computation was "the restoration, in part at least, of the Jewish computation," which established itself during Saint Peter's time. For a brief, intelligible discussion of Anatolius's system, see E. L. Oulton, *Eusebius: Ecclesiastical History* (Cambridge, Mass. 1980) 244–45.

51. *ODCC*, 50.

52. *ODCC*, 1037.

Mondays and Thursdays, but as for you, fast on Wednesdays and Fridays." The end of this fragment returns to the theme of the Lord's Day and the day of resurrection, and it is probable that it belongs to *On Easter*.

VI. Miscellaneous Fragments

VI.1 From the Teaching of Saint Peter of Alexandria

Several fragments have come down under the title Διδασκαλία Πέτρου. The *PG* (18:521B) prints one fragment (VI.1 in this work) from "Leontius of Byzantium and John." This fragment appears, along with another, under the title Διδασκαλία Πέτρου in the *Sacra parallela* of John of Damascus (fragments 502 and 503 in Holl's numbering).[53] Dobschütz suggested that these fragments might come from a work by Peter of Alexandria, but this seems very unlikely.[54] Fragment 503 makes no mention of Peter of Alexandria, and fragment 502 (VI.1 of this work) according to Holl is attributed to Peter *of Alexandria* in only one of the five manuscripts.[55] W. Schneemelcher has aptly said that these texts are so general "that it would hardly be possible to assign them to one particular work."[56]

VI.2 Untitled Fragment

This Syriac fragment is too short for any discussion. It is not attested in Greek.

Conclusion: Peter's Theology

Is Peter's theology, as Harnack says about the saint's life, doomed to be "obscure" and lost "in an impenetrable fog"?[57] If one exercises caution in dealing with such fragmentary evidence and avoids making sweeping generalization, it is possible to dispel at least some of the fog.

In the eyes of those who later quoted him Peter was supremely orthodox, and one might think from their opinion that his theological language was just waiting to be adopted against all heretics by the councils of the fifth and sixth centuries. Peter's crown of martyrdom, already lauded by Eusebius early in the fourth century, assuredly made

---

53. Holl, "Fragmente," 233. These can be more conveniently found in *NTApo* 2:98.
54. E. Dobschütz, *Das Kerygma Petri*, TU 11 (1894) 110–21.
55. Holl, "Fragmente," 233.
56. *NTApo* 2:98.
57. Harnack, *Geschichte* 1/1:73.

him an attractive witness against Origen; if he had any pre-Nicene "unorthodoxies," they were quietly passed over—and hence forgotten. Still, any judgment about Peter's theology based on the extant fragments must be an extremely cautious one.

If the judgments reached above are sound, only four (or five) theological works of Peter survive:

1. *On the Deity and Humanity [of Christ]*
2. *On the Soul*
3. *Paschal Letter (On the Resurrection)*
4. *On the Resurrection*
5. *On Easter* (a paschal letter?)

All of these are very fragmentary.[58] Moreover, many of the fragments attributed to Peter under these titles are secondary and cannot be used to establish Peter's theology. It also becomes clear that only a few pieces of Peter's writing survived into the fifth century and these were then passed down through various hands. Justinian, for example, probably did not have any of Peter's work in hand, but instead quoted from extracts.

In discussing Peter's theology, therefore, only the following fragments, all in Greek, may be used. The rest are either secondary, have very tenuous attestation, or are too brief to be of any help.

1. *On the Deity and Humanity [of Christ]*:   Frags. I.1–3 and I.4–5
2. *On the Soul*:   Frag. II.1
3. *Paschal Letter (On the Resurrection)*:   Frags. III.1–2
4. *On Easter* (paschal letter):   Frags. V.1–5

If *On the Deity* and *On the Soul* are related works, which is probable (see above, 91–92), then Peter wrote two major treatises, one on the nature of Christ (Περὶ θεότητος καὶ ἀνθρωπότητος) and one on the soul (Περὶ ψυχῆς). Fragments I.1–3 follow scripture very closely, affirm the two natures of Christ (without using technical creedal language), and emphasize the activity of the Logos in Christ's becoming human. Fragment II.1 states that the things concerning the deity and humanity of Christ were explained "according to the blessed apostle," which suggests that *On the Deity and Humanity [of Christ]* may have been a commentary on Paul's teaching about Christ.

Fragment II.1 on the soul is perhaps the most important piece of

58. They total five columns in *PG* 18.

Peter's theological writings to be preserved because in it he clearly denies one of Origen's teachings, the preexistence of the soul. If the testimony of frag. II.T is added to this, then it is likely that Peter also denied the allegorical interpretation of Gen. 3:21: that the coats of skins that Adam and Eve received were bodies. Before Peter's anti-Origenism can be assumed, several things must be stressed: Peter does not use language such as *hypostasis*, nor does he attack Greek philosophy. Where he appears to do either are secondary texts which do not belong to him. In addition, as far as we can tell, Peter did not attack Origen specifically, or Origenism or allegory in general (see below, 110–26, for a discussion of Peter and anti-Origenism). Peter affirms that humanity was made, body and soul, at one time by God.

Fragments III.1–2 preserve part of an Easter letter. In III.2 the bishop sets the date for Easter, an Alexandrian custom, and discusses, appropriately, the resurrection. In this fragment Peter does not go beyond Paul's (and Pauline) thought on the resurrection body. He quotes Paul extensively and affirms that the dead will be changed, taking on imperishability and immortality. In frag. III.2, in fact, Peter has an understanding of "realized" resurrection for the faithful. The Syriac fragments (IV.1–7) on the resurrection are heavily interpolated, and the identification there of the heavenly and earthly body cannot be safely attributed to Peter.

Fragments V.1–5, probably from a paschal homily or letter, discuss the dating of Easter. In these fragments Peter follows the Alexandrian custom of observing Easter after the vernal equinox.

Taken together, these four major fragments are considerably shorter than even Origen's preface to his *Contra Celsum*. It is easier to say what they are not than what they are. Peter does not once use, in the clearly authentic fragments, such post-Chalcedonian technical terms as *hypostasis*, *physis*, or *theotokos*. To say that his work is orthodox is almost meaningless: those who quoted his work determined that. Most of those writers were anti-Origenists, and it has been suggested that Eusebius says nothing about Peter's writing because the latter was anti-Origenist.[59] Furthermore, almost all of the scholarship about these fragments has taken their anti-Origenism as a given. It remains to be considered whether this is a valid inference.

---

59. Quasten 2:114. Yet Eusebius also does not mention Theognostus, who is "pro-Origen."

ANTI-ORIGENISM[60]

"Origenism" can be defined as "the group of theories enunciated by, or attributed to, Origen."[61] The most prominent—and controversial— aspects of Origen's teaching were those on the preexistence of the soul, the nature of the resurrection body, and his trinitarian theology (his "subordinationism"). Origen's allegorical method also received censure and support. These topics are also the ones around which the name of Peter of Alexandria figures. The discussion to follow focuses on the writings of Bishop Peter and the uses to which those writings were put, primarily in the fourth through sixth centuries, but as late as in the ninth.

Although Origen had critics during his lifetime, anti-Origenism seems to have begun in earnest with Peter's contemporary, Methodius of Olympus (d. 311), and about fifty years later, with Epiphanius's attack on Origen in *Adv. haer.* 64. Late in the fourth century the controversy broadened with the attacks by Theophilus of Alexandria and Jerome, and the defense by Rufinus, and continued through the fifth and sixth centuries. The emperor Justinian was able to have Origen condemned at Constantinople in 553.

Origen's supporters were many, among them Eusebius of Caesarea and Pamphilius (d. 309), the latter the author of an "Apology" of Origen. Basil and Gregory of Nazianzus thought highly of many of Origen's teachings and preserved in their *Philocalia* those writings they thought beneficial. I do not deal in the main with the supporters of Origen; rather, because Peter has been identified as an opponent of Origen, the focus here is primarily on anti-Origenism.

Saint Peter is almost universally regarded by modern scholarship as being an anti-Origenist. L. B. Radford, in *Three Teachers of Alexandria*, says that it is Peter's "antagonism to the peculiar doctrines of Origen which constitutes the special theological interest of Peter's work as a

---

60. For background discussion of "The Problem of Origenism," see Wolfgang A. Bienert, *Dionysius von Alexandrien: Zur Frage des Origenismus im dritten Jahrhundert* (Berlin/New York 1978) 6–25, esp. 15–25. Since Bienert's focus is the third century, Peter is mentioned only once in those pages. For a good discussion of the late fourth c., see J. N. D. Kelly, *Jerome* (London 1975), esp. 227–42, and see the index. B. Th. Stauridos, "Hai ōrigenistikai erides," *Theologia* 28 (1957) 550–77, is not reliable.
61. *ODCC*, 1010, s.v. "Origenism."

teacher and writer."[62] Quasten, Bardenhewer, Altaner and Stuiber, Harnack, Baus, Lebreton, Bienert, Sauget, and Barnes agree.[63]

If scholarship has achieved consensus on seeing Peter as an anti-Origenist, it has with equal agreement viewed his precursors at the catechetical school in Alexandria as Origenists. Dionysius (248–65), Theognostus (265–82), and Pierius (282–300) have long been regarded as followers of Origen, while Peter has been seen as the one who first broke ranks. As W. Bienert has concluded in his survey of the subject: "Previously one in general started from the premise that, after Demetrius, who had first banned Origen from Alexandria, it was Peter I (d. 311) who was the second Alexandrian bishop who had turned against the famous teacher, or against his teaching."[64]

Bienert's conclusion raises several important questions: Was Peter anti-Origenist? And if he was, was he reacting against a long-held tradition of Origenism at Alexandria, both in the catechetical school and in the episcopacy? These questions are important because if it is accepted that Peter was an anti-Origenist, anti-Origenism must be located in Alexandria as early as 300, and one must consider what importance this has with regard to the theology of Alexander and Athanasius.

In addressing these issues I review Peter's theological writings and the ecclesiastical tradition of the fifth and sixth centuries that preserved them, especially with regard to Origen. But first, it is necessary to look at

62. Radford, 60–61; see ibid., 58ff.

63. Quasten 2:114; Bardenhewer 2:239; Altaner and Stuiber, *Patrologie* (Freiburg 1966), 213; A. Harnack, *History of Dogma* (repr. Gloucester, Mass. [c. 1900] 1976) 3:99; K. Baus, *Handbook of Church History* (New York 1965) 1:241; J. Lebreton and J. Zeiler, *The History of the Primitive Church* (New York 1949) 2:1045; J.-M. Sauget, "Pietro I.," *Bibliotheca Sanctorum* 10:765; T. D. Barnes, *Constantine and Eusebius* (Cambridge, Mass. 1981), 198. Bienert, *Dionysius: Zur Frage*, 16, sums up Peter's anti-Origenism in two points: "he spoke out against a spiritualizing teaching on the resurrection as well as the teaching of the pre-existence of the soul"; L. W. Barnard, "The Antecedents of Arius," *Vigiliae Christianae* 24 (1970) 183, cites three: anti-allegorism, denial of the preexistence of the soul, and a repudiation of Origen's teaching on the resurrection body. B. Th. Stauridos, 566–67, lists Peter first among the anti-Origenists, although he nuances this by saying that Peter opposed "certain opinions" of Origen, and he points out that Origen is not named. In any case, the fragments Stauridos quotes are among the most doubtful of those preserved. The *ODCC*, 1010, does not list Peter as either a proponent or an opponent of Origen.

64. Bienert, *Dionysius: Zur Frage*, 1–2, who cites Harnack, *Geschichte*, 1/1:444. With regard to scholarly views on Dionysius, Theognostus, and Pierius, Bienert is undoubtedly correct. See, e.g., Quasten 2:101, 110: "The most remarkable of Origen's pupils was Dionysius of Alexandria. . . . the work of Theognostus was a kind of dogmatic summa which followed the doctrine of Origen and especially his subordinationism." For Pierius, see ibid. 2:111.

the writings of Peter's predecessors, beginning with Dionysius, with special attention to their views on Origenist positions. Finally I survey very briefly some of Philo's writings and then some of the works of Origen himself.

Bienert notes that Dionysius has been considered a "champion, disciple, and friend of Origen," but he believes that new fragments throw doubt on these conclusions.[65] He refers in particular to a new fragment from codex Vatopédi 236 (see also 99 n. 31 above), "From the *Commentary* (ἑρμηνείας) *On Ecclesiastes* of Dionysius, Bishop of Alexandria":[66]

> (1) Therefore (this) is also added in order: "and the dust returns to the earth" from where it was taken—and these things (are said) concerning the human body. But concerning the soul, which very thing itself, the one who formed (humanity) [ὁ πλάσας] created at the same time as the body at (the time of) creation, (it is said): "And the spirit returns to God who gave it" [Eccl. 12:7].
>
> (2) And after other things. Thus again souls (are) properly [ἴδιαι] from God, for it is by his commandment and creation that they come into being [παρέχονται], (and they do) not exist [οὖσαι] or preexist [προγεγονυῖαι] before. Therefore we ought on every occasion to give thanks to him.

C. L. Feltoe published several fragments of a work on Ecclesiastes attributed to Dionysius, some of whose authenticity is very doubtful.[67] Feltoe concluded that, in general, Dionysius "was a loyal but not uncritical pupil of Origen in the interpretation of scripture. . . . [and] accepts the allegorical interpretation rather than the literal."[68] More specifically in question is the allegorical or literal interpretation of Gen. 3:21, the passage on the "coats of skins," which closely follows Gen. 3:19b, "for you are earth, and to the earth you shall return) (LXX). This passage, as has been seen (98–99), is crucial with regard to Origen's teaching on the preexistence of the soul (see also 121ff. below).

Procopius of Gaza reports that "'all the teachers' speak against the allegorical interpretation of the leather tunics and of other things in Paradise, and he gives by name, among many others, 'Dionysius. . . and Peter.'" Although it is clear that Procopius is correct with regard to Peter (see 100 above), up until now no corroboration existed for Dionysius.

65. Bienert, *Dionysius, Zur Frage*, 2.
66. Bienert, "Neue Fragmente," 310. My translation from Bienert's text.
67. *Dionysius: Letters*, 209. Eng. trans., ANF 6:111–14. On the question of authenticity, see also Bienert, "Neue Fragmente," 311.
68. *Dionysius: Letters*, 209.

Bienert agrees with Feltoe that the previously published fragments on Ecclesiastes do not show opposition to allegory or, more specifically, to Origenist exegesis.[69] He sees in this new fragment, however, a confirmation of Procopius's statement:

> We possess for the first time through the two new fragments evidence for Procopius' statement and clear proof that Dionysius came to a critical understanding of Origen's teaching on the preexistence of the soul. The authenticity of the two fragments seems to be without doubt; the citation from Eccl. 12:7 underscores [their] origin from the commentary on Ecclesiastes.[70]

Bienert is undoubtedly right that in these new fragments we have a refutation by Dionysius of one of Origen's teachings, as Procopius had testified, one which Peter also refuted. However, caution must be exercised on several points. The passage in Eccl. 12:7 may have reminded Dionysius of Gen. 3:19b, but we cannot be certain. Nothing is said about the coats of skins or allegory. All that can be concluded is that Dionysius, like Peter, taught that God created body and soul "at the same time."

As was shown above (97–99), the fragments attributed to Peter from codex Vatopédi are interpolated with secondary, anti-Origenist material. This is undoubtedly not the case with the first of Bienert's fragments; however, the second is not as secure. As is common in catenae of this sort (see e.g., frags. I.1–3 and I.4–5), the second piece is separated from the first by an editorial "and after other things," and, despite Bienert's assertion, does not necessarily belong to the first fragment. It could be an editorial summary. However, given this caveat, the fact remains that it is very close in language to frag. II.1 of Peter.

Most important, care must be exercised in the conclusions one draws from these two small fragments. Bienert correctly concludes that Dionysius, like Peter, criticized Origen's teaching on the preexistence of the soul.[71] Further, in his larger work on Dionysius he asserts that these fragments throw "considerable doubt" on the long-held view of Dionysius as the "genuine champion of Origenism."[72] Indeed, "champion" (*genuiner Vertreter*), as Feltoe would agree, is indeed too strong a word

69. Bienert, "Neue Fragmente," 311.
70. Ibid.
71. Ibid., 310–11.
72. Bienert, *Dionysius: Zur Frage*, 2. The other fragment Bienert publishes ("Neue Fragmente," 309) has little bearing on the present discussion. In it, Dionysius accepts the literal nature of Paradise as "part of the cosmos," rather than a place "beyond the cosmos" (ὑπερκόσμιον χῶρον). See Bienert, "Neue Fragmente," 309–10; Harnack, *Geschichte* 1/1:422; *Dionysius: Letters*, 199–200.

for Dionysius's attitude toward Origen, and if Bienert is opposing that word, then he is undoubtedly correct.[73]

However, unlike Feltoe, Bienert is willing to see Dionysius as more of an opponent to Origen. He makes much of the fact that Dionysius was the head of the catechetical school at Alexandria while Heraklas was bishop—Heraklas who had succeeded Demetrius who had originally driven Origen into exile.[74]

Therefore, Bienert implies, there is an "anti-Origenist" succession from Demetrius to Heraklas to Dionysius.[75] If one accepts this, then Alexandrian theology from Origen to Peter looks like this:

Origen
Anti-Origenists: Demetrius
                   Heraklas
                   Dionysius
Origenists: Theognostus
                   Pierius
Anti-Origenist: Peter[76]

This is very unlikely. As I show below, Peter is not an anti-Origenist, at least as that term has commonly been applied to him. We know very little about Demetrius and Heraklas, and with regard to Dionysius, Bienert's suggestion of an "anti-Origenist succession" is very dubious.[77] None of Dionysius's previously extant works suggests this, and the new fragments published by Bienert do not support such a conclusion. The most one can say is that Dionysius opposed in some sense the pre-existence of the soul; that he also opposed the allegorical interpretation of Gen. 3:21, as Procopius says, is not unlikely.[78]

73. Other epithets he questions—"Anhänger," "Freund des Origenes" (*Dionysius: Zur Frage*, 2), and "Verehrer" (ibid., 222)—are certainly overdrawn. However, since he does not cite sources for these names, one wonders whether they are strawmen. Bienert unfortunately applies similar terms to Dionysius: "Dionysius, as disciple or perhaps confidant [Anhänger oder gar Vertrauter] of Heraklas, shared in the renunciation of Origen by the Alexandrian Church" (ibid., 131).
74. Ibid., 5. See *Dionysius: Letters*, xxv–xxix.
75. The break between Demetrius and Origen was doubtless due more to church politics than theology. Demetrius simply wanted to put the catechetical school more directly under his own control.
76. For Bienert's views on Peter, see *Dionysius: Zur Frage*, 2, 223.
77. Ibid., 222, says that Dionysius "shared" (mitgetragen hat) in Heraklas's banishment of Origen. Such a succession, with its alternating Origenists and anti-Origenists, is difficult to imagine, and does not help explain the "Origenism" of Athanasius.
78. For fragments dealing with allegory, see *Dionysius: Letters*, 199–200; Bienert, "Neue Fragmente," 309, where allegory is rejected; and *Dionysius: Letters*, 228; W. A. Bienert, *Dionysius von Alexandrien: Das erhaltene Werk* (Stuttgart, 1972) 95, where allegory is used. For a discussion of these passages, see *Dionysius: Letters*, 208, 228, and xxviii; and Bienert, *Dionysius: Werk*, 122 nn. 263, 265.

Theognostus and Pierius, successors of Dionysius at the catechetical school, are generally considered to be Origenists.[79] Unfortunately, very little survives by Theognostus and almost nothing by Pierius.[80] For the historian, the interpretation of both their works and their position in the controversy over Origen is beset by a major obstacle: most of the fragments are preserved (or, more accurately, summarized) by Photius who, as an anti-Origenist, is a very dubious witness (see above, 96). Both Quasten and Radford are willing to accept at face value what Photius says about Theognostus: "that the contents of the *Hypotyposeis* bore witness to the Origenistic sympathies of their writer it is impossible to doubt in view of the comments of Photius."[81]

Radford at first seems to accept without comment that the *Hypotyposeis* is epitomized by Photius and says nothing about Photius's bias.[82] However, when Photius says that Theognostus described the Son as a creature, Radford correctly observes that the "actual use of the word κτίσμα is doubtful. Photius may be quoting the exact word used by Theognostus, but the language of Photius (κτίσμα αὐτὸν ἀποφαίνει) looks rather as though he were simply giving the gist of what he took Theognostus to mean."[83] With regard to this "subordinationism" of Theognostus, Radford points out, but does not make enough of, that Photius's report of Theognostus's subordinationism "echoes" Justinian (see 116 below).[84]

Undoubtedly, Theognostus was Origenist in his teaching; Photius's censure of him shows this. But with regard to the details of that Origenism, Photius must be used with extreme caution. So little is known about Theognostus or his work that very little can be said. Radford observes that he was appealed to by both Origenists and Arians, and quotes Diekamp: "The mind of Theognostus, like that of Origen, worked alternately on two lines, 'one leading to Arianism, the other to Homoousianism.'"[85]

Pierius, the successor of Theognostus, was also accused by Photius of

79. See Quasten 2:110–11.

80. For their works, see: PG 10:235–41; ANF 6:155–56; Radford, 1–43 (Theognostus); and PG 10:241–46; ANF 6:156–57; Radford, 44–57 (Pierius).

81. Radford, 10. See Quasten 2:110.

82. Radford, 10–11.

83. Ibid., 12. He goes on to discuss the doubts he has about Justinian's attribution of κτίσμα to Origen. Harnack accepts Photius's statement that Theognostus used κτίσμα (TU 24.3 (1903) 86; cited by Radford, 17–18). Photius seems to be implying that Theognostus was an Arian! It appears that one did not have to be an Origenist to be suspect to Photius—just pre-Nicene.

84. Radford, 31–32.

85. Ibid., 18, 23. Athanasius *De decretis* 25 cites Theognostus as an excellent teacher.

subordinationism:[86] "Pierius, he [Photius] says, talks mysteriously about the pre-existence of souls just [as] in Origen's absurd fashion. But the few scattered fragments of his works that remain and the references of Photius to the contents of other works go far to prove that he was a close follower as well as a not unworthy successor of Origen."[87] Once again, Photius must be trusted only in a general sense—that is, Pierius was undoubtedly "Origenist"—but when Photius reports that Pierius spoke of two οὐσίαι and two φύσεις, considerable skepticism is warranted.[88]

Pierius was known later as "Origen the Younger," and Bienert, following Harnack, says that this shows "how alive was the heritage of Origen in the Alexandrian Church."[89] Bienert sees a dichotomy at Alexandria: the catechetical school of Theognostus and Pierius was clearly Origenist, while the bishops, from Demetrius to Peter, had continued in opposition to Origen.[90] Like most scholars, he sees in Peter a "reaction" against Origenism, but the Origenism is that of the catechetical school, not, as commonly held, that of his predecessors in the episcopacy.

This judgment about Peter, although it is traditional, must be questioned. There are several reasons for doing so: (1) Many scholars have made their conclusions based on material that cannot be assigned to Peter, have read too much into the authentic texts, or have made generalizations that, based on the evidence at hand, are much too broad. (2) There has been, as far as I can determine, no discussion of the circumstances surrounding the preservation of Peter's writing. (3) Scholarship has taken for granted certain views attributed to Origen (usually by his enemies) without checking more closely to see if these attributions are correct.

Radford made a serious mistake when he cited an obviously apocryphal passage from the Acta Sancti Petri to confirm Peter's anti-Origenism. Shortly before his martyrdom, in a prayer to Saint Mark, founder of the see of Alexandria, Peter rails against "that madman Origen who caused schisms in the Church which to this day have raised up con-

---

86. Radford, 35, 52. As he notes (44) of Pierius: "the fragments of his writings and teaching which have survived are even more rare and disconnected than those which enable us to reconstruct the theology of Theognostus."

87. Ibid., 49. His discussion of Pierius is almost wholly dependent on Photius, yet he never discusses Photius's bias.

88. See ibid., 51, who, however, accepts Photius's statements.

89. Bienert, Dionysius: Zur Frage, 223. The epithet goes back to Jerome De vir. ill. 76; cf. Radford, 48.

90. Bienert, Dionysius: Zur Frage, 223. He does not discuss why Theognostus and Pierius would turn against the "anti-Origenism" of Dionysius and become "Origenists." The suggestion is very doubtful.

fusion and disorder."[91] W. Telfer, in his detailed attempt to restore the Urtext of Peter's *Acta*, rejects this portion, and is undoubtedly right in doing so—it is a later polemic.[92] Radford's error, interestingly, is not a modern one only. The same anti-Origenist statement that he quotes occurs in Justinian's *Contra Origenem*, where it is quoted along with a fragment of Peter's work in order to show that Peter had opposed Origen (see 98–99 above).[93]

This failure to take into account the tendentious and polemical has been a common one among scholars with regard to Peter. The titles attributed to Peter's work *On the Soul* cannot possibly be his (namely, that "the soul did not preexist the body," and longer titles; see above, 97–98), yet the *PG* prints them and even Harnack accepts them without comment.[94] This gives the reader the impression that Peter gave his work a deliberately anti-Origenistic title, when in fact the title is redactional and reflects only the substance of a very small fragment.

O. Bardenhewer sums up his discussion of *On the Soul* (frag. II.1 according to the numbering used here) by saying that "it gives testimony to nothing less than a detailed polemic which numbers at least two books and is directed against one of the main supports of the Origenist system."[95] Surely Bardenhewer is inferring too much from one small fragment. It cannot possibly be determined, based on the extant evidence, that the work was a polemic "directed against" Origen (see 97–100 above); one can say, at most, that it attacked *one* of Origen's teachings. Bardenhewer also accepts the passage from *On the Soul* attacking Greek philosophy.[96] This passage (compare the expansions in frag. II.1b with frag. II.1) is a later addition and does not occur in the earliest preserved text (see 99 above).

Bardenhewer, Quasten, and Barnes also accept the seven Syriac fragments on the resurrection (frags. IV.1–7) and say that they are anti-Origenistic.[97] Peter did write at least one work on the resurrection (see frags. III.1–2), but it is impossible to say with confidence that these Syriac fragments are Peter's (see above, 103–4). Even if they do go back

91. Radford, 60–61.
92. W. Telfer, "St. Peter of Alexandria and Arius," *AnBol* 67 (1949) 117–30. See also A. Athanassakis (trans.), *The Life of Pachomius* (Missoula, Mont. 1975) 40–43 (par. 31), for anti-Origenist additions to the story of Pachomius's life.
93. *ACO* 3:197.
94. Harnack, *Dogma* 3:99.
95. Bardenhewer 2:246.
96. Ibid. 2:246; see also Radford, 90.
97. Bardenhewer 2:246; Quasten 2:115; Barnes, *Constantine and Eusebius*, 199; Stauridos, 567; Barnard, "Antecedents," 183.

to Peter, which is possible, they have undoubtedly been heavily interpolated. Barnes goes further when, citing M. Richard's fragments from
the Easter homily of 309 (frags. III.1–2), he says that "Peter attacked
Origen's ideas in the Easter letters which he sent each year to the
churches throughout Egypt."[98] This cannot be demonstrated.

Such generalizations are common in the literature. G. W. H. Lampe, in
his study of Christian theology in the patristic period, says that the term
theotokos was used by Peter.[99] He cites the Easter homily printed in *PG*
18:517, although frag. VII in the *PG* (the piece after frag. V.4 of this
study), where *theotokos* occurs, comes from Athanasius (or at least his
time) and not Peter (see above, 105–6). Concerning Peter's supposed
theological language, M. Bardy says: "his doctrine proved that the belief
in the union in Christ of the two natures in one person ($\mu\iota\alpha\nu$ $\upsilon\pi\delta\sigma\tau\alpha\sigma\iota\nu$
$\kappa\alpha\iota$ $\pi\rho\delta\sigma\omega\pi\sigma\nu$ $\epsilon\nu$) was orthodox and apostolic."[100] M. Richard has shown
that such technical language belongs, not to Peter, but to Photius (ninth
c.), and that the fragment preserved "is a question neither of person nor
of hypostasis."[101]

Peter's works were largely preserved and translated by those who,
like Photius, were anti-Origenist—or thought they were: the Council of
Ephesus, Marius Mercator, Leontius of Jerusalem, and the emperor
Justinian.[102] (It is interesting to note that Epiphanius does not preserve
any of Peter's "anti-Origenistic" writings.) Origen was, posthumously,
perhaps the greatest casualty of the theological wars of the fourth

98. Barnes, *Constantine and Eusebius*, 198–99.
99. "Christian Theology," 128. J. Pelikan, *The Christian Tradition* (Chicago 1971) 1:241,
does not include Peter in his discussion: "Despite the effort to find evidence of it
elsewhere, there is reason to believe that the title [*theotokos*] originated in Alexandria,
where it harmonized with and epitomized the general Alexandrian tradition. The
earliest incontestable instance of the term Theotokos was in the encyclical of Alexander
directed against Arianism in 324." However, see Lampe, 639A for citations before
Alexander. Radford 47, reports that according to Philip Sidetes, Pierius wrote a treatise
or sermon ($\lambda\delta\gamma\sigma$s) on the Theotokos. He further comments (56): "Of the $\lambda\delta\gamma\sigma$s $\pi\epsilon\rho\iota$ $\tau\eta$s
$\theta\epsilon\sigma\tau\delta\kappa\sigma\upsilon$ we have only the title so quoted by Phillipus. If the title came in that shape
from the pen of Pierius, it would be the earliest example of the use of the expression
$\theta\epsilon\delta\tau\sigma\kappa\sigma$s by itself. . . . yet it is improbable that the title was already in such general use
as to stand by itself as a proper name in the heading of a treatise." Origen *Sel. in Deut.*
22:23 (*PG* 12.813C) uses the term: ' $E\alpha\nu$ $\delta\epsilon$ $\gamma\epsilon\nu\eta\tau\alpha\iota$ $\pi\alpha$ιs $\pi\alpha\rho\theta\epsilon\nu\sigma$s $\mu\epsilon\mu\nu\eta\sigma\tau\epsilon\upsilon\mu\epsilon\nu\eta$ $\alpha\nu\delta\rho\iota$ [cf.
Deut. 22:23 (LXX)] $\tau\eta\nu$ $\eta\delta\eta$ $\mu\epsilon\mu\nu\eta\sigma\tau\epsilon\upsilon\mu\epsilon\nu\eta\nu$ $\gamma\upsilon\nu\alpha\iota\kappa\alpha$ $\kappa\alpha\lambda\epsilon\iota$· $\sigma\upsilon\tau\omega$ $\kappa\alpha\iota$ $\epsilon\pi\iota$ $\tau\sigma\upsilon$ $I\omega\sigma\eta\phi$ $\kappa\alpha\iota$ $\tau\eta$s
$\theta\epsilon\sigma\tau\delta\kappa\sigma\upsilon$ $\epsilon\lambda\epsilon\chi\theta\eta$. Socrates *HE* 7.32.17 (*PG* 67:812B; NPNF 2d ser., 2:171) reports: "Origen
also in the first volume of his *Commentaries* on the apostle's epistle to the Romans, gives
an ample exposition of the sense in which the term Theotokos is used."
100. Richard, "Pierre Ier," 357.
101. Ibid., 358.
102. See *RS* 46–51; and *PG* 18:512Aff. Interestingly, it is to Photius that we are
indebted for the transmission of Peter's canons into the canons of the Eastern Church.

through sixth centuries, and interestingly, Peter seems to have been one of those who did him in. But this owes much more to those who preserved the bishop's writings than it does to Peter himself.

The Council of Ephesus preserves three fragments from *On the Deity* (frags. I.1–3) which cannot possibly be construed as anti-Origenistic. The emperor Justinian quotes one of the three fragments, and probably did not have an independent text of Peter's writing before him. Leontius of Byzantium preserves a fragment from *On the Soul* (frag. II.1) which Justinian borrows and clearly interpolates (frag. II.1a). A later anti-Origenist florilegium further interpolates the text, making it into an attack on Origenists (frag. II.1b; see above, 98–99, for details).

The tendency here is clear. Later writers almost always quoted Peter's writings in a polemical context. Some of these works, like Leontius's, were not expressly anti-Origenistic, but Justinian's work was a tractate expressly attacking Origen.[103] Codex Vatopédi is also anti-Origenistic.[104] Probably none of the writers or editors after Leontius had a complete text of Peter, and it is even doubtful whether Leontius or those at Ephesus did.

Peter is preserved only in a few small fragments which were passed down in increasingly polemical contexts. What later polemicists preserve of Peter's work is very incomplete, quoted out of context, and fashioned into theological weapons. If Peter's writings are removed from their later, polemical contexts, if the texts have their interpolations removed, and if the tendentious titles are ignored, then Peter's theology can be seen more closely as it originally was. It was not anti-Origenistic, and it does not appear that Peter wrote specifically in order to combat Origen. He did, however, refute some of Origen's teachings. We now turn our attention to those refutations.

The fragments preserved under the title *On the Soul* are the most important with regard to anti-Origenism. In this work Peter expressly denies the preexistence of the soul (frag. II.1) and, if frag. II.T is a testimony to the same work, the allegorical interpretation of the coats of skins (cf. Gen. 3:21), both held to be tenets of Origen's thought. Does this make Peter an opponent both of Origen and allegory, as has been

---

103. See Justinian, "Ad Mennam," *PG* 86¹:945D–993B. Stauridos, 567, seems to accept Peter as an anti-Origenist in large part because Justinian says he is. For Leontius, see M. Richard, "Léonce de Byzance était-il Origéniste?" *Opera Minora* 2:31–66 (#57).

104. M. Richard, apropos Vatopédi 236, fol. 113r–127r, says that it is an anti-Origenist florilegium from the second quarter of the sixth century in a "Palestinian monastic milieu in opposition" to Origenistic monks. See his "Nouveaux fragments de Theophile d'Alexandrie," *Opera Minora* 2:57[3] (#39).

claimed?[105] Almost all of the scholarship on Peter's writings accepts, without comment, that Origen held the coats of skins to be bodies (which presumes preexistence of the soul) and that Peter denied this.[106]

Jerome, about a century after Peter, reports that Origen "interprets the coats of skins, with which Adam and Eve were clothed after their fall and ejection from Paradise, to be human bodies, and we are to suppose, of course, that previously in Paradise they had neither flesh, sinews, nor bones."[107] The question is, however, whether Origen expressly held this view and, if so, whether Peter was attacking him.

Methodius of Olympus (d. c. 311), in his *De resurrectione*, many scholars agree, was the first person to attack Origen for his interpretation of the coats of skins.[108] In fact, Peter and Methodius are linked together by Harnack: they "trumped" Origen's views and "protected the principles transmitted by the Church from [Origen's] spiritualizing and artificial interpretations."[109] J. F. Dechow says that Peter's views "are found amplified extensively throughout Methodius' *De resurrectione* and Epiphanius' *Panarion* 64."[110] A closer look at these works, however, reveals that neither author quotes Peter, nor even mentions him, and that neither of their works can be connected to Peter's extant writings.

The *De resurrectione* of Methodius exists in Greek only in fragments, the Greek being preserved mostly by Epiphanius and Photius.[111] In the part preserved by Epiphanius, Methodius affirms that the coats of skins are not bodies and that the resurrection is not without flesh, and he attacks those who allegorize.[112] In some of the fragments preserved by Photius, Methodius attacks Origen, but the speaker is actually Photius, not Methodius: the third-person voice is used for Methodius, and

---

105. See Barnes, *Constantine and Eusebius*, 198–99; J. F. Dechow, "Dogma and Mysticism in Early Christianity" (Ph.D. diss.: Univ. Pennsylvania 1975), 300. W. Bienert, "Petrusfragmenten," 241, maintains that Peter "polemicizes" against the Origenist teaching on the preexistence of the soul, and says that the three fragments tell us something of the arguments over Origen at the beginning of the fourth century in Alexandria. However, the sure presence of an editorial hand (see Bienert, "Neue Fragmente," for the text) cautions against such a judgment. See n. 31 above.

106. H. Chadwick, in his edition of the *Contra Celsum* (Cambridge 1980) 216 n. 5, defends Origen.

107. Jerome *Adv. Ioann. Hier.* 7; cited in J. Stevenson, *Creeds, Councils, and Controversies* (London 1981) 174 (#123).

108. *Contra Celsum* (Chadwick, 216 n. 5). Chadwick does not, however, mention Peter.

109. Harnack, *Dogma* 3:104.

110. Dechow, 99. See also 19 where he suggests that Peter's writings *On the Soul* and *On the Resurrection* may have influenced Epiphanius "in an anti-Origenist direction."

111. PG 18:265D–329D. For the critical edition, see D. G. N. Bonwetsch, *Methodius* (Leipzig 1917).

112. *De resurrectione* I.20–II.8; Bonwetsch, 242–345. PG 18:265–89.

Gregory Nazianzus (329–89) is criticized![113] As M. Richard has pointed out (see above, 96), Photius cannot be trusted to preserve accurately the text of the author he is quoting: he reformulates the author's views according to the language and theology of his own time. More important, since the bishop of Olympus shows no knowledge of Peter's writings, it is impossible to make any connection between him and the bishop of Alexandria.

Can we determine with greater accuracy what Origen actually said about these matters? H. Chadwick has noted that Philo understood the "coats of skins" as bodies;[114] one would expect that Origen would have received this tradition in Alexandria from Philo's writings. Origen also may have been influenced by rabbinic tradition.[115] Philo certainly understood the body to be in some sense evil (*Leg. Alleg.* 3.69); since the body was of a lower order than the spiritual, it was symbolically called a "tunic of skin." It should be noted, however, that he in no way associates the coats of skins with the Fall; in another passage where he speaks of the body as a skin (*Quaest. Gen.* 1.53) he does not refer to Gen. 3:21, but speaks of Rebecca and Hagar.

Clement of Alexandria, in a work against Gnostics, *Extracts from Theodotus*, states that his opponents held views very similar to those Philo expressed in *Quaest. Gen.* 1.53: there are various levels of being or creation, and the body, called the "coat of skin," is the lowest. In *Stromateis* 3.14 Clement says that "the 'coats of skins' in Cassian's view are bodies. That both he and those who teach the same as he does are

---

113. Photius, *Bibliotheca*, cod. 234. K. Holl, in *Amphilochius von Ikonium* (repr., Darmstadt [1904] 1969) 202, points out that Gregory of Nyssa interpreted the coats of skins symbolically and quoted Gregory Nazianzus extensively. It appears that Origen was condemned for views that the Cappadocian saints held also.

114. *Contra Celsum* (Chadwick, 85 n. 9). For a recent full treatment of the subject, see P. F. Beatrice, "Le tuniche di pelle," in *La tradizione dell' enkrateia* (Milan 1982), 433–84, who emphasizes the use of the coats of skins story in early Christian encratism.

115. Jonathan Z. Smith, "The Garments of Shame," *History of Religions* 5 (1966) 217–38 (repr. in idem, *Map Is Not Territory: Studies in the History of Religion* [Leiden 1978] 1–23), esp. 231ff., gives a fascinating account of the coats of skins and logion 37 of the *Gospel of Thomas*. According to Smith, parts of the early Christian baptismal ceremony, e.g., being baptized naked and the trampling of goatskins, can be "traced back to Jewish exegesis of Gen. 3:21, the clothing of Adam and Eve by God with 'tunics of skins.' Some rabbis interpreted this to mean that before the expulsion from Eden, Adam and Eve had bodies or garments of light, but that after the expulsion, they received bodies of flesh or a covering of skin" (231). Smith sees in logion 37 "an interpretation of this archaic Christian baptismal rite" (238). If Smith is correct, Origen's interpretation of Gen. 3:21 has roots in Jewish exegesis and primitive Christian baptismal symbolism. For an equally fascinating recent discussion of logion 37, Clement's "Secret Gospel of Mark," and primitive Christian baptism, see John Dominic Crossan, *Four Other Gospels* (Minneapolis, Minn. 1985) 116–18.

wrong."[116] He does not discuss the connection between the coats and the Fall. Nor does Irenaeus in his discussion of the gnostic view of the coats of skins.[117]

Origen himself does not definitively commit himself on the question. In *Contra Celsum* 4.40, he clearly connects the coats of skins with the Fall, but says that the passage "has a certain secret and mysterious meaning." In *Selecta in Genesim* (PG 12:101), he ridicules the idea that the coats of skins can be taken literally, but will not commit himself on their exact nature: "it is plausible to say that the coats of skins are nothing other than bodies, but it is possible to assert for the sake of argument that it is not at all clear what is true."[118] He follows this passage, however, with a rhetorical question and answer that indicates that he believed the coats of skins to be "flesh and bone," that is, bodies.

Only one meager scrap of evidence, preserved by Procopius of Gaza (frag. II.T), indicates that Peter attacked the allegorical interpretation of the coats of skins. Because of the more trustworthy evidence given in frag. II.1 that Peter denied the preexistence of the soul, this is plausible, but we have no first-hand evidence that Peter attacked allegory per se. L. W. Barnard has suggested that Peter represented a "literalist, scriptural approach," and that this was opposed by followers of Origen.[119] This seems to be a reasonable inference, but because Peter denied preexistence does not mean he opposed the use of allegory, as many scholars have assumed. Based on the extant fragments, one should not press too hard a literalist-allegorist conflict between Peter and Origenists.[120]

In his recent work on the "coats of skins" passage, P. F. Beatrice says that Peter did not like the Origenist interpretation that the preexistent souls sinned and thus fell into bodies. This is probably true, but caution is warranted: Beatrice bases his conclusion on both Procopius's state-

---

116. *Stromateis* 3.14 (Stählin 3.95.2; PG 8:1196), trans. H. Chadwick, in *Alexandrian Christianity* (Philadelphia 1954) 84–85.

117. *Adv. Haer.* 1.1.5 (Harvey 1.1.10).

118. Origen's attack on literalism is worth quoting in full: "Therefore, it is exceedingly stupid and old-womanish and unworthy of God to think that God made the skins stripped off of some animals that were destroyed or in some other way killed into the forms of coats, (working) shredded skins in the manner of a shoemaker. . . . One must not cling to the literal nature [lit.: letter] of scripture as (the only) truth, but (one must) seek the hidden treasure in the literal [lit.: letter]."

119. Barnard, "Antecedents," 183–84.

120. As Barnard does (ibid., 184); and his conclusions on anti-Origenism (ibid., 183–85) seem overdrawn.

ment and the expanded fragments preserved by Justinian where Peter speaks against the notion that souls sin in heaven (II.1a; see 130 below).[121] The authentic fragment, II.1 (see 130), however, speaks only against preexistence and not the idea of sinning in heaven. That Peter attacked Origen cannot be proved; the work from which frag. II.1 comes, *On the Soul* (or possibly, *On the Deity and Humanity [of Christ]*), cannot be labeled a treatise against Origen.[122] The most that can be said is that Peter criticized a widespread view *probably* held also by Origen, one which his followers probably adopted too.

Many scholars also assume that Peter in his work on the resurrection (frags. III.1–2) is attacking Origen. J. Quasten, for example, says that this work "was most probably a refutation of Origen, stressing as it does, the identity of the body in the resurrection with that of the present life, a doctrine that Origen denied."[123] Of the fragments attributed to Peter on the resurrection, frags. III.1–2 are the ones most likely to be genuine and uninterpolated (see 100–103 above). The Greek fragments do not claim the identity of the resurrection body with the risen body: Jesus, when he rose from the dead, "received his *own* body" (τὸ ἴδιον ἀπέλαβε σῶμα), not the *same* (τὸ αὐτὸν σῶμα) body. Peter follows Saint Paul's thinking here and quotes him extensively. Nothing in frags. III.1–2 claims identity.

The question remains: could Peter be attacking here a position held by Origen? In the *Contra Celsum*, Origen quotes Celsus: "And it follows from this that Jesus could not have risen with his body; for God would not have received back the spirit which he gave after it had been defiled by the nature of the body," and replies, "It is silly for us to reply to statements put into our mouths which we should never say."[124]

In *Contra Celsum* 5.14, Celsus again attacks Christians for believing that the dead "will rise up from the earth possessing the same bodies as before."[125] In reply, Origen quotes 1 Cor. 15:51–52 and emphasizes the same point as Peter: "we shall be changed." Origen gives in *Contra Celsum* 5.18 a "brief account" of his views: the resurrection of the flesh, "while preached in the churches, is understood more clearly by the intelligent" (συνετωτέρων)—but he does not say what that understand-

---

121. Beatrice, 437. On the fragments, see the discussion above, 97–100.
122. Contra Bardenhewer 2:246.
123. Quasten 2:115.
124. *Contra Celsum* 6.72 (Chadwick, 386). In *Contra Celsum* 2.77 (Chadwick, 126), Origen, provoked by Celsus, raises questions about the resurrection, but does not discuss them.
125. Chadwick, 274.

ing is. Origen's "gnostic" understanding comes forth here, the same understanding that reads Gen. 3:21 as a "mystery."[126]

However, in *Contra Celsum* 5.19, Origen quotes 1 Cor. 15:35–38 and says that the dead "at the appropriate time out of the bodies that are sown take up the body which is appointed by God for each man in accordance with his merits." Origen quotes much of 1 Corinthians 15 in this passage of the *Contra Celsum* and says that Paul "wants to hide the secret truths" from the simple-minded.[127] He strongly implies, quoting Paul, that there is a change.

In *De principiis* 2.10, Origen, in answering "heretics," affirms the teaching of the church:

1. "It is of the body, then, that there will be a resurrection."

2. "It is a body which arises, [and] in the resurrection we are to make use of bodies."

3. "It can be a matter of doubt to no one that they rise again, in order that we may be clothed with them a second time at the resurrection."[128]

The above quotations are found only in Latin; consequently, there is the difficulty here that Rufinus may be more responsible than Origen for what is being said. However, a passage in *De principiis* 2.10.3 seems unlikely to have been altered. In it, Origen admits to a "spiritual" body, yet his metaphor of the seed and the germ insists on the resurrection of the earthly body.[129]

In his careful study "Origen, Celsus, and the Resurrection of the Body," H. Chadwick states that "the evidence points to the conclusion that [Origen] held to the continuance of personal identity in some form." Chadwick goes on to say that the idea that Origen denied the resurrection body "was an inference drawn either by his followers or by his opponents."[130]

Peter was not, it seems, one of those opponents. But Justinian and Photius were, and it is to them that Peter's "anti-Origenism" must now be attributed. Henry Chadwick, in his discussion of Origen and the resurrection body, finds that "critical examination of the evidence

---

126. Lest Origen, by his use of the word "mystery," be criticized for evading the issue, one should note that Ignatius of Antioch sees the virginity of Mary and the birth and death of Jesus as "three resounding mysteries wrought in the silence of God." See also the *Paschal Homily* of Melito, pars. 34 and 46. Also see, inter alia, 1 Cor. 2:7, 15:51; Eph. 5:32.

127. Chadwick, 278.

128. ANF 4:293.

129. ANF 4:294.

130. H. Chadwick, "Origen, Celsus, and the Resurrection of the Body," *HTR* 41 (1948) 102.

should warn us to be on our guard against blindly following Justinian, as is done by Koetschau and de Faye." He concludes, "if we are dealing with Justinian as an authority for the actual doctrine of Origin himself, difficulties immediately arise. I venture to think that the only question is how far he can safely be distrusted."[131]

As Chadwick has concluded, "In short, what we have in the anathemas of Origen at Constantinople is an ecclesiastical action arising directly out of the contemporary situation in the sixth century."[132]

To paraphrase Chadwick, it is vital to distinguish between Peter and those who claimed to be quoting Peter.[133] For the actual teaching of Peter, Justinian and Photius must be distrusted.[134] I hope that I have shown that the "anti-Origenism" of Peter lies in Photius, Justinian, and secondary or doubtful texts. Even if one allows the criticisms of Origen's teaching by Dionysius and Peter, one can conclude only that they criticized or modified certain positions of Origen.[135] It cannot be said that they were anti-Origenists.[136]

Similarly, J. Dechow has suggested that "the fragments do not demonstrate that Peter was primarily opposing Origen himself rather than some of Origen's interpreters."[137] Harnack suggested that Peter "only deprived Origen's doctrines of their extreme conclusion, while otherwise he maintained them, in so far as they did not come into direct conflict with the rule of faith"; while E. R. Hardy concluded that "Peter was an able theologian of the moderate Origenist school, disposed to

131. Ibid., 102. I would say the same about Photius.
132. Chadwick, "Origen," 95. Socrates HE 6.7 does not list Peter among the detractors of Origen. In HE 6.13 Socrates (an Origenist) puts Methodius first in that list, and puts Athanasius in the forefront of his defenders.
133. One has to wonder if Peter had been such an anti-Origenist, wouldn't more than snippets of his theological writings have survived (e.g., as with Methodius's works, preserved by Epiphanius and Photius)?
134. Ibid., 95, has this to say about Justinian: "But it is difficult to know how far the opinions attributed to Origen really go back to Origen himself. . . . at least, one of the anathemas of the council at Constantinople in 543 is now known to be a quotation from Evagrius Ponticus and not from Origen at all, so that it is clear that Justinian was not too careful to verify his references."
135. For Dionysius, see Bienert, "Neue Fragmente," 308–14; and above, 112–14.
136. "Anti-Origenism" really begins with the abrupt "about face" of Theophilus (d. 412). See Socrates HE 6.7 and esp. 6.13.
137. Dechow, 96–97. See also Solignac, 1500–1501. Just as I complete my own study, I find that Solignac has reached many of the same conclusions. He states (1500) that the traditional view which numbers Peter among the anti-Origenists must be "nuanced." He goes on to add (1501) that Peter was more likely criticizing certain followers of Origen; that Peter's works do not show a "combative anti-Origenism"; and that in at least some of those works Peter's methods of argument and conclusions are much the same as Origen's.

discourage the more daring speculations of the master and some of his followers."[138]

These conclusions of Dechow, Harnack, and Hardy are more accurate than the view that holds Peter to be an anti-Origenist. Nothing more can be said about Peter and Origen than that the former opposed one or two of the latter's ideas. It cannot be said that Peter attacked Origen. As preserved, Peter's theology is orthodox (as defined by later councils) and Alexandrian.

With regard to Peter's place in Alexandrian theology, I think it best to place him with those after Demetrius (and Heraklas?) who were moderate Origenists or, more accurately, simply Christian platonists: Dionysius, Theognostus, and Pierius. At least two heads of the catechetical school, Dionysius and Peter (when they were bishops?), criticized some of Origen's teachings. Little more than this can be said. Ironically, with regard to his theological writings, Peter is important not so much for what he said as he is for those who preserved his writings and what and whom they were attacking.

Appendix
TEXTS OF THE THEOLOGICAL FRAGMENTS

See table 1 (90) for a list of the fragments and the synoptic table (91) for their cross-references.

Abbreviations: A: Armenian
G: Greek
S: Syriac
T: Testimonium
Exp: Expansion

I. On the Deity and Humanity [of Christ]

I.1–3 *On the Deity* (Περὶ θεότητος). Greek. *PG* 18:509A–512A; *RS* 4:46–47.

[I.1] Truly "grace and truth came through Jesus Christ" [John 1:17], from which fact we also are saved by grace, according to the word of the apostle: "and this is not your own doing, it is the gift of God—not because of works, lest any man should boast" [Eph. 2:8–9]. By the will of God, although "the Word became flesh" [John 1:14], "being found in human form" [Phil. 2:7], it was not deprived of its deity.

Although he was rich, he became poor, not in order to be separated completely from his power or glory, but in order to take death upon himself on behalf of us sinners [cf. 2 Cor. 8:9], "the righteous for the unrighteous, that he

---

138. Harnack, *Dogma* 3:99; Hardy, *Christian Egypt*, 145.

might bring us to God, being put to death in the flesh but made alive in the spirit [1 Pet. 3:18].

And after other things.

[I.2] Therefore, the evangelist also speaks the truth when he says, "the Word became flesh and dwelt among us" [John 1:14]. It dwelt among us even from the moment when the angel greeted the Virgin, saying, "Hail, O favored one, the Lord is with you" [Luke 1:28]. Now when Gabriel said, "The Lord is with you," he meant "God the Word (ὁ θεὸς λόγος) is with you." He means that the Lord came (γενόμενον) into the womb and thus became (γενόμενον) flesh, as it is written: "The Holy Spirit will come upon you, and the power of the Most High will overshadow you; therefore the child to be born will be called holy, the Son of God" [Luke 1:35].

And again, after other things.

[I.3] God the Word, in the absence of man, by the will of God who has the power to work all things, became flesh in the Virgin's womb without need of man's help (ἐνεργείας) and (without his) presence (ἀπουσία). For the power of God worked more effectively (ἐνεργέστερον) than a man when he overshadowed the Virgin with the Holy Spirit who came upon her.

From a Sermon (or Book) of Theology (Ex sermone [vel libro] de theologia). Latin. *PG* 18:521C–522C.

[I.2a] Meanwhile the evangelist firmly says: "The Word became flesh, and dwelt among us" [John 1:14]. From this we learn that that angel, when he greeted the Virgin, saying, "Greetings, (you who are) full of gladness, the Lord is with you" [Luke 1:28], wished to signify: "God the Word is with you." He also wished to show that he (the Word) would be born from her womb and would be made flesh, as it is written: "The Holy Spirit will come upon you and the power of the Most High will descend upon you; therefore the child to be born of you will be called holy, the Son of God" [Luke 1:35].

On the Resurrection. Syriac. *AS* 4:189; Latin trans., 4:426 (Pitra IIA).

[I.2b] This same thing therefore the evangelist confirms, saying, "And the Word became flesh and dwelled among us" [John 1:14]. This moreover is known from the fact that the angel greeted the Virgin, saying, "Hail, full of grace, the Lord is with you" [Luke 1:28]. For Gabriel meant by "The Lord is with you" (this:) "God the Word is with you." For the angel shows that he is to be conceived in the womb and made flesh according to what is written: "The Holy Spirit will come upon you and the power of the Most High will shade you. Therefore, that which will be born from you will be called holy, the Son of God" [Luke 1:35].

From the Book *On the Deity.* Syriac. *AS* 4:187–8; Latin trans., 4.425–26. (Pitra IA–D).

[I.1a] Since grace and truth have truly been given through Jesus Christ, therefore we are saved through grace, according to the word of the apostle: "And not from us, for it is a gift from God. Not because of works, lest anyone boast" [Eph. 2:9]. Further, since by the will of God "the Word was made flesh" [John 1:14] and "was found in a man's likeness" [cf. Phil. 2:7], it has not fallen away from God. For it was not "made poor" [2 Cor. 8:9] in order to fall away from its goodness and glory, since it was (already) rich, but in order to suffer death for us sinners, "the righteous for the unrighteous, that he might bring us to God, being put to death in the flesh, but made alive in the spirit" [1 Pet. 3:18].

[I.2c] "Therefore that which shall be born from you is holy (and) will be called the Son of God" [Luke 1:35]. And that which is born from flesh is flesh; but Mary by the flesh brought forth our Lord Jesus Christ, who truly is one and the same and is not now this, now that. Far from it! For truly we say Jesus is Lord, believing especially that Jesus is the Son of God and that Jesus is the Christ, as Jesus himself was seen by the apostles after his ascension.

[I.3a] Moreover, God the Word was made flesh in the Virgin's womb without (her having) intercourse with a man, but solely by the will of God who is able to do all things, without need of the operation or presence of man. For the power of God, which descended upon her with the Holy Spirit who came to her, was more efficacious than man('s power).

[I.3 (S Exp)] Therefore, when Emmanuel was brought forth, he made the Virgin the Mother of God, (and) from her he was gloriously made incarnate and was born.

Five Armenian Fragments. AS 4:194–95; Latin trans., 4:430.

[I.A1] Why do we say that since Mary bore our Lord Jesus Christ by the body he was made holy and the Son of God, the same Word, and not something else? (The latter) is impossible! Jesus Christ is truly the Son of God and truly Jesus is the Christ, and truly he suffered torments for us.

[I.A2] Mary gave birth to the Word of God made flesh, one and the same—and not now this, now that, which is impossible!

[I.A3] Those who dare to say that the union was corrupted by the body or (dare to) divide God from the body, let them be struck down by anathema!

[I.A4] And God and the body are one nature, and one person, which comes by its own will and the dispensation of the Spirit. We must adore this indivisible God in his indivisible unity.

[I.A5] Those who, after the indivisible union, speak of two natures, two figures, two Sons, one of whom (is) from the Father and the other from Mary (his) mother, spurn the Father and act foolishly when they acknowledge two Sons, one of whom is natural, the other foreign, whence they introduce a Quaternity and by their words deny the Holy Trinity. A new God is adored, having its origins from Mary. Furthermore, if these matters are as they believe, all peoples err in their adoration of a crucified man and in their eating his body and blood.

From his (Peter's) Work Concerning Deity and Humanity, That the Lord Accepted Natural and Sinless Emotions. Greek. M. Richard, "Le Florilège du Cod. Vatopédi 236 sur le corruptible et l' incorruptible," 86 (1973) 268–69 (Richard 15 and 16).

[I.4] And that "growing weary from walking, he sat down near a stream" [John 4:6]. And that he wept over Lazarus [cf. John 11:35]. And that he said at the time of (his) passion: "My soul is deeply grieved unto death" [Matt. 26:38], and going out he fell to the ground and was praying [cf. Matt. 26:39; Mark 14:35]. And that they seized and bound him and led him to the chief priests [cf. Luke 22:54; John 18:12–13]. And that the servant standing by slapped Jesus [cf. John 18:22]. And that they clothed him in purple and placed upon his head a crown they had woven from thorns [cf. Matt. 27:28], and that they led him outside in order to crucify (him), and crucifying him, they nailed him to the cross. And that when he said "I thirst" [John 19:28], they placed a sponge on a reed and gave him vinegar to drink, and that "when he tasted it, he refused to drink" [Matt. 27:34]. And that "bowing his head, he gave up the spirit" [John 19:20], and he breathed his last. And that taking him down from the cross they wrapped him in a burial sheet [cf. Mark 15:46], and with a mixture of "myrrh and bitter aloes" [John 19:39], "just as it is the custom of the Jews, they buried (him)" [John 19:40]. And that they placed him in a new tomb [cf. Matt. 27:60].

These and similar things written down here and there in the scriptures make it clear that the Word became flesh and appeared as man [cf. John 1:14], Jesus the Christ, the Son of God, like all men in likeness (but) without a single sin. For if the Word in likeness did not become like all men, nothing great, no paradox, nothing marvelous (if someone wishes the Word to be something else) has come about other than our own weakness. And if, according to the will of the God and Father of all, for our salvation God the Word became flesh in dignity, this (is) the grace of God—and more, (is) the divine power in him who became man for us. Wherefore, confessing that he also exchanged human weakness, we glorify and give thanks to God who is Word, the Son of God.

Similarly from his same work.

[I.5] By the will of God the Word—and it was given life by the Spirit.

"On the Advent of our Savior." Greek. *RS* 4:48. Latin. *RS* 4:48, and *PG* 18:511A–512.

[I.6] And he said to Judas, "Would you betray the Son of Man with a kiss? [Luke 22:48] These things and things similar to these, and all the signs and miracles which he performed, show that he is God made man. Therefore, both things are demonstrated: that he was God by nature, and that he became man by nature.

"On the Advent of Christ." Greek. *PG* 18:511–12.

[I.6a] Therefore, both things are demonstrated: that he was God by nature, and that he became man by nature.

"On Matthew." Latin. *PG* 18:521C.

[I.6b] And in the Gospel according to Matthew, the Lord says to the one who betrays him: "Would you betray the Son of man with a kiss?" [Luke 22:48] This passage Peter the martyr and archbishop of Alexandria explains, saying these things and things similar to them: "And all the signs and miracles which he performed show that he was God by nature, and that he became man by nature."

"On the Union of Two Natures." Latin. *RS* 4:50.

[I.T] Concerning Saint Peter along with many other fathers, Ephrem, patriarch of Antioch, speaks thus: "That confessing the union of two natures and the one hypostasis and one person is the preaching of the fathers and of orthodox thought. John Chrysostom, reflecting on the Gospel according to John, bears witness in his eleventh homily—and also Peter of Alexandria the martyr, and Basil of Caesarea, etc."

II. On the Soul (Περὶ ψυχῆς).

"That the Soul Did Not Preexist the Body." Greek. *PG* 18:520C–521A; *RS* 4:48–50.

[II.1] We have explained earlier [ἐν πρώτοις; see 91–92 and n. 7] the things concerning the deity and humanity (περὶ τῆς θεότητος καὶ ἀνθρωπότητος) of the Second Man, according to the blessed apostle. It is necessary also to relate and set down the things concerning the First Earthly Man who was born from the earth, to show that he came into being one and the same at one time, even if sometimes he is separately called the inner and outer man. For if, according to the word of salvation, the one who made the outside also made the inside [cf. Luke 11:40], then certainly (the Creator did this) once and at the same time, that is, on that day when God said, "Let us make man in our image, after our likeness" [Gen. 1:26]. From this it is perfectly clear that (man) did not come about from a union, as if joined to another preexistent being from another place. For if the earth, at (God's) command, brought forth the other living animals, much greater was the dust, raised by God from the earth, which received life according to the will and working of God.

From the First Sermon of Saint Peter, Bishop and Martyr, of the Great City of Alexandria, "Concerning the Soul. That It Did Not Preexist nor Sin (and) On Account of This Was Cast into the Body." Greek. *ACO* 3:197; *PG* 86¹:961B.

[II.1a] We note that the things concerning the First Earthly Man who came from the earth are provided to show that he came into being at one and the same time, even if sometimes he is separately called the inner and outer man. For if according to the word of salvation, the one who made the outside also made the inside [cf. Luke 11:40], then certainly (the Creator did this) once and at one time, that is, on the same day when God said, "Let us make man according to our image and likeness." From this it is perfectly clear that (man) did not come about from a union, as if joined to a preexistent being of some kind. For if there had been (such) a union, why was it also written, "it was made"?

And after other things.

[II.1a (G Exp-1)] So that it is not possible for souls to sin in heaven before they assume corporeal form, nor for that matter is hypostasis possible before corporeal existence. This teaching is a precept of Greek philosophy which is foreign and alien to those who desire to live piously in Christ.

From the same (author), from the spiritual teaching which he gave to the church when he was going to receive the crown of martyrdom.

[II.1a (G Exp-2)] Therefore, I ask, keep awake, because you are going to enter again into affliction. You know how many dangers my father and bishop, Theonas—he who raised me (whose throne I also received; would that I [had] also [received his] way of life!)—suffered at the hands of those who were mad for idols. When the great Dionysius was also in hiding from place to place, at this time also Sabellius was causing grief. And what should I say about Heraclas and Demetrius, the blessed bishops who suffered such great trials under the madman Origen who also threw the church into schisms which even until today cause it trouble?

Concerning the Soul. That It Did Not Preexist or Sin Before. Of Peter, Bishop of Alexandria and Martyr. Greek. W. Bienert, "Neue Fragmente des Dionysius und des Petrus von Alexandrien aus Cod. Vatop. 236," *Kleronomia* 5 (1973) 311– 12.

[II.1b] "God said, 'Let us make man in our image and after our likeness'" [Gen. 1:26]. From this it is quite clear that (man) did not come about from a union, as if joined to a preexistent being of some kind from another place, for if there had been such a union, why was it also written, "it was made"?

From him (Peter), from the same (work).

[II.1b (G Exp-1)] And if, as they [Origenists?] say, in this life (the souls) enjoy the goodness of God, shown mercy according to (their) amendment, even this does not follow, especially because—according to them—the sins of the souls were smaller and half-finished inasmuch as coming about by desire alone, it was not forgiven (them) through repentance and amendment in heaven according to the mercy and goodness of God, but they were cast below. For if up above they did not refuse, for what reason were they possessed by bodies when they were cast down and added to measure and quantity and terribleness of sins?

From him, from the same work.

[II.1b. (G Exp-2)] Since it is not possible for the souls to sin in heaven before (they have) bodies, nor in a word take on substance (ὑποστάσας) before (they have) bodies, this doctrine is from foreign Greek philosophy and is alien to those who wish to live in accordance with right teaching in Christ. Concerning which (foreign philosophy) we hear: "Do not know well another; do not embrace one not your own" [Prov. 5:20 (LXX)]. We who pursue (the Christian life) far distant and removed from this (philosophy) maintain strongly that neither do the inspired scriptures teach any such thing, nor has the holy and catholic church (ever) taught in such a way, but rather (it teaches) that men sin while dwelling upon the earth, while (still) being able to attain heaven.

And in order that I not cite the whole thing, he shows throughout the whole work that souls in no way preexist bodies.

"That the Soul Did Not Preexist (the Body), nor Did It Sin (Before)." Syriac. *AS* 4:193–94; Latin trans., 4:429 (Pitra III).

[II.2] For what (Jesus) said is true: "And do not fear those who kill the body, but cannot kill the soul. But rather fear him who can destroy both soul and body in Gehenna" [Matt. 10:28]. Whence it is known that the body, which is killed by men, also arises united again with the soul in order that both might receive retribution in judgment for those things which they did in this life.

From the "First Sermon on the Soul." Latin. *RS* 4:50.

[II.T] Procopius of Gaza says that "all the teachers" speak against the allegorical interpretation of the leather tunics [cf. Gen. 3:21] and of other things in Paradise, and he gives by name, among many others, "Dionysius, Bishop of Alexandria in an 'Exposition which He Gave in Church,' and of the same city the bishop and martyr Peter in the 'First Sermon on the Soul.'"

III. On the Resurrection (Paschal Letter)

From the *Paschal Letter* of Peter, Archbishop of Alexandria and Martyr. Greek. Richard, "Le Florilège," 267–69.

[III.1] For we know the faithful who in good faith maintain strongly and say: If the beginning of all things, "the first-born of creation [Col. 1:15], and the "first fruit of those who sleep (in death)" [1 Cor. 15:20] has become "also the first-born of the dead" [Col. 1:18] in order that he might cause us to rise together with him, and (that) he might sit "at the right hand of greatness among the most high" [Heb. 1:3], through whom he received (a) body from the Virgin—it is clear that like the first fruit of those who sleep (in death), (and like) the first-born of the dead, all the dead will rise, changing their form and being conformed "to his body of glory" [Phil. 3:21]. This very thing was said by the apostle with assurance: "For it is necessary that this perishable (nature) be clothed with imperishability and this mortal (nature) be clothed with immortality" [1 Cor. 15:53], (and) thus it is fulfilled.

After other matters, again from him (Peter).

[III.2] Just as when we arise from the dead we receive a different body, not according to substance, but according to the quality made manifest in him. "For it is necessary that this perishable (nature) be clothed with imperishability" [1 Cor. 15:53]. And thus the Lord gave life to his own body, (and) after he arose from the dead he made (it) imperishable, that is, impassible and eternal. For this is the change to which the teacher [v. l. : the apostle] says the Lord submitted. For he does not teach that he changed the substance of (his) body. Not at all!

Performing (this) spiritual service in a pure way, let us lift up "holy hands without anger and arguments" [1 Tim. 2:8], being hopeful that we are being brought to life again. We will cease (our) fasts in the evening on Saturday when holy Sunday begins to dawn four days before the Ides of April, which is the fifteenth of Pharmouth [10 April 309], on which day arose the one who was living and became (one of the) dead and again lives for ever [cf. Rev. 1:18]. He aroused the thought(s) of his disciples who thought they "saw a ghost" [Luke 24:37], saying, "'Why are you troubled, and why do questionings rise in your hearts? Feel me and see that a ghost does not have flesh and bones as you see me having.' And having said this, he showed them (his) hands and feet" [Luke 24:39–41].

(These) very things he established as reasonable through the change which happened in him, through which "they were prevented from recognizing him" [Luke 24:16], since even in this it was necessary for him to take precedence according to the apostolic word [cf. Col. 1:18]. Whence also someone took pains to feel him, who also truly becoming fully assured concerning his resurrection, called him both Lord (and) God . . . [cf. John 20:27–28].

IV. On the Resurrection (from the Syriac)

On the Resurrection. Syriac. *AS* 4:189–93; Latin trans., 4:426–29 (Pitra IIB–H).

[IV.1] Further, they call a building that which provides for terrestrial man born from the earth. Therefore, even if the soul leaves the body at the time of separation and dissolution, we are nevertheless a work of art and the work of an artificer, whence we are able to return from the dead since it is known that at the resurrection our mortal bodies put on immortality in order that the body united with the soul might receive the reward which it deserves.

[IV.2] Therefore the resurrection will not be otherwise. For it is known only through a comparison with him who was the first-born from the dead. Wherefore "we know that when he appears we shall be like him, for we shall see him as he is" [1 John 3:2]. And this too was heard in the beginning, at the creation of man, when God said, "Let us make man in our image and likeness [Gen. 1:26]. Therefore, another saying is rightly placed beside this one: in the likeness of "the first fruits of those who have fallen asleep" [1 Cor. 15:20]. For we know that Christ is our first fruits; therefore the first fruits which (we will have) afterward are Christ's through his advent. When the dead arise in his likeness who is the first fruits of the sleeping, it is clear that this body also, which was in the grave, will be resurrected, made perfect in its members, in the manner that Christ rose again from his own tomb—at that time when he had shown that his spirit was (still) in his body (and) said to all his disciples: "Touch me and see that a ghost does not have flesh and bones as you see that I do" [Luke 24:39]. To Thomas in particular he said, "Put your finger here, and see my hands, and put out your hand, and place it in my side; do not be faithless, but believing" [John 20:27].

[IV.3] Therefore, paying attention to the marvelous works which God has done from the beginning up to today, we also say to the unbelieving what the apostle said in the Acts of the Apostles when he was speaking about the resurrection: "How can I be judged by you when you do not believe that God will raise the dead?" [cf. Acts 23:6]. How fully the divine books testify that these same bodies, which are of the earth, as we believe, are buried (and) will arise faster than a seed!

[IV.4] But if then this saying of the apostle—"This, moreover, I say, brethren, that flesh and blood can not inherit the kingdom of God" [1 Cor. 15:50]—disturbs one of the nonbelievers, we ought carefully to understand that the apostle did not say "they can not rise again," but "they can not inherit." Indeed, that they can not inherit is clear from the two following points, namely, from the corruption in the human body and from perverse acts which man does, as the apostle says, adding: "Nor will the perishable possess the imperishable" [1 Cor. 15:50]. (The apostle means) to make two points especially, namely that unless this perishable flesh first acquire imperishability, it will not be able to possess the kingdom of God, and that flesh is not powerful enough to take on imperishability as long as something (perishable) remains in man because of the foul works which he does; he can not ever possess the kingdom of God, because he is corrupted by his works. Whence Paul also says: "If someone violates the temple of God, God will destroy him" [1 Cor. 3:17]. Therefore, when the whole man is called flesh, indeed (it is meant) in another sense.

[IV.5] Therefore, by this phrase "(we) shall all be changed" [1 Cor. 15:51], we mean this: when indeed "we shall all arise" together, we shall again wear the appropriate aspects of the body, good or bad, according to the way we lived [cf. 2 Cor. 5:10]. "We shall be changed" [1 Cor. 15:52] signifies one thing: that we are perfected in glory and honor, (and) thus pass over strong and powerful so that the body can sustain the splendor of the air since each person will be led to immortality and incorruptibility. "For the trumpet will sound," it says, "and the dead shall arise imperishable" and "we shall be changed" [1 Cor. 15:52]. For this signifies one thing, namely that in whatever manner, those who arise shall be changed by putting on incorruption; thus too, those who are left behind alive shall be changed and become incorruptible. Therefore, we know that we will not receive other bodies for our (present) bodies, but our bodies which were placed in the tomb. Moreover, those who remain alive shall relinquish their bodies; therefore we are able to add (this quotation) and say: "For this perishable nature must put on the imperishable, and this mortal (nature) must put on immortality [1 Cor. 15:53]. When therefore all these things are completed in perfection, then we can say: "Death is swallowed up in victory. O Death, where is your sting?" [1 Cor 15:54].

[IV.6] It is evident that our Lord and Savior Jesus Christ was changed when he was transfigured on the mountain, but nevertheless, he did not assume another body in place of his own body, but when he ascended (the mountain) with his disciples he retained the body that he had from the line of David. "And his face," so says Matthew, "shone like the sun, and his clothing became white as light" [Matt 17:2].

And indeed this happened not only when he was a man; truly, after the resurrection he appeared changed and, on account of this, his disciples believed that they were seeing a ghost and did not know him. Therefore in a similar way, our bodies also are changed by putting on, according to the saying of the apostle, not just some physical body, but a spiritual body [cf. 1 Cor. 15:44]. For it is known through experience that the blessed Paul calls "change" what is simply "difference." This I say according to custom and frequency of experience, because change is another thing entirely, which is used in figures of speech and parables, each (of which) is praised in divine Scriptures, especially in the law when it is said, "The first born of an ass you will exchange (with a) sheep but you will not exchange good for evil" [cf. Exod. 13:13; 34:30].

[IV.7] "He blew breath into his face and he became man" [Gen. 2:7]. And again: "I will lay sinews upon you, and will cause flesh to come upon you, and cover you with skin" [Ezek. 37:6]. Therefore, step by step he formed a creature. Again it is written: "I will give my spirit to you" in order that the glory of the Holy Spirit might show that the bodies of the just are illumined with immortality, incorruptibility, glory, and splendid brilliance. Whence it is fitting that the resurrection not consist of a change of essence, but of a covering brought forth by grace by which, when death and corruption have fled, an eternal length of time is given, with glorious communication in the essence of God.

Therefore, one and the same is the body which is sown in corruption. "What is destroyed and goes to the grave," says Paul, speaking of the hope of resurrection, "rises in imperishability. It is sown in dishonor, it will rise in glory; it is sown in weakness, it will rise in power. It is sown a physical body, it will arise a spiritual body" [1 Cor. 15:42–45]. But if the body which was sown did not rise, but another (body) in its place, so that another body was given to the soul, what wonder would there be in the resurrection? Is the resurrection something, properly speaking, which does not raise that which it has killed, nor arouses that which has been dissolved, nor restores that which has become old?

V. On Easter (Περὶ τοῦ πάσχα)

On Easter. That the Jews Correctly Fixed the Fourteenth Day of the Lunar Month up to the Destruction of Jerusalem. Greek. PG 18:512B–520B.

[V.1] Let us give thanks to God, since his mercy is everywhere great, and because he sent the Spirit of Truth to us to lead us to all truth.

Therefore, the month of the new months was established by law as the beginning of the months and was made known to us as the first of the months of the year. Both the ancient writers who lived before the destruction of Jerusalem and those who lived after have shown that this month has a very clear and evidently fixed period. (That it is fixed) is especially (made clear), since in some places the first fruits are gathered early, while in other places they are gathered late, with the result that sometimes they are gathered before the month and sometimes after—just as it was in the very beginning of the law before the Passover. As it is written: "But the wheat and the rye were not ruined, for they were late (in coming up)" [Exod. 9:32]. Therefore it has been rightfully established by law that after the most proper and suitable songs of praise have been given, from the time of the vernal equinox the Passover is to be celebrated in whatever week the fourteenth day of the first month falls.

For, as it says: "This month shall be for you the first month; it shall be the beginning of the months of the year" [Exod. 12:2], it is written, when the sun in the summertime gives forth a clearer and brighter light, and the days lengthen and become longer, while the nights are contracted and shortened. When the new seeds have come up as flowers they are thoroughly cleared and gathered to the threshing floors and, what is more, all the fruit trees blossom and send forth flowers. Immediately then one discovers that (they send forth) a variety of various and diverse fruits, so that in that same time one finds clusters of grapes, just as the lawgiver says: "It was the days of spring and the first clusters of grapes" [Num. 12:24]. When he sent men to scout out the land, they brought a great cluster of grapes on a litter, and pomegranates and figs too. For then, as they say, our eternal God, the creator and maker of all things, set together all things which he had chosen: "Let the earth put forth vegetation, plants yielding seed according to their kind and likeness, and fruit trees bearing fruit, whose seed according to their kind is upon the earth." And then it adds, "And it was so" [Gen. 1:11–12].

Moreover, he justly and rightfully makes clear that the first month was established by law among the Hebrews, which we know was observed by the Jews until the destruction of Jerusalem. This is so, moreover, because the Jews (themselves) have handed down the tradition. But after the destruction of Jerusalem, through foolishness this practice was mocked. We have received through tradition this practice, lawfully and sincerely observing it.

And on this subject, according to what has been said (in Scripture), saying < . . . > the day of our holy feast, which election has obtained (for us) [cf. Rom. 11:7]. But the rest have become hardened, as Scripture has said.

And after other things.

[V.2] And he has the following things to say: "They will do all things to you because they do not know him who sent me" [John 15:21]. And if they were ignorant of him who sent and him who was sent, there is no doubt that they have been ignorant of the ordinance concerning the Passover. Therefore, not only do they err in their choice of location, but (they err also in reckoning) the beginning of that month which is the first month among the months of the year. On the fourteenth of this month, the ancients celebrated the Passover, which they religiously observed *after* the equinox according to divine command. But the men of today erroneously and through utter carelessness celebrate it *before* the equinox, ignorant of the way they (the ancient Jews) did it every year, as he also witnesses in the scriptures.

Therefore, it does not make any difference to us whether the Jews sometimes celebrate their own Passover in the month of Phamenoth, erroneously (reckoning) according to the course of the moon, or every third year in the month of Pharmuthi according to the intercalary month. For we have no other concern than to keep the remembrance of his passion—and at this very time, as eyewitnesses have handed down from the beginning, before the Egyptians believed. For even now, observing the course of the moon, they do not necessarily celebrate it on the sixteenth of Phamenoth, but once every three years in Pharmuthi. They seem always to have done it in this manner from the beginning and before the advent of Christ. Because of this, [you say,] God censures them through the prophet when he says: "They always err in their hearts. Therefore I swore in my anger that they shall not enter my rest" [Ps. 94:10–11].

Therefore, as you can see, even in this you appear to be lying greatly, not only against men, but also against God. First of all, the Jews never erred in this matter since there were with them from the beginning eyewitnesses and ministers. How much more (sure it is that we have) not (erred) since the coming of Christ! For God does not say they always erred in their hearts concerning the ordinance of the Passover, as you have written, but rather because of all their other disobedience and because of their ugly and evil deeds, seeing that he indeed saw them turning to idolatry and fornication.

And after a few things.

[V.3] Since you have been asleep, it is important concerning this matter—it is very important—to get yourself up and use the cattle prod of Ecclesiasticus, especially recalling to mind where he speaks of "slipping on the pavement, or with the tongue" [Sir. 20:18]. As you can see again, the accusation which you have brought against their leaders has overtaken you, and I suspect that great danger will follow. Don't we hear that the stone which a man has heaved up to a height falls back on his head?

But even more reckless is anyone who dares in this matter to accuse Moses, that great servant of God, or Joshua, the son of Nun, who succeeded him, or those who in succession followed them and ruled—I mean the judges and the kings who appeared or indeed the inspired prophets and furthermore those who among the high priests were blameless, and those who followed who changed nothing but agreed concerning the observance of the Passover and their other feasts at the proper time.

And after other things.

[V.4] Therefore you should have pursued a safer and more reverent course. You should not have recklessly and slanderously written that they from the beginning and always seem to be in error concerning the Passover. You cannot prove this, no matter what things you may speechify against those who are now caught up in error, who have fallen away from the commandment of the law concerning the Passover and other things. For the ancients seem to have kept it after the vernal equinox—which you just by chance might learn from the ancient writings, especially those which the wise Hebrews wrote.

[V.G Exp] Therefore, it has been briefly demonstrated that up to the time of the Lord's passion and at the time of the final destruction of Jerusalem which took place when Vespasian was emperor of the Romans, the people of Israel, correctly observing the fourteenth day of the first lunar month, celebrated the Passover according to the law. Therefore, the holy prophets, and everyone, as I have said, who with them righteously and justly conducted themselves according to the law of the Lord, with the entire people, celebrated a symbolic and shadowy Passover. (The Lord) himself, the Creator and Lord of every unseen and seen creation, the only-begotten Son, the Word coeternal and, with the Father and Holy Spirit, of the same substance (ὁμοούσιος) in divine nature, our Lord and God, Jesus Christ, who at the end of the world was born according to the flesh from our holy and glorious Lady, Mother of God and Ever-Virgin (θεοτόκου καὶ ἀειπαρθένου), truly of Mary the Mother of God (θεοτόκου), who appeared upon the earth and truly lived as a man, with men who were of the same substance (ὁμοούσιος) (as he), according to the nature of man, with the people, in the years before his preaching, and at the time of his preaching, celebrated the legal and shadowy Passover, eating the symbolic lamb. For "I did not come to destroy the law or the prophets, but to fulfill them," the Savior himself said in the Gospels.

After he preached, he did not eat of the lamb, but himself suffered as the true lamb in the paschal feast, as John, the theologian and evangelist says in the Gospel according to John: "Then they led Jesus from the house of Caiaphas to the praetorium. It was early. They themselves did not enter the praetorium, so that they might not be defiled, but might eat the Passover [John 18:28]. And a little later: "When Pilate heard this word, he brought Jesus out and sat down on the judgment seat at a place called the Pavement, and in Hebrew, Gabbatha. Now it was the day of Preparation of the Passover; it was about the third hour" [John 19:13–14]. (This is the way) the correct book has it, and the autograph manuscript itself of the evangelist by the grace of God is preserved to this day in the most holy church of Ephesus and is there revered by the faithful.

Again the same evangelist says: "In order to prevent the bodies from remaining on the cross on the Sabbath—since it was the Day of Preparation, for that Sabbath was a high day—the Jews asked Pilate that their legs might be broken and that they might be taken away" [John 19:13–14]. Therefore, on that day in which the Jews were about to eat the Passover in the evening, our Lord and Savior Jesus Christ was crucified, becoming the victim for those who were going to share, by faith, in the mystery [or: sacrament (μυστήριον)] concerning him, according to what is written by the blessed Paul: "For Christ our Paschal Lamb has been sacrificed for us." Not, as some, swept away by their ignorance, maintain: that when he had eaten the Passover, he was betrayed. We have learned this neither from the holy evangelists, nor have any of the blessed apostles handed it down to us. At that time, therefore, when our Lord and God Jesus Christ suffered for us according to the flesh, he did not eat of the legal Passover but, as I have said, he himself, as the true lamb, was sacrificed for us in the feast of the shadowy Passover, on the day of Preparation, the fourteenth of the lunar month. Furthermore, the symbolic Passover passed away, since the true Passover was (now) present. "For Christ our Passover was sacrificed for us," as has been stated before, and as the apostle Paul, the chosen vessel, teaches.

Canon 15 of the *Canonical Letter*

[V.5] No one shall find fault with us for observing the fourth and sixth days of the week, on which days we are reasonably commanded to fast according to tradition. On the fourth day the Jews made their plans for the betrayal of the Lord; on the sixth he himself suffered for us. But we celebrated the Lord's Day as a day of joy because on this day he rose again. We have received it as a custom not even to bend the knee on this day.

VI. Miscellaneous Fragments

From the "Teaching of Saint Peter of Alexandria." Greek. *PG* 18:521B.

[VI.1] What a wretch I am for not remembering that God pays careful attention to the mind and hears the voice of the soul! I was aware of (my) sin, and said to myself, "God is merciful and will keep his trust in me." And when I was not immediately struck (down), I did not cease (from sinning) but rather despised his forbearance and exhausted the long suffering of God.

Untitled Fragment ("Opus Christianisimi"). Syriac. *AS* 4:194; Latin trans., 4:429 (Pitra IV).

[VI.2] It is properly the work of Christianity to hand down knowledge devoid of errors and to lead those who are perfected by this to the blessed life.

3

The *Canonical Letter*

INTRODUCTION

The *Canonical Letter* is the most important extant work of Saint Peter of Alexandria.[1] It is first attested, although indirectly, by the canons of the Trullan Synod which met at Justinian II's request in 692 at Constantinople. The second canon of that synod states that among the early canons of the church which it accepts are "also the canons of Dionysius who was archbishop of the great city of the Alexandrians and of Peter who was archbishop of Alexandria and (a) martyr."[2]

By the ninth century Peter's canons had been incorporated into the great canon collections of the eastern church. In the *Syntagma Canonum* of Photius, patriarch of Constantinople (c. 810–c. 895), Peter's canons are collected in a chapter "concerning apostates and sacrificers, and magicians and enchanters, and astrologers, soothsayers, and charmers."[3] Peter's canons are preceded by some "apostles' canons" and canons from the sixth ecumenical council, and they are followed by some canons of Basil and Gregory of Nyssa. As far as can be known, the canons, like the

---

1. For the question of the authenticity of the two Coptic homilies attributed to Peter, see chap. 1, 59–64. The *Canonical Letter* is also called the *Canonical Epistle(s)* and *On Penance*. E. Schwartz, "Zur Geschichte des Athanasius," *NGG* (1905) 170, regards the last title as the original one. The text of the canons can be found in A. Mai's 1842 edition of Photius's *Syntagma Canonum: Specilegium Romanum* 7:443–55; Paul Anton de Lagarde, *Reliquiae Iuris Ecclesiastici Antiquissimae* (Leipzig 1856) 63–73 (Greek), 99–117 (Syriac); *RS* 4:21–82; and most conveniently in *PG* 18:467–508. The only English translation heretofore is that done by the Rev. James B. H. Hawkins, ANF 6:255–84.

2. J. Mansi, *Sacrorum Conciliorum Collectio Nova et Amplissima* (Venice 1759) 11:940E. Dionysius's letter to Conon is remarkably similar to Peter's canons in its expression and judgments. For it, see C. L. Feltoe, *St. Dionysius of Alexandria: Letters and Treatises* (London 1918) 60–61; and idem, *DIONYSIOU LEIPSANA: The Letters and Other Remains of Dionysius of Alexandria* (Cambridge 1904) 59ff. (hereafter, *Dionysius: Letters*).

3. Photius's *Syntagma* is collected in A. Mai, *Spicilegium Romanum* 7:75ff. See Mai's preface to the *Syntagma*, viii–xxxii. Peter's canons are on 444–55.

theological fragments, did not survive in Coptic or Arabic; the Arabic collection of canons of the Alexandrian patriarchs includes canons attributed to Athanasius, but nothing to Peter.[4]

Peter's canons, as we have them, are epitomes or excerpts—possibly made at one of the councils—from what must have been a longer work. Unfortunately, what that work was and precisely when it was written cannot be determined for certain. The first canon states that "this is now the fourth Easter under persecution." Since the persecution under Diocletian began during Lent of 303, these canons must have been written in 306, but the text does not make it clear whether they were written before or after Easter.[5] Many scholars, accepting the former, believe that the canons comprise or are part of the Easter letter of 306; others term the *Canonical Letter* an "encyclical" and place it after Easter. Edouard Schwartz prefers to see it as a work entitled *De lapsis*.[6]

Interestingly, a late, and largely hagiographical, work, *An Encomium Proclaimed by Abba Alexander of Alexandria on Saint Peter* (see 78–84) mentions the "catholic epistles" of Saint Peter, which might point to an encyclical letter or letters. However, the *Encomium* could easily reflect a later period when Saint Peter and his writings had been "canonized."[7] At any rate, the *Encomium* does not state what these epistles were.

Given the evidence, it is best to see the *Canonical Letter* as an encyclical on penance. The mention of Easter at the beginning of Canon 1 may point to an Easter letter, but this is not certain: the season is noted by the

4. This may not be as significant as it seems since nor are canons for Peter's episcopal predecessors or immediate successors there. See W. Riedel, *Die Kirchenrechtsquellen des Patriarchats Alexandrien* (Leipzig [1900] repr., 1968).

5. This date enjoys unanimous agreement among modern scholars. See O. Bardenhewer, *Geschichte der altkirchlichen Literatur* (2d ed.; Freiburg 1914) 243; F. H. Kettler, "Petros 1," in *Realencyklopaedie der klassischen Altertumswissenschaft* (1938) 19/2:1281; A. von Harnack, *Geschichte der altchristlichen Literatur* (2d ed.; Leipzig [1893] 1958) 1/1:444; B. Altaner and A. Stuiber, *Patrologie* (Freiburg 1966) 212; Schwartz, "Zur Geschichte," 171; and J. Quasten *Patrology* (repr., Westminster, Md. [1953] 1984) 2:115–16. On the subject of Easter letters at Alexandria, see 105–7 and notes ad loc.

6. Easter letter: J. Lebreton and J. Zeiller, *The History of the Primitive Church* (New York 1948) 2:1046; Quasten 2:115–16; Altaner and Stuiber, 212; G. Fritz, "Pierre d'Alexandrie," *Dictionnaire de théologie catholique* (1935) 12/2:1802; Bardenhewer, *Geschichte* 2:242. Encyclical letter written after Easter: Kettler, "Petros 1," 1281; see also W. H. C. Frend, *Martyrdom and Persecution in the Early Church* (repr., Grand Rapids, Mich. [1965] 1981), 540; Schwartz, "Zur Geschichte," 170–71; and S. L. Greenslade, *Schism in the Early Church* (London 1953) 54. I wish to thank Professor Robert Renehan of the University of California at Santa Barbara for help with the Greek text of the opening sentence of Canon 1.

7. H. Hyvernat (ed.), *Les Actes des martyres de l'Égypte* (Hildesheim 1977) 248. On the slippery use of the term "canon" in the history of Christianity, see R. Grove, "Canon and Community: Authority in the History of Religions" (Ph.D. diss. Univ. California at Santa Barbara, 1983).

bishop as one reason among several for the mitigation of ecclesiastically imposed punishment (see Canon 1, 185). The extant canons do not mention setting the date for Easter, customary in an Easter letter, nor is the festal day mentioned again after the first canon. What is important is that the persecution is continuing into its fourth year.

Given the state of siege under which the *Canonical Letter* must have been written, the most surprising thing about it is its pervasive calm. The letter has little or none of the emotion, zealousness, rancor, and right-eousness of other Christian works written in times of persecution. Martyrdom and apostasy were among the most divisive issues of the ante-Nicene Church, yet there is no polemical spirit here, as there is with the Novatianists and Donatists on the schismatic side, and Eusebius, Cyprian, and Tertullian among the orthodox. If it were not that the fourteen canons impose various punishments for apostasy, one could imagine that one was reading canons from any post-Nicene council when peace had made the persecutions a memory, at least in the official business of the church.

In Peter's letter there is neither a theology of martyrdom nor an eschatological exultation that regards martyrdom as "the highest good,"[8] such as that seen from the Maccabees through Eusebius. What W. H. C. Frend says of Clement applies equally to his fellow Alexandrian Peter: "There is no hatred of the judges, no rejoicing over the fate of the damned and no eschatology in Clement's concept of martyrdom, such as we find in Tertullian (*De spectaculis* 30)."[9]

The question arises: does such an attitude as Peter's represent a culmination in the church's thinking, "in agreement with the course of the Church's development," as Lietzmann believes?[10] It is true that, by

8. See, e.g., (Pseudo-)Cyprian, *De laude martyriis*, ed. Aloysius Hayden (Washington, D.C. 1955), 73. See also Eusebius *Martyrs of Palestine*, in *The Ecclesiastical History and The Martyrs of Palestine*, ed. H. J. Lawlor and J. E. L. Oulton (London 1928); and Ignatius of Antioch's letters for a telling comparison. Cyprian Ep. 58.3 offers a vivid contrast: "The Lord wished us to rejoice and to exult in persecutions since, when persecutions are carried on, then crowns of faith are given; then the soldiers of God are tested; then the heavens lie open to the martyrs." *Letters of St. Cyprian*, trans. Sister Rose Bernard Donna, C.S.J. (Washington, D.C. 1965). All translations from Cyprian's epistles and Eusebius's *The Martyrs of Palestine* are taken from these editions.

9. Frend, *Martyrdom*, 357. T. D. Barnes, however, in *Tertullian: A Historical and Literary Study* (Oxford 1971), 170, does not have a high opinion of Peter's attitude; for Barnes, Peter "equated apostasy with sacrifice and argued that any Christian who had not himself sacrificed and who had not compelled his Christian slaves to sacrifice in his stead had acted impeccably. Accordingly, he imposed penitential discipline on those who had succumbed, and wrote a theological justification of those who had evaded the issue."

10. Hans Lietzmann, *A History of the Early Church* (Cleveland 1961) 3:104–5.

the time of the Great Persecution, the episcopal right to forgive even the worst of sins—apostasy and murder—and thereby set appropriate penance had been firmly established for more than fifty years.[11] Peter's canons are well within the tradition of the church's developing penitential system.[12]

Given this it would be convenient to see Peter as the "good moderate" who steered a middle course between rigorism and laxity, and who just before the "peace of the church" wrote a kind of *Summa* on apostasy and penance: "he had put an end, in good catholic fashion, to the radicalism of the primitive church, and to the privileges claimed by and granted to Confessors as men of special spiritual quality."[13] Peter, however, did not end that "radicalism," for his canons explicitly exclude fallen priests from full forgiveness (that is, they could return to communion, but could no longer exercise their priestly functions). Also, the fact that the Melitians continued well into Athanasius's time shows that Peter did not end the power of the confessors.[14]

The simple truth is that it is very difficult to place Peter within a straight line of development on the question of apostasy and penance. There are too many gaps in our knowledge to do this, and what evidence we do have is sometimes conflicting. Much has to be argued from silence. For example, Peter makes no mention of *traditio*, the handing over of sacred books by the clergy to the civil authorities, which Frend finds "astonishing."[15] Nor does he mention forgiveness in extremis, an issue in the writings of both Cyprian and Dionysius. Can we infer from

11. As J. N. D. Kelly, *Early Christian Doctrines* (London 1977) 216, has remarked: "With the dawn of the third century the rough outlines of a recognized penitential discipline were beginning to take shape. . . . The system which seems to have existed in the Church at this time, and for centuries afterwards, was wholly public, involving confession, a period of penance and exclusion from communion, a formal absolution and restoration—the whole process being called *exomologesis*." For a brief survey of the third century, see ibid., 216–19.

12. See William Telfer, *Forgiveness of Sins* (London 1969) 67; and Frend, *Martyrdom*, 416. Karl Baus, *Handbook of Church History* (New York 1965) 1:345, therefore is not accurate when he says that Peter's canons "show no real development in penitential practice since Origen." For Origen, see 162–63 below. This chapter cannot deal with two crucial, and very complex, issues in church history: the rise of the episcopate, and the development of a penitential system. For the first, one should consult the works in the bibliography by or on Cyprian. For the second, W. Telfer's brief discussion, *Forgiveness of Sins*, is a good introduction. See also W. H. C. Frend, *The Donatist Church* (Oxford 1952) 133ff. For a discussion of the Great Persecution, see N. H. Baynes, "The Great Persecution," chap. 19 in *Cambridge Ancient History* (Cambridge 1971) 12:646–91.

13. Lietzmann 3:104–5. For a discussion of rigorism and lenience, see Frend, *Martyrdom*, 415–29.

14. See chap. 1, 33–34, for a discussion of the *Canonical Letter* and Melitianism.

15. Frend, *Donatist Church*, 22–23. See Frend, *Martyrdom*, 624, s.v. "traditor" for references.

Peter's silence that these were no longer issues in Alexandria at the turn of the fourth century? If we say yes, then we are faced with another question: did Peter cause this silence, or does this reflect decisions made by previous bishops? It is very difficult to say.

There can be no doubt that Peter in many ways is more moderate than Cyprian or even Dionysius,[16] but one cannot say that he moderated their positions, since no evidence exists to show any direct link between the works on penance by those bishops with Peter's *Canonical Letter* (which points up the paucity of our information; Dionysius had held the episcopacy at Alexandria only a half century before Peter). Similarly a study of the canons of Nicea shows that Peter's canons probably had no direct influence upon that council.[17] Therefore both Lietzmann's statement quoted above and the belief that "the decisions and directions given by St. Peter were inspired by the same spirit as those of St. Dionysius, St. Cyprian and St. Cornelius" must be looked at more closely.[18]

Eusebius says (*HE* 6.43.2) that a synod was held in Rome to discuss the question of rigorism and leniency, "while in the rest of the provinces the pastors ($\pi o\iota\mu\acute{\epsilon}\nu\omega\nu$) in their several regions individually considered the questions as to what was to be done." This seems to have been the case at Alexandria as well. However that may be, it is nevertheless profitable to view Saint Peter within the context of the persecutions and how the church responded to those who apostatized. Peter's *Canonical Letter* and Cyprian's *De lapsis* and epistles are our major surviving documents, along with the fragmentary letters of Dionysius of Alexandria.

Here I discuss the question of apostasy and penance in the works of these three bishops (with a brief glance at Origen). I conclude with a discussion of the canons of the councils of Elvira, Ancyra, and Nicea since the latter two councils close the discussion of apostasy and penance. An annotated translation of the *Canonical Letter* then follows.

There is no modern annotated edition of Saint Peter's canons, and they have received little scholarly attention.[19] M. J. Routh in 1846 published the canons with a brief commentary in Latin. Edouard Schwartz in 1904 discussed them at length in his work on Athanasius.[20]

16. See Schwartz, "Zur Geschichte," 172, who says that Peter's canons are milder.
17. See 179–80 below.
18. Lebreton and Zeiler 2:1046.
19. Henri Gregoire, *Les persécutions dans l'empire romain* (Brussels 1950); and J. Moreau, *La persécution du Christianisme dans l'empire romain* (Paris 1956), mention neither Paris nor his canons. Frend, *Martyrdom*, mentions Peter briefly several times and, in a footnote, his canons.
20. *RS* 4:19–82; Schwartz, "Zur Geschichte," 164ff. W. Bright, "Petrus I., St.," in *DCB* 4:331–34, gives a summary of the canons.

The following table provides a brief summary of the canons:[21]

TABLE 3

Canon	Description	Penance
1	those who lapsed after torture	3 years (already served) + 40 days more
2	those who lapsed without torture (but were imprisoned)	3 years (already served) + 1 year
3	those who lapsed without torture or imprisonment	3 (or 4) years
4	those who lapsed and are unrepentant	they are cursed
5	dissembled: did not sacrifice but instead sent non-Christian slaves, or used some other ruse	6 months
6	Christian slaves who sacrificed	1 year
7	masters of Christian slaves who dissembled and forced their slaves to sacrifice for them	3 years
8	lapsed, but then repented and confessed the faith	none; accepted into communion
9	zealots who gave themselves up voluntarily (no mention of lapse)	rebukes them; accepted into full communion
10	clergy who fell but later "took up the struggle" (zealots?)	removed from office, but accepted into Christian fellowship
11	approves of confessors' (even if zealots) prayers for the fallen	
12	gave money to avoid sacrificing	none
13	gave up property and withdrew	none
14	those who lapsed under torture and who have witnesses	none; regarded as confessors

During the Decian and Diocletianic persecutions, a Christian could lapse in two ways: sacrificing (*sacrificatio*), which included offering incense (*turificatio*) or eating food offered to idols; or by handing over sacred books or vessels to the authorities (*traditio*). As G. M. de Ste. Croix has pointed out with regard to Peter's canons:

> Although the nature of the act constituting the lapse is seldom specified, it is obviously assumed throughout the document to be something in the nature of sacrificing, offering incense, or partaking of food previously offered to idols; there is no reference whatever to *traditio*, direct or indirect.[22]

21. For other summaries see Bright, "Petros I.," 331–34; and Schwartz, "Zur Geschichte," 170ff.

22. Geoffrey de Ste. Croix, "Aspects of the 'Great' Persecution," *HTR* 47 (1954) 75ff. Eating foods offered to idols is forbidden in the "apostolic decrees" of Acts 15:29 (but see Paul in 1 Cor. 8:1–6).

Ste. Croix's observation raises the important question why *traditio* is not mentioned by Peter. There are two possible answers: (1) *traditio* was not an issue in Alexandria in 306, or (2) mention of *traditio* has fallen out of the extant canons. While the first choice is more likely, I offer this second possibility as a caution.

A quick glance at the canons shows that they are not of a piece. Canons 1–4 seem to go together in a logical fashion; each succeeding canon orders a longer penance. Canons 5–7, grouped around the theme of dissembling, also go together, but 8–14 show no distinct order (although canons 8 and 9 belong together). Canon 15 has been tacked on the manuscript; canons 12 and 13 go better with 5–7; canon 8 would go better with canon 4, as would 14.

Thematically, then, the canons are somewhat of a jumble. In addition, the Greek of the canons is in some places abominable; the text reads like an epitome and seems to be a patchwork: Greek that one would expect an Alexandrian bishop to write alternates with an execrable idiom. Given this situation, it seems likely that we do not possess the complete text of Peter's canons; the Syriac fragments published by Lagarde (and absent from the Greek text) would seem to confirm this.[23]

However, what we do have shows some very clear positions on Peter's part. During the persecutions, Christians had three options: they could conform (i.e., sacrifice); they could flee; they could stay, resist, and face the consequences. Peter's canons deal with all three of these situations. The first he condemns, the second he approves, and the third he has varying opinions on.

For those who sacrificed and fell, Peter orders varying periods of penance, depending on the nature of the fall. J. Quasten has pointed out that "in none of the canons is the reconciliation postponed to the day of death, as it had been previously."[24] This is true, except for those who lapsed and are unrepentant and who receive no specific punishment (i.e., excommunication) because, it is assumed, they have excommunicated themselves.

Peter clearly approves of flight from persecution. This attitude has drawn the opprobrium of at least one scholar, but it is within the precedent set by Cyprian and Dionysius.[25] It is only natural that if Peter

---

23. If one accepts Schwartz's verdict on the Syriac text, then this is a certainty. See Schwartz, "Zur Geschichte," 164ff., and see appendix 2 for a translation of the Syriac fragments (from Schwartz's Greek retroversion).

24. Quasten 2:116. Compare Dionysius's letter to Fabius.

25. T. D. Barnes, *Tertullian*, 171 n. 6, traces Peter's views to Clement of Alexandria

could approve of flight, he could approve also of "stationary flight," that is, dissembling. As T. D. Barnes has observed, Peter "equated apostasy with sacrifice";[26] he approved of any method to avoid sacrificing—except the use of Christian slaves. He looks upon the use of "brother slaves" severely (Canon 7), equating masters who do this to those who apostatized without torture or imprisonment (Canon 3). However, none of Peter's punishments is as severe as those given before and after him.

Although Peter rebukes the zealots who voluntarily gave themselves up, he accepts them into full communion (Canons 9 and 11). He even restores to full communion those who fell but then repented and confessed the faith (Canon 8). The bishop is severe only with clergy who lapsed (Canon 10); he removes them from office, but does accept them into "Christian fellowship (κοινωνία)."

How do these positions differ from or agree with those of Cyprian, Origen, and Dionysius? Is there a tradition, or is Peter acting independently? In what follows I try to answer these questions and place Peter within the larger context of Alexandrian and church attitudes of the third and fourth centuries on apostasy and penance.

SAINT CYPRIAN AND SAINT PETER

In Ep. 55.6–7 Cyprian states that each of the *lapsi* "should be examined according to what is contained in the treatise which, I trust, has come to you, in which separate headings of our decisions are drawn up."[27] This treatise is, unfortunately, lost. It may well have been an encyclical much like Peter's *Canonical Letter*. Since we are without it, Cyprian's decisions must be gathered from his extant correspondence and his treatise *De lapsis*. In general, these are his views:[28]

1. "Peace," that is, fellowship and communion, is not to be given to the lapsed without repentance.

2. He emphasizes the authority of the church, the bishop, and the council of clergy.

(*Strom.* 4.76.1ff.) and says this "brings Clement close to the views of Basilides and Heracleon." See 200 and n. 4 below.

26. Barnes, *Tertullian*, 170.

27. The Latin text may be found in Le Chanoine Bayard (ed.), *Saint Cyprien, Correspondance*, 2 vols. (Paris 1961).

28. See Epistles 55.6–7, 57, 64, and 67. For a thorough discussion of Cyprian and the Decian persecution, see Michael M. Sage, *Cyprian* (Philadelphia 1975), esp. chap. 4 (165–265). For Cyprian and penance, see K. Rahner, "Die Busslehre des hl. Cyprian von Karthago," *Zeitschrift für Katholische Theologie* 74 (1952) 257–76, 381–438; see also H. Koch, "Die Bussfrage bei Cyprian," chap. 6 in *Cyprianische Untersuchungen* (Bonn 1926) 211–285.

3. The case of each of the lapsi should be examined and, after appropriate penance, they should be reinstated to fellowship.

4. Those who flee should not die without peace.

5. The clergy are to be spotless, and fallen clergy are to be defrocked.

The Necessity for Repentance

Cyprian regarded the lapsed as "dead" who, he hopes, "may be brought back to life" (Ep. 33.1); they are in "a state of ritual sin."[29] But if this attitude seems harsh, Cyprian did not adopt his master Tertullian's position that the fallen were beyond forgiveness.[30] He divided the lapsed into two categories, those who had received certificates (*libellatici*), and those who had sacrificed (*sacrificati*):

It seemed fitting . . . when the cases of each had been examined, for those who had received the certificates to be admitted meanwhile (libellaticos interim admitti), [and] for those who had sacrificed to be received at death (sacrificatis in exitu subveniri). (Ep. 55.17)[31]

When it came to working out conditions of penance on a pastoral level, Cyprian showed an ability to discern differences among the various cases brought to his attention. Once the bishops were granted (or assumed) the power to forgive sins, this ability to make distinctions among sinners marks the beginning of a penitential system supervised by the episcopacy.

Cyprian always insisted on repentance and a time of penance. In Ep. 36.3 he strikes a note that Peter will sound later with very similar language in his first canon:

It is time, therefore, that they should do penance for the sin, that they should show reserve, that they should manifest humility, that they should demonstrate modesty, that they should arouse the clemency of God toward themselves by their submission, and that they should draw divine mercy upon themselves by due honor to the bishop of God.[32]

As a penitent, "you must beg and pray assiduously, spend the day sorrowing and the night in vigils and tears, fill every moment with

29. Frend, *Martyrdom*, 418. Cf. Cyprian *De lapsis* 34 and *De ecclesiae catholicae unitate* 23; both are in the edition of Maurice Bévenot, S.J. (Oxford 1971) 50–51, 92–95.

30. P. B. Hinchliff, *Cyprian of Carthage and the Unity of the Christian Church* (London 1974) 65.

31. As far as I know, Cyprian does not mention *traditores*. Nor does Peter, and one can plausibly assume that it was not regarded as a form of apostasy. See Frend, *Martyrdom*, 624, s.v. "traditor," and canons 13 and 14 of the Council of Arles. For the *libellatici* and *sacrificati*, see Sage, 200, 263, and 263 n. 1. See also the commentary on Canon 5 n. 2, 197 below.

32. Although the tone of Cyprian's Ep. 36.3 and Peter's Canon 1 are very similar, there is no mention by Peter of episcopal authority. He probably takes it for granted.

weeping and lamentation; you must lie on the ground amidst clinging ashes, toss about chaffing in sackcloth and foulness" (*De lapsis* 35).

Even if a certain amount of this severity is attributed to rhetoric, one comes away from reading Cyprian with the feeling that the duties of a penitent were rigorous—and long. In Peter's day too the penitents had their duties: "And during these days through hard spiritual exercise and keener vigilance they will turn an alert mind to prayer and to profound study of what was said by the Lord. . . .'You shall worship the Lord your God and him only shall you serve' [Matt. 4:10]" (Canon 1).

Both Cyprian and Peter spend a great deal of time dealing with the fallen and repentant. They are curt with the unrepentant: these are cursed like the fig tree, and the prophet Isaiah has prophesied concerning them, "their worm shall not die, their fire shall not be quenched" (Is. 66:24 [LXX]). The passage just quoted is from Peter (Canon 4), but it could just as well have come from Cyprian. In *De lapsis* 30–34, Cyprian inveighs against the unrepentant and in chapters 22–26 relates, in gruesome detail, the sufferings that will come to those who do not confess their sin. In Ep. 55.23, he bluntly states his position: "We have decreed that those who do not do penance and testify to sorrow for their sins with their whole heart and with a manifest profession of their lamentation must be completely cut off from the hope of communion and peace."

Cyprian saw a fundamental connection between the communion of fellowship and the eucharistic communion with Christ. For the bishop of Carthage, then, a penitential system was closely related to sacrament and liturgy. Lapsed Christians who claimed communion without doing penance "do violence to His body and blood, and sin more heinously against the Lord with their hands and mouths than when they denied Him."[33] In Canon 8 Peter also equates *koinonia*, fellowship, with the eucharistic body and blood of Christ (see 188 below).

The Authority of the Church

Both Cyprian and Peter insist that forgiveness can come only through proper ecclesiastical channels.[34] Cyprian says that authority rests with the church, the bishop, and the council of clergy. Although Peter makes

---

33. See Kelly, *Doctrines*, 211–12. See also Cyprian *De lapsis* 16 and Ep. 15.1.

34. Bévenot notes (viii) concerning the *De lapsis* that "this address presupposes a background of custom in dealing with serious public sins, such as murder, adultery and apostasy. . . . The fierceness of the persecution of Decius had, however, caused so many to 'lapse' that it was difficult to decide how the customary process could be followed." See Telfer, *Forgiveness*, 40–41, for the Roman church's attitudes toward repentance.

no such explicit statement, he assumes what Cyprian is forced to defend.[35]

Both Peter and Cyprian had to face the question of whether "martyrs" or "confessors of the faith" (see appendix 5, 216–19 for a discussion of these terms) could in any way forgive the sins of the lapsed and mitigate their punishments. Cyprian's Epistle 21 shows that some in Carthage were urging that the lapsed be received back because of the intercession of the martyrs. Cyprian dealt with this in two ways. He downgraded the virtue of confessing, and then denied that those who had confessed had thereby gained any authority: "Let not anyone say: 'He who receives martyrdom is baptized in his own blood and no peace from the bishop is necessary to him. . . .' He who is not armed for the battle by the Church cannot be fit for martyrdom" (Ep. 57.4).[36]

A certain Lucian claimed to have had a special dispensation from Paul "the blessed martyr" (not the apostle) while he "was still in the body" to forgive (da pacem) anyone who requested it (Ep. 22.2).[37] Epistle 23 is addressed to Cyprian by others like Lucian, by "all the confessors," who "have given peace to those whose record of what they have done after the transgression was *agreeable*" to Cyprian (emphasis added). In Epistle 26 Cyprian denies them the right to do this until he can call an assembly "to examine the case" of each lapsed. In Epistle 27 he says the actions of the confessors are subterfuge and should be "opposed as much as possible."

Cyprian states in Epistle 15 that peace can be given to the lapsed only (1) when the persecution is over, (2) an assembly of clergy tries the cases, (3) penance is done, and (4) hands have been imposed by a bishop and priest. This passage is very interesting with respect to Peter's canons

35. In Ep. 14.4 Cyprian insists, as often elsewhere, that he does nothing without his clergy's advice and the consent of the people. In Ep. 33.1, he cites Matt. 16:18–19 on the primacy of Peter to emphasize that "the Church is established upon the bishops and every action of the Church is governed through these same prelates."

36. In *De lapsis* 17 Cyprian seems to accede to the martyrs, but then postpones their authority to the heavenly kingdom. Authority deferred to heaven is no authority at all. Cyprian says, "We do not call in question the power which the merits of the martyrs and the works of the just have with the Judge, but that will be when the day of judgement comes." In *De lapsis* 3 "confessing" is equated with *not* apostatizing: "Once the period prescribed for apostasizing had passed, whoever had failed to declare himself (professus) within the time, thereby confessed (confessus est) that he was a Christian." See also the commentary on Canon 5 n. 5, 199.

37. Cyprian denies Lucian's right to grant petitions "indiscriminately" to all comers, but interestingly says that "Mappalicus, the martyr, cautious and modest, mindful of the law and of discipline [i.e., mindful of the bishop?], wrote no letter contrary to the Gospel but, moved only by filial piety, he requested that peace be given to his mother and to his sister who had lapsed" (Epistle 27).

because the bishop of Alexandria deals with only the third condition. He does not defer forgiveness (or the imposition of penance) until after the persecution is over; he makes no mention of an assembly of clergy; he does not mention the imposition of hands, although it may be assumed that this was done after the appropriate penance had been fulfilled. It is interesting that Cyprian in his letters refers to the first two conditions as means by which he can assert episcopal authority. Peter feels no need to do this and clearly feels that he has no need of an assembly and does not have to wait for peace.

Both Peter and Cyprian have to deal with those lapsi who have been aided by the martyrs. In Ep. 19.2 Cyprian summarizes his position as to when they may be received in peace: (1) they must be ill or in danger; only then (2) after they make confession and (3) hands are imposed upon them by authorized clergy, (3) may they be restored to the Lord.[38]

Although Peter is much briefer and does not deal with the question of deathbed forgiveness or the necessity of the laying on of hands, he retains the same attitude as Cyprian: the bishop is the only one who has the right to forgive sins and set penance. In Canon 5 he deals with those who have been forgiven by confessors, and asserts his authority:

> Certain ones of those who confessed the faith, as I have heard, have forgiven them since, above all, with great piety they have avoided lighting the sacrificial fire with their own hands and have avoided the smoke rising from the unclean demons, and since indeed they were unaware, because of their thoughtlessness, of what they were doing. Nevertheless, six months of penance will be given to them.[39]

Individual Cases

Peter and Cyprian agree that the bishop is the final authority (at least on earth) in judging the lapsed and imposing penance. Each bishop

---

38. See Sage, 214. In Ep. 18.1 Cyprian states that the lapsed "who have received petitions from the martyrs and may be helped by their prerogative, if they should be seized with any injury and danger of illness when our presence is not expected, may make confession of their sin before whatever priest may be present or, if a priest has not been found and death begins to be imminent, before even a deacon that they may come to the Lord when hands have been imposed upon them in penance with the peace which, in letters sent to us, the martyrs have desired to be given." For Cyprian's struggles with confessors and clergy who opposed him, see Sage, 211ff.

39. In Canon 11 Peter approved "prayers and petitions" (δεήσεις) on behalf of the fallen and says that "because of the faith of others some have had the benefit of God's goodness in the forgiveness of sins, in the health of their bodies, and in the resurrection of the dead." "The forgiveness of sins" might imply that acts of the confessors are involved, but nothing else in the canon points to a conclusion that Peter has the confessors' actions in mind.

believes that the lapsed should be treated individually, and that no one, except the unrepentant, is to be excluded from forgiveness.[40] Cyprian does not set forth a detailed system of penance; there is no discussion of crime and punishment. He remains vague about the length of penance and does not have a system in mind such as Peter's and such as developed later in the church.[41] Perhaps his lost treatise resembled Peter's canons, but since none of his extant works indicates this, it must remain a question whether it was anything as detailed as Peter's *Canonical Letter*.

In general, Peter considers three kinds of lapse: (1) those who lapsed without torture or imprisonment (this includes those who sent Christian slaves to sacrifice for them), (2) those who lapsed after torture or imprisonment, and (3) those who lapsed but then confessed the faith. The first of these is the worst and earns three to four years of penance, while the second receives a milder sentence and the third no penance at all. A comparison of Peter's canons to Cyprian's statements is fruitful in exploring whether such a system as Peter's and that of the later church exists, either explicitly or implicitly, in the thinking of the bishop of Carthage.

In *De lapsis* 8 Cyprian speaks of those who voluntarily sacrificed, who "did not even wait to be arrested." They "were defeated before the battle was joined, they collapsed without any encounter, thus even depriving themselves of the plea that they had sacrificed to the idols against their will." Peter, in Canon 3, speaks of those who "of their own free will . . . have gone over to evil [i.e., apostasy], betrayed by cowardice and fear."

---

40. See Ep. 8.3 and 55.13. Epistle 55.13 has a statement which bears witness to bizarre practices: "If there are any who are stricken with infirmities, assistance is given to them in danger as it has been decided. Yet after they have been aided and peace has been given to them in danger, they cannot be suffocated by us, or destroyed by force, or be urged forward at our hands to the departure of death, as if, because peace is given to the dying, it is necessary for those who have received peace to die." The question of death-bed repentance appears again in Dionysius's writings, but not in Peter's. It is clear that the practice was common in Cyprian and Dionysius's times. It is not clear whether punishment was always assigned to the lapsed *until* just before their death, or whether those who had need of forgiveness in extremis had taken sick *before their time of penance was up*. It is also unclear whether Peter did away with the practice. Cyprian allowed penance to last until just before death; therefore he had to deal with deathbed forgiveness; see Ep. 55.13. On the other hand, Peter did not impose punishments that were to last until the point of death. He imposed set sentences and, since the longest was three or four years, few people had to worry about dying unforgiven. That some did face that situation must not be doubted, and Peter certainly had to deal with the problem later.

41. See Basil's epistle to Amphilochius (Ep. 199.22); and Gregory Thaumaturgus "Canonical Letter" 11 (*PG* 10:1048), given in n. 128 below.

The bishop of Alexandria punished these lapsi with three years of penance, as he did those who sent their Christian slaves to sacrifice in their stead. This is his harshest judgment in the canons; nevertheless, he has no particularly harsh words for these people, unlike Cyprian who in *De lapsis* 8 equates the altar where the apostates sacrificed with their funeral pyre:

> Poor fellow . . . you yourself are the offering and the victim come to the altar; there you have slain your hope of salvation, there in those fatal fires you have reduced your faith to ashes.

Although Cyprian regards such apostasy as evil, in *De lapsis* 9 and 10 he considers those who encouraged others to apostatize and those who apostatized to save their property as worse than those who did so out of cowardice. Given Cyprian's attitude toward property, it is not surprising that he, like Peter (see Canons 12 and 13), does not condemn those who used any means possible (e.g., flight or the purchase of *libelli*) to avoid sacrificing. Although in Ep. 20.2 Cyprian seems to equate the purchase of certificates with actual sacrificing, the weight of his testimony shows that he did not regard them as equal.[42] In Ep. 55.14 he says that it shows a "lack of mercy" and "bitter hardness" to equate libellatici with sacrificati, for the former have given a bribe to avoid doing what is not lawful.[43] Although the person has "sinned" and has been beguiled, it is "not so much by sin as by error," and "he gives testimony that he is now instructed and prepared for the future."

The libellatici, in Cyprian's thought, seem to have occupied a middle position between those who sacrificed and those who fled (see 157–59 below for a discussion of the latter). They had in a sense sacrificed, but had not performed actual *sacrificatio*, and therefore had not sinned (or sinned as badly) as the sacrificati. This is an important distinction, and Peter held much the same belief.

---

42. However, in *De lapsis* 27 Cyprian says that "a certificate is itself a confession of apostasy, it is a testimonial that the Christian has renounced what he was." Bévenot (viii) dates the *De lapsis* to 251, and if Epistle 55 is dated to late 251 or 252 (see *St. Cyprian, Letters,* 134; and Sage, 370), then Cyprian may have changed his mind. Ste. Croix, "Aspects," 87 n. 58, believes that Cyprian regarded libellatici as less sinful than adulterers; see Ep. 55.26.1. In Ep. 55.13 Cyprian says that "those with certificates" ought not to be considered "in the same category with those who have sacrificed."

43. Peter reaches the same conclusion in Canon 12: "No accusation is to be brought against those who gave money in order to remain completely undisturbed by any evil. In order not to damage or destroy their souls they have borne a fine and loss of property which others, because of shameful greed, have not done." Acts of "dissembling" such as Peter speaks of in Canon 5 are given verification by the papyri. See the commentary on Canon 5 n. 3, 199.

In Peter's thought those who dissembled (Canons 5–7; there are no libellatici, as Cyprian understood the term) by sending slaves have in a sense apostatized and will do three-years of penance with other apostates. However, their offense does not seem as grievous. Those who gave up money or property (Canons 12 and 13) did so correctly, are not apostates, and will do no penance—the same judgment which is given to those who fled. Although in the thinking of both bishops these dissemblers in a sense fell, their fall is excusable, or at least more excusable than those who apostatized. They "fell" without undergoing torture or imprisonment; therefore both Peter and Cyprian reckon them among the apostates. Yet at the same time both bishops regard them as a special case, and therefore either regard their offense as less serious, or mitigate their punishment, or both.

Both bishops were also willing to look with mercy upon those who had lapsed under torture or imprisonment.[44] In *De lapsis* 13 Cyprian deals with the question of those who fell under torture and those who, having fallen, returned to the struggle (cf. Canon 8). He says that a plea of torture "may truly avail for forgiveness, such a defense deserves our pity." He then goes on to tell the story of Castus and Aemilius who, "having been worsted in the first engagement [i.e., under torture]. . . . were pardoned by the Lord" and were made "victors in the second."

The context here might suggest that their "pardon" by the Lord consisted of receiving strength to do battle again and that it was not unconditional forgiveness—in other words, they had to do battle again in order to receive pardon. However, Cyprian's views in his letters indicate that he held a more lenient position. In Epistle 25 he approves of Bishop Caldonius's actions in forgiving a certain Bona "who was dragged by her husband to sacrifice, who did not pollute her conscience":

> Since, therefore, they have washed away all sin and wiped out the first stain by their later virtue, with the assistance of the Lord, they who, banished and despoiled of all their goods, have redeemed themselves. (Epistle 24, Caldonius to Cyprian)

Bona had her hands held by the authorities and, like Castus and Aemilia, was forced to sacrifice; her circumstances are exactly like those of the people in Canon 14 who "have suffered great violence and torture, and have had chains put in their mouths; through the working of their faith they have steadfastly endured having their hands burned when

44. For Cyprian's list of tortures, see *De lapsis* 13–14.

they were forced, against their will, to offer unholy sacrifice." Peter goes on to say in Canon 14 that those who "were mortified through many tortures . . . may be placed in the ministry among those who confessed the faith." Cyprian agrees: "that peace which they had regained for themselves by true penance and the glory of the confession of the Lord ought to be bestowed upon our brethren" (Epistle 25).

It must be noted that Cyprian, although he grants peace to the lapsi, still requires them to do penance. In Canon 14 Peter does not, but he, unlike Cyprian, makes a distinction for those who lapsed under torture: there are two kinds—those who were forced to eat and drink the sacrificial offerings (that is, had them forced down their throats), and those who voluntarily ate and drank (but under duress). The former he absolves in Canon 14; the latter he gives penance to (in Canon 1), but clearly views their guilt as less because of the tortures they have endured.

Cyprian and Peter agree completely that those who have fallen under torture have indeed lapsed and, although they must do penance, it will not be as severe as for others, because their crime was not as bad. As Cyprian states in Epistle 52:

> For since it was decided in Council that those doing penance should be aided in the danger of sickness and peace given to them, assuredly, they ought to precede in receiving peace who, we see, did not fall through weakness of soul but, assembled in battle and wounded, were not able to endure to the end the crown of their confession through the weakness of the flesh, especially since it was not permitted to those who desired to die to be killed, but for so long a time, tortures lacerated weary men as they [the persecutors] conquered, not their faith which is invincible, but they wore out their flesh which is weak.

Peter, however, takes Cyprian's attitude a step further and declares (in Canon 14) that those who were forced to sacrifice had in reality not sacrificed.

In Canon 1 Peter agrees with Cyprian that the flesh is weak and that those who lapsed because of its weakness should not be unduly punished:

> There are those who, after they were reported to the authorities and were imprisoned, at first endured intolerable tortures and unbearable whippings and many other terrible hardships but who were later betrayed by the weakness of the flesh. It is true that in the beginning they were not received back into the church because of their great fall; nevertheless, they have gone through many struggles and have fought long and hard. To this, one should add that they have not come to their present condition by choice,

but because they were betrayed by the weakness of the flesh, and that some of them now show on their bodies the marks of Jesus.

Epistle 56.1 of Cyprian offers an almost exact parallel to Peter's first canon:

[Three men confessed the faith.] Afterward, when they were tortured before the proconsul with excruciating torments, they were overcome by the force of the torments and through the continued tortures, fell. . . . Yet, after this grave lapse, brought about not through their free will but by compulsion, they have not ceased from doing penance throughout these three years.

This idea of the sufficiency of penance performed de facto (that is, by "doing time" in prison or exiled from the church) rather than de jure (that is, imposed by the bishop) occurs in Canon 1 also, and, interestingly, the period of "penance" there is also three years:

because they have spent three years in grievous mourning and we have just celebrated our fourth Easter still under persecution, it is indeed sufficient that from the time of their presenting themselves to the church another forty days of forced absence be added as penance.

This *sufficit* of Peter amounts to an amnesty, one which Cyprian also grants:

Yet we ought not to close to them the opportunity for pardon and deprive them of the love of their Father and of communion with us. For them we think that it can suffice to beg the clemency of the Lord because for three years continually and sorrowfully . . . they have lamented with the greatest sorrow of penance (Ep. 56.2).

It is tempting to suggest that Peter is dependent on Cyprian for his views, but that is unlikely. The language is remarkably similar, but that alone does not suffice to establish a connection between the two bishops. Nevertheless, there are great similarities between Canon 1 and Epistle 56. These two bishops, although separated by time, distance, and language, held virtually identical views toward those who lapsed under torture.

As is clear from the discussion above, Cyprian was lenient both to those who lapsed under torture and to those who fell but later redeemed themselves. In Ep. 56.2 the bishop of Carthage talks about readying the lapsed for battle again. In Ep. 8.3 the Roman clergy urge the clergy of Carthage to encourage the fallen, that they "may confess, if they should be taken again, in order that they may be able to correct their former error." This idea of *priorem errorem corrigere* was held in Africa as well as at Rome. Caldonius, a bishop and confessor, reports to Cyprian in Epistle 24 that some who had sacrificed, "when they were tried a second time, became exiles. They seem, therefore, to me to have wiped out their previous sin since they are losing their possessions and homes and, doing penance, are following Christ."

It is not clear here whether the penance Caldonius speaks of was an officially imposed one or whether it was de facto, as in Canon 1 and Epistle 56. It seems likely that it was the latter and that there was here a kind of "substitutionary penance"; that is, one suffers through exile and loss of property, and such suffering is counted as time "served" in penance. It is also important to note here that a lapsed person could confess the faith—and therefore be forgiven—*by means other than martyrdom* (in the modern sense of the word; see appendix 5). To Caldonius, deprivation of property and banishment was "martyrdom" or "confession."

Caldonius thus stood opposed to the Novatianists and to Tertullian who saw the lapse of an apostate as irremediable.[45] However, he had on his side the Roman clergy, Cyprian, and later, Peter. Cyprian in Epistle 25 fully agrees with Caldonius and does not regard his actions as "rash." In that letter he concludes that these lapsed "have redeemed themselves and have begun to stand with Christ[; they] ought not to lie any longer, as it were, prostrate under the devil."

Peter, like Caldonius, urges that the faithful, "with a joyful heart, join together in supporting" the fallen:

> We do this so that if they contend more vigorously, they too may be considered worthy "of the prize of the upward call." For "a righteous man falls seven times and rises again"; if all those who had fallen had done this, they would have demonstrated with their whole heart a most perfect repentance (Canon 8).

It is clear from this canon that repentance involves imprisonment and torture; nevertheless, it is important to see that Peter views the former

45. See Barnes, *Tertullian*, 170; and Bévenot, 21. Barnes insists on Peter's "affinities with Clement" and cites Clement *Stromateis* 4.76.1 (Stählin = *PG* 4:10). In chapter 10 Clement cites with approval Matt. 10:23, as does Peter in Canon 9. Clement says that Christians should avoid persecution; zealots become "accomplices" in the "crime" of their persecutors. Barnes *Tertullian*, 171 n. 6, claims that this "again brings Clement close to the views of Basilides and Heracleon," and infers a genealogy from the Alexandrian Gnostics to Clement to Peter. Such an inference is surely overdrawn. In any case, the Gnostics were not of one mind on martyrdom. Ptolemaeus, a Valentinian, may have died a martyr's death. See Justin 2 *Apol.* 2. On Gnostic views of martyrdom, see K. Koscherbe, *Die Polemik der Gnostischer gegen das kirchliche Christentum* (Leiden 1970) 134–37.

sins of the lapsi as forgiven. He views substitutionary penance favorably. He does not, it is true, discuss the loss of property or banishment as a result of a second appearance of the lapsed before the persecutors. Therefore, his position cannot be equated to that of the African bishops; however, Peter does regard the giving up of property or flight as an act of *confession*: he does, then, have an idea of a "substitutionary confession of faith" whereby one who confesses the faith through loss of property or homeland is equal to the one who confesses before the magistrates.[46]

In Canon 12 Peter says that "no accusation is to be brought against those who gave money in order to remain completely undisturbed by any evil. In order not to damage or destroy their souls they have borne a fine and loss of property which others, because of shameful greed, have not done." In Canon 13 he says, "therefore, neither is it right to accuse those who gave up everything for the safety of their lives and withdrew, *even if others were detained because of them*" (emphasis added).

Flight from Persecution

The Roman clergy write to Cyprian approving of his flight.[47] In Ep. 20.1 he defends himself: "considering not so much my safety as public peace for the brethren, I withdrew for a time lest the sedition which had begun be further provoked through our indiscreet presence." There is no reason to doubt the sincerity of this statement,[48] and it probably resembles what Peter said about his own flight. In Canon 9 he says that Christ "wishes us [like him] to move about from place to place when we are being persecuted for his name," and "wishes us to wait patiently and to take heed for ourselves, to watch and pray so that we may not enter into temptation."

The beginning of Canon 9 makes it clear that Peter is opposing these discreet actions to those of the zealots who "throw themselves" into the conflict. As he does in Canon 13, he here approves of flight. Canons 9 and 13, therefore, encapsulate the long struggle in the church between the zealots and the bishops, a struggle common to both Cyprian and Peter.

Cyprian believes with Peter that "the Lord commanded us to withdraw and flee from persecution, and to encourage us to it, he both taught

---

46. As Barnes, *Tertullian*, 170, notes with disapproval.
47. Epistle 8. On Cyprian's flight, see Sage, 193ff.
48. "In this case self-interest and community good pointed to the same course"; Sage, 196.

and did so himself" (*De lapsis* 10).[49] Like Peter, Cyprian defends flight as a way of avoiding apostasy: "A man had only to leave the country and sacrifice his property" (*De lapsis* 10).[50] In fact Cyprian asserts that many stayed to face the sacrifice test only out of "blind attachment" (*De lapsis* 11) to their property![51]

To Cyprian's way of thinking, those who flee to save their faith are clothed in the same armor as those who fight in the prisons and are, therefore, soldiers of Christ:

> If anyone flees after having abandoned all of his things and, having found himself in hiding and in solitude, perchance falls among robbers or dies from fever or from weakness, will it not be imputed to us that so good a soldier who has left all his belongings and, having cast aside his home and his parents and his children, has preferred to follow his Lord, should die without peace and communion? (Ep. 57.4).

It is not clear whether Cyprian in this letter equates the fugi with the lapsi, both of whom are without peace. It is more likely that he is referring to the common practice of equating the two, a practice which he no longer follows. If the one who fled is still in need of peace—whereas the confessor in prison is not—Cyprian's tone here shows that such peace will not be given under stringent terms. It is important to observe Cyprian's list of sorrows suffered by the one who flees; it corresponds to the usual lists of sorrows that those in prison undergo. In Cyprian's mind, both are martyrs. The letter clearly has behind it the Gospel passages where Jesus demands sacrifice of his followers; to Cyprian, those who fled are implicitly ranked with the apostles, whom they by their sacrifices imitate:

> If the primary claim to victory is that, having fallen into the hands of the pagans, a man should confess the Lord, the next title to glory is that he should have gone underground and preserved himself for further service of the Lord (*De lapsis* 3).

Peter's thinking on this subject is the same as Cyprian's: a Christian's duty was to confess the faith, and that could be done both "positively"

---

49. See Sage, 22, 217–20, for a discussion of Cyprian's change of attitude.

50. See Epistle 81. Cyprian, like Polycarp, flees, and when he is captured accepts his role as confessor. He takes pains to instruct the people in what they have learned from the Lord and "very often" from their bishop: "keep quiet and tranquility, lest anyone of you should stir up any tumult for the brethren or offer himself to the Gentiles" (Ep. 81). See Canon 9 and commentary.

51. See *De lapsis* 11–12 for a discussion of property and its worthlessness. See also Sage, 235.

(that is, by confessing before the authorities) and "negatively" (that is, by affirming that one is a Christian by fleeing the authorities who would force apostasy). Neither Cyprian nor Peter saw this second route as negative in any moral sense; they considered those who acted this way to be in the first, or second, rank of the "martyrs."

T. D. Barnes has stated that Peter thus did away with the martyr's ideal of the *imitatio Christi*: "By Peter's argument that ideal was now transformed: the true disciple was not he who endured, but he who ran away."[52] Undoubtedly one could have the same judgment of Cyprian, who, like Peter, "ran away." But such a judgment is not to the point. The churches of Carthage in 250 and Alexandria in 306 were not the same as the one Tertullian knew. One could certainly argue whether that church was better or worse (without ever, in my opinion, coming to a conclusion), but one cannot argue that its bishops did not have different responsibilities later. If they were now encouraging their flock to live, rather than die, for Christ, that is not cowardly; it reflects the view of a church which in the third and early fourth centuries was established and trying to make peace with the Roman world. Both Peter and Cyprian strongly condemn apostasy; they are, however, working with different definitions of apostasy, confession, and martyrdom from those of Tertullian.[53] One cannot make comparisons without recognizing that fact. Saying more than this is making a value judgment on which definition was better.

The Clergy

Cyprian and Peter, by their example and in their writings, also approved of clergy who fled persecution. They severely condemned those who remained and fell. Cyprian follows the traditional African thinking that "we ought to choose none but spotless and upright priests who, offering sacrifices holily and worthily to God, may be able to be heard in the prayers which they offer for the safety of the people of the Lord" (Ep. 67.2; see also Ep. 65.2). Why did the priest need to be spotless? J. N. D. Kelly has remarked that for Cyprian "the priest, it would appear,

52. *Tertullian*, 170.
53. For a brief discussion of a similar change in the definition of "heresy" between the time of Irenaeus and that of Tertullian and Origen, see R. A. Markus, "The Problem of Self-Definition: From Sect to Church," chap. 1 in *From Augustine to Gregory the Great: History and Christianity in Late Antiquity* (London 1983) 10–11: "What had changed was the concept of 'heresy.' Previously used to define the *locus* of the true church among the competing sects, it was now becoming the name for teaching at variance with its obverse, an emerging 'orthodoxy.'"

sacramentally re-enacts the oblation of His passion, which the Savior originally presented to the Father."[54] It is interesting to speculate, given the similar attitudes toward apostate clergy held by Cyprian and Peter, whether the latter held the same sacramental theology as Cyprian.

In Ep. 67.3 Cyprian quotes Hos. 9:4 to the effect that those who take the sacraments from a sinful priest are defiled. When Bishop Stephen of Rome restored the Spanish bishops Martial and Stephen who were libellatici, Cyprian objected: "If any priests or deacons have been first ordained in the Catholic Church and afterwards have stood against the Church . . . and have attempted to offer in opposition to the one and divine altar false and sacrilegious sacrifices . . . they should receive Communion as laymen" (Ep. 72.2).[55]

The punishment Cyprian imposes here is identical with that given by Peter in Canon 10: Cyprian's "ut communicent laici et satis habent quod admittuntur ad pacem" equals Peter's "᾿Αρκεῖ γὰρ αὐτοῖς ἡ κοινωνία." Just as Cyprian has two standards for libellatici—one for laity and one for clergy—so does Peter for lapsi who fell but later confessed. In Canon 8 these are forgiven, but he must be referring to laypersons, since in Canon 10 clergy in a similar position are not completely forgiven; they may be received to full communion, but will lose their ecclesiastical office.[56]

It is possible that, given Peter's dislike of zealotry (see Canon 9), the bishop of Alexandria is not referring in Canon 10 to all clergy but only to those who "sought to justify the faith in prison," "who boast and bring blame upon themselves." What they had done (their zealotry?) was "contrary to reason." Thus it is important to keep this caveat in mind: Cyprian and Peter's views on fallen clergy cannot be equated without caution. Peter does not speak elsewhere of fallen clergy and he does not give the *de opere operantis* justification for a pure clergy that Cyprian does. However, the punishment for fallen clergy is the same in both bishops' writings: they are to remain in church communion, but are to be deprived of their office. Given this fact, it is not unlikely that Peter

54. Kelly, 215.
55. Frend, *Martyrdom*, 419, says that "Stephen was evidently following Callistus' precedent in granting pardons even to clergy who had repented of deadly sin." In Ep. 67.6 Cyprian speaks of two priests who "have been contaminated with the abominable certificate of idolatry (nefando idolatriae libello contamini sint)." Apparently there were two standards for libellatici as well as for sacrificati: one for laypersons and one for clergy.
56. An attitude seen in Origen too (*Contra Celsum* 3.51; Chadwick, 164): Christians "do not select those who have fallen after their conversion to Christianity for any office or administration in the Church of God, as it is called."

assumes Cyprian's justification of a pure clergy and in Canon 10 is referring to all fallen clergy.

Conclusion

J. N. D. Kelly has pointed out that before the outbreak of the Decian persecution, Cyprian, like Tertullian his master, considered idolatry to be an irremissible sin, but that later his policy was "more merciful."[57] Although it is difficult to establish Cyprian's final attitude toward libellatici and sacrificati, it is clear that in his mind the former could receive peace soon while the latter could obtain it at least before they died, if not sooner.[58] In the case of those who lapsed under torture, Cyprian was willing to limit penance to the time already "served," and he was willing to see differences among cases and circumstances. Epistle 57.5 offers the suggestion that he, like Peter, was willing to give peace immediately because the struggle was imminent.

Neither Cyprian nor Peter had a fully developed penitential system like that of Basil or Gregory Thaumaturgus (see 169 below)—at least as far as can be determined from their extant writings. One can see, however, the beginnings of that system: distinctions were being made, categories given, and different penances assigned.[59] Although Cyprian left no canons such as Peter's, it is not too much to say that he was working toward the development of a system and that he was adding to the tradition of episcopal and conciliar authority over the forgiving of sins.

Both Peter and Cyprian were concerned that denying peace (communion) to the lapsed might drive them from the fold.[60] None but the unrepentant were to go unforgiven, and those who were tortured and those who returned to the conflict after their fall were given special consideration. Both bishops stressed episcopal authority and denied the power of the "confessors" to absolve the fallen.

A direct connection cannot readily be made between Cyprian and Peter, between Latin-speaking Carthage and Greek-speaking Alexandria, concerning the lapsed, but the two bishops did have a great deal in common: both fled their sees during persecution, defended that flight, administered their bishoprics in absentia, and dealt with usurpers. Both

---

57. Kelly, 218.
58. See Ep. 55.17 for this view, but in Ep. 55.6 he considers the lapsi as a group and says that repentance "should endure for a time (diu)."
59. See Basil Ep. 199.22.
60. Cyprian Ep. 57.5. See Canon 10 and Cyprian Ep. 8.2.

dealt with the fallen with mercy, especially when one compares their positions with those of Tertullian, the Novatianists, Donatists, and Melitians.

Mention was made earlier of a cautious episcopate trying to hold together a church under siege. Zealotry was discouraged and even condemned, and a more conservative position was taken by those in authority. W. H. C. Frend seems at times exasperated with the zealotry of the martyrs and suggests that some of them deserved what they got;[61] it is not unlikely that many bishops felt the same. Raymond Brown has pointed out that the church at Rome continued to identify itself with the state, even after persecution, and it is likely that Cyprian and Peter, as heads of vast church governments, adopted the conservatism of the Roman state.[62] Caution and pragmatism could be combined with mercy, and a merciful judgment given the lapsed could also be a "conservative" one. Such, it seems, is what happened at Rome, Carthage, and Alexandria.

ORIGEN AND SAINT PETER

Cyprian's contemporary Origen (c. 185–c. 254) provides the oldest information about a penitential system at Alexandria.[63] In his "Second Homily on Leviticus" (2.4), Origen says that there are seven ways for sins to be forgiven: (1) baptism, (2) martyrdom, (3) almsgiving, (4) forgiving our brother's sins, (5) restoring a sinner, (6) abundance of charity, and (7) "there is also a seventh way, a hard and painful one, and that is by penance, when the sinner drenches his pillow with his tears . . . and is not ashamed to confess his sin to one of the Lord's priests and ask him for a remedy [quare medicinam]."[64] J. Daniélou believes that in this passage "the reference to sacramental confession is quite plain."[65]

Origen, like both Cyprian and Peter (see 147–48), sees penance as a trial, a purgation which the penitent must undergo. But when is penance necessary, and when may one be forgiven by a less "hard and painful" way? The evidence is not certain, but Origen seems to make a distinction among sins, some being graver than others, "one involving exclusion

---

61. See Frend, *Martyrdom*.
62. Raymond E. Brown and John P. Meier, *Antioch and Rome* (New York 1983) 159ff.
63. For a full study of Origen, see K. Rahner, "La doctrine d'Origène sur la pénitence," *Recherches de science religieuse* 37 (1950) 47–97, 252–86.
64. J. Daniélou, *Origen* (London/New York 1975) 69. Daniélou (or his translator) misquotes slightly; see *Homélies sur le Lévitique*, ed. M. Borret (Paris 1981) 106–13. Peter also uses the medical imagery; see the Syriac fragment, 193–95 below.
65. Daniélou, *Origen*, 69.

from the community, and the other not."[66] What he terms "trifling sins" seem not to need the absolution of a priest or the doing of penance.[67]

In *De oratione* 28 Origen implies that the graver sins are idolatry, adultery, and fornication (apostasy and murder are not mentioned), and that these can be forgiven only by a priest.[68] In *Hom. Num.* 10.1 Origen makes a clear distinction between laity and clergy, and their powers: "The layman (Israelita, id est laicus) cannot remove his sins on his own, he must have a priest (Levitam, indiget sacerdote)." Yet he adds a curious sentence: "If, however, he lacks priests (sacerdos) or bishop (pontifex), he can cleanse (purgare) his own sins—if, however, he does not sin against God."[69]

Origen does not say here what sins against God are, but it is likely that they included graver sins such as blasphemy, idolatry, apostasy, and adultery (?). It is clear that Origen does not approve of those who "arrogate to themselves a greater power than priests possess" and forgive weighty sins.[70]

Daniélou believes that "Origen's witness is of exceptional value."[71] Origen does indeed share four views with Cyprian and Peter: (1) there are different classes of sins; (2) penance is necessary for forgiveness, at least for major sins; (3) priestly absolution is necessary—again, at least for some sins—(4) laypersons are not to assume the powers of forgiveness, at least for major sins. Since Peter in the *Canonical Letter* does not deal with "trifling" sins, it cannot be determined whether he allowed other than sacerdotal forgiveness for them. Therefore a development of priestly powers with regard to absolution cannot be traced from Origen to Peter. It is clear, however, that Peter shares Origen's views at least in the four ways given above. Therefore it seems reasonable to conclude that the views Origen gives on penance are not merely personal but rather reflect the custom of the Alexandrian church of his day. This was the custom and tradition handed down to the bishops Dionysius and Peter.

SAINT DIONYSIUS AND SAINT PETER

Dionysius of Alexandria (c. 200–265) was bishop from 247 to 265 and thus shepherded his flock through both the Decian and Valerian perse-

66. Ibid., 70–71.
67. Origen, *Hom. Jos.* 76.; Daniélou, *Origen*, 71.
68. Daniélou, *Origen*, 70.
69. *PG* 12:635–36.
70. Daniélou, *Origen*, 70.
71. Ibid., 71.

cutions. He, like Cyprian and Peter, had to deal with the effects of the persecutions against the Christians: martyrdom, flight, apostasy, and reconciliation. According to Eusebius *HE* 6.46.1–5, Dionysius wrote at least five letters on repentance (or possibly the same letter to different groups or persons); these are all lost except for such fragments, allusions, or repetitions as exist in other letters which are extant, for example, "To Fabius."[72] Those Eusebius lists are:

1. "To the Egyptians," "in which he has set forth his opinions with reference to those who had fallen, outlining degrees of failures (τάξεις παραπτωμάτων)" (an encyclical letter like Peter's?)
2. To the bishop of Armenia
3. To Laodicea (on repentance?)
4. To Rome
5. To Conon (Konon) or Colon

The letter "to the Egyptians" may be similar to Cyprian's lost "treatise" on the lapsed (see above 146) and to Peter's *Canonical Letter*. What Eusebius terms the "degrees of failures" may well have provided "terms of reconciliation" as well, that is, a period of penance set for each "failure." It is a great loss to church history and to the history of the development of a penitential system in the church that we do not have these lost works of Cyprian and Dionysius; without them it is virtually impossible to trace a development, whether direct or indirect, from Cyprian to Dionysius to Peter and on to the conciliar canons of the early fourth century.[73]

It is not unimportant that the Third Council of Constantinople, "in Trullo" (692), joined Dionysius and Peter as "canonical." That council accepted their canons along with those of Nicea and the other ecumenical councils and the canons of many of the great writers of the

---

72. For Dionysius' works, see Feltoe, *St. Dionysius*. For the Greek text, consult most conveniently the Loeb edition of Eusebius, *HE*, vol. 2 ed. J. E. L. Oulton (LCL; Cambridge [1932] repr. 1980). The Greek text, with commentary, may also be found in *Dionysius: Letters*. On the works of Dionysius, see now also W. Bienert, *Dionysius von Alexandrien: Zur Frage des Origenismus im Dritten Jahrhundert* (Berlin 1978), esp. chap. IID, "Das erhaltene Werk des Dionysius," 51–70. For the collected works of Dionysius, see also idem, *Dionysius von Alexandrien: Das erhaltene Werk* (Stuttgart 1972). Bienert's German translation is based on Feltoe's collection of 1904. For a discussion of Dionysius and repentance, see Bienert, *Dionysius: Zur Frage*, esp. chap. IVC, "Der Streit um die Busse, das Schisma Novatians und die Folgen," 177–93.

73. Bienert, *Dionysius: Zur Frage*, 178–80, gives a brief overview, beginning with Callistus of Rome, of the policy of allowing sinners readmission to the church after an appropriate time of penance.

eastern church.[74] One of Dionysius's canonical writings has survived, a letter to Basilides in which the bishop of Alexandria sets down rules concerning the Easter celebration. This letter was accepted by the Trullan Synod as canonical; undoubtedly the canons of Saint Peter were also. This offers a link, however tenuous, between the two bishops and shows how their letters were taken into the canons of the church.[75] Dionysius is called *kanonikos* by Basil in a letter on the canons, and it is probable that Peter was so regarded before the synod made it official in 692.[76]

The writings of Dionysius and Peter eventually took on the nature of canons or authoritative statements of the church. How early this occurred is impossible to tell, but the fact that Peter's *Canonical Letter* survived (even though not quoted by Eusebius), while most of his theological writing did not, offers evidence that his canons were used early by the church. His death as a martyr undoubtedly lent them even greater authority. The question arises, given the canonical status of the two bishops and the fact that Dionysius presided sixty years before Peter, whether Peter used Dionysius's canons on repentance. A definitive answer cannot be given, but it is possible to sketch some details of Dionysius's thought on apostasy and penance and to compare these views to Peter's.[77]

In a fragment on repentance, Dionysius argues against severity toward apostates: "Let us then not repel those who return, but gladly welcome them and number them with those who have not strayed, and thus supply that which is wanting in them."[78] Dionysius here is arguing that sinners and saints are equal in the church, but he points out that those who have strayed are in need of the church's teaching. The attitude expressed here is very similar to that found in a Syriac fragment on repentance attributed to Peter (and to the fourteen canons as a whole):[79]

In order that we might make finally and willingly repentant those who, of their own accord, have fallen into the snare(s) of the devil . . . let us restore

---

74. Karl Joseph Hefele, *History of the Ecclesiastical Councils* (repr., New York, [1894] 1972) 5:224.

75. See *Dionysius: Letters*, 91. Bienert, *Dionysius: Zur Frage*, 180, notes that of the numerous letters on penance the letter to Conon is "canonical."

76. Basil Ep. 188.1.

77. Bienert, *Dionysius: Zur Frage*, 177–93, does not mention Peter in his discussion of Dionysius and penance.

78. Feltoe, *St. Dionysius*, 62; *Dionysius: Letters*, 62–64.

79. For the Syriac see Schwartz "Zur Geschichte," 166ff. See appendix 2 of this chapter, 193–95, for a translation.

those who with all (their) might flee him. . . . By this time it is just to determine the means of healing which comes especially through repentance.

In the letter to Fabius (or Fabian) Dionysius recounts the horrors of the persecution and the bravery of the confessors and martyrs.[80] He also lists, as does Peter, the various ways that Christians apostatized and fell (the numbers in brackets refer to the canons where Peter refers to the same subject):

And of many of the more eminent persons, some came forward immediately through fear [3], others in public positions were compelled to do so by their business, and others were dragged by those around them [14]. Called by name they approached the impure and unholy sacrifices, some pale and trembling. . . . and it was evident that they were by nature cowards in everything, cowards both to die and to sacrifice [3]. But others ran eagerly towards the altars. . . . Of the rest, some followed one or other of these, others fled [9]; some were captured, and of these some went as far as bonds and imprisonment, and certain (ones), when they had been shut up for many days, then forswore themselves even before coming into court [2], while others, who remained firm for a certain time under tortures, subsequently gave in [1, 14]. (HE 6.41.11–13)

Dionysius is particularly hard on those who "ran eagerly towards the altars"; he says that "they will be saved with difficulty."

Dionysius goes on in the letter to give a list of the martyrs and stories about them. Unlike Peter, he speaks approvingly of those zealots who voluntarily gave themselves up to the courts (HE 6.41.23; cf. Canon 9), and does not refer, as Peter does, to those who "dissembled" by sending slaves or offering bribes (cf. Canons 5–7, 12). However, he does speak of those who fled:

What need is there to speak of the multitude of those who wandered in deserts and mountains, and perished by hunger and thirst and frost and diseases and robbers and wild beasts? Such of them as survive *bear testimony to their election and victory* (εἰσὶν ἐκλογῆς καὶ νικῆς μάρτυρες) [cf. Heb. 11:38] (HE 6.42.2; emphasis added).

The language here is very similar to Cyprian's about flight (see 157–59 above) and agrees with Cyprian and Peter's ideas of "substitutionary confession." The "tortures"—hunger, thirst, cold, disease, robbers, and wild beasts—equal those of the martyrs in prison (see HE 6.41.15–17). Those who fled are, in fact, "martyrs" and "elect": they are martyrs

---

80. HE 6.41.1–42.6; Feltoe, *St. Dionysius*, 35–43. For Dionysius and the question of martyrdom and Novatianism, see Bienert, *Dionysius: Zur Frage*, 183–93.

without dying, confessors without imprisonment (see also appendix 5, 216–19). Dionysius, in his letter to Germanicus (*HE* 6.40), argues that since these people are God's elect, they act with God's approval—just as he does himself when he flees: "Acting not on my judgment nor apart from God have I taken flight." This sounds very much like Cyprian and Peter (in Canon 9 God "wishes" the persecuted to flee).

Although a bishop, along with many of his flock, might flee and justify his (and their) actions, he still has to deal with those who stayed and either confessed the faith or lapsed. Dionysius, confronted with the fact that confessors are forgiving the lapsed, asks Fabius, bishop of Antioch, what the two of them are to do (*HE* 6.42.5f.). The passage is important enough to quote at length:

> Therefore the divine martyrs (οἱ θεοὶ μάρτυρες) themselves among us, who now are assessors of Christ, and share the fellowship of his kingdom, and take part in his decisions and judge along with him, have espoused the cause of certain of the fallen brethren who became answerable for the charge of sacrificing; and seeing their conversion and repentance, they judged it had the power to prove acceptable to him who has no pleasure at all in the death of a sinner, but rather his repentance; and admitted them to the worship of the Church as *consistentes* (συνέστησαν) and gave them fellowship in their prayers and feasts. What then do you counsel us, brethren, on these matters? What are we to do? Are we to be of like opinion and mind with them, uphold their decision and concession, and deal kindly with those they pitied? Or shall we esteem their decision unjust, and set ourselves up as critics of their opinion, cause grief to kindness, and do away with their arrangement? (*HE* 6.42.5–6; translation modernized).

This letter suggests a great many things. First, it is clear that Dionysius is dealing with acts of forgiveness already granted by the confessors which, his letter implies, go against episcopal authority and tradition. Nevertheless, he disapproves neither of the acts nor of the actors. His praise of the confessors, unlike Cyprian and Peter's, is fulsome: they are now sitting at God's table.[81] His compassion for the fallen is genuine. As for his query regarding the acts of forgiveness, it may be a real question on his part, but it seems more likely that it is a rhetorical question to which Dionysius has already answered "No": he will not be hard-hearted and undo the confessors' actions.[82] The tone of the letter strongly suggests that Dionysius looked upon the confessors and their

---

81. See 148–50 for Cyprian. Peter is more circumspect with regard to the confessors. See Canons 5 and 11.

82. Bienert, *Dionysius: Zur Frage*, 182, says it is a rhetorical question and that Dionysius "leaves the decision up to Fabius."

actions favorably. Feltoe infers that confessor pardon was practiced at Alexandria, but only by the martyred before they died; that is, their forgiveness had efficacy only because of their subsequent death.[83] This is possible, but cannot be proved.

Feltoe is correct in saying that confessor pardon existed at Alexandria—unlike at Carthage. In Canons 5 and 11 Peter assumes the existence of confessor pardon. He approves of the confessor's petitions, *but does not give them the power of direct forgiveness.* This is probably the case with Dionysius also. He approves of the petitions and allows the lapsi to be received as penitents (of the *consistens* class? see below). However, he does not hand over his episcopal authority to the confessors; instead, like Peter, Dionysius uses the petition to confirm his episcopal power. He will allow the lapsed who are thus forgiven to enter the ranks of the penitents; the petitions have had effect, but nevertheless the sinner must do penance and cannot receive communion until the bishop approves.

The term *consistens,* pl. *consistentes,* in addition to giving evidence of the bishop's power, seems to point to a developing penitential system at Alexandria. E. L. Oulton notes, referring to the letter to Fabius (see 166), that the consistentes were the highest (or fourth) order of penitents "admitted to eucharistic prayers, but debarred from communion."[84] However, one must use extreme caution here. Dionysius uses συνίστημι twice in his extant letters, here (*HE* 6.42.5) and in his letter to Xystus, bishop of Rome (*HE* 7.9.5). It is very uncertain whether he is talking about an actual class or rank of penitents—those standing—or whether he means the verb in a more general sense of "organize," "bring together," "stand together," "act in support." It must also be noted that Dionysius uses the verb in both passages, not the technical noun ἡ σύστασις which Gregory Thaumaturgus and Basil use to denote the fourth class of penitents.[85]

---

83. *Dionysius: Letters,* 5.

84. Eusebius *HE;* Lawler and Oulton 2:112 n. 2. G. A. Williamson, *Eusebius: The History of the Church* (Minneapolis, Minn. 1965 = Penguin edition), translates συνέστησαν as "bystander," probably following the Loeb translation. See n. 85.

85. Basil Ep. 199.22 (to Amphilochius). Gregory Thaumaturgus, "Canonical Letter" 11 (*PG* 10:1048). See n. 128 below for a translation of Gregory's letter. Bienert, *Dionysius: Zur Frage,* 182 n. 22, says that *HE* 7.9.5 gives perhaps a clearer indication that a rank of consistentes existed. This seems unlikely. In his translation, Bienert, *Dionysius: Werk,* 31, seems to interpret συνέστησαν, and the entire sentence (*HE* 6.42.5), in a general sense: "versammelten sich mit ihnen, standen ihnen bei und hielten Gebets- und Mahlgemeinschaft mit ihnen."

None of Dionysius's extant letters (and only one of Cyprian's)[86] offers evidence that an *ordo* or *taxis* existed where various types of apostasy were listed with the assigned penance due and an appropriate level assigned to the penitent. However, one can judge from Cyprian's letters that a change was occurring from the times of the early church when lapsi could not be forgiven. Cyprian shows that this earlier attitude is no longer so and also shows that he is making distinctions among the fallen. His lost "treatise" and Dionysius's lost "to the Egyptians" might have given an *ordo penitentiae*. If to this (admittedly meager) evidence is added Peter's system of crime and punishment and the possible existence of consistentes in Dionysius's day, one could argue that a system of penance for lapsi did exist at Alexandria by 250.

The fully developed system, as given by Gregory Thaumaturgus (d. 270) and Basil (in 375), includes four stages of penance (Basil's terms are given first; the terms in parentheses are those of Gregory in his "Canonical Letter"):[87]

1. The excluded and weepers; ἐκβάλλεσθαι (weeping: ἡ πρόσκλαυσις)
2. The hearers (hearers): εἰς ἀκρόασιν
3. The penitents: εἰς μετάνοιαν (kneeling: ἡ ὑπόπτωσις)
4. Those standing—consistentes: εἰς σύστασιν μετὰ τοῦ λαοῦ ἀπεχομένους τῆς προσφορᾶς (participants or standing: ἡ σύστασις)
5. Communion

Although Dionysius certainly made distinctions among penitents, one should probably not infer that he knew of a penitential system with four ranks. However, consistentes certainly designates some kind of order, whether or not it is an actual rank, and it is not improbable that it meant those allowed into worship, but still excluded from the Eucharist and full fellowship (communion). Given this evidence, it is not unreasonable to hypothesize at least a two-order system for penitents at Alexandria: the excluded and the consistentes.

Peter's canons offer no evidence for a graded penitential system at Alexandria. The canons presuppose, by the imposition of penance, a time when penitents will be received back into the church, but these canons say nothing about their status as penitents. It is clear that they are outside of the church, that is, debarred from the Eucharist, but it is impossible to tell whether they could participate in the worship service as consistentes or were excluded altogether. If there had been a full

86. The lost "treatise." See 146 above.
87. *PG* 10:1048A. See n. 128.

penitential system at Alexandria in 250, it is very unlikely that it would have disappeared by Peter's time; therefore, it is striking that Peter makes no clear mention of such a system. One may suppose that if Peter had known of such technical vocabulary as that used by Gregory and Basil (and hence their systems), he would have used it. It is highly unlikely that such language, if used, would fall out of the text. One is forced to conclude that Peter did not know of the system and, if this is granted, neither did Dionysius (his use of συνίστημι being general rather than technical).[88]

Since Gregory Thaumaturgus, bishop of Neo-Caesarea in Cappadocia, takes for granted a full penitential system during Dionysius's lifetime and since Basil speaks of one in Cappadocia late in the fourth century, it is probable that its use arose to the east of Alexandria and was not known either to Dionysius or Peter who used a simpler system, one that was not graded.

Dionysius's letter to Fabius (HE 6.44) further complicates matters. Eusebius says that Dionysius wrote Fabius "a certain astonishing tale" about one Serapion, "an old man and a believer, who lived blamelessly for a long time, but in the trial [persecution] fell." He "often begged to be restored but no one heeded him."[89] Finally, he lay on his deathbed but would not die until he had received the sacrament and, thus, forgiveness. When he received communion, he died.[90]

This tale is "astonishing," but in a way Eusebius did not realize. The phrase "he often begged to be restored, but no one heeded him" is very ambiguous, as is "there was a certain Serapion among us (παρ᾿ ἡμῖν)," since it does not say whether he was in Alexandria or elsewhere. We do not know whether he was a penitent and asked for reconciliation because of his former blameless life, or whether for the same reason he asked for communion without doing penance. Dionysius (or Eusebius)

88. Bienert, Dionysius: Zur Frage, 180, notes that the letter to Conon shows both that "the institution of penance is therefore familiar to Dionysius" and, 182 n. 22, that "Dionysius differentiates different degrees of lapse is certain (cf. Eusebius HE 6.46.1)." As to the most difficult question of the consistentes, Bienert, 182 n. 22, cites B. Poschmann who sees in the word an allusion to the later-attested rank of penance which is first to be seen in Gregory Thaumaturgus. He also cites E. Schwartz and J. Grotz; the former opts for the later development of the ranks, while the latter, because of Gregory Thaumaturgus, is willing to see such a rank in Dionysius's time. Bienert himself is more inclined than I to accept the possibility of ranks of penitents at Alexandria in the mid-third century. He says that we can not know for certain, but "it seems possible" that such ranks were known by Dionysius.

89. Feltoe, St. Dionysius, 42.

90. Bienert, Dionysius: Zur Frage, 181, points out that since Serapion was able to receive the Eucharist, "the sacramental character of absolution is made evident."

reports only that he received communion on his deathbed because of an order Dionysius had given (the language implies that either the man lived at a distance or that Dionysius was at a distance—in exile?): "Yet since I had given an order that those who were departing this life, if they besought it, and especially if they had made supplication before, should be absolved, that they might depart in hope."

Dionysius seems here to accept postponement of absolution until death, which we have also seen in Cyprian (see 151 n. 40). However, caution is again necessary: we do not know whether this Serapion was unable to receive absolution *until* near death or whether he was dying unforeseen *before the term of his penance was over*. The passage implies the former, but certainty is impossible. More important, it shows Dionysius, like Cyprian, ordering that no one is to die *unabsolved*. Eusebius approvingly quotes the passage, saying Dionysius wrote it to Fabius while the latter "was inclining somewhat towards the schism [rigorism? Novatianism?]." If Eusebius is right and Dionysius is upholding the practice of forgiveness, then one can conclude that some were dying unabsolved in Antioch, but that forgiveness was granted at the end in Alexandria. Dionysius quotes this "astonishing" story as proof that the miraculous end of this man is a sign of God's approval of the actions taken at Alexandria.[91]

In another letter, "To Conon" (or Colon), Dionysius insists that "it is part of the divine mercy to send on their way free" those repentant who are near death.[92] Feltoe suggests that in the letter to Conon we have the "order" (ἐντολὴ ὑπ' ἐμοῦ δεδομένη) Dionysius mentions in the fragment concerning Serapion.[93] Eusebius *HE* 6.46.1 says that Dionysius wrote "to Colon (he was bishop of the community of the Hermopolitans) a personal letter . . . On Repentance." The connection that Feltoe sees is certainly possible, since Dionysius expresses in both letters the same attitude toward those in extremis: they are to receive absolution.

In the letter to Conon, Dionysius goes farther and states that if those so absolved "continue to live, it does not appear to me consistent to bind them again and load them with their sins . . . so long as nothing wrong has been done by them in the meantime to bring them back into bondage for the sins.[94] Dionysius shows that he is aware of practice

91. See ibid., 182, for a discussion of the letter.
92. Feltoe, *St. Dionysius*, 61. For a discussion of the Greek text, see *Dionysius: Letters*, 59–60.
93. *Dionysius: Letters*, 60.
94. Feltoe, *St. Dionysius*, 61.

contrary to his own: some who have been absolved in extremis and have recovered are being remanded to their former sins. He objects to this.

Feltoe says that this judgment shows "Dionysius' abundantly illustrated broad-mindedness," and he refers the reader to Cyprian's Ep. 55.23, and 29.[95] Epistle 55.23 does indeed show Cyprian's "broad-mindedness," because here he asserts that no repentant sinner is without hope of peace. However, Cyprian insists that if a lapsus repents only on his deathbed, he will receive no peace, because "he who has not reflected that he is destined to die is not worthy to receive solace in death." The bishop of Alexandria, by contrast, says that those near death are to be absolved if they seek absolution, "and *especially* if they had made supplication before" (*HE* 6.44.4; emphasis added).[96] Dionysius seems to be saying that those already penitent (and doing penance?) before danger of death are especially to be forgiven, but unlike Cyprian he does not exclude the formerly unrepentant.

Both Cyprian and Dionysius seem to assume that those who are near death (or at least most of them) have been doing penance. This would suggest that neither in Carthage nor in Alexandria was absolution put off until death; rather, it was the reward for the penitents after they had completed their penance. If, by chance, one were to fall ill and be near death, forgiveness was to be granted. For Dionysius, such forgiveness, like baptism, was not to be rescinded.

Unfortunately, Peter has nothing to say about absolution in extremis. It is clear, however, that he does not foresee the postponement of absolution until death; he assigns very specific penance for specific crimes. It is logical to conclude from this that those doing penance, if in danger of death, would be given absolution by Peter—and here he would follow both Cyprian and Dionysius. It is not clear what he would do about the unrepentant who, near death, suddenly repent. Although his attitudes are generally moderate, in Canon 4 he curses the unrepentant. Whether he would change his mind if they were dying cannot be determined but, given the attitudes expressed in the canons, it is probable that he would be lenient.

E. R. Hardy, in summarizing Dionysius' position, compares him to Cyprian:

When the persecution ended Dionysius, like Cyprian in the West, took a serious but moderate view of the proper treatment of those who lapsed but

95. *Dionysius: Letters*, 60.
96. Bienert, *Dionysius: Zur Frage*, 183, remarks that it is difficult to ascertain how far the "milde Busstheologie" of Dionysius is influenced by Origen.

now desired readmittance to the Church. They were allowed absolution after varying degrees of penance, especially in view of the intercession for them by some of the confessors.[97]

This description also fits Peter very well; in fact, it fits Peter better than the other two bishops: Dionysius does not speak explicitly of "varying degrees of penance," as does Peter, but his lost letter to the Egyptians may have set forth canons on apostasy and penance. Hardy has inferred such a *taxis* from Dionysius's work as a whole, and it seems reasonable to conclude that Peter inherited from Dionysius (and his successors) at least an incipient penitential system.

ELVIRA, ANCYRA, AND NICEA
AND SAINT PETER

C. J. Hefele, in his study of church councils, regarded those held at Rome in 251 concerning Novatianism and the lapsi as among the first councils of the church. He concluded that their decrees, collected by Cyprian, but now lost, constituted "the first penitential book" of the church.[98] This "penitential book" is the treatise Cyprian speaks of in Epistle 55 (see 146 above). Hefele summarizes the conclusions of Cyprian's council: that none of the lapsi is without hope, providing that one is repentant and does penance; that distinctions must be made between the various cases; that there is a difference between the crimes of the sacrificati and libellatici, the sins of the former being worse; and that lapsed clergy are to be admitted to penance but may not resume their former offices.[99] A synod called by pope Cornelius affirmed these decisions at Rome in 251. Cyprian called another synod on the lapsed in 252, and in Epistle 57 upholds the positions taken earlier.

The Council of Elvira met concerning the lapsed in 305 or 306 in southern Spain.[100] As Hefele notes, "the decisions of Elvira about the *lapsi* are much more rigorous than those of Nicea." This severity even led an ancient commentator, Morinus, to the conclusion that the council must have met before 250; "otherwise the Fathers of Elvira, by their first canon, must have taken the side of the Novatians."[101] The first canon states:

97. E. R. Hardy, *Christian Egypt* (New York 1952) 25–26; see Dionysius's letter to Novatian, *HE* 6.45.
98. Hefele, 1:94.
99. Ibid., 94–95.
100. For the date, see ibid., 132–38.
101. Ibid., 134.

> Whoever, after the profession of faith as an adult by means of the baptism of salvation, goes to the temple of idols to commit idolatry and has done so—which is a capital offense because it is the worst crime—is not to be received into communion (communionem), even at the end of his life.[102]

Hefele believes that *communio* means not only "communion with the Church, but sacramental communion as well," and attributes the severity of this canon to its being promulgated during or soon after violent persecution.[103] According to Frend, the canons of Elvira show how the "crimes of apostasy, bloodshed and immorality remain those for which no pardon could be granted to full members of the Church."[104]

Such an attitude was held by Cyprian before 250 and the onset of persecution, but Cyprian became less rather than more severe during and after persecution. Thus the canons of Elvira may reflect the traditionally rigorist attitudes common to the early church, rather than any immediate event. Hefele correctly points out, however, the difference between the fathers of Elvira and the Novatianists (and Hippolytus and Tertullian): "the Novatians pretended that the Church had not the *right* to admit to communion a Christian who had apostasized; the Fathers of Elvira acknowledged this right," but preferred to decide how it was to be applied.[105]

Canon 2 of Elvira agrees with Canon 1 and says that *flamens* who sacrifice "shall not receive communion even at the last," but Canon 3 states that flamens who "dissembled" by giving money (as a bribe) and therefore kept themselves from sacrificing are to be given communion at the last after having performed due penance.[106] Although this decision is harsher than either Cyprian or Peter allowed, the canons of Elvira, like the two bishops, allow for distinctions among the lapsi and also judge less harshly those who dissemble.

Once a council or bishop begins to make distinctions between the cases of the lapsed, it is natural that varying periods of penance will be assigned. The canons of Elvira make a distinction between flamens who had fulfilled their imperial duties and had given games and sacrificed, and those who had only given games. The former are refused communion forever while the latter might be admitted at the end of their lives.[107] Further, Canon 4 states that flamens who were only cate-

---

102. Latin text in ibid., 138.
103. On *communio* see ibid., 138, and on the severity of the canon, ibid., 134.
104. Frend, *Martyrdom*, 562 n. 5.
105. Hefele 1:134.
106. For the Latin text, see ibid., 138–39.
107. Ibid., 139.

chumens were to be treated less severely; if they performed their duties, but did not sacrifice, they were to be baptized after three years.[108] Canon 46 declares that Christians may apostatize by staying away from church; if they do, they are to be received into communion after a penance of ten years.[109]

We can see at Elvira what Cyprian hints at and what Peter assumes: a system of crimes and punishment. The canons, like Cyprian and Peter, insist on the church's authority, and they prove that in the same year Peter wrote his canons (306) a penitential system existed in southern Spain. The canons of Elvira, unlike Peter's, deal with issues other than apostasy. They, like Cyprian and Peter, also insist on the purity of the clergy (those caught in usury are to be degraded). Interestingly, although conservative, even rigorist, the canons reflect strong ecclesiastical control. Canon 60 discourages zealotry; those who destroy idols and are consequently killed are not to be considered martyrs.

The Council of Ancyra is the next important council to consider apostasy and penance; it met in 314, three years after Peter's death. The bishops were almost all from Asia Minor and Syria, and none from Egypt.[110] Ancyra and Nicea are the only councils after the Great Persecution to consider the problem of the lapsi; therefore, they are of the utmost importance in making any decision concerning Peter's influence on subsequent canons.

Canons 1 and 2 of Ancyra (like Peter's Canon 10) concern clergy who lapsed and returned to the battle. They are no longer allowed to perform any priestly duties although they continue to "enjoy the honors of their office (τῆς μὲν τιμῆς τῆς κατὰ τὴν καθέδραν)."[111] Peter does not speak of the honor (τιμή) of office still belonging to lapsed clergy, but he does allow them "Christian fellowship" (κοινωνία—communio), which must include the Eucharist. Perhaps this τιμή mentioned by Ancyra Canons 1 and 2 equals the κοινωνία of Peter's Canon 10. Clergy who did not take up the struggle again are not mentioned by the canons of Ancyra. It must be assumed, de fortiore, that these clergy are debarred from their office; perhaps they also suffered loss of τιμή.

In the case of deacons who have lapsed but returned to the struggle, they may keep the other honor(s) of their rank (τὴν μὲν ἄλλην τιμὴν

108. Ibid., 139–40.
109. Ibid., 156–57.
110. Ste. Croix, "Aspects," 84; Hefele 1:199–200. For the list of bishops, see Hefele 1:200. He considers the lists to be of little value.
111. Hefele 1:201.

ἔχειν) but lose all liturgical functions (πεπαῦσθαι δὲ αὐτοὺς πάσης τῆς ἱερᾶς λειτουργίας).[112] Hefele suggests that these deacons "continued their offices as almoners to the poor, and administrators of the property of the Church." This might explain the τιμή still allowed the priests (πρεσ-βύτεροι) in Canon 1, since the same term (τιμή) is used for both priests and deacons.

Canons 1 and 2 of Ancyra define the "office" (λειτουργία) that these have fallen from as consisting of (1) the eucharistic function and (2) preaching. Although Peter does not define the λειτουργία, undoubtedly he means that the fallen priests can no longer be celebrants (or even assistants) or preachers.[113] It is not clear whether he also denied them the τιμή of minor functions.

The canons of Ancyra, like those of Peter, make distinctions among lapsi. Canon 3 pardons fully those who lapsed under duress and there-fore gives the same judgment as Peter does in Canon 14: they did not assent and therefore did no wrong. Canon 3 sounds remarkably like Cyprian's Ep. 57.4 and Peter's Canons 12 and 13 (see above, 157–59):

> Those who fled before persecution, but were caught, or were betrayed by those of their own houses, or in any other way, who have borne with resignation the confiscation of their property, tortures, and imprisonment, declaring themselves to be Christians, but who have subsequently been vanquished by force and [in spite of this] have persevered in avowing themselves Christians, and have evinced their sorrow for what had be-fallen them by their dejection and humility—such, not having committed any fault, are not to be deprived of the communion of the Church.[114]

This canon combines the "list of sufferings" of substitutionary martyr-dom which we have seen above with Cyprian and Dionysius (155–59 and 166); it also affirms (indirectly) the decisions taken by Peter: those who are vanquished but return to battle are forgiven (Canon 8) and those who gave up money or property to escape persecution have done no wrong (Canons 12 and 13). It also pardons fully those who lapsed under duress and therefore gives the same judgment as Peter in Canon 14. Ancyra Canon 3 allows those who sacrificed under force and who have witnesses that they were tortured to be "placed in the ministry among those who confessed the faith": (ἐν τῇ λειτουργίᾳ ταχθέντες ἐν τοῖς ὁμολογηταῖς), that is, among the confessors. This canon says that these people, if qualified, may be promoted to the ministry (τάξις).

112. Ibid., 202–3.
113. See Ancyra Canon 2 and ibid.
114. Ibid., 204.

Apparently some were arguing at Ancyra and Alexandria that these unfortunates had been somehow stained by their forced lapse. But both Canon 3 of Ancyra and Canon 14 of Peter insist that there is no fault in them; they are eligible for promotion to the λειτουργία of confessors and, one would assume, according to Peter to the τάξις of clergy.

The first three canons of Ancyra do not assign specific terms of penance, but Canons 4–6, like Peter's canons, do. Canon 4 is very similar to Canon 3 of Peter: both deal with those Christians who willingly sacrificed, that is, under force but without torture or imprisonment. Peter assigns them three (or four) years of penance without making any mention of an *ordo penitentiae*. Canon 4 of Ancyra assigns six years of penance—which is similar to Peter—but much more important, assumes a penitential order. The penitents are to serve:

1. one year as hearers (ἀκροάσθαι),
2. three years as *substrati* (ὑποπεσεῖν),
3. two years as participants in prayer (εὐχῆς δὲ μόνης κοινωνῆσαι),
4. and then (ἐπὶ τὸ τέλειον) communion.[115]

These steps equal the second through fourth ranks of penance given by Basil and Gregory Thaumaturgus (see 169 above) but about which Peter is silent. Canons 5 and 6 also use this penitential system. In Canon 5 those who fell, but did so under protest, and ate of the sacrificial meat are to serve three years as *substrati* and then be admitted to fellowship without taking part in the offering (κοινωνησάτωσαν χωρὶς προσφορᾶς).[116] Those who were present at the sacrifice but did not eat have a milder term of two years as substrati and one year as consistentes. This canon does not have an exact parallel with Peter's canons, but since there is no mention of torture or imprisonment, it could be compared to Peter's Canon 3 where the punishment is three or four years. Its tone, however, is similar to his Canon 1 which assigns an additional forty days to three years already "served."

Canon 6 of Ancyra also deals with those who lapsed without punishment, but only "on the mere threat of punishment, or of the confiscation of their property, or of exile."[117] This canon punishes them with six years of penance, partly because they had not repented until the time of the synod. They will serve one year as *audientes* or hearers, two years as substrati, and two years as consistentes. As with Peter's first canon, this

115. Ibid., 205.
116. Ibid., 206. For a discussion of *prosphora* see 206–7.
117. Ibid., 207.

canon allows for "time already served"; it also allows for pardon if there is danger of death or for "any other important reason."[118] This canon is most like Peter's Canon 3 where the lapsed are given three years penance.

The other canons regarding the lapsed deal with subjects not treated by Peter:

Canon 7. Those who sat at pagan festivals but did not eat: two years of penance.

Canon 8. Those who sacrificed two or three times under compulsion: six years.

Canon 9. Those who apostatized and betrayed others: ten years.

Canon 12. Catechumens who apostatized, but then later received baptism, are forgiven and are eligible for the priesthood.

The Council of Ancyra does not deal, as Peter does, with the questions of flight or of dissembling by sending slaves or giving money. However, it does not *disapprove* of those who did these things. Could it be that there were different traditions of resistance in the two areas, with flight being less common in Asia than in Egypt? Once again, we are faced with silence. However, it is possible to infer from that silence that those who fled or dissembled were considered worthy of "no accusation," as Peter says in Canon 12. No mention is made in the Ancyra canons of those who lapsed under torture, while canons have to be written to deal with those who lapsed voluntarily. Presumably, the former were considered not to have fallen, and the same might be said at least of those who fled (Peter's Canon 9) or those who gave up their property and withdrew (Peter's Canon 13). In any case, at Ancyra apostasy was viewed as sacrificing or—what is really the same thing—eating sacrificial meats. As with Peter, there is no mention of *traditio*, and, also in agreement with Peter, flight was probably not considered as a lapse.

The spirit of these canons is very similar to Peter's.[119] They are moderate in their imposition of penance, and they assume, as does Peter, that specific terms of penance are to be set and that none of the lapsi is to be excluded until death. Penance is even seen as working retroactively, as in Peter's first canon.

The question arises whether Peter had any influence on these canons. Linguistically and thematically, the answer has to be no: there is not

---

118. Ibid., 208.

119. T. D. Barnes, *Constantine and Eusebius* (Cambridge, Mass. 1981) 201, notes that the decisions of the *Canonical Letter* "strongly resemble the decisions of a council held in Ancyra eight years later."

enough evidence to establish any connection between Alexandria and Ancyra. Still it is clear that there is a *Zeitgeist* at work here: the church, whether through bishop or council, is acting to reinstate the lapsed after they have done appropriate penance, and it has developed a penitential system to effect this reconciliation. Since this system is in use only three years after Peter's death and since Dionysius shows some knowledge of it, it must be assumed that it existed in Peter's lifetime. As was shown above, such a penitential system is likely to be eastern in origin, at least as it fully developed into a system of ranks or grades such as we see for Gregory and Basil in Cappadocia.

The last council to deal with the lapsi was Nicea, in 325. The lists of bishops shows that Alexander of Alexandria was present, yet little or no influence of Peter is to be found in Canons 9–14 which deal with the lapsed.[120]

Nicean Canon 10 insists, as does Peter, that clergy be "blameless." As Peter in his tenth canon deposes clergy who have fallen, so Canon 10 of Nicea deposes lapsi who have subsequently been ordained. This canon shows that through 325 all parts of the church, east and west, rigorist and moderate alike, insisted on the purity of the clergy: Tertullian, Novatianists, Cyprian, Dionysius, Peter, and Nicea.[121]

Canons 11–14 of Nicea deal, not with the persecution of Diocletian and Maximin, but rather with that of Licinius. Canon 11 deals with those who lapsed "without being driven to it by necessity ($\chi\omega\rho\grave{\iota}\varsigma$ $\mathring{\alpha}\nu\acute{\alpha}\gamma\chi\eta\varsigma$), or by the confiscation of their goods, or by any danger whatever," and is, therefore, very similar to Canon 6 of Ancyra and Peter's Canon 3. Since confiscation of property is listed in addition to "necessity," "$\mathring{\alpha}\nu\acute{\alpha}\gamma\chi\eta$" might mean torture and imprisonment. If this is so, and it seems possible, one can see how the argument of Peter's Canon 13 has been incorporated into these later canons: the danger of losing one's property is cause now for mitigating a charge of apostasy; certainly if one were to give up one's property and flee, one would be considered to have sacrificed a great deal for the faith.

Although the fallen mentioned in Canon 11 of Nicea are "unworthy," the Synod "decides that they ought to be treated with gentleness."[122] Those who are penitent are to serve (with the terms of Canon 6 of Ancyra in parentheses):

120. Hefele, 1:272.
121. Canon 10 of the *Canonical Letter* "refutes Epiphanius' opinion, derived from Melitianising documents, that Peter was in favor of restoring lapsed clerics to their ministry" (Bright, "Petrus I.," 332).
122. Hefele, 1:416.

1. 3 years as audientes (Ancyra: 1)
2. 7 years as substrati (Ancyra: 3)
3. 2 years as consistentes (Ancyra: 2)

for a total of twelve years. In Peter's Canon 3, which is comparable, Peter commands three (or four) years of repentance.

Canons 12–14 of Nicea have no exact parallels with those of Peter; they are concerned with, respectively, the military, readmission in extremis, and catechumens. Nevertheless, they are similar in tone to Peter's canons:

> Those among [the fallen] who, by fear and with tears, together with patience and good works, show by deeds that their conversion is real, and not merely in appearance, after having finished the time of their penance among the audientes, may perhaps take part among those who pray [substrati or consistentes]; and it is in the power of the bishop to treat them with greater leniency. (Canon 12)[123]

Canon 13 allows communion to those in danger of dying, and in doing so, says it is following "the old rule of the Church."[124] This "old rule" must be Canon 6 of Ancyra and can be traced backed to Dionysius of Alexandria (but is absent from Peter's canons).[125] This is all that the First Ecumenical Council has to say on apostasy and penance, and none of the councils that follow is concerned with the lapsed.

CONCLUSION

The most important conclusion that can be drawn from this survey is that the issue of apostasy and penance was part of two larger issues (which could not be addressed in the scope of this chapter): the growing power of the episcopacy and the rise of a penitential system. Just as one can plausibly argue that the "single episcopacy" of Ignatius of Antioch grew out of the church's struggle for unity and against heresy, so one could argue that the episcopacy grew in the second and third centuries because of the church's struggle against Roman persecution and orthodox and unorthodox rigorism. Moreover, one can see in Cyprian, Dionysius, and Peter, as well as in the conciliar canons, an absolute insistence on the authority of the bishops, as against the confessors.

123. Ibid., 417.
124. Ibid., 419.
125. So ibid., 420.

This authority invested in the bishop, clergy, and councils the right to assign penance to sinners. Cyprian claims that right for himself, acting in council, although he is vague about how to implement a system of penance. By Dionysius's time, there is more evidence of a penitential system, and Peter assumes the authority to assign varying terms of penance.[126] Finally, by the time of the councils of Ancyra (314) and Nicea (325), a full penitential system (already outlined by Gregory Thaumaturgus by the mid-third century in Cappadocia), one that is governed by bishop, clergy, and council, is taken for granted.

Given the evidence outlined above that some kind of system of penance existed in Alexandria around 250 and that the Council of Ancyra presupposes that one had existed for some time, can anything more specific be said about such a system in Alexandria during Peter's time (300–311)? Some scholars closely familiar with the third-century church have assumed the existence of a full penitential system in Egypt during Peter's episcopacy. W. Bright, in referring to Canon 1, says that there were "mourners" or "weepers" at Alexandria.[127] These are the lapsi who belonged to the lowest rank of penitents (the "excluded" of Basil's system) and who, in the words of Gregory Thaumaturgus, are "outside the door(s) of the house of prayer [= church]."[128] They have not been admitted to penance and have been noncommunicants for three years: "The mourners or weepers, as is well-known, were 'candidates for penance' who besought the faithful as they passed into the church to plead for their admission into the class of penitents."[129]

---

126. Origen *Contra Celsum* 3.51 (Chadwick, 163–64), written at the same time as Dionysius and Cyprian held their sees (c. 248), shows knowledge of a penitential system: "But Christians mourn as dead men those who have been overcome by licentiousness or some outrageous sin because they have perished and died to God. They admit them some time later as though they had risen from the dead provided that they show a real conversion, though their period of probation is longer than that required of those who are joining the community for the first time." Note the baptismal language; see 153 above for Cyprian's use of similar language—language absent in Peter's extant canons.

127. Bright, "Petrus I.," 331.

128. PG 10:1048. Gregory's Canon 11 reads in full: "Weeping (ἡ πρόσκλαυσις) is (done) outside the gates of the house of prayer. It is necessary that the sinner stand there to ask the faithful who are coming in to pray for him. Hearing (ἡ ἀκρόασις) (is) within the gates, in the narthex; it is necessary that the sinner stand there until the catechumens come in, and to make his exit from the same place. For, it is said, after he hears the Scriptures and teaching, let him be removed (from the church) and not be thought fit (to participate in) prayer. Kneeling (ἡ ὑπόπτωσις) is done within the gates of the sanctuary so that (the penitent) might go out with the catechumens. Standing (ἡ σύστασις) (is within the sanctuary) so that (the penitent) might stand with the faithful and not go out with the catechumens. Last of all (is) the participation in the sacraments."

129. Bright, "Petrus I.," 331.

Bright's conclusion is an important one. If he is right, Canon 1 offers strong evidence for a full penitential system, one with ranks, and similar to the one that Gregory and Basil know. However, the evidence is far from certain. Peter's word for "mourners" is καταπενθοῦντες, a general word (see, for example, Basil Ep. 131.2), while Gregory uses ἡ πρό-σκλαυσις, a technical term (Basil, Ep. 188.1, uses ἐκβάλλεσθαι for this rank).[130] Peter also uses a verb with general meaning, while Gregory uses a technical noun. Indeed, Peter seems to suggest that these mourners have not yet presented themselves to the church; once they do, they are to receive forty days of penance. On the basis of καταπενθοῦντες, however, I can not agree with Bright that these are the "mourners" of whom Gregory and Basil speak, that is, a distinct class (the lowest) of penitents.

W. H. C. Frend goes a step further than Bright.[131] He agrees with E. Schwartz's conclusion that Canon 3, which allowed those who con-fessed their offense "to begin their restoration as 'penitents' (ὑποπίπ-τοντες) without going through the two meanest grades of ecclesiastical penance," implies the existence of a graded structure of penance.[132] However, nowhere in Peter's canons do the technical terms ὑποπε-σοῦνται or ὑποπίπτοντες occur. A judgment that Peter is admitting lapsi to the third stage of penance (Gregory: ὑποπεσοῦνται; Basil: εἰς μετάνοιαν) must rest on an interpretation of the use of μετάνοια in the canons.[133] In Canon 3, εἰς μετάνοιαν is a general term, like καταπενθοῦντες in Canon 1, and is not the technical term that Basil makes of it. Μετάνοια occurs in Canons 3, 5, 6–8, and 11, and in none of these does it mean the third class of penitent. Canon 7 (ἐν τρίσιν ἔτεσιν ἐξετασθήσονται ἐν μετανοίᾳ) could possibly suggest that those lapsi are to be ὑποπίπτοντες for three years. But this leads to a further problem: nowhere in the canons does Peter mention the fourth class of penitents, the consistentes. One would have to assume that the lapsi, after three years, would pass directly into full communion. The canons of Nicea and Ancyra show that this would be very unlikely.

130. For καταπενθοῦντες, see Lampe, 714; for ἡ πρόσκλαυσις, 1173.
131. Frend, Martyrdom, 540.
132. Schwartz, "Zur Geschichte," 171–72: "Peter determines that all those who have come forward [that is, presented themselves] should be readmitted; indeed, he will impose on those who have been πρόσκλαυσις up until now a certain set period [of penance]—depending on the type of apostasy—which they are to complete as penitents, that is, as ὑποπίπτοντες: this category of penitents is above that of ἀκροώμενοι, not to mention that of προσκλαίοντες."
133. See Lampe, 855, s.v. μετάνοια, II & IIF.

Of all the canons in the *Canonical Letter*, Canon 8 suggests most strongly that Peter knew of a graded penitential system: "It is fair that we ... join with them in every way in Christian fellowship (κοινωνεῖν ἐν πᾶσιν)—in prayer (ταῖς προσευχαῖς), and in receiving the body and blood of Christ (τῇ μεταλήψεω τοῦ σώματος καὶ τοῦ αἵματος), and in the consolation of the Word (τῇ παρακλήσει τοῦ λόγου)." The difficulty here is one of both vocabulary and word order. *Koinonia*, fellowship or communion (L. communio), can be either general or specific in meaning —or both.[134] It can mean, generally, Christian community or, specifically, the eucharistic celebration. The three elements of *koinonia* that Peter lists—prayer, receiving the Eucharist, and hearing the Word—are, generally, three central parts of Christian community. Specifically, however, they are also distinct parts of the Sunday worship service in the ancient church—from which various classes of penitents were excluded. In other words, is Peter's list apposed to—and merely descriptive of— koinonia, or is he, by listing the various parts of the service, listing also the various classes of penitents?

Arguing against the latter is the fact that in Canon 8 Peter uses none of the technical vocabulary known to Basil and Gregory. Also, the order in Peter's list does not fit well into an *ordo penitentiae*. Gregory, in his eleventh "Canonical Letter," has this order (1) hearing of scripture and teaching, (2) prayers, and (3) participation in the sacraments. Whereas Peter lists the "consolation of the Word" last, Gregory says that after "the scriptures and teaching," the penitent leaves the sanctuary because he is not "thought fit (to participate in) prayer"—much less in the Eucharist. Thus it seems unlikely that Peter was listing the specific parts of the service, in all of which the people referred to in Canon 8 may participate but from some of which others are excluded. Rather, because there is no indication of rank in any of the other canons, it seems best to take Peter's remarks here as general: he is listing the benefits of community.

One must conclude, in opposition to Bright, Frend, and Schwartz, that there is no clear evidence for assuming that the full penitential system of Gregory and Basil was used at Alexandria by Peter. Peter does not seem to know the technical vocabulary of such a system (although, as just discussed, he seems very close!). The most one can say—and it is significant—is that there is a two-tiered system: those excluded and those doing penance. Perhaps Peter's contribution was to abolish the

134. See ibid., 762Bff.

former class by moving all of its members (if they were contrite) into the latter, and from there, after doing assigned penance, they would be eligible for full communion.

From a study of the material presented in this chapter, it cannot be said that a clear development can be traced from Cyprian to Nicea. There are too many gaps in our sources and there is too much geographical distance to come to absolute conclusions. However, it would seem that from Cyprian to Origen to Dionysius to Peter and on to Nicea there is the gradual development of a penitential system. The evidence also seems to show that it developed, at least with regard to the lapsed, more quickly in the East.

Given the state of the sources, it is not possible to show direct or indirect influence among these bishops or councils, but if one looks chronologically, there is certainly a logic of development from Cyprian to Nicea, a development into which Peter of Alexandria clearly fits: the church was saying that it had the right to forgive sinners and vested that authority in its clergy, especially in the bishops.[135] These clergy, at least as represented by the bishops, tended toward moderation, as opposed to the rigorists, most of whom ended up outside the church. Questions like whether this moderation was Christlike mercy or the self-interest of an establishment, whether it was a falling away from the original ideal of a pure church or a realistic compromise with the world, have been and will continue to be debated. It is clear, however, that the spirit of the church during the third and fourth centuries, at least with regard to the fallen, was slowly moving toward the *philanthropia* held forth by the eleventh canon of the Council of Nicea.

The canons of Peter of Alexandria exhibit to an even larger extent than those of Nicea what *philanthropia* could mean: compassion, mercy, moderation, and forgiveness. Saint Peter was most remembered in the Greek church as a martyr and heretic-fighter, but the Coptic church

---

135. Kelly, 219, cites the Syriac *Didascalia Apostolorum* 2.23, where the bishop "is exhorted to reconcile all repentant sinners—idolaters, murderers and adulterers included. He is depicted [2.18] as sitting in the Church as a judge appointed by God and charged by Him with the power of binding and loosing. His authority is from on high, and he should be loved like a father, feared like a king and honored as God." Canons attributed to Athanasius have come down in Coptic and Arabic. For these, see W. Riedel and W. E. Crum, *The Canons of Athanasius of Alexandria* (London 1904). Riedel dates the canons to 350–500 (xiii) and concludes that it is possible that the canons are derived from a work of Athanasius (xxvi). See his discussion of the problems of attribution, vii–xxx. It is worth noting that in these canons, various degrees of penance are assigned, e.g., three years to a priest for seeing a sorcerer (#4), and one year of penance for an adulterous priest (#42).

came to venerate him as a pastor also. His canons show that the respect accorded him was well-deserved.

Appendix 1
THE *CANONICAL LETTER* OF SAINT PETER, BISHOP OF ALEXANDRIA AND MARTYR

[Superscripts refer to the commentary on each canon, appendix 3, which begins on 195.]

[468A][1]

Canons[2] of the Blessed Peter, Archbishop of Alexandria and Martyr, Which Are Given in His Work on Repentance

Canon 1

There are those who, after they were reported to the authorities and were imprisoned, at first endured intolerable tortures and unbearable whippings and many other terrible hardships but who were later betrayed by the weakness of the flesh.[3] It is true that in the beginning they were not received back into the church because of their great fall;[4] nevertheless, they have gone through many struggles and have fought long and hard.[5] To this, one should add that they have not come [468B] to their present condition by choice, but because they were betrayed by the weakness of the flesh, and that some of them now show on their bodies the marks of Jesus [cf. Gal. 6:17]. Because of these reasons and because they have spent three years in grievous mourning[6] and this is now our fourth Easter under persecution,[7] it is indeed sufficient that from the time of their presenting themselves to the church another forty days [of forced absence] be added as punishment.[8]

During these forty days they should remember that, even though our Lord and Savior Jesus Christ fasted for the same number of days after he was baptized, he was still tempted by the devil [Matt. 4:1ff.].[9] And during these days through hard spiritual exercise and keener vigilance[10] they will turn an alert mind to prayer and to profound study of what was said by the Lord to the one who tempted him and sought to make our Lord worship him: "Get behind me, Satan, for it is written, 'You shall worship the Lord your God and him only shall you serve'" [Matt. 4:10; 16:23].

Canon 2

A year [of penance] added to the other time of suffering[1] will suffice for those who were only imprisoned and, as if under siege, endured the afflictions and foul stench of their prison cells, but who, afterward, were broken down through a great lack of will power and some sort of blindness, and without the hardships of struggle became captives.[2]

This time of penance suffices since actually [469D] they too gave themselves to be punished for the name of Christ, even if they did have while in prison the great benefit of aid and comfort from their brothers. This help they will more than return since they desire to be released from the most bitter imprisonment of the devil, especially remembering the one who said: "The Spirit of the Lord is upon me, because he has anointed me to preach good news to the poor. He has sent me to proclaim release to the captives and recovery of sight to the blind, to set at liberty those who are oppressed, to proclaim the acceptable year of the Lord and the day of vengeance" [Isa. 61:1–2 (LXX)].

Canon 3

But there are those who have suffered none of these things and have shown none of the fruit of faith; [472C] rather, of their own free will they have gone over to evil, betrayed by cowardice and fear,[1] and now repent.[2] For these it is fitting and necessary to set forth the parable of the unfruitful fig tree. As the Lord says: "A man had a fig tree planted in his vineyard; and he came seeking fruit on it and found none. And he said to the vinedresser, 'Lo, these three years I have come seeking fruit on this fig tree, and I find none. Cut it down; why should it use up the ground?' And he answered him, 'Let it alone, sir, this year also, till I dig about it and put on manure. And if it bears fruit, well and good; but if not, next year you can cut it down'" [Luke 13:6–9].

If they keep this parable before their eyes [472D] and show fruit worthy of repentance for the same period of time, they will be helped greatly.[3]

Canon 4[1]

What was said concerning the other fig tree will be spoken to those who have completely given up hope and have not repented,[2] and have the Ethiopian's unchanging skin and the leopard's spots: "May no fruit ever come from you again!" [Matt. 21:19] And therefore the fig tree withers at once. For in such people what was also said by Ecclesiastes is surely fulfilled: [473B] "What is crooked cannot be adorned, and what is lacking cannot be numbered" [Eccl. 1:15]. For unless what is crooked is first made straight, it is impossible for it to be adorned; and unless what is lacking is made up, it is impossible for it to be numbered.

Therefore, what was spoken by the prophet Isaiah will happen to them in the end: "And they shall look on the dead bodies of the men that have rebelled against me; for their worm shall not die, their fire shall not be quenched, and they shall be seen by all men" [Isa. 66:24 (LXX)]. Since also it has thus been prophesied by him: "But the wicked, like the churning sea, will be thrown into confusion, and they will not be able to find rest. There is no joy for the wicked, said God" [Isa. 57:20–21 (LXX)].

Canon 5

But there are those who dissembled in order to escape death, as David did when he pretended to have an epileptic fit [cf. 1 Sam. 21:13]. And there are those who have not nakedly written down a denial [of their faith][1] but rather, when in great distress, like boys who are sensible and deliberate among their foolish fellows, have mocked the schemes of their enemies: they have either [476A] passed by the altars, or have made a written declaration,[2] or have sent non-Christians [to sacrifice] in their place.[3]

Certain ones of those who confessed the faith,[4] as I have heard, have forgiven[5] them since, above all, with great piety they have avoided lighting the sacrificial fire with their own hands and have avoided the smoke rising from the unclean demons, and since indeed they were unaware, because of their thoughtlessness, of what they were doing. Nevertheless, six months of penance will be given to them.

For in this way, they also will exceedingly be profited, meditating on the prophetic words, and saying [Isa. 9:6 (LXX)]:

To us a child is born,
   and to us [he] is given;
the government will be upon his shoulders
   and his name will be called
"Messenger of My mighty counsel."

This very child, as you know, was himself conceived to preach repentance, [476B] being conceived six months after the conception of another child who later, before his (the Lord's) advent, preached repentance for the forgiveness of sins [Luke 1:26, 36, 76–77].

Furthermore we also hear both preaching, in the first place, not only concerning repentance, but also concerning the kingdom of heaven, which, just as we have learned, is at hand [cf. Luke 17:21]. Therefore this fact which we believe with our lips and with our hearts is near to us. Concerning the kingdom of heaven, they also will remember and will learn to confess with their own lips that Jesus is Christ, believing with their own hearts that God has raised him from the dead—indeed, learning that "man believes with his heart and so is made righteous, and he confesses with his lips and so is saved" [Rom. 10:8–10].

[477C]

Canon 6

There are those who sent Christian slaves [to sacrifice] in their place. The slaves are under their masters' hand and in a way are themselves in the custody of their masters and have been threatened by them; on account of their fear they have come to their present situation and have lapsed. They will show for one year the works of repentance, learning for the future, as the slaves of Christ, to do the will of Christ and to fear him.[1] They will especially listen to this: "Whatever good anyone does, he will receive the same again from the Lord, whether he is slave or free" [Eph. 6:8].

Canon 7

But those who are free [1] will be under careful scrutiny during three years of repentance since they both dissembled and forced their fellow slaves to offer sacrifice. They have not heeded the apostle, who wishes masters to treat their slaves as they treat themselves, and to forbear threatening, as he says, knowing that he who is both their master and ours is in heaven, and [480B] that there is no partiality with him [cf. Eph. 6:9; Rom. 2:11].

If we all have one master, one who shows no partiality since Christ is both all and in all, in barbarian and Scythian, slave and free [cf. Col. 3:11; Gal. 3:28], they ought to consider what they have done: wishing to save their own souls, they have dragged into idolatry their fellow slaves who themselves would have been able to escape if [their masters] had given to them what is just and equitable, as the apostle again says.

Canon 8

There are those who have been handed over [to the authorities] and have fallen, who then of their own accord have entered into the conflict confessing themselves to be Christians, and have been thrown into prison and tortured. It is fair that we, with a joyful heart, join together in supporting them and join with them in every way in Christian fellowship—both in prayers and in receiving the body and blood of Christ, and in the consolation of the [481A] Word.[1]

We do this so that if they contend more vigorously, they too may be considered worthy "of the prize of the upward call" [Phil. 3:14]. For "a righteous man falls seven times and rises again" [Prov. 24:16]; if all those who had fallen had done this, they would have demonstrated with their whole heart a most perfect repentance.

[484A]

Canon 9

There are those who, as if from sleep, throw themselves into a conflict which is painful and promises to be a protracted one; they bring upon themselves a temptation which is like fighting against the sea and its many waves—or rather, they are as it were heaping up coals to inflame the sinners against the brethren. With these also we must join in Christian fellowship,[1] since they enter into the conflict in the name of Christ, even if they do not heed his words when he teaches, "Pray that you may not enter into temptation," and when again he says to the Father in prayer, "And lead us not into temptation, but deliver us from evil" [Matt. 26:41; 6:13].

And perhaps they also do not know that our Master and Teacher withdrew many times from those who wished to set traps for him, and that [484B] there were times when he did not walk about openly because of these people [cf. John 11:54]. Even when the time of his passion drew near, he did not hand himself over, but rather waited until they came for him with "swords and clubs" [Matt. 26:55].[2] He said to them, "Have you come out against a robber, with swords and clubs to capture me?" And they "delivered him," [the Gospel] says, "to Pilate" [Matt 27:2].

Therefore, those who walk keeping him as an example experience the same things he did, as they keep in mind his divine words, through which he strengthens us as he speaks about persecution: "Take heed to yourselves; for they will deliver you up to councils, and flog you in their synagogues" [Matt. 10:17]. He says "they will deliver you up," not "you shall deliver yourselves up"

[Matt. 10:17], and "you will be brought before governors and kings on account of my name" [484C] [Matt. 10:18], not "you shall bring yourselves."

He also wishes us to move about from place to place when we are being persecuted for his name, as we again hear him saying: "And when they persecute you from this town, flee to the next" [Matt. 10:23].[3] For he does not wish us of our own accord to go over to the supporters and accomplices of the devil, for if we did so we would become the cause of many deaths and would be forcing them to become harsher and to carry out their works of death.[4]

Rather, he wishes us to wait patiently and to take heed for ourselves, to watch and pray so that we may not enter into temptation. Thus Stephen, following in his footsteps, was the first to suffer martyrdom. He was seized by lawbreakers in Jerusalem and brought before the council; when he [484D] was stoned he was glorified in the name of Christ, and crying out he said: "Lord, do not hold this against them" [Acts 7:59; cf. Luke 23:24].[5]

Thus James, the second [martyr], was seized by Herod and beheaded with a sword. In the same way Peter, the first-chosen among the apostles, was often seized and thrown into prison and [485A] dishonored, and was finally crucified in Rome. And the famous Paul time after time was handed over [to the authorities] and was in danger of dying. He undertook many struggles and boasted about the many times he was persecuted and his many afflictions; in the same city he also was beheaded with the sword and ended his life doing those things about which he boasted. In Damascus he was lowered at night in a basket over the wall and escaped the hands of the one who sought to arrest him [cf. Acts 9:23–25; 2 Cor. 11:32–33].

They set before themselves first to preach the good news and teach the Word of God, in which "they strengthened the brethren to continue in the faith" [Acts 14:22]. They also said that "through many tribulations we must enter the kingdom of God" [Acts 14:22]. For they did not seek what was beneficial to themselves but rather what would benefit the many, in order that the many might be saved. And he told them many things about these matters, that they might act according to the Word. [I say this in conclusion] lest, in the words of the apostle, "the time fail us" as we explain these matters [Heb. 11:32].

Canon 10

Therefore it is not fair that those who of their own accord deserted and fell from the [ranks of the] clergy and [later] took up the struggle again remain any longer in church office.[1] They abandoned the Lord's flock and brought blame upon themselves—which none of the apostles ever did. For indeed the blessed apostle Paul, after he had undergone many persecutions, and was able to display the trophies from many contests, and though he knew that it was better "to depart and be with Christ," still was able to say: "To remain in the flesh is more necessary on your account" [Phil. 1:23–24]. Since he did not consider what was beneficial for himself, [488C] but rather what was beneficial for the many in order that they might be saved, he believed that staying with the brethren and caring for them was more important than rest for himself. He also wished the teacher to be for the faithful "a model in his teaching" [Tit. 2:7].

Therefore, those who sought to justify the faith in prison, but who fell from their ministry and [afterward] took up the struggle again, clearly lack perception. For why else do they seek that which they have abandoned when they are able for the present to be of some benefit to their brethren? As long as they remained steadfast, they were forgiven for what they had done contrary to reason, but since they have lapsed—as people who boast[2] and bring blame upon themselves—they are no longer able to minister in the church. Therefore, let them in humility give thought to how they might "perform,"[3] ceasing from vanity and self-delusion.

[488D] Christian fellowship is sufficient for them. This [judgment] is given with care and scrupulousness for two reasons: that they not think that they are distressed and therefore look for a violent departure from here; and that some of the lapsed not have a pretext because of their punishment, to slacken [from what the faith requires]. [489A] These will have more shame and reproach than all the others, like the one who laid the foundation and was not able to finish it. For all those who are passing by, [the Gospel] says, will begin to mock him, saying, "This man laid a foundation, and was not able to finish it" [Luke 14:29–30].

Canon 11

There are those who leaped into the turmoil of the persecution and gathered around the law court watching the holy martyrs hasten to "the prize of the[ir] high calling" [Phil. 3:14] and with noble zeal desired to hand themselves over too. They were courageous and fearless, especially when they saw those who had been brought down and lapsed; on their account they became fired up and [496B] were urged on from within to wage war against the exultant Adversary. They hastened to do this in order that he not seem "wise in his own conceit" [Rom. 12:16 (KJV)], thinking that he had defeated them through cunning. He hadn't noticed that he himself had been defeated by those who endured the torment of flesh-scrapers and whips, the sharpness of swords, burning of fires, and submersion under water.[1]

It is right that we give our approval to those who according to faith think it right that prayers and petitions ought to be made, either on behalf of those who have been punished in prison and have been betrayed by hunger and thirst, or on behalf of those who outside of prison have been tortured before the judges with skin-scrapers and whips and afterward have been defeated by the weakness of the flesh.[2] [496C] For indeed it harms no one to sympathize with and share in the sufferings of those who weep and mourn on behalf of parents, brethren, or children who have been defeated in the struggle by the great strength of the evil-scheming devil.

We know indeed that because of the faith of others some have had the benefit of God's goodness in the forgiveness of sin, in the health of their bodies, and in the resurrection of the dead. Therefore we are mindful of the many miseries and troubles they have undergone in the name of Christ; not only have they repented, but they also mourn for what they did when they were betrayed by the weakness and mortality of the flesh. Furthermore they testify that they, as it were, have been disenfranchised from the faith. Let us pray with them and plead together for their reconciliation, [496D] and for other proper things, through him who is "our Advocate with the Father," who makes propitiation for our sins. And, [scripture] says, "if anyone sins, we have an Advocate with the Father, Jesus Christ the righteous, and he is the propitiation for our sins" [1 John 2:1].

Canon 12

No accusation is to be brought against those who gave money in order to remain completely undisturbed by any evil.[1] In order not to damage or destroy their souls they have borne a fine and loss of property which others, because of shameful greed, have not done. For the Lord says, "What will it profit a man, if he gains the whole world and forfeits [500C] his soul, or loses it? [Matt. 16:26]. Again he says, "You cannot serve God and mammon" [Matt. 6:24]. Therefore in these things they have shown that they are servants of God because they have hated, trampled, and despised their money and have fulfilled what is written: "The ransom of a man's life is his wealth" [Prov. 13:8 (LXX)].[2]

We also read in the Acts of the Apostles that there were those who were dragged in place of Paul and Silas before the civic magistrates in Thessalonica, and were released after giving satisfaction. For after they [the Jews] burdened them greatly on account of his name and disturbed the crowd and the civic magistrates, [scripture] says that "when they had taken security from Jason and the rest, they let them go. [500D] The brethren immediately sent Paul and Silas away by night to Beroea" [Acts 17:5ff.].

Canon 13

Therefore, nor is it right to accuse those who gave up everything for the safety of their lives and withdrew, even if others were detained because of them.[1] For at Ephesus also, instead of Paul they seized Gaius and Aristarchus, Paul's traveling companions, [and took them to] the theatre [cf. Acts 19:26–30]. Since the uproar came about because Paul had persuaded a large group of them and brought them over to the worship of God, "he wished to enter the crowd," but his disciples would not let him" [Acts 19:30]. What is more, "some of the Asiarchs also, who were friends of his, sent to him and begged him not to venture into the theatre" [Acts 19:31].

But if anyone continues to quibble against those who sincerely hold [501C] to the saying "Flee for your life; do not look back" [Gen. 19:17], let him also remember what happened to Peter, the leader of the apostles. He was thrown into prison and handed over to four squads of soldiers who were to guard him [cf. Acts 12:4]. After he fled at night and was rescued from the hands of the Jews by the command of the angel of the Lord, it says that "when day came, there was no small stir among the soldiers over what had become of Peter. And when Herod had sought for him and could not find him, he interrogated the sentries and ordered that they should be put to death" [Acts 12:18–19].

No blame is reckoned to Peter for their death, for it was possible for them, when they heard what had happened, to escape—just as [501D] all the children in Bethlehem and in the territory around the city [might have escaped] if their parents had known what was going to happen [Matt. 12:13–16]. These children were killed by the cruel murderer Herod because he was seeking to kill the child—who also escaped by the command of the angel of the Lord. [504A] This child now quickly began to strip the slain enemy of his arms and quickly began to plunder, in accord with the meaning of his name, as it is written: "Call his name 'The one who quickly strips his enemy and quickly plunders'; for before the child knows how to cry 'Father' or 'Mother,' the wealth of Damascus and the spoils of Samaria will be carried away before the King of Assyria" [Isa. 8:3–4 (LXX)].[2]

The Magi therefore, since they have been "stripped" and "plundered," sub-missively and as suppliants adore the Child, opening their treasures and offering to him the most fitting and proper gifts, gold and frankincense and myrrh, as to a king, to God and to man. Being assisted by Providence, they no longer thought it right to return to the Assyrian king. [504B] For "being warned in a dream not to return to Herod, they departed to their own country by another way." Then the bloodthirsty Herod, "when he saw that he had been tricked by the wise men, was in a furious rage, and he sent and killed all the male children in Bethlehem and in all that region who were two years old or under, according to the time which he had ascertained from the wise men" [Matt. 2:16–17]. In addition to the wise men, he had sought to kill another child who had been born previously, and when he did not find him, he murdered his father "between the sanctuary and the alter" [cf. Matt. 23:55; 2 Chron. 24:10–22],[3] the child escaping with this mother Elizabeth. On account of these things, they have no blame.

Canon 14

Some have suffered great violence and torture, and have had chains put in their mouths; through the working of their faith they have steadfastly endured having their hands burned when they were forced, against their will, to offer unholy sacrifice.[1]

From prison the thrice-blessed witnesses for the faith, and others of their fellow ministers, have written to me concerning these same things which were done to those in Libya. Such witnesses as these who have had others—espe-cially others of the brethren—bear witness for them [505B] may be placed in the ministry among those who confessed the faith.[2] They were mortified through many tortures, and no longer had the strength to speak or even utter a sound or make any movement of resistance against those who in vain were acting violently against them. They did not assent to their brutal conduct.[3]

In the same way I have again heard from their fellow ministers that each person who conducts himself as Timothy did will be placed among those who confessed the faith. He too obeyed the one who said, "Aim at righteousness, godliness, faith, love, steadfastness, gentleness. Fight the good fight of the faith; take hold of the eternal life to which you were called when you made the good confession in the presence of many witnesses" [1 Tim. 6:11–12].

[For "Canon 15," see chap. 2, 138]

Appendix 2
TWO SYRIAC FRAGMENTS CONCERNING THE
LAPSED ATTRIBUTED TO SAINT PETER
OF ALEXANDRIA

In 1856 Paul Lagarde published the Greek text of Saint Peter's *Canonical Letter*, along with a Syriac translation from Paris Syriac codex 62.[136] The Syriac contains two pieces not found in the received Greek text, one before Canon 1 and one between Canons 13 and 14. Edouard Schwartz considered them authentic,[137] as did F. H. Kettler and, apparently, Harnack and Bardenhewer.[138] Their opinions seem to be justified. There is nothing hagiographical about the fragments, and they fit well within the context of the canons preserved in Greek.

Lagarde and Schwartz both gave Greek retroversions from the Syriac, and I have used the latter's in making my translation into English.[139] There has heretofore been no English translation.

Fragment 1

From the Teaching of Saint Peter, Bishop of Alexandria and Martyr, Concerning Those Who Lapsed during the Persecution.

In order that we might make finally and willingly repentant those who, of their own accord, have fallen into the snare(s) of the devil[140]—those who were caught by him according to his will—let us restore those who with all (their) might flee him, praying[141] especially for them to have faith in God and a good conscience in Jesus Christ our Lord who said, "Be merciful, even as your heavenly Father is merciful. Judge not, that you might not be judged; condemn not, that you might not be condemned; forgive, and it will be forgiven to you; give, and it will be given to you; good measure, running over, will be put in your lap. For the measure you give will be the measure you get back" [Luke 6:36–38].[142]

By this time it is just to determine the means of healing which comes especially through repentance, because we hear that not every wound is healed by the same compress. With regard to these things, all of you must in every way heed the Lord who says, "Take heed to yourselves lest your hearts be weighed down with dissipation and drunkenness and the cares of this life, and that day come upon you like a snare; for it will come upon all who dwell upon the face of

136. Lagarde, 62–73 (Greek); 99–117 (Syriac).
137. Schwartz, "Zur Geschichte," 164–87.
138. Kettler, "Petros 1," 1286: "Der Briefcharacter, welcher durch die gegenwartigen Überschriften im Griechischen und Syrischen verdunkelt ist, wird noch durch den Schluss des Syrers τέλος τῆς ἐπιστολῆς Πέτρου usw. bezeugt." See Harnack, *Geschichte* 1/1:445; 2/2:73; Bardenhewer 2:243.
139. Lagarde, 46–54; Schwartz, "Zur Geschichte," 166–69.
140. See Ignatius of Antioch *Trall.* 8; *Phld.* 6, for similar language. See Canon 11.
141. See Basil Epistle 217, can. 84 (Schwartz).
142. The tone of the fragment is very similar to Dionysius's writings on repentance. See Feltoe, *St. Dionysius*, 62.

the whole earth. But watch at all times, praying that you may have strength to escape all these things that will take place, and to stand before the Son of man" [Luke 21:34–36].

Fragment 2

These things I have written with great urgency, brothers, groaning and weeping greatly over the evils that have happened, in order that we might once again remember the things which the Lord spoke at the end: "In the world you have tribulation; but take courage, I have overcome the world" [John 16:33]. Therefore, encouraging our brothers who have fallen, let us adduce what was spoken by the prophet to those in captivity. He said to them: "Have courage, children, and call upon God, for the one who is leading (you) into captivity will remember you. For just as you purposed to go astray from God, return with tenfold zeal to him to seek him" [Bar. 4:27–28].

Another prophet says: "Seek God while he may be found (and) call upon him when he is near to you. Let the wicked man forsake his ways, and the unrighteous man his counsels [Isa. 55:6–7 (LXX)]. For if you thus approach (God) and uphold the canon in the fashion of the sinful woman about whom we hear in the Gospel of Luke [cf. Luke 7:38ff.], (and) stand behind the Lord and wet his feet with many tears of repentance and amendment from (your) shattered heart, and with the hairs of your head wipe (his feet clean) by (bearing) fruit worthy of repentance, (that is), good works, and remember the word which was said: "From it too you will come away with your hands upon your head" [Jer. 2:37 (LXX)], unceasingly kissing his feet with the great love of one who is not a hypocrite, and anointing with myrrh to create in addition a sweet fragrance through amendment, then the gentle and merciful Lord will speak on your behalf to those who grumble to themselves, the double-minded, the leprous, those of little faith and those who do no such thing (i.e., repent) for the Lord, those who justify themselves before men. Just as (Jesus said) for the sake of Simon the leper, I say to you: Your sins, which are many, are forgiven, for you have loved much. But he to whom little is forgiven, also loves little [cf. Luke 7:47].[143]

Therefore, even if certain limits and forms and regulations for repentance be set down, nevertheless the ardent faith of each person and the firm steadfast zeal and especially good deeds done both before and after this great temptation, and the pure way of (a) life in Christ all constitute (even) stronger and more powerful healing agents. For it was so that the woman with the hemorrhage, filled with great faith, having touched the Lord, came up and received health before the daughter of the ruler of the synagogue [cf. Mark 5:21ff.].

Therefore, it is necessary for those who interpret[144] to the catechumens, imparting (to them) baptism and (giving) to the laity the distribution (of the

---

143. Luke has "one of the Pharisees" (7:36), but the parallels in Matt. 26:6 and Mark 14:3 have "Simon the leper." Only Luke has the saying quoted here (Luke 7:47). This is a nice case of harmonization.

144. ἐξοδεύουσιν. See Nicea Canon 13 and Basil Epistle 217, can. 73 (Schwartz).

Eucharist) to show fruit worthy of repentance.[145] If it is pleasing to you, let these things be applied in general to those from the laity and those from the clergy, even if it is written that "the powerful will be afflicted powerfully, and the least will be shown mercy" [Wis. 6:7], "and the one to whom much has been given, more will be demanded from him" [Luke 12:48].

But it suffices for them, that is, to those of the clergy, the other additional penalty: they no longer can boast of taking part in the eucharistic liturgy[146]—not only them but also those who were considered worthy of the spiritual gifts[147] and later fell—except if someone renews the struggle and overcomes (his fall) by his own patient endurance.[148] For the divine Word wishes those in authority over the people to be without reproach[149] [cf. 1 Tim. 3:2, 10] and the teaching through works is very clear and precise for the teacher. (Jesus) himself says, "He who does (the least of these commandments) and teaches (them), this one shall be called great in the kingdom of heaven" [Matt. 5:19]. For on account of this the apostle also exhorts Timothy, saying, "Let no one despise your youth, but set the believers an example in speech, in conduct, in love, in faith, and purity" [1 Tim. 4:12].

Appendix 3
COMMENTARY ON THE CANONS OF
THE *CANONICAL LETTER*

Canon 1 (see 140–41, 144, 154–55, 166, 174, 177, 178)

1. The bracketed figures refer to the column numbers in *PG* 18.

2. W. Bright, "Petrus I, St." *DCB* 4:331–32, gives a summary of the canons; as does Edouard Schwartz, "Zur Geschichte des Athanasius," *NGG* (1905) 170. Geoffrey de Ste. Croix, "Aspects of the 'Great' Persecution," *HTR* 47 (1954) 84, calls the work a "Canonical Letter." W. H. C. Frend, *Martyrdom and Persecution in the Early Church* (Grand Rapids, Mich. 1981) 540, terms it an "encyclical." For the use of "canon," see Eusebius *HE* 7.20.1. In discussing a paschal letter of Dionysius, Eusebius says that Dionysius "sets forth a canon (κανόνα)." Dionysius is called κανονικός by Basil (Ep. 188.1, περὶ κανόνων). The 692 synod "In Trullo" joins Peter and Dionysius as "canonical." See C. L. Feltoe, *DIONYSIOU LEIPSANA: The Letters and Other Remains of Dionysius of Alexandria* (Cambridge 1904) x and 91 (hereafter, *Dionysius: Letters*). See also Dionysius's letters to Conon (*Dionysius: Letters*, 59ff.) and to Fabius (Eusebius *HE* 6.41) for letters on the same subject as Peter's.

3. For a list of tortures, see Eusebius *The Martyrs of Palestine* 1.33 (shorter version), in *The Ecclesiastical History and the Martyrs of Palestine*, ed. H. J. Lawlor

---

145. See Canon 3 for the same phrase.
146. λειτουργίας. See Canon 10.
147. πνευματικοῦ χαρίσματος.
148. "The rulings of Canons 1 and 2 of Ancyra are harsher" (Schwartz); see Canon 8.
149. See the ninth canon of Nicea (Schwartz) and Peter's Canon 10.

and J. E. L. Oulton (London 1928, 1954) 333. For Tertullian on torture as a sign of God's favor, see *De fuga* 5. For Dionysius, see the letter to Fabius (*HE* 6.41). Cyprian, in *De lapsis* 13–14, says that a plea of torture "may truly avail for forgiveness, such a defense deserves our pity." See also Cyprian Ep. 56.1 and Ste. Croix, "Aspects," 80. On the church's willingness to receive fallen brethren, see Cyprian Epp. 8.2; 57.5. Dionysius, in C. L. Feltoe, *St. Dionysius of Alexandria: Letters and Treatises* (New York, 1918) 62, is representative: "Let us then not repel those who return, but gladly welcome them and number them with those who have not strayed, and thus supply that which is wanting in them."

4. This must refer to their sacrificing. See Ste. Croix, "Aspects," 79ff.

5. Canon 1 distinguishes those who willingly sacrificed after torture from those in Canon 14 who were forced to sacrifice by eating and drinking; the latter had the food and drink shoved down their throats. The fourth canon of Ancyra punishes the former with six years of penance, while the fifth punishes the latter with three years.

6. See 154–55.

7. This sentence dates the canons to Eastertime 306, but it cannot be determined whether they were written before or after Easter. Τέταρτον ἤδη πάσχα ἐπικατείληφε τὸν διωγμόν in Greek idiom does not necessarily mean that Easter is past. The clause states that this is the fourth Easter spent under persecution, but does not indicate whether the writer is saying this before or after Easter. See 139–40 above and 140 n. 5.

8. For a comparison to Peter's leniency, see Canons 1 and 2 of the canons of the Council of Elvira, where apostasy is a "capital offense," and the offender "is not to be received into communion, even at the end of his life." See Origen *Exhortation to Martyrdom* 7–10, trans. John J. O'Meara (Westminster, Md. 1954), where apostasy is the greatest corruption. See also Heb. 6:4–8, where apostates are equated with crucifiers of Christ. Balsamon, in his commentary (205 below), draws attention to the canons of Ancyra.

9. In translating the canons, I have followed the Revised Standard Version (RSV). I have, however, silently altered the RSV version where necessary to conform to Peter's text.

10. See Zonaras's commentary on this canon (205–6 below).

Canon 2 (see 144–45)

1. The Greek here is ambiguous. What the "other time of suffering" refers to is not clear. It could refer to the "forty days" of penance imposed in Canon 1, but there is no guarantee that the extant canons are in their original order. Possibly the "time of suffering" refers to imprisonment, and a year of penance is to be added to that. Both Balsamon and Zonaras understand the "other time" to be the three years mentioned in Canon 1. This is most likely to be correct. The penance is longer here because these sinners have suffered a bit less, and also because (1) their term of imprisonment may not have been as long as three years, and (2) they show no "stigmata."

2. See Cyprian Ep. 57.3 for the beginnings of a penitential system that allows for distinctions such as Peter makes in Canons 1–4 between various lapsi. References to Cyprian's letters are from *Letters of Saint Cyprian*, trans. Sister Rose

Bernard Donna, C.S.J. (Washington, D.C. 1965); the Latin text may be found in *Saint Cyprien: Correspondance*, ed. Le Chanoine Bayard (Paris 1961). Dionysius's letter to Fabius (*HE* 6.41.13) deals with the same problem as this canon.

Canon 3 (see 144–45, 151, 166, 177–79)

1. See Cyprian *De lapsis* 8 for possibly a fuller description. Dionysius (*HE* 6.41.12) says that such as these "will be saved with difficulty." Canon 6 of Ancyra gives those who lapsed after punishment six years of penance. Canon 11 of Nicea punishes those who lapsed "without being driven to it by necessity, or by the confiscation of their goods, or by any danger whatever," with twelve years of penance—and considers this judgment to be "philanthropia." See C. J. Hefele, *History of the Ecclesiastical Councils* (repr., Edinburgh [1894] 1972) 1:416.

2. See 147–48 above.

3. Again, the text as we have it is ambiguous. Balsamon takes the penance to be for three years, Zonaras four. Either is possible. Since there are no extenuating circumstances in these people's apostasy such as torture (Canon 1) or imprisonment (Canon 2), their penance is longer. Frend, *Martyrdom*, 540, 563 n. 25, says that Canon 3 refers to the "eventual rehabilitation" of the clergy. This must be a mistake, for Canon 3 makes no mention of clergy. See Canon 10 and notes.

Canon 4 (see 144–45, 148, 154)

1. Bright, "Petrus I., 331, notes, with justification, that this canon "is not, strictly speaking, a canon, but a lamentation over *lapsi* who had not repented." See W. Telfer, *Forgiveness of Sins* (London 1969) 40: "It goes without saying that Christians who sinned and did not repent, were held to be lost, alike to the Church and to the hope of final salvation." Canon 22 of Arles states that those who apostatize and do not do penance will not be given communion until they show fruits worthy of repentance.

2. See *De lapsis* 24–26 for Cyprian's stories about what happens to the unrepentant. In Epistle 35 Cyprian berates those "who refuse to do penance," and in Ep. 55.23 he says that these are "completely cut off from the hope of communion and peace." Zonaras says that they are unrepentant "out of despair, or from evil motives."

Canon 5 (see 144–45, 150, 153, 166, 168)

1. μὴ γυμνῶς ἀπογραψαμένοις τὰ πρὸς ἄρνησιν. Zonaras interprets this phrase: "Some pretend to approach the altars or write a denial of their faith but did not nakedly (that is, clearly and openly) write down a denial." Routh, in his commentary on the canons, assumes that these written denials are *libelli* and that the writers are libellatici; see *RS* 4:57. See n. 3 below.

2. χειρογραφήσαντες. Lampe, 1522A, s.v. χειρογραφέω, cites this passage: "acknowledge in writing, of recanting persons." Does this refer to a *libellus*? John R. Knipfing, "The Libelli of the Decian Persecution," *HTR* 16 (1923) 358, says that the libellatici were Christians "who had obtained a libellus, and had had it attested without having actually performed the sacrifice. This group were distinguished from the *sacrificati*, or Christians who had actually sacrificed." E. A.

Judge and S. R. Pickering, "Papyrus Documentation of Church and Community in Egypt to the Mid-Fourth Century," *JAC* 20 (1977) 47 n. 1, refer to a "forthcoming" article in *ANRW* by B. F. Harris and S. R. Pickering which will be the most comprehensive work on the Decian libelli.

G. W. Clarke, "Some Observations on the Persecution of Decius," *Anticthon* 3 (1969) 74, points out that "in the West what was purchased [i.e., a *libellus*] was significant (for the East our sources are comparatively meagre). For a Christian it was tantamount to a formal declaration of apostasy, and by acknowledging a *libellus* as his own a Christian was, technically, guilty of denying his faith. He joined the ranks of the *lapsi*, the fallen." Geoffrey de Ste. Croix, "The Persecutions," in *The Crucible of Christianity*, ed. A. J. Toynbee (New York 1969) 349, rightly points out that even in the West there were degrees of lapsed, and the libellatici were treated more leniently; they "were deemed to have apostasized, but their offense was treated as a much more venial one than sacrificing itself: Cyprian insists that it is a less grave sin than, for instance, adultery. These *libellatici* were accepted back into the Church on very easy terms; the *sacrificati* and *turificati*, who had actually sacrificed or offered incense, were only readmitted on proof of penitence and after a long probation."

Ste. Croix, "The Persecutions," 350, insists that there were no libellatici in the East: "the purchase of exemptions did take place, but was not regarded as sinful, so that those who had obtained false certificates by bribery or otherwise were not regarded as apostates in any sense." He cites Canons 12 and 13 as evidence, but Canon 5 seems to offer opposing evidence: Peter speaks of "nakedly writing down a denial" (see n. 2 above) and opposes that to those who have not done so.

Clarke, 74, disagrees with Ste. Croix; he says these persons are indeed libellatici, but suggests that the wording "may have differed widely" between the Decian and Great Persecution (see Knipfing, 345ff., for examples of *libelli*). The wording, he says, was unequivocal during the Decian Persecution—one had sacrificed (see Knipfing, 346–47)—but during the Great Persecution one could avoid making a statement of apostasy. He hypothesizes a *libellus*: "'I hereby command that no further action is required on the part of inhabitant X concerning the fulfillment of the terms of edict Y. Signed Magistrate Z.' No technical apostasy need have been involved in the *libelli* of the Great Persecution, and hence those who have obtained them were not censured by Peter of Alexandria." He concludes that "practice in this sort of casuistry makes for perfection."

T. D. Barnes, *Tertullian* (Oxford 1971) 171 n. 4, considers Clarke's study an "exculpation," which, given the last sentence quoted above, is surprising. Is it "casuistry" on Peter's part? Clarke suggests that the definition of a *libellus*—and its owner, a libellaticus—had changed from the time of Decius to that of Diocletian. As I suggest (216–19) the definition of "martyr" changed also—and the definitions go closely together. Already in Cyprian (see 155–59) one can see that the definitions are close to what they would be in Peter's time. Just as a martyr changes from a "blood-witness" (Frend) to one who professes the faith by any means, including flight (Canons 9 and 13), so too might the definition of libellaticus change: from a person who has apostatized to one who has avoided apostasy (by obtaining a writ). It is difficult to be absolutely certain about these things, but given the tenor of Peter's canons, such a conclusion does not seem unreasonable. For an analogous change in the word "heresy," see R. A. Markus, "The Problem of Self-Definition: From Sect to Church," chap. 1 in *From Augustine to Gregory the Great: History and Christianity in Late Antiquity* (London 1983) 10–11.

3. Balsamon and Zonaras try to clarify this sentence. Apparently, Peter lists different ways of dissembling, the first two of which are rather vague. Evidence for such dissembling is now provided by the papyri. In a papyrus fragment (Papyrus Oxyrhyncus xxxi [1966], 2601), a certain Copres who is involved in a lawsuit must sacrifice as part of that legal action. E. A. Judge and S. R. Pickering, "Papyrus Documentation of Church and Community in Egypt to the Mid-Fourth Century," *JAC* 20 (1977) 48, date this fragment to the beginning of the fourth century. They say (53) it "documents a requirement to sacrifice such as we know Diocletian imposed on all litigants in his edict of 23 February, 303." The litigant "does not seem unduly put out and evades it by giving power of attorney to his 'brother' (an unbeliever?). One can only assume that this was an acceptable device for circumventing the difficulty, or that the situation was so novel that it had not yet occurred to people such as Copres that a serious crisis of conscience was posed." The former explanation is more likely. See n. 2 above.

4. ὁμολογεῖν.

5. From the beginning of the persecution to its end, the question of confessors forgiving the lapsed was a troublesome one in the church. Eusebius, at the end of the persecution, speaks (*HE* 9.1.9) of the lapsed "begging the strong for the right hand of safety, and supplicating God to be merciful to them." He reports that at the beginning of the persecutions, the martyrs of Lyons forgave those who were not martyrs (*HE* 5.1.45). Epiphanius reports (*Adv. haer.* 68) that at Alexandria those who had fallen "went to those who had confessed and borne witness [martyrs] in order to obtain mercy through repentance."

For a discussion of confessor and lapsed, see Telfer, *Forgiveness*, 67–69. On the power of the martyrs, see W. H. C. Frend, *The Donatist Church* (Oxford 1952) 116; and Tertullian *Ad martyres* 1. Frend notes (*Donatist Church*, 121) that "Tertullian was as hostile as Cyprian to the popular claim that a confessor could forgive deadly sins while still on earth." For the opposition of Cyprian, Dionysius, and Peter to confessor forgiveness, see 148–50, 167–68 above.

Canon 6 (see 144–46, 153, 166)

1. Balsamon says that Peter "pardons" these slaves who sacrificed for their masters—which is not strictly correct. He is correct, however, in seeing that Peter "does not place a heavy burden on them; he does indeed treat them leniently."

Canon 7 (see 144–45, 153, 166)

1. That is, the masters of the slaves mentioned in Canon 6.

Canon 8 (see 144–46, 157, 160, 166–67, 178)

1. That is, in full communion. See Cyprian, Epistles 24 and 25 for similar judgments. Epistle 8.3 gives the Roman view that one could "correct" one's "former error," or fall. See also Ep. 55.16, 19. See Eusebius *HE* 5.1.25 where Biblis,

a martyr of Lyons, falls and returns to the faith. Ste. Croix "Aspects," 83, comments: "Voluntary martyrdom was officially condemned by the orthodox, except in the case of those who were seeking to redeem an earlier lapse."

Canon 9 (see 144–46, 157, 160, 166–67, 178)

1. The phrasing here is interesting. Peter appears to be saying that the zealots in Canon 9 are to be equated with the fallen (and restored) of Canon 8, although his tone here is begrudging: he seems to have more doubts about the zealots.

2. *The Martyrdom of Polycarp*, following the Gospel accounts, has similar details.

3. See Clement of Alexandria *Stromateis* 4.10 (Stählin, 4.76.1); Tertullian *De fuga* 9 (ANF 4:119); Origen *Contra Celsum* 1.65 (*Contra Celsum*, ed. Henry Chadwick [Cambridge 1980] 60). See n. 4 below.

4. Clement of Alexandria *Stromateis* 4.10 (*PG* 8:1285 = Stählin 4.76.1) advises the same thing. See also Canon 13. Scholars disagree greatly in their opinions of Peter's counsel. C. Schmidt, "Fragmente einer Schrift des Martyrerbischof Petrus von Alexandrien," TU, V/4b (1901) 18–20, regards Peter's canons as an exculpation for his flight; O. Bardenhewer, *Geschichte der altkirchlichen Literatur* (2d ed., Freiburg 1914) 2:306 n. 1, disagrees with Schmidt. W. H. C. Frend, *Martyrdom*, 498, calls Peter "chicken-hearted" (!), although he accepts the flight of Gregory Thaumaturgus with equanimity (410). T. D. Barnes, *Tertullian*, 171, gives a gnostic genealogy to Peter's actions by tracing his defense of flight to Clement and thence to Basilides and Heracleon! Edgar J. Goodspeed and Robert M. Grant, *A History of Early Christian Literature* (Chicago 1966) 128, suggest that Origen disapproved of Clement's flight, and that is the reason Clement is not mentioned once in any of Origen's works.

The story of the precocious zealotry of Origen's youth is well-known, and he did write an exhortation to martyrdom in 235. However, in the *Contra Celsum*, written 246–48, he seems to have modified his views (1.65; Chadwick, 60):

> Jesus taught his disciples not to be rash, saying to them: 'If they persecute you in this city flee to another; and if they persecute you in that, flee again to yet another.' And he gave them this example of his teaching by his tranquil life; he was careful not to meet dangers unnecessarily or at the wrong time or for no good reason.

See also *Contra Celsum* 1.66 (Chadwick, 61). In 8.44 (Chadwick, 484) he says that "even if a Christian were to run away, he would not do so for cowardice, but because he was keeping the commandment of his Master [i.e., in Matt. 10:23] and preserving himself free from harm *that others might be helped to gain salvation*" (emphasis added).

Tertullian, of course, disagreed with such advice and says that those who use Matt. 10:23 in such a way are doing so as a "cloak for their cowardice" (*De fuga* 6). He offers (*De fuga* 9; ANF 4:119) an interesting piece of exegesis on Matt. 10:23: "We maintain that this belongs specially to the persons of the apostles, and to their times and circumstances." For Tertullian persecution was given by God and is not to be avoided (*De fuga* 4). Barnes, *Tertullian*, 177, concludes that for

Tertullian flight "is permitted and better than apostasy under torture, but what is permitted is not necessarily good. . . . Flight from persecution he no longer regards as normal: he now condemns it as a *pis aller* for the weaker brethren." In *De fuga* 9.4 Tertullian says, "Desire not to die in bed, in childbirth or from fever, but in martyrdom, to glorify him who suffered for us."

Martyrdom was used by Tertullian to set off and define Christianity. See Markus, 6: "Here, after all, had been the most visible expression of the line that divided the church from the world outside it. The line was shifting and beginning to break in Tertullian's generation; as he was himself, sometimes, keenly aware, church and world were growing together and beginning to interpenetrate."

Cyprian held views entirely opposed to Tertullian. For Cyprian "going underground" was an act of confession (*De lapsis* 3; see also *De lapsis* 10, Epistles 8, 20, 57.4, and 58.3). In Epistle 81, his last letter, Cyprian offers the same advice as Origen: "keep quiet and tranquility [sic], lest anyone of you should stir up any tumult for the brethren or offer himself voluntarily to the Gentiles." See 155–59 above for a discussion of "substitutionary confession" and martyrdom.

Eusebius, though a zealous advocate of martyrdom (see *Martyrs of Palestine* 1.3 [shorter recension]; Lawlor and Oulton 1:333), approves of Dionysius's flight (*HE* 6.40.2). Like Cyprian, Dionysius considered flight a victory over the Enemy; it is even a sign of election (*HE* 6.42.2). See 167 above.

Clement, Origen, Cyprian, Dionysius, and Peter all defend flight from persecution—their own, and that of the brethren. Athanasius gives the imprimatur to flight (*De fuga* 22; J. Stevenson, *A New Eusebius* [London 1963] 170):

Thus the saints, as I said before, were abundantly preserved in their flight by the providence of God, as physicians for the sake of them that had need. And to all men generally, even to us is this given, that we should flee when we are persecuted, and hide ourselves when we are sought after, and not rashly tempt the Lord, but should wait. . . . This rule the blessed martyrs observed in their several persecutions. When persecuted, they fled; while concealing themselves, they showed fortitude; and when discovered they submitted themselves to martyrdom.

One can hardly escape the conclusion that the rigorists (Montanists, Melitians, Novatianists, Donatists), who advocated martyrdom, stood outside the church, while orthodoxy (the bishops ruling a growing and more established church) opposed martyrdom. Ignatius of Antioch is not held up as an example by any of the bishops discussed here.

At Alexandria there was a tradition, going back at least to Clement, that a martyr is not one who dies, but one who is perfected (*Stromateis* 4.4; ANF 2:411–12): "We call martyrdom perfection, not because the man comes to the end of his life as others, but because he has exhibited the perfect work of love." In *Stromateis* 4.7.43 (cited by Frend, *Martyrdom*, 355) Clement says that "whoever follows out the commands of the Savior bears witness ($\mu\alpha\rho\tau\upsilon\rho\epsilon\hat{\iota}$) . . . crucifying the flesh with its desires and passions." The Christian gnostic tractate *The Testimony of Truth*, which was probably written in the third century in the area around Alexandria (*NHLE*, 406), speaks against seeking "perfection" through martyrdom (*NHLE*, 408 par. 34).

Eusebius could say that a Christian is "perfected" in dying for Christ, but Clement ordinarily saw perfection in gnostic terms. He attacks both the Gnostics, who say that "the man is a self-murderer and a suicide who makes confession by death" (this is, says Clement, the "sophistries of cowardice"), and the zealots "who are in haste to give themselves up." They are "poor wretches dying through hatred of the Creator," "not belonging to us [Christians], but sharing the name merely."

By contrast, as Frend notes (*Donatist Church*, 100), martyrdom in North Africa "was regarded both as the crowning achievement in the Christian's life and a personal sacrifice to God, which automatically released the sinner from all guilt." This attitude runs very strongly through the works of Ignatius, *The Martyrdom of Polycarp*, and Eusebius; Ste. Croix correctly concludes ("Aspects," 83, 93, 101–3; "Why Were the Early Christians Persecuted?" *Past and Present* 26 (1963) 21ff.) that voluntary martyrdoms were common among the orthodox and not confined to heretics or schismatics. For the most part, however, they were condemned by church authorities such as Peter and Cyprian. As an example of "official" disapproval, one can "detect a reaction against voluntary martyrdom in the early recension of the Acts of Polycarp preserved in Eusebius *HE* 4.15" (Frend, *Martyrdom*, 288). For Cyprian's disapproval, see Ep. 55.13. Canon 60 of Elvira says that those who destroy idols and are consequently killed are not to be considered martyrs.

With regard to this question, one must be careful of making simplistic distinctions of orthodox vs. rigorist. Bright ("Petrus I.," 332) says that in Canon 9 "Peter states the Catholic as opposed to the Montanistic principle of action." While this is true, it should be remembered that Catholics were rigorists and zealots too. In his letter to Fabius (*HE* 6.41.23) Dionysius approves, at least in one instance, of the zealots' actions. Although in Canon 9 Peter rebukes the zealots, he does not deny the principle of voluntary martyrdom. As a pastor he is worried that they bring temptation on themselves and will "inflame" the persecutors against the faithful. As Frend concludes (*Martyrdom*, 15), "the line between Christian 'boldness' ($\pi\alpha\rho\rho\eta\sigma\iota\alpha$) . . . and 'provocation' must have been difficult to draw." For a full discussion, see Ste. Croix, "Aspects," 75ff.

5. This too becomes a motif in Christian martyrology.

Canon 10 (see 144–46, 160–61, 175)

1. Frend, *Martyrdom*, 540, says that Peter implies "that clergy were to have the chance of eventual rehabilitation, provided they first did penance as laymen." (He cites Canon 3 for evidence, which must be an error.) Peter, indeed, does offer "rehabilitation," that is, communion, but lapsed clergy are not to retain their offices. Bright, "Petrus I.," 332, rightly concludes that this canon "refutes Epiphanius's opinion, derived from Melitianizing documents, that Peter was in favor of restoring lapsed clerics to their ministry." See Epiphanius *Adv. haer.* 6 for language similar to Peter's on lapsed clergy.

In his thinking Peter is in the mainstream of the church, from Cyprian to the canons of the councils. Cyprian expressly states (Ep. 65.2) that the prayers of a sinful priest will not be heard. Epistle 72.2 sounds remarkably like Canon 10 in its conclusions: lapsed clerics will receive communion as laypersons. See also Epistles 64.1 and 67. Origen asserts (*Contra Celsum* 3.51; Chadwick, 163–64) that Christians "do not select those who have fallen after their conversion to Christianity for any office or administration in the Church of God, as it is called."

Canon 10 of Nicea insists that clergy be "blameless," and Canons 1 and 2 of Ancyra agree with Peter's conclusions. With regard to lapsed clergy, Peter undoubtedly agreed with Tertullian (*De exhortatione castitatis* 10; cited by Frend, *Donatist Church*, 120): "quod sanctus minister sanctimoniam noverit ministrare." What Jaroslav Pelikan says about Cyprian also holds true for Peter (*The Christian Tradition* [Chicago 1971] 158): "Cyprian seems to have concluded that the very condition of the church as a mixed body required that the bishops and clergy be pure, so that they might administer the sacraments by which the members of the church could become pure."

Balsamon concludes: "Observe, therefore, that not even a confession for Christ's sake restores to church office the one who once, because of his fall, became a stranger."

See also appendix 2, 193–95. The Syriac fragment agrees with what Peter says in this canon.

2 περπερευσαμένοι: cf. 1 Cor. 13:4.

3. ἐκτελεῖν in Patristic Greek can mean to perform the Eucharist or baptism. Since Peter is here addressing himself to clergy, I am reading "perform" as a play on words: they will perform penance rather than sacraments. Balsamon says "'perform' their confession."

Canon 11 (see 144–46, 160–61, 175)

1. Cf. Eusebius *HE* 6.41.17. See also *Passio S. Perpetuae* 3 and Eusebius *HE* 8.9 for lists of tortures.

With regard to "scrapers and scourges," an interesting motif runs through the persecution literature back to the Maccabean writings. Cyprian Ep. 58.6 refers to the "blessed martyrs of the Maccabees." For the Maccabees and Christian martyrdom, see the index to Frend, *Martyrdom*, 617.

Peter Canon 11: ξυστήρων καὶ μαστίγων βασάνους.

HE 6.41.17: ξυστῆρας μάστιγας.

Origen *Exhortation to Martyrdom* 23: μάστιξι καὶ νεύροις ᾐκίσατο.

2 Macc. 7:1: μάστιξιν καὶ νευραῖς αἰκιζομένους.

2. See the commentary on Canon 10, and Canon 14 and commentary.

Canon 12 (see 144–45, 152–53, 157, 166, 176)

1. Zonaras says: "The passage 'remain completely undisturbed by any evil' means either 'they have not been moved to deny their faith' which conquers all evil, or it means 'the evils and affliction of punishment.'" See Ste. Croix, "The Persecutions," 349. See Cyprian Ep. 55.14 for his leniency toward (and tacit

approval of) those who gave bribes. Canon 3 of Elvira is much harsher toward those who gave money; it postpones communion for them until "at the last." Nevertheless, it judges them more leniently than those who actually sacrificed. See also Clarke, 73ff.

The distance between Tertullian and Peter on this issue is immense. Tertullian "equates flight and bribery" (Barnes, *Tertullian*, 182; see *De fuga* 12), while Peter, as Ste. Croix, "Aspects," 87–88, points out, speaks of those who offered bribes "almost with respect. After this we hear nothing more about the practice. Anyone who reads the canons of the Council of Ancyra with Cyprian's *De lapsis* and letters in mind may well be astonished at the lack of any reference to the sale of immunities in the first nine canons, which deal in detail with the various grades of apostasy during the persecution. The one satisfactory explanation is that the device was not regarded as sinful by the Eastern churches, and therefore did not require to be dealt with in the disciplinary canons. . . . by countenancing the purchase of exemptions the Eastern churches made it possible for very many Christians to avoid the alternatives of apostasy or death without the least stain on their consciences."

2. This passage shows the danger of quoting scripture out of context. The second half of Prov. 13:8 continues, "but a poor man has no means of redemption"! It is ironic that Prov. 13:8, taken as a whole, supports what Peter implicitly affirms: the rich can buy their release, while the poor are out of luck.

Canon 13 (see 144–45, 152–53, 157, 176, 178–79)

1. See Canon 9 and commentary.

2. What follows is tortured—and tortuous—exegesis.

3. Early Christians sought to equate this Zechariah, the priestly son of Jehoiada (see Gen. 4:8; 2 Chron. 24:20–22), with the father of John the Baptist. So Balsamon and Zonoras. See also the Protevangelium of James 23:1; *NTApo* 1:387.

Canon 14 (see 144–45, 153, 166, 176–77)

1. Eusebius *Martyrs of Palestine* 1.3–4 (shorter recension; Lawlor and Oulton 1:333–34) corroborates Peter's statements about the tortures used to compel sacrifice: "At one time it was lashes without number, at another time the rack, the laceration of the sides, and unbearable fetters." He goes on in considerable—and gruesome—detail.

2. Note that confessors can *witness* that a person did not voluntarily sacrifice, but that they cannot forgive. Balsamon says that those referred to in this sentence are clergy. He is taking "ministry" (λειτουργία) in the technical sense, but it need not be taken so. The Greek is ἐν τῇ λειτουργίᾳ ταχθέντες ἐν τοῖς ὁμολογηταῖς. Zonaras says they "may be counted among the clergy (λειτουργίᾳ), or rather be placed among the confessors," which doesn't help elucidate the text.

3. Peter's leniency finds precedent in Cyprian (Epistles 24 and 55) and approval in Ancyra Canon 3 which pardons fully those who lapsed under duress. Canon 5 of Ancyra deals leniently with those who under protest ate of the sacrificial meats.

Appendix 4
THE COMMENTARIES OF THEODORE BALSAMON
AND JOHN ZONARAS ON THE *CANONICAL*
LETTER OF SAINT PETER
OF ALEXANDRIA

Canon 1

[486C][150]

BALSAMON:[151] The present canons deal with those who denied their own faith during persecution and later repented. The first canon directs that for those who sacrificed to the gods after great tortures, since they were not able to persevere on account of their weakness, and since they have spent three years in repentance, another forty days be added, and that in this way they are to be received into the church.

Observe carefully these present canons [469A] which define various necessary rules on behalf of those who have denied their faith and now seek repentance, and which concern those who of their own accord sought martyrdom, but then lapsed, and once again confessed their faith, and which concern others in similar situations. It is necessary that you consult also most of the canons from the Council of Ancyra.

ZONARAS:[152] The holy father makes a distinction among those who during persecution denied their own faith. His words concern those who had been brought before the tyrant and had been thrown into prison, and endured among other hardships dangerous (ἀνηκέστους) tortures and unbearable whippings which are hardly capable of cure or healing (for ἄκος means "cure" and ἀνήκεστον means "that which cannot be healed"), and after these they submitted and sacrificed to the gods. He says that since they were betrayed by the weakness of the flesh which, [469B] because of the pain, could not hold out to the end, the time which has passed suffices as penance, since this is the fourth Easter from the time of their great fall.

And even if perhaps at first they were not received back when they came forth as penitents, nevertheless he has determined that, instead of any further punishment, another forty days from the time when they came forward asking to be received be added as penance. He dictates this because they resisted for a long time and did not of their own free will offer sacrifice, and because they show the marks of Jesus (that is, the scars of the wounds which on behalf of Christ they have patiently borne), and the third year has now passed for those who mourn their fall.

---

150. The bracketed figures refer to the column numbers in *PG* 18.

151. Theodore Balsamon (c. 1140–after 1195). Greek canonist. See the *ODCC*, 124; and the *NCE* 2:32, for brief articles.

152. Johannes Zonaras (twelfth c., or thirteenth?). Byzantine canonist and historian. See the *ODCC*, 1512; and *NCE* 14:1129.

During these forty days of penance, after they have given proof of additional spiritual exercise and keener vigilance, that is, after they have given themselves to more serious reflection, they will turn an alert mind to [469C] prayer and to profound study. Indeed, they will meditate on and utter the words which the Lord said to the one who tempted him: "Get behind me, Satan, for it is written, 'You shall worship the Lord your God and him only shall you serve.'"

[472A]
Canon 2

BALSAMON: This canon directs that those who were only mistreated in prison and fell without suffering torture be punished with another year of penance in addition to the three years. For even if, as he says, these received consolation, since some of the faithful supplied them with the necessities of life, nevertheless they are worthy to be pardoned since they have indeed been mistreated on behalf of the faith.

ZONARAS: In the second ordinance he places those who were only imprisoned and were mistreated while in confinement, and fell, even though they were not tortured. For these he orders punishment in addition to the time that has already passed, that is, the three years he spoke of above. For they also, he says, have endured afflictions for the name of Christ, even if, as may well be, they received consolation from their [472B] brothers while in prison.

For, as seems probable, the faithful who were not being held in custody supplied the necessities of life to those who were imprisoned, and gave them relief. This help they will more than return, for they will now repent those things which they enjoyed in prison, and they will "afflict" and "punish" themselves even more, if they wish to be released from the imprisonment of the devil: through their denial of Christ they became his captive and slaves. Finally he adds the prophetic words taken from Isaiah, which he says they are to remember.

Canon 3

BALSAMON: The canon, in accordance with the parable of the fig tree in the Gospels, punishes with three years of penance those who deserted through fear and cowardice and afterward had it in mind to repent. For the Lord said, "'Three years I have come to it seeking fruit, and I find none.' And the vinedresser said, 'Let it alone, sir, this year also.'"

ZONARAS:
[473A] The parable of the fig tree according to the Gospel fits those, he says, who underwent no suffering but deserted through fear and cowardice alone; they willingly went over to evil and afterward had it in mind to repent. If they keep this parable before their eyes, and do labor worthy of repentance for the same period of time (i.e., for four years), they will be helped. For the Lord said, "'Three years I have come to it seeking fruit, and I find none.' And the vinedresser said, 'Let it alone, sir, this year also.'"

[473C]

Canon 4

BALSAMON: What has been said previously about the fallen has been said with regard to those who repented. But against those who have not repented, he brings the curse of the other fig tree, the one to which the Lord spoke because of its unfruitfulness: "May no fruit ever come from you again!"

ZONARAS: What has been said previously about the fallen has been said with regard to those who repented. But against those who have not repented he brings the curse of the other fig tree, the one to which the Lord spoke because of its unfruitfulness: "May no fruit ever come from you again!"

He does this because these are unrepentant out of despair or from evil motives. They also wear the unalterable and indelible blackness of sin, as the Ethiopians wear their dark skin and a leopard its spots. And he says that for such people the words of Ecclesiastes are fulfilled: [473D] "What is crooked cannot be adorned, and what is lacking will not be able to be numbered." After he has made these things clear, he adds also the words of Isaiah.

[476C]

Canon 5

BALSAMON: Some pretended to approach the altars or write a denial of their faith, and did not do this nakedly and openly. Rather through some kind of a ruse they have mocked those who were with violence forcing them [to sacrifice], as David did when, fleeing from Saul and among foreigners, he pretended to have an epileptic fit and in this way escaped death. These mocked the schemes of their enemies, as sensible and deliberate boys mock their foolish fellows. For they deceived the ungodly by seeming to sacrifice when in reality they were not—or perhaps they sent as substitutes non-Christians and unbelievers, and through these they thought they were sacrificing.

For such people, he says, a period of six months suffices for repentance. For although they did not sacrifice, nevertheless they did make an agreement to do so or sent others in their place. Therefore, they were thought to be in need of repentance, even if certain ones [476D] of those who confessed the faith forgave some of them. He compares them to boys because they did not bravely resist the idolaters, but nevertheless he calls them sensible because by a clever ruse they avoided making sacrifice.

ZONARAS: Some pretended to approach the altars or write a denial of their faith [477A] but did not nakedly (that is, clearly and openly) write down a denial. Rather, through some kind of a ruse they mocked those who with violence were forcing them to sacrifice, as David did when, fleeing from Saul and among foreigners, he pretended to have an epileptic fit and in this way escaped death.

He says that these mocked the schemes of their enemies, as deliberate, sensible, and prudent boys who intelligently make plans mock their foolish fellows. He likens them to sensible people because they deceived the ungodly and seemed to sacrifice when they were not. They were sensible in that they so long avoided making a sacrifice, but they were children in that they did not show a mature and brave resolution and did not nobly resist the idolators. After all, they did make an agreement to offer sacrifice, even if they sent non-Christians, that is, [477B] unbelievers, in their place, and when these offered sacrifice, they were considered to have sacrificed.

For such people, he says, a period of six months will suffice for repentance. For although they did not sacrifice, nevertheless they did make an agreement to do so or sent others as substitutes and seemed to have sacrificed. Therefore, they were thought to be in need of repentance, even if certain ones of those who confessed the faith forgave some of them. For some of those who were witnesses to their faith and suffered on behalf of it forgave those who—by a ruse it is said—did not sacrifice, and received them into the company of the faithful because they had used every means of avoiding sacrificing to demons.

Because he has set down a period of six months, he calls to mind the message of Gabriel which came six months after the conception of the Forerunner, at which time the Lord was conceived. Finally he adds the words of the apostle.

Canon 6

BALSAMON: This father punishes with a year [of penance] the slaves who sacrificed because of the commands and threats of their masters. First he pardons those who [477D] obeyed their masters, and does not place a heavy burden on them; second, since they are rather the slaves of Christ and ought to fear him more, he punishes them moderately. For, he says, in the words of the great Paul, "Whatever good anyone does, he will receive the same again from the Lord, whether he is slave or free."

ZONARAS: There are those who sent their own Christian [480A] slaves, even against their will, to sacrifice in their place. Although these slaves sacrificed by command of their masters, they were forced to do so, and did not do it of their own free will. Therefore, this Father has determined that they spend a year in repentance and learn, because they are of the faithful, that they are the slaves of Christ and ought rather to fear him and that, according to the great Paul, "Whatever good anyone does, he will receive [the same again], whether he is slave or free."

Canon 7

BALSAMON: But he imposes a punishment of three years on those who are free, that is, the masters of the slaves who were forced to offer sacrifice. He does this because they pretended to sacrifice and, in short, seemed to assent to it. They compelled their fellow slaves to sacrifice and did not heed the apostle who ordered [them] to forbear threatening their [480C] slaves since, although they are masters, they are still slaves of Christ and are fellow slaves with their own house slaves. Those [he punishes] were eager to save their own souls but were forcing into idolatry their fellow slaves who [otherwise] would have been able to escape.

ZONARAS: But he imposes a punishment of three years on those who are free, that is, the masters of the slaves who were forced to offer sacrifice. He does this because they pretended to sacrifice and, in short, seemed to bow under the yoke. They compelled their fellow slaves to sacrifice and did not heed the apostle who ordered [them] to forbear threatening their slaves since, although they are masters, they are still slaves of Christ and are fellow slaves with their own house slaves. Those [he punishes] were eager to save their own souls, but forced into idolatry their fellow slaves who [otherwise] [480D] would have been able to escape.

Canon 8

BALSAMON: Some were denounced and handed over to the tyrants, or voluntarily handed themselves over and, when they were defeated by punishment, fell, and failed to witness. Afterward, they repented and acknowledged what is good and confessed that they were Christians, with the result that they were thrown into prison and submitted to torture.

Therefore the holy [father] judges that it is fair to receive with joy such people as these and to strengthen them in the orthodox faith, to join with them in Christian fellowship, [481B] both in prayer and in receiving the Eucharist, and to exhort them through the Word so that they will take a more vigorous part in the conflict and be considered worthy of the heavenly kingdom.

In order that they might not be considered by some, because of their fall, to be unworthy of being received [into the church], he adds testimony from scripture: "Seven times," that is, often, "a righteous man falls and rises again." He says that if all those who fell and failed to confess had done this, that is, had taken up the struggle again and confessed themselves to be Christians before the tyrants, they would have demonstrated a most perfect repentance.

Therefore, there is a difference between the things dealt with in the present canon and those things included in the first canon. There those who had lapsed because of torture did not [later] change their minds and make a confession of faith before [481C] the tyrants; here those who had lapsed because of torture [later] confessed the Lord before the tyrants with a worthy repentance. On account of this they are not considered to have fallen.

ZONARAS: Some, he says, were denounced and handed over to the tyrants, or handed themselves over. They fell and failed to witness after they had been defeated by punishment and were not able to bear while in prison bad treatment and torture. Afterward, they took up the struggle again, and confessed that they were Christians, with the result that they were thrown into prison and submitted to torture.

The holy [father] judges that it is fair to receive with joy such people as these and to strengthen them, that is, give them the resolve, power, and courage to confess the faith. [He says] to join with them in Christian fellowship, both in [481D] prayer and in receiving the Eucharist, and to exhort them through the Word, indeed to rouse them to give testimony, so that they will take a more vigorous part in the conflict and be considered worthy of the heavenly kingdom.

In order that they might not be considered by some to be unworthy, because of their fall, of being received [into the church], he adds testimony from scripture: "Seven times," that is, often, "a righteous man falls and rises again." He says that if all those who fell and failed to confess had done this, that is, had taken up the struggle again and confessed themselves to be Christians before the tyrants, they would have demonstrated a most perfect repentance.

[485B]

Canon 9

BALSAMON: Those who have just risen from sleep, especially if they were in a deep sleep, do not use proper reason; rather, their thoughts are confused and unsteady. To such persons as these this holy martyr compares those who throw themselves into the conflict, that is to say, those who, not in an orderly way but rather rashly and thoughtlessly, thrust themselves into a conflict which is painful and promises to be a protracted one. It has not yet broken open but instead threatens to break open and delays, slowly drawing in the combatants who bring temptation upon themselves, that is, they *pull* temptation toward themselves.

Instead of doing good for the other faithful, they are kindling the coals of the sinners, and it is clear that by this he means the punishment [inflicted by] the tyrants. Although he censures those who act in this way, at the same time he directs the faithful to join with them in Christian fellowship. For these people entered into the conflict for the sake of Christ, [485C] and were ignorant of his teaching since he teaches [us] to ask that we not be tempted. Also, he did not hand himself over [to the authorities], but rather was handed over. Nor are we of our own accord to go over to those who torture us, for if we did so we would cause them to be guilty of many murders, as those do who incite them to punish the godly. The canon adds various examples from scripture.

ZONARAS: Those who have just risen from sleep, especially if they were in deep sleep, do not use proper reason; rather, their thoughts are confused and unsteady. To such persons as these this holy martyr compares those who throw themselves into the conflict, that is to say, those who, not in an orderly way but rather rashly and thoughtlessly, thrust themselves into a conflict which is painful and promises to be a protracted one. It has not yet broken open but instead [485D] threatens to break open and delays, slowly drawing in the combatants who bring temptation upon themselves, that is, they *pull* temptation toward themselves.

Instead of doing good for the other faithful, they are kindling the coals of the sinners, and it clear that by this he means the punishment [488A] [inflicted by] the tyrants. Although he censures those who act in this way, at the same time he directs the faithful to join with them in Christian fellowship. For these enter the conflict in the name of Christ, quite clearly having confidence in Christ, or they undertake the conflict in behalf of the name of Christ, even if, perhaps, they are not following his teaching. For he teaches [us] to ask that we not be tempted. Also, they are ignorant that the Lord withdrew from those who were laying traps for him, and that there were times when he did not walk about openly. Nor did he hand himself over to suffer, but rather was handed over. He also commanded his disciples to flee during persecution from city to city and not of their own accord to go over to those who would torture them, for if they did so they would be the cause of many murders, as those are who incite them to punish the godly. [488B] And he adds the apostles as an example: Stephen, James, and the chiefs of the apostles, Peter and Paul.

Canon 10

BALSAMON: The father spoke earlier about those who of their own accord entered into the conflict concerning witnessing the faith; now he speaks concerning those of the clergy [who did the same]. He says that there are those of the clergy who of their own accord [entered into the conflict], and then were unable to endure their punishment, and fell. Later, coming to their senses, they took up the struggle again, making up for their own fall, and confessed themselves to be Christians before the tyrants. Such persons shall no longer hold church office, because they abandoned the Lord's flock and because they, of their own accord, sought the conflict and were unable to bear up under torture, and thus brought blame upon themselves. [489B] For surely the apostles never did what such as they have done: to be disdainful of teaching the people and to prefer what is beneficial for oneself. The great Paul, after he had endured many tortures, and though he considered it better to leave this life, still preferred to live and be tortured for the salvation and teaching of the people.

Therefore these lack perception who seek the ministry from which they fell of their own accord. For how can they seek that which they abandoned, when they were able to be of some benefit to their brethren at such a time, that is, during a time of persecution? If indeed they had not fallen, he says, they would have been forgiven for what they had done contrary to reason, namely, for their entering the conflict of their own accord and for their laziness concerning teaching and strengthening the brethren. [489C] But since they fell because of boastfulness, that is, because of pretension and arrogance, they are no longer able to minister in the church. For such a nature causes one recklessly to dare face torture and then not be able to endure it, and thus causes others to triumph over that person. Therefore let them rather be concerned about how they might "perform" their confession in humility, ceasing from the vanity of seeking the ministry.

Fellowship with the faithful is sufficient for them, for two reasons which are given with scrupulous care and concern for order. For if we say that we do not hold them in Christian fellowship, we will cause them distress, making it clear that they are condemned to a violent departure from here, that is, death. And we will cause others who may have lapsed and who wish to return to what is good to slacken and be negligent; they will have the pretext that, even if they confess their faith after their fall, [489D] they are not going to be in Christian fellowship with the faithful. Such people who do not reform will be shamed and reproached more than all others, like the one who laid the foundation, but did not finish the house. For those who of their own accord took on torture are like this person [in the parable]: for Christ they, as it were, laid a good foundation but, because of their fall, were unable to perfect that which is good.

Observe, therefore, that not even a confession for Christ's sake restores to church office the one who once, because of his fall, became a stranger.

[492A]

ZONARAS: The father spoke earlier about those who of their own accord entered into the conflict concerning witnessing the faith; now he speaks concerning those of the clergy [who did the same]. He says that there are those of the clergy who of their own accord [entered into the conflict], and then were unable to endure their punishment, and fell. Later, coming to their senses, they took up the struggle again, making up for their own fall, and confessed themselves to be Christians before the tyrants. Such persons shall no longer hold church office, and he adds the reason, which is this: because they abandoned the Lord's flock and because they of their own accord sought the conflict and were unable to bear up under torture, and [thus] brought blame upon themselves. For surely the apostles never did what such as they have done: to be disdainful of teaching the people and to prefer what is beneficial for oneself. The great Paul, after he had endured many tortures, and though he considered it better [492B] to leave this life, still preferred to live and be tortured for the salvation and teaching of the people.

[The father] demonstrates that these lack perception who seek the ministry from which they fell of their own accord. For, he says, how can they seek that which they abandoned when they were able to be of such benefit to their brethren at such a time, that is, during a time of persecution? Indeed, as long as they remained steadfast, they were forgiven for what they had done contrary to reason, namely, for their entering the conflict of their own accord and for their laziness concerning the teaching of the brethren. [492C] But since they have lapsed—as people who boast—they are no longer able to minister in the church. If indeed they had not fallen, he says, they would have been forgiven for what they had done contrary to reason—for it was contrary to reason. Not only did they abandon the good, but they also deserted the Lord's flock and did not remain with it; then too, they did not strengthen the brethren who were being driven into confusion during the time of persecution. But since they fell because of boastfulness—and he calls "boastfulness" here "self-conceit" and "arrogance" because they had confidence in themselves through their arrogance, and [later] gave up the struggle, bringing shame upon themselves (that is, because of their fall, they brought disgrace upon themselves)—they are no longer able to minister in the church. Therefore, he says, let them rather be concerned about how they might "perform" their confession in humility, that is, ceasing from vanity and self-delusion; their seeking the ministry comes about, he says, through vanity and self-delusion.

[492D] Christian fellowship is sufficient for them, that is, to have the faithful in fellowship with them, in other words, to pray with them or to partake of the divine sacraments. And this must be done with care and scrupulousness, that they may not think themselves distressed and therefore reach for a violent departure from here. He says [in other words] that this should be done in this fashion so that they will not depart from this world, exiting as it were from their bodies by means of the violence which comes from the punishments and suffering of imprisonment. This order is given also that some might not have a pretext to become slack and give up the struggle of confessing the faith, and on account of this [pretext] of punishment, to fall. These will be the more ashamed, just as it is said in the Gospels: the man was not able to finish the foundation.

[Omitted here is Zonaras's commentary directed against Muzalon, a Byzantine statesman and writer of the thirteenth century. In it, Zonaras says that since priests are defrocked for deserting their flocks, how much more culpable are bishops when they desert their churches.]

Canon 11

BALSAMON: The saint said earlier that those who of their own accord [entered into the conflict] and lapsed, and did not retract or repent their fall, would have more shame; they are like builders who do not put a roof on a foundation, [497A] that is, they do not complete and make perfect what is good. Now he adds a confirmation of this and other matters. He says that there are those who took a stand amid the turmoil, that is, at the height of the persecution, and, when they saw the saints' confession of faith and how they hastened with godly zeal to receive their heavenly crowns, courageously gave themselves up in order to confess the faith. [They did this] especially when they saw that some had been brought down (that is, stolen away and deceived by the devil) and lapsed, that is, they denied their faith. On account of these people they became fired up inside, that is, their hearts were kindled, since they heard that through this they could wage war, that is, conquer their boasting opponent, the devil.

They hastened to take on martyrdom so the devil would not be able to boast and seem "wise in his own conceit" [497B] because he had conquered through his cunning those who of their own accord entered into the conflict. He hadn't noticed, however, that he had been defeated by the athletes who had endured torture. Therefore it is right that we concur with or give our approval to the faithful who pray for those who were punished and defeated. Indeed, this seems good, for it doesn't do any harm to sympathize and grieve with parents or other relatives on behalf of those who confessed the faith and fell because of the machinations of the devil.

We know that many have had the benefit of God's mercy and goodness through the prayers of others. Therefore, we will ask that they be forgiven their sins by God. [497C] Mindful of the conflicts [they underwent] for the sake of God before their fall, mindful of the worthy repentance they later made and of the fact that they testify they have been considered disenfranchised because of their sin, we will have communion with those who have fallen and afterward repented their error and confessed their faith. Not only will we have communion with them, but we will also pray with them for their reconciliation and for other proper things, that is, for good works which ought to be done by them—fasting, for example, almsgiving, and penance. Through these things the one who is our Advocate makes propitiation to the Father on our behalf.

Finally, he makes use of scripture which is taken from the first catholic epistle of the holy apostle and evangelist John.

ZONARAS: The meaning of the present canon is this. [497D] He says that there are those who took a stand amid the seething turmoil of persecution, that is, at its height, and, when they saw the saints' confession of faith and how they hastened to receive their heavenly crowns, with godly zeal they gave themselves up in order to confess the faith; with great courage they rushed into the conflict, emulating the saints who were suffering, willingly giving themselves up to martyrdom. They did this especially when they saw that some had been brought down, that is, stolen away and deceived, denying their faith. They became fired up inside, that is, their hearts were kindled.

They hastened to make war against the evil one who had dragged down [the others], so he would not be able to boast that he had defeated the godly. Indeed he himself hadn't noticed that, on the contrary, he had been defeated by them because many demonstrated the constancy of their faith even unto death. [500A] They hastened, he says, to do these things, but were defeated by their tortures due to the weakness of the flesh; some suffered evils in prison, some were punished before the judges, and they were unable to bear their punishment.

It is right to suffer with those who mourn in their behalf. He says that some of them mourn for parents, some for brothers, and some for children who lapsed. Indeed it harms no one to mourn with those who mourn the fallen, nor to join in prayer with or share in the sufferings of those who are praying for themselves by other proper means. That is, those who have fallen might do other things for penance, such things as fasting and tears and other humiliations, observing the punishment imposed on them and, if they have the means, giving money to the poor. [500B] Through these things the one who is our Advocate makes propitiation to the Father in our behalf.

Finally he makes use of scripture which is taken from the first epistle of the holy apostle and evangelist John.

Canon 12

BALSAMON: After the saint finished concerning those who of their own accord became witnesses for the faith, he said that those who were undisturbed by the affliction of punishment and defended themselves by giving money were blameless, for they chose to lose their property rather than their souls. Then he confirms this by offering [501A] different scriptures and examples from the Acts of the Apostles concerning the blessed apostle Paul and others.

ZONARAS: He says that those who gave money and escaped and preserved their faith will not be accused, nor for this reason will anyone lay a charge against them, for they chose to lose their property rather than their souls and showed that they wished to serve God and not mammon, that is, money. He adduces words from scripture, and examples from the Acts concerning the blessed apostle Paul and others.

The passage "remain completely undisturbed by any evil" means either "they have not been moved to deny their faith" which conquers all evil, or it means "the evils and afflictions of [501B] punishment."

Canon 13

BALSAMON: But, he says, if some left behind their wealth and withdrew so that they wouldn't be held [504C] and have their lives endangered—perhaps because they would not be able to endure to the end in the confession of their faith on account of the cruelty of their tortures—they are not to be accused even though others were held on their account.

He offers in support of this statement the example of Gaius and Aristarchus, who were detained instead of Paul; the soldiers who were guarding Peter; the children who were killed by Herod for Christ's sake; and Zacharias, the father of the honored and holy Forerunner.

ZONARAS: But, he says, if some left behind their wealth and withdrew so that they wouldn't be held and have their lives endangered—perhaps because they would not be able to endure to the end in the confession of their faith on account of the cruelty of their torturers—they are not to be accused, not even if others were held and tortured on their account.

Again from [504D] the Acts he adduces examples, saying that in Ephesus also Gaius and Aristarchus were seized instead of Paul, but Paul was not blamed for this. Nor was Peter when he was brought out of prison by the angel. He escaped danger, but the soldiers who were guarding him were punished because of him. He also cites as an example from the Gospel the children who were killed by Herod. He says that the Lord was not [505A] blamed for their deaths. And when Elizabeth fled with John and was protecting him, his father, Zacharias, was killed because his son had been demanded from him. But John was not blamed for this.

[505C]

Canon 14

BALSAMON: There are those who, because of a tyrant's violence, seemed to eat meat that had been offered to idols or drink wine from the pagan libations. For it happened that the tyrants threw them on the ground and put hooks, that is, pieces of iron, into their mouths so they would be wide open, and then poured wine down their throats or forced down pieces of meat; or they placed hot coals in their hands along with incense and—in very truth—made them sacrifice.

For the clergy the canon determines that they, each according to his own rank, be placed with those who have confessed the faith. For laymen the canon determines that they be considered martyrs, because these people did not do these things of their own free will nor did they assent in any way to what was done.

There are also those who, because of the torture of punishment, lost the strength of their bodies and were not able to oppose those who were pouring libation wine into their mouths—these are to be placed among those who confessed the faith. Next in order he speaks of those who persevered in making witness of a good conscience, and he numbers these among the confessors.

ZONARAS: There are those who punished the holy witnesses, and [inflicted] great torture upon some; [508A] with violence they poured libation wine into their mouths or placed in their mouths meat that had been offered to idols. They also put incense into their hands and dragged them to the altar where they violently seized their hands and poured out the incense upon the altar, or else they placed burning coals along with incense in their hands so that they would not be able to bear the pain caused by the burning and would let go of the incense along with the coals over the altar. [Those who confessed] were forced by [their torturers] to do this.

He says that such persons as these [who were forced to sacrifice] may be counted among the clergy, or rather be placed among the confessors. For they did not by their own choice either taste the libation wine or place the libations upon the altar, but rather did so by force and did not assent with their own reason to what was done.

Also there are those who because of the torture of punishment lost the strength of their bodies and thus were unable either to move or to utter a sound and were unable to oppose those who were violently pouring libation wine into their mouths. These also will be placed among those who confessed. Next in order he speaks of those who persevered in making witness of a good conscience, and he numbers these among the confessors.

Canon 15

BALSAMON: The present canon rules in accordance with the sixty-fourth Apostolic Canon which has determined that we are not to fast on the Sabbath—except for one exception, that is, the Great Sabbath. It is also in accord with the sixty-ninth canon which severely punishes those who do not fast during Holy Lent and on every fourth and sixth day.

ZONARAS: He says that the fourth and sixth days of each week are always to be days of fasting, nor will anyone find fault with us for fasting [on these days]. He also states his reasons. But we ought not to fast on the Lord's Day, which is a day of joy because of the resurrection of the Lord. He says that, as a custom which we have received, nor are we to bend the knee on this day. The phrases "received as custom" and "commanded according to tradition" are especially significant, because from these words it is clear that long-established custom was considered as law. The great Basil also puts forward reasons why it was forbidden to bend the knee on the Lord's Day, and from Passover to Pentecost. Read also the sixty-sixth and sixty-ninth Apostolic Canons.

Appendix 5
A BRIEF DISCUSSION OF ΜΑΡΤΥΣ, ETC.

A great problem confronts the historian of the persecutions and the church; it is semantic: how to translate the word "martyr," which in Greek literally means "witness." Kirsopp Lake, in his translation of Eusebius's *Ecclesiastical History*, comments:

The translation of all this passage is rendered difficult by the impossibility of translating the Greek word μάρτυς by the same English word in all passages. "Martyr" has been adopted as far as possible but the sense of "witness" is much more present than it is in the English word, for though it is used in a more or less technical sense, it does not as yet imply death.[153]

W. H. C. Frend asserts that in the Book of Revelation, μαρτυρία "is used in the technical sense of being a blood-witness, the sense it was to retain from now onwards."[154] However, he also points out, when referring to the martyrs of Lyons, that "in the mind of the writer, though death alone rendered the Christian a 'perfected martyr'—Stephen is called ὁ τέλειος μάρτυς—the act of witnessing itself gave the Christian a qualification for this honor."[155] The two quotations by Frend show the tension in the word μάρτυς and related words: it can refer both to the living and the dead and, apparently, was not used in any systematic sense.

Lack of consistency in a word should not be too bothersome (words are seldom consistent!). In common usage today, "martyr" can still refer to the living and the dead. We speak of martyrs, whether religious or political, as people who have died (or "died") for a cause. We can also say to someone who is very much alive, "Quit being a martyr." However, in ecclesiastical usage today, the use of "martyr" is consistent—it means one who died for the faith—and causes the problem Lake discusses above: how to refer to early Christian "martyrs," some of whom died for the faith while others did not.[156]

Eusebius *HE* 5.4.3 distinguishes between martyrs (μαρτύρων) and confessors (ὁμολογητῶν). The former were obviously killed, "some consecrated by beheading, some cast out to be eaten by the wild beasts, others who fell asleep in jail, while the latter "still survived at that time." E. L. Hummel, in his book on Cyprian, says that Tertullian uses the term "confessor" only for those who have died.[157] T. D. Barnes disagrees: "Some Christians suffered nothing more severe than temporary imprisonment. Around the year 200, this category appears to become numerous, and for it comes into use the technical term 'confessor.'"[158]

Cyprian calls those who are in prison "confessors" and generally reserves "martyr" for those who have died. However, he also uses the term "martyr"—in a specialized sense, to be sure—for those who are still alive. Hummel summarizes:

---

153. Eusebius *HE*; Lawlor and Oulton 1:438 n. 1.

154. Frend, *Martyrdom*, 91. For the New Testament, see C. Schneider, *TDNT* 4:474–514. On the connection between Christian martyrdom and Judaism of the Maccabean period, see Frend, *Donatist Church*, 486.

155. Frend, *Martyrdom*, 14; see 1–23 for Frend's discussion of martyrdom. Also see Hans von Campenhausen, *Die Idee des Martyriums in der alten Kirche* (2d ed.; Göttingen 1964).

156. A check of the Episcopal Church's *Lesser Feasts and Fasts* shows that "martyr" refers only to those who died for the faith. On both the word and the concept see also E. L. Hummel, *The Concept of Martyrdom According to St. Cyprian of Carthage* (Washington, D.C. 1946).

157. Hummel, 4, 11–12. On the term "confessor," see *HE* 5.4.3; 6.8.7.

158. Barnes, *Tertullian*, 148.

Cyprian makes it clear that in contrast to the simple confessors these men [in prison] already had been subjected to torture, and therefore already stood at the threshold of death. From this, then, we may safely conclude that when the word "martyr" is used for a person who is still living, the idea of death is included, or, in other words, that the idea of death is in the background. The concept of confessor does not in any sense include this idea.[159]

A letter of 250, from Lucian to Celerinus, confirms this definition. Celerinus, a Roman priest, had been tortured, confessed the faith, and was released. Lucian, in a letter to Celerinus himself, praises him as one who "is already to be numbered among the martyrs (iam inter martyribus deputande)." In the same letter Paul, who is dead, is a "blessed martyr."[160]

The same tension can be observed in the writing of Dionysius of Alexandria. In his letter to Fabius (HE 6.41.14–15), Dionysius clearly defines martyrs (μάρτυρες) as those who are killed for the faith; he then goes on to give a list of those killed in the persecution. In this letter, Dionysius, with Cyprian, generally defines a martyr "with the idea of death in the background." He speaks (HE 6.42.5f.) of "the divine martyrs" (οἱ θεοὶ μάρτυρες) who, before their deaths, pleaded the case of some of the fallen. In another passage, however, he means "martyr" quite differently (HE 6.42.2): those who, having fled persecution and surviving hardships in "deserts and mountains," "bear testimony to their election and victory" (εἰσὶν ἐκλογῆς καὶ νικῆς μάρτυρες). This is the "substitutionary confession" discussed above (155–59), and the phrase can only be translated with the English "witness" or "bear testimony," or something of the sort. By "martyr," Dionysius no longer means only those who die for the faith, although one could argue that death is still "in the background."

Peter's use of μάρτυς and related words generally conforms to Hummel's definition given above. In Canon 9, Stephen, James, Peter, and Paul are "martyrs" (μάρτυρες) who "suffered martyrdom" (μαρτύριον) by dying for the faith. However, for Peter "martyr" does not always mean one who has died. In Canon 11 the "holy martyrs" (ἁγίους μάρτυρες) are those standing trial before the court. (Who are going to their deaths? It's uncertain.) In Canon 14, the "thrice-blessed witnesses for the faith" (τρισμακάριοι μάρτυρες) are alive and have spoken up for their "fellow witnesses" (συμμαρτυρούντων) who have suffered violence and torture; these latter were forced to confess, but were not killed. In the same canon ὁμολογητής is a "confessor" and equals μάρτυς: both mean someone who is tortured and imprisoned (unlike in Cyprian's usage). In Canon 8 ὁμολογεῖν, "to confess," means to confess under torture.

Unfortunately, in the other canons Peter does not use the words "martyr" or "confessor" when speaking about others who confessed the faith by fleeing (and of whom he clearly approves). It is painful to note that Peter speaks of "confession" as occurring only under torture or imprisonment; as we know from Eusebius, this was the rule during the persecutions.

159. Hummel, 18.
160. Cyprian Ep. 22.1.

It is clear that the Greek word μάρτυς retained its root meaning of "witness," whether witnessing involved death or not. The English word "martyr" no longer carries such a meaning. From Peter's canons it is clear that some, probably many, confessors or "martyrs" survived their punishments. Although they are martyrs (μάρτυρες) in Peter's eyes, to use our word "martyr" for them would be misleading. Therefore, in this chapter I have used "martyr" only when the person referred to has died, and "confessor" when the person clearly is alive.

Bibliography

Achelis, H. "Meletius von Lykopolis." *Realencyklopädie für protestantische Theologie und Kirche* 12: 558–62.

Acta conciliorum oecumenicorum. Ed. E. Schwartz. Berlin 1940.

Altaner, Berthold, and Alfred Stuiber. *Patrologie.* Freiburg 1966.

Amann, E. "Mélèce de Lycopolis." *Dictionnaire de théologie catholique* 10: 531–36. Paris 1928.

Athenagoras. *Legatio and De resurrectione.* Ed. and trans. William R. Schoedel. Oxford 1972.

Bardenhewer, Otto. *Geschichte der altkirchlichen Literatur.* 2d ed. Freiburg 1914.

Barnard, L. W. "The Antecedents of Arius." *Vigiliae Christianae* 24 (1970) 172–88.

———. "Athanasius and the Meletian Schism in Egypt." *Journal of Egyptian Archeology* 59 (1973) 181–89.

———. "Some Notes on the Meletian Schism in Egypt." *Studia Patristica* 12 (1971) 399–405.

Barnes, Timothy David. *Constantine and Eusebius.* Cambridge, Mass. 1981.

———. *Tertullian: A Historical and Literary Study.* Oxford 1971.

Barns, J., and Henry Chadwick. "A Letter Ascribed to Peter of Alexandria." *Journal of Theological Studies* 24 (1973) 443–55.

Basil, Saint. *The Letters.* Trans. Roy J. Deferrari. Cambridge, Mass. 1952.

Basset, R. "Synaxaire Arabe Jacobite." *Patrologia orientalis* 3 (1909) 353–59.

Baus, Karl. *Handbook of Church History.* New York 1965.

Bayard, Le Chanoine, ed. *Saint Cyprien: Correspondance.* Paris 1961.

Baynes, N. H. "The Great Persecution." Chap. 19 in *Cambridge Ancient History* 12:646–91. Cambridge 1971.

———. "Sozomen I.15." *Journal of Theological Studies* 49 (1948) 165–68.

Beatrice, P. F. "Le tuniche di pelle." In *La tradizione dell' enkrateia: motivazioni ontologiche e protologiche.* Atti de Colloquio Internazionale Milano, 20–23 aprile 1982. 433–84.

Bedjan, Paul, ed. *Acta martyrorum et sanctorum* 5:543–61. Paris 1895.

Bell, H. I., and W. E. Crum. *Jews and Christians in Egypt.* London 1924.

Benson, Edward White. *Cyprian.* London 1897.

Bienert, Wolfgang A. *Dionysius von Alexandrien: Das erhaltene Werk.* Stuttgart 1972.

220

———. *Dionysius von Alexandrien: Zur Frage des Origenismus im dritten Jahrhundert*. Berlin/New York 1978.

———. "Neue Fragmente des Dionysius und des Petrus von Alexandrien aus Cod. Vatop. 236." *Kleronomia* 5 (1973) 308–14.

———. "Zu den neuen Petrusfragmenten aus Cod. Vatop. 236." *Kleronomia* 6 (1974) 237–41.

Bigg, Charles, *Christian Platonists of Alexandria*. Repr. Oxford (1913) 1968.

Bonwetsch, D. G. Nathanael, ed. *Methodius*. Leipzig 1917.

Bright, W. *Canons of the First Four General Councils*. 2d ed. Oxford 1892.

———. "Petrus I., St." *Dictionary of Christian Biography* 4:331–34.

Brooks, E. W. "The Ordination of the Early Bishops of Alexandria." *Journal of Theological Studies* 2 (1901) 612–13.

Budge, E. A. Wallis. *The Book of the Saints of the Ethiopian Church*. Hildesheim/New York 1976.

———. *Coptic Texts*. Volume 1, *Coptic Homilies in the Dialect of Upper Egypt*. Repr. London (1910) 1977.

Burmester, O. H. E. "The Homilies or Exhortations of the Holy Week Lectionary." *Le Muséon* 45 (1932) 21–23, 50–51, 68– 69.

Campenhausen, H. von. *Die Idee des Martyriums in der alten Kirche*. Göttingen 1936, 1964.

Chadwick, Henry. *The Early Church*. New York 1980.

———. *History and Thought of the Early Church*. Variorum Reprints. London 1982.

———. "Origen, Celsus and the Resurrection of the Body." *Harvard Theological Review* 41 (1948) 82–102.

———. "The Role of the Christian Bishop in Ancient Society." *Protocol of the Colloquy of the Center for Hermeneutical Studies*. Berkeley 1979.

———., ed. *Alexandrian Christianity*. Philadelphia 1954.

Chaîne, M. *La chronologie des temps Chrétiens de l'Égypte et de l'Éthiope*. Paris 1925.

Clarke, G. W. "Some Observations on the Persecution of Decius." *Antichthon* 3 (1969) 63–76.

Clement of Alexandria. *Extraits de Théodote*. Ed. F. Sagnard. Paris 1948.

———. *Stromata*. In *Ante-Nicene Fathers*. Vol. 2. Grand Rapids, Mich. 1979.

Crum, W. E. *Catalogue of the Coptic Manuscripts in the British Museum*. London 1905.

———. "Hagiographica from Leipzig Manuscripts." *Society of Biblical Archaeology, Proceedings* 29 (1907) 289–96, 301–07.

———. "Some Further Meletian Documents." *Journal of Egyptian Archaeology* 13 (1927) 19–26.

———. "Texts Attributed to Peter of Alexandria." *Journal of Theological Studies* 4 (1902–3) 387–97.

Cunliff-Jones, Hubert, ed. *A History of Christian Doctrine*. Philadelphia 1981.

Cureton, William, ed. *The Festal Letters of Athanasius*. London 1848.

Cyprian, *Correspondance*. Ed. Le Chanoine Bayard. Paris 1961.

———. *De lapsis and De ecclesiae catholicae unitate*. Trans. Maurice Bévenot, S.J. Oxford 1971.

———. *Letters of Saint Cyprian*. Trans. Sister Rose Bernard Donna, C.S.J. Washington, D.C. 1965.

———. *Treatises*. Trans. and ed. Roy J. Deferrari. New York 1958.

(Pseudo-)Cyprianus. *De laude martyrii*. Ed. Aloysius Hayden. Washington, D.C. 1955.

Daniélou, Jean. *Origen*. London/New York 1955.

———. *The Theology of Jewish Christianity*. Chicago 1964.

Daniélou, Jean, and Henri Marrou. *Christian Centuries: The First Six Hundred Years*. New York 1964.

Dechow, Jon Frederick. "Dogma and Mysticism in Early Christianity: Epiphanius of Cyprus and the Legacy of Origen." Ph.D. diss. Univ. Pennsylvania 1975.

Delahaye, H. Review of Carl Schmidt, "Fragment einer Schrift des Martyrerbischofs Petrus von Alexandrien," Texte und Untersuchungen, n.f., 5/4 (= *Analecta Bollandiana* 20 [1901]) 101–3.

Devos, P. "La Passion copte de saint Théonoé d'Alexandrie." *Analecta Bollandiana* 71 (1953) 415–49.

———. "Une Passione grecque inédite de S. Pierre d'Alexandrie et sa traduction par Anastase le Bibliothécaire." *Analecta Bollandiana* 83 (1965) 157–87.

Dobschütz, Ernst von. *Das Kerygma Petri*. Texte und Untersuchungen 11. 1894. 1–162.

Eusebius. *The Ecclesiastical History*. 2 vols. Vol. 1, trans. Kirsopp Lake. Vol. 2, trans. J. E. L. Oulton. Cambridge, Mass. 1926, 1975.

———. *The Ecclesiastical History and The Martyrs of Palestine*. Ed. H. J. Lawlor and J. E. L. Oulton. London 1928, 1954.

———. *The History of the Church*. Trans. G. A. Williamson. Minneapolis, Minn. 1965.

Feltoe, Charles Lett. *DIONYSIOU LEIPSANA: The Letters and Other Remains of Dionysius of Alexandria*. Cambridge 1904.

———. *St. Dionysius of Alexandria: Letters and Treatises*. London/New York 1918.

The Festal Epistles of S. Athanasius, Bishop of Alexandria. London 1854.

Foakes-Jackson, F. J. "Meletianism." *Encyclopaedia of Religion and Ethics* 8 (1915): 538–39.

Foerster, Werner. *Gnosis: A Selection of Gnostic Texts*. Oxford 1972.

Frend. W. H. C. *The Donatist Church: A Movement of Protest in North Africa*. Oxford 1952.

———. *Martyrdom and Persecution in the Early Church*. Grand Rapids, Mich. 1965, 1981.

———. *Religion Popular and Unpopular in the Early Christian Centuries*. Variorum Reprints. London 1976.

———. *The Rise of Christianity*. Philadelphia/London 1984.

———. *Town and Country in the Early Christian Centuries*. Variorum Reprints. London 1980.

Fritz, G. "Pierre d'Alexandrie." *Dictionnaire de théologie catholique* 12/2:1802–4. Paris 1935.

Goodspeed, Edgar J., and Robert M. Grant. *A History of Early Christian Literature.* Chicago 1966.

Grant, R. M. *Early Christianity and Society: Seven Studies.* London 1978.

Greenslade, S. L. *Schism in the Early Church.* London 1953.

Gregg, Robert C., and Dennis E. Groh. *Early Arianism: A View of Salvation.* Philadelphia 1981.

Grégoire, Henri. *Les persécutions dans l'empire romain.* Brussels 1950.

Guérard, O. "Note préliminaire sur les papyrus d'Origène découverts a Toura." *Revue de l'histoire des religions* 131 (1946) 85–108.

Haile, Getachew. "The Martyrdom of St. Peter Archbishop of Alexandria." *Analecta Bollandiana* 98 (1980) 85–87.

Halkin, F., ed. Hagiographi Bollandiani ex recensio Francisci Halkin. *Sancti Pachomii Vitae Graecae.* Brussels 1932.

Hardy, E. R. *Christian Egypt.* New York 1952.

Harnack, Adolf von. *Geschichte der altchristlichen Literatur.* 2d ed. Repr. Leipzig (1893) 1958.

———. *History of Dogma.* Repr. Gloucester, Mass. (1894–99) 1976.

Harvey, W., ed. *Sancti Irenaei: Libros quinque adversus haereses.* Cambridge 1857.

Haslehurst, R. S. T. *Some Account of the Penitential Discipline of the Early Church in the First Four Centuries.* London 1921.

Hebbelynck, A., and A. van Lantschoot. *Codices Coptici Vaticani Barberiniani Borgiani Rossiani.* Vatican City 1937.

Heer, J. M. "Ein Neues Fragment der Didaskalie des Martyrerbischofs Petros von Alexandrien." *Oriens christianus* 2 (1902) 344–51.

Hefele, Carl Joseph. *History of the Ecclesiastical Councils.* Trans. William R. Clark. Repr. New York (1894) 1972.

Hennecke, Edgar, and Wilhelm Schneemelcher. *New Testament Apocrypha.* Philadelphia 1964.

Hinchliff, Peter Bingham. *Cyprian of Carthage and the Unity of the Christian Church.* London 1974.

Holl, Karl. *Amphilochius von Ikonium.* Repr. Darmstadt (1904) 1969.

———. "Fragmente Vornicänisher Kirchenväter aus den Sacra Parallela." Texte und Untersuchungen 5/2. 1899. 1–241.

Hummel, E. L. *The Concept of Martyrdom According to St. Cyprian of Carthage.* Washington, D.C. 1946.

Hyvernat, Henri. *Bibliothecae Pierpont Morgan Codices Coptici photographice expressi.* Romae 1922.

———. *A Checklist of Coptic Manuscripts in the Pierpont Morgan Library.* New York 1919.

———. "The J. P. Morgan Collection of Coptic Manuscripts." *Journal of Biblical Literature* 31 (1912) 54–57.

———., ed. *Les Actes des martyrs de l'Égypte.* Hildesheim 1977.

Judge, E. A., and S. R. Pickering. "Papyrus Documentation of Church and Community in Egypt to the Mid-Fourth Century." *Jahrbuch für Antike und Christentum* 20 (1977) 47–71.

Kelly, J. N. D. *Early Christian Doctrines.* 5th ed. London 1977.

Kemp, Eric Waldram. "Bishops and Presbyters at Alexandria." *Journal of Ecclesiastical History* 6 (1955) 125–42.

Kettler, F. H. "Der meletanische Streit in Ägypten." *Zeitschrift für die neutestamentliche Wissenschaft und die Kunde des Urchristentums* 35 (1936) 155–93.

————. "Petros. 1." *Realencyklopaedie der klassischen Altertumswissenschaft*, 19/2 (1938) 1281–88.

Kidd, B. J. *A History of the Church*. London 1922.

Knipfing, John R. "The Libelli of the Decian Persecution." *Harvard Theological Review* 16 (1923) 345–90.

Knox, W. L. "Origen's Conception of the Resurrection Body." *Journal of Theological Studies* 39 (1938) 247–48.

Koch, Hugo. "Die Bussfrage bei Cyprian." Chap. 6 in *Cyprianische Untersuchungen* 211–85. Bonn 1926.

Koscherbe, K. *Die Polemik der Gnosticher gegen das kirchliche Christentum*. Leiden 1970.

Lagarde, P. A. de, ed. *Reliquiae iuris ecclesiatici antiquissimae*. Leipzig 1856.

Lampe, G. W. H. "Christian Theology in the Patristic Period." In *A History of Christian Doctrine*, ed. Hubert Cunliffe-Jones. Philadelphia 1980.

————., ed. *A Patristic Greek Lexicon*. Oxford 1961, 1978.

Lebreton, J., and J. Zeiler. *The History of the Primitive Church*. New York 1949.

Lefort, L.-Th. "Coptica Louvaniensia." *Le Muséon* 53 (1940) 126–28.

————. *S. Athanase: lettres festales et pastorales*. Scriptores Coptici Tomus 20. Louvain 1955.

————. "St. Athanase, écrivain copte." *Le Muséon* 46 (1933) 31.

Lemm, Oscar von. *Koptischen Studien*. Leipzig 1972.

Lietzmann, Hans. *A History of the Early Church*. Vol. 2 *The Founding of the Church Universal*. Cleveland 1961.

Lilla, Salvatore R. C. *Clement of Alexandria*. Oxford 1971.

Lucchesi, Enzo. *Repertoire des manuscrits coptes (Sahidiques) publiés de la Bibliothèque Nationale de Paris*. Geneva 1981.

MacMullen, Ramsey. *Christianizing the Roman Empire (AD 100–400)*. New Haven 1984.

Mai, Angelo, ed. *Scriptorum veterum nova collectio*. Rome 1825–38.

————. *Specilegium Romanum*. Rome 1842.

Markus, R. A. *From Augustine to Gregory the Great: History and Christianity in Late Antiquity*. London 1983.

Martin, Annik. "Athanase et les Mélitiens (325–335)." In *Politique et théologie chez Athanase d'Alexandrie*, ed. C. Kannengiesser. Actes due colloque de Chantilly 23–25 Septembre 1973. Paris 1974.

Meinardus, Otto. *Christian Egypt Ancient and Modern*. 2d ed. Cairo 1977.

Mercatti, G. "Note di letteratura biblica cristiana antica." *Studi E Testi* 5 (1901) 87–98.

————. "Un preteso scritto di S. Pietro, vescovo d'Alesandria e martire, sulla bestimmia e filone l'istoriografico." *Rivista storico-critica dell scienza teologica* 1 (1905) 162–80.

Methodius of Olympus. *De resurrectione*. In *Patrologia Graeca* 18:265–333.

Moreau, J. *La persécution du Christianisme dans l'empire romain*. Paris 1956.

Müller, Caspar Detlef Gustav. *Die alte Koptische Predigt*. Berlin 1954.

―――. *Die Engellehre der Koptischen Kirche*. Wiesbaden 1959.

Musurillo, Herbert. *The Acts of the Christian Martyrs*. Oxford 1972.

―――. "Peter of Alexandria." *New Catholic Encyclopedia* 11:209.

Nautin, Pierre. *Homélies Pascales*. 3 vols. Paris 1950, 1953, 1957 (= *Sources Chrétiennes*. Vols. 27, 36, 48).

―――. *Lettres et écrivains chrétiens des IIe et IIIe siècles*. Paris 1961.

Neale, John Mason. *A History of the Holy Eastern Church. The Patriarchate of Alexandria*. London 1847.

Origen. *Commentaries on the Gospel of John and the Gospel of Matthew*. In *Ante-Nicene Fathers* 10:297–528.

―――. *Contra Celsum*. Trans. Henry Chadwick. Cambridge 1980.

―――. *Exhortation to Martyrdom*. Trans. John J. O'Meara. Westminster, Md. 1954.

―――. *Homélies sur le Lévitique*. Trans. Marcel Borret. 2 Vols. Paris 1981.

―――. *Homilies on Genesis and Exodus*. Trans. Ronald E. Heine. Washington, D.C. 1982.

―――. *Sur la Pâque*. Ed. and trans. O. Guérard and P. Nautin. Paris 1979.

Orlandi, Tito. "Coptic Literature." In *The Roots of Egyptian Christianity*, ed. Birger A. Pearson and James E. Goehring. Philadelphia 1986.

―――. "The Future of Studies in Coptic Biblical and Ecclesiastical Literature." In *The Future of Coptic Studies*, ed. R. McL. Wilson, 143–63. Leiden 1978.

―――. "La raccolta copta delle lettere attribuite a Pietro Alesandrino." *Analecta Bollandiana* 93 (1975) 127–32.

―――. "Ricerche su una storia ecclesiastica alesandrina del IV sec." *Vetera Christianorum* 11 (1974) 269–312.

―――. "Sull' Apologia secunda (contra Arianos) di Atanasio di Alessandria." *Augustinianum* 15 (1975) 49–79.

―――. "La Versione copta (Saidica) dell' 'Encomio di Pietro Alesandrino'." *Rivista degli Studi Orientali* 45 (1970) 151–75.

The Oxford Dictionary of the Christian Church. 2d ed. Ed. F. L. Cross and E. A. Livingstone. Oxford 1978.

Papadopoulos, C. A. *Historia tēs Ekklēsias Alexandreias*. Alexandria 1935.

Papadopoulos, K. N. "Eis Petron Alexandreias." *Kleronomia* 6 (1974) 235–36.

Pearson, Birger A. "Hypostasis." In *Encyclopaedia of Religion*. Forthcoming.

―――. "Two Homilies Attributed to St. Peter of Alexandria." In *Proceedings of the Warsaw Congress of Coptic Studies*. Forthcoming.

Pelikan, Jaroslav. *The Christian Tradition*. Vol. 1, *The Emergence of the Catholic Tradition (100–600)*. Chicago 1971.

Peter of Alexandria. *The Canonical Epistles and Other Works*. In *Ante-Nicene Fathers* 6:255–84.

―――. *Opera*. In *Patrologia Graeca* 18:467–522.

Philo of Alexandria. *Questions and Answers on Genesis*. Loeb Classical Library, Supplement, vol. 1. Cambridge, Mass. 1961.

Pitra, J. B. *Analecta Sacra*. Repr. Paris (1883) 1966.

―――. *Iuris ecclesiastici Graecorum historia et monumenta*. Vol. 1. Romae 1864.

Quasten, Johannes. *Patrology*. Repr. Westminster, Md. [1953] 1984.

Rackham, R. B. "The Texts of the Canons of Ancyra." *Studia biblica et ecclesiastica* 3 (1891) 139–216.

Radford, L. B. *Three Teachers of Alexandria: Theognostus, Pierius and Peter. A Study in the Early History of Origenism and Anti-Origenism.* Cambridge 1908.

Rahner, Karl. "Die Busslehre des hl. Cyprian von Karthago." *Zeitschrift für Katholische Theologie* 74 (1952) 257–76, 381–438.

––––––. "La doctrine d'Origène sur la pénitence." *Recherches de science religieuse* 37 (1950) 47–97, 252–86.

Reymond, E. A. E., and J. W. B. Barns. *Four Martyrdoms from the Pierpont Morgan Coptic Codices.* Oxford 1973.

Richard, M. "Le Florilège du Cod. Vatopédi 236 sur le corruptible et l'incorruptible." *Le Muséon* 86 (1973) 249– 50, 267–69.

––––––. "L'introduction du mot 'Hypostase' dans la théologie de l'Incarnation." *Mélanges de Science Religieuse* 2 (1945) 5–32, 243–70.

––––––. *Opera Minora.* 3 vols. Turnhout Brepolis 1976.

––––––. "Pierre Ier d'Alexandrie et l'unique hypostase du Christ." *Mélanges de Science Religieuse* 3 (1946) 357–58.

Richardson, C. C. "The Condemnation of Origen." *Church History* 6 (1937) 59–60.

Riedel, Wilhelm. *Die Kirchenrechtsquellen des Patriarchats Alexandrien.* Repr. Leipzig (1900) 1968.

Riedel, Wilhelm, and W. C. Crum. *The Canons of Athanasius of Alexandria.* London 1904.

Robinson, James M., ed. *The Nag Hammadi Library.* New York 1977.

Rousseau, Philip. *Pachomius: The Making of a Community in Fourth-Century Egypt.* Berkeley 1985.

Routh, M. J. *Reliquiae Sacrae.* 2d ed. Oxford 1846.

Sauget, Joseph-Marie. "Pietro I." *Bibliotheca Sanctorum* 1:761–70.

Schmidt, Carl. "Fragmente einer Schrift des Martyrerbischof Petrus von Alexandrien." Texte und Untersuchungen, n.f., 5/4b (1901) 1–50.

Schwartz, Edouard. *Gesammelte Schriften.* Berlin 1959.

––––––. "Zur Geschichte des Athanasius." *Nachrichten von der Gessellschaft der Wissenschaften zu Goettingen (Phil-hist- Klasse)* (1905) 164–87.

Septuaginta. Ed. Alfred Rahlfs. Stuttgart 1935.

Severus. *History of the Patriarchs of the Coptic Church of Alexandria.* Trans. B. Evetts. In *Patrologia Orientalis* 1 (1907) 103–211, 383–518.

Smith, Jonathan Z. "The Garments of Shame." *History of Religions* 5 (1966) 217–38.

Socrates. *Ecclesiastical History.* Trans. A. C. Zenos. In *Nicene and Post-Nicene Fathers,* 2d ser., 2:1–178.

Solignac, Aimé. "Pierre I d'Alexandrie." In *Dictionnaire de spiritualité, ascetique et mystique, doctrine et histoire,* ed. M. Viller et. al. Fasc. 80–82. Paris 1985. Cols. 1495–1502.

Sozomen. *Ecclesiastical History.* Trans. C. D. Hartranft. In *Nicene and Post-Nicene Fathers,* 2d ser., 2:181–427.

Spanel, D. B. "Two Fragmentary Sa'idic Coptic Texts Pertaining to Peter I, Patriarch of Alexandria." *Bulletin de la Société d'Archéologie Copte* 24 (1979–82) 85–102.

Spanel, D. B., and Tim Vivian. "Peter I, Seventeenth Archbishop of Alexandria (300–311)." In *The Coptic Encyclopedia*, ed. A. Atiya et al. Forthcoming.

Stählin, Otto, ed. *Clemens Alexandrinus*. Leipzig 1909.

Stauridos, B. Th. "Hai ōrigenistikai erides." *Theologia* 28 (1957) 556ff.

Ste. Croix, Geoffrey de. "Aspects of the 'Great' Persecution." *Harvard Theological Review* 47 (1954) 75ff.

———. "The Persecutions." Chap. 15 in *The Crucible of Christianity*, ed. A. J. Toynbee. New York 1969.

———. "Why Were the Early Christians Persecuted?" *Past and Present* 26 (1963) 6–38.

Stevenson, James. *Creeds, Councils and Controversies*. London 1981.

———. *A New Eusebius*. London 1963.

Telfer, W. "The Codex Verona LX (58)." *Harvard Theological Review* 48 (1955) 227–37.

———. "Episcopal Succession in Egypt." *The Journal of Ecclesiastical History* 3 (1952) 1–13.

———. *Forgiveness of Sins*. London 1969.

———. "Meletius of Lycopolis and Episcopal Succession in Egypt." *Harvard Theological Review* 48 (1955) 227–37.

———. "St. Peter of Alexandria and Arius." *Analecta Bollandiana* 67 (1949) 117–30.

Tertullian. *Disciplinary, Moral and Ascetical Works*. Trans. Rudolph Arbesmann, O.S.A., et al. New York 1959.

———. *Treatises on Penance*. Trans. P. Le Saint, S.J. Westminster, Md. 1959.

Veilleux, Armand, ed. *Pachomian Koinonia*. 3 vols. Kalamazoo, Mich. 1980.

Viteau, J. *Passions des Saints Ecaterine et Pierre d'Alexandrie*. Paris 1897.

Wessely, Carl. *Studien zur Palaeographie und Papyruskunde*. Repr. Amsterdam [1914] 1967.

Williams, R. "Arius and the Melitian Schism." *Journal of Theological Studies*, n.s., 37/1 (1986) 35–52.

Index

228